An Introduction to Law and Regul

Text and Materials

D1383985

In recent years, regulation has emerged as one of the most distinct and important fields of study in the social sciences, both for policy-makers and for scholars who require a theoretical framework that can be applied to any social sector. This timely textbook provides a conceptual map of the field and an accessible and critical introduction to the subject. Morgan and Yeung set out a diverse and stimulating selection of materials and give them context with a comprehensive and critical commentary. By adopting an interdisciplinary approach and emphasising the role of law in its broader social and political context, it will be an invaluable tool for the student coming to regulation for the first time. This clearly structured, academically rigorous title, with a contextualised perspective is essential reading for all students of the subject.

BRONWEN MORGAN is Professor of Socio-legal Studies at the University of Bristol. Her research focuses on the political economy of regulatory reform and global governance. She is the author of *Social Citizenship in the Shadow of Competition* (2003).

KAREN YEUNG is Professor of Law at Kings' College London. She was a university lecturer at Oxford University and a Tutorial Fellow in Law at St Anne's College from 1996 until 2006. Her research lies in the intersection of public law and socio-economic regulation.

The Law in Context Series

Editors: William Twining (University College London) and Christopher McCrudden (Lincoln College, Oxford)

Since 1970 the Law in Context series has been in the forefront of the movement to broaden the study of law. It has been a vehicle for the publication of innovative scholarly books that treat law and legal phenomena critically in their social, political and economic contexts from a variety of perspectives. The series particularly aims to publish scholarly legal writing that brings fresh perspectives to bear on new and existing areas of law taught in universities. A contextual approach involves treating legal subjects broadly, using materials from other social sciences, and from any other discipline that helps to explain the operation in practice of the subject under discussion. It is hoped that this orientation is at once more stimulating and more realistic than the bare exposition of legal rules. The series includes original books that have a different emphasis from traditional legal textbooks, while maintaining the same high standards of scholarship. They are written primarily for undergraduate and graduate students of law and of other disciplines, but most also appeal to wider readership. In the past, most books in the series have focused on English law, but recent publications include books on Europe law, globalisation, transnational legal processes and comparative law.

Books in the Series

Anderson, Schum & Twining: *Analysis of Evidence*
Ashworth: *Sentencing and Criminal Justice*
Barton & Douglas: *Law and Parenthood*
Beecher-Monas: *Evaluating Scientific Evidence: An Interdisciplinary Framework for Intellectual Due Process*
Bell: *French Legal Cultures*
Bercusson: *European Labour Law*
Birkinshaw: *European Public law*
Birkinshaw: *Freedom of Information: The Law, the Practice and the Ideal*
Cane: *Atiyah's Accidents, Compensation and the Law*
Clarke & Kohler: *Property Law: Commentary and Materials*
Collins: *The Law of Contract*
Davies: *Perspectives on Labour Law*
Dembour: *Who Believes in Human Rights?: The European Convention in Question*
de Sousa Santos: *Toward a New Legal Common Sense*
Diduck: *Law's Families*
Elworthy & Holder: *Environmental Protection: Text and Materials*
Fortin: *Children's Rights and the Developing Law*
Glover-Thomas: *Reconstructing Mental Health Law and Policy*
Gobert & Punch: *Rethinking Corporate Crime*
Harlow & Rawlings: *Law and Administration*
Harris: *An Introduction to Law*
Harris, Campbell & Halson: *Remedies in Contract and Tort*
Harvey: *Seeking Asylum in the UK: Problems and Prospects*
Hervey & McHale: *Health Law and the European Union*

An Introduction to Law and Regulation
Text and Materials

Bronwen Morgan and Karen Yeung

CAMBRIDGE UNIVERSITY PRESS
Cambridge, New York, Melbourne, Madrid, Cape Town, Singapore,
São Paulo, Delhi, Dubai, Tokyo, Mexico City

Cambridge University Press
The Edinburgh Building, Cambridge CB2 8RU, UK

Published in the United States of America by Cambridge University Press, New York

www.cambridge.org
Information on this title: www.cambridge.org/9780521685658

First published 2007
Reprinted 2009

A catalogue record for this publication is available from the British Library

Library of Congress Cataloguing in Publication Data

Morgan, Bronwen, 1966-
  An introduction to law and regulation : text and materials / Bronwen Morgan and Karen
Yeung. – 1st ed.
    p. cm. – (The law in context series)
Includes bibliographical references and index.
ISBN-13: 978-0-521-68565-8 (pbk.)
ISBN-10: 0-521-68565-6 (pbk.)
1. Administrative law. 2. Delegated legislation. I. Yeung, Karen, Dr. II. Title. III. Series.
K3400.M67 2007
340–dc22   2006037260

ISBN 978-0-521-68565-8 Paperback

To Jim
To Duncan

Contents

Preface and Acknowledgements

The origins of this book can be traced back to an informal conversation between us in 1999 as two young legal academics at Oxford University shortly after discovering our shared interest in the nature and workings of the administrative state. This prompted us to consider the possibility of putting together a post-graduate course with the rather broad title 'Regulation'. As neither of us had previous experience in teaching such a course, we began somewhat tentatively, seeking to devise a course that would encourage students to interrogate legal institutions beyond the confines of a narrow focus on legal doctrine. Our ambition was to cultivate in our students what Roberto Unger calls an 'institutional imagination', one that highlights the challenges of institutional design in public policy-making and practice so as to enrich and enliven their understanding of the law and its contribution to the regulatory enterprise.

It was in the process of locating suitable material for our proposed course that we discovered the lack of any textbook to guide us and our students. Although there were several valuable essay collections, as well as books that adopted one particular disciplinary orientation in examining regulation, there was no single book which satisfactorily fulfilled our pedagogical objectives. What we wanted was a scholarly yet accessible text which both drew together a broad range of perspectives and examined a wide range of regulatory issues. In the absence of such a text, we proceeded by gathering rather disparate materials from legal, social-scientific and policy sources, organising them around our conceptual frame and amalgamating them into a course-pack. But problems remained. In particular, we were asking our students to engage with somewhat disparate strands of social scientific literature which they had not previously encountered. Many often struggled to identify how these strands related to each other or, indeed, to the legal tradition to which they were accustomed. In short, there was an acute need for a text that provided an organising frame for interrogating the variety of disciplinary approaches to regulation, and this provided us with the impetus to write this book.

Although the original course was constructed with postgraduate law students in mind, this book is intended to introduce both lawyers and non-lawyers alike to the study of regulation. While the meaning of the term 'regulation' is heavily contested and subject to multiple academic interpretations, our approach to the subject is much broader than many lawyers' understandings of the term. We were reminded of just how narrow a lawyer's understanding of the term can be from the incredulity expressed by a newly arrived law student, who thought that our entire course was devoted to delegated legislation — and who was much relieved to discover that this was not the case. We understand 'regulation' scholarship as a broad and open-ended category that can readily apply to many forms of intellectual inquiry concerning the purposive shaping of social behaviour, particularly state and non-state standard-setting, monitoring and behaviour-modification processes. Seen in this light, the topic may be of general interest to social scientists who are not lawyers, particularly those who find 'regulation' as a category of inquiry cropping up in the course of their work. Those concerned with globalisation and supranational governance may also find the chapter on regulation above and beyond the state of direct relevance.

Given that one of our aims is to help lawyers and legal scholars engage with a considerable body of scholarship that does not always directly focus on law, we have woven an argument about the role of law in regulation into our commentary. This argument is complementary to our more general mapping of the field, so that the resulting survey should still be valuable to readers who are less concerned with the role of law. Readers may also disagree with our argument about the role of law without it affecting the integrity of the general mapping exercise.

Although the structure of the book broadly reflects the conceptual framework which we originally adopted when we first offered our Regulation course, we have continually revised and refined the course over the years in light of feedback from our students. Some have continued to pursue their academic inquiry into regulation in the form of research degrees, while others are now embarking on their own academic careers. Still others have gone on to work in regulatory contexts as varied as public sector reform in Singapore and gas operations in Bolivia. Thus, it is to our former students that we owe our primary debt of gratitude. We have learned much from them, and their input was invaluable in refining the structure and presentation of this book as well as the material we have chosen to extract. Several former students have told us that studying regulation provoked them to think about the law and social institutions in an entirely fresh light, and bearing witness to their intellectual enthusiasm has been one of our richest rewards. Special thanks are due to the Oxford University postgraduate law students who took the course in 2005–6, many of whom read the entire manuscript, identifying areas where further clarification, explanation or restructuring were needed.

We are also enormously indebted to Roger Brownsword, Denis Galligan, Simon Halliday, Kathy Liddell, Anne Meuwese, Tony Prosser and Stephen Weatherill, who provided critical yet encouraging feedback on the first draft of the manuscript and were able to offer a more dispassionate and objective critique of our work than we could provide to each other. Oxford University Law Faculty and the Oxford Centre for Socio-legal Studies provided support and assistance both in developing the course and in bringing the book to completion, not least by making it possible to employ our indispensable research assistants, Anna Oldmeadow and Elen Stokes, without whose help the task of completing the manuscript would have been considerably more painful and protracted. We are also grateful to Sinead Moloney, Anjana Narayanan and Finola O'Sullivan for skilfully steering the manuscript through the production process. Finally, we wish to thank each other. Teaching and writing together has been a privilege, not only in terms of intellectual stimulation but also for the sheer fun involved. Our hope is that this book reflects our enthusiasm for the study of regulation and demonstrates how stimulating and rewarding such a study can be.

KY and BM
London and Bristol
18.10.06

Figures

1

Introduction

Regulation is increasingly seen as a distinct field of academic inquiry. Yet it is often difficult to obtain a holistic sense of its contours and the nature of its terrain. The primary aim of this book is to provide a map that will help to orientate those encountering this field for the first time. We construct this map by drawing together material from a range of disciplinary perspectives from law and the social sciences. Three objectives flesh out our broad aim. Firstly, we seek to challenge lawyers to look beyond conventional legal sources. Secondly, as a corollary objective for those who are not lawyers, this book seeks to examine the role of law as an instrument of social control within regulation broadly understood. Thirdly, we aim to break down a subject which can be rather daunting for newcomers into digestible and accessible form. The map we draw is structured around four core conceptual facets of regulation: (i) theories of regulation, (ii) techniques and instruments for regulating, (iii) compliance with and enforcement of regulation and (iv) issues of accountability and legitimacy in relation to regulation. We then extend this map, in the penultimate chapter, by applying our conceptual framework to regulation in the supranational context. The resulting taxonomy is intended to provide a descriptive sense of the breadth and variety in approaches to regulation across political studies, economics, law, criminology and sociology.

Although the perception of regulation as a distinct field of social inquiry is a relatively recent development, purposive attempts to influence and control economic and social activity have a long pedigree. Continuity and change in the practice and debates surrounding regulation may be illustrated by comparing Marie Antoinette's indignant response to complaints about rising bread prices in pre-revolutionary France, to France Telecom's contemporary response to complaints about fears of rising local telephone call charges in rural France as a consequence of telecommunications privatisation. Like the latter's protestations that international calls would be so much cheaper (Silbey 1997: 207–208), Marie Antoinette similarly claimed, 'But then let them eat cake.' In other words, both justified the potentially negative distributional impact of a refusal to regulate the price of important goods by invoking the expansion of choice available to citizens. Yet both failed to give credence to the incapacity of particular sectors of the community to avail themselves of essential commodities, be they bread or local phone calls. Such a failure demonstrates that insensitivity to the political and moral dimensions of regulatory policy and practice has endured, despite the long sweep of time separating the two events.

While bread and local telephone calls may, at first sight, be surprising comparators, these contrasting anecdotes have conceptual parallels that a broad-based study of regulation may illuminate. This book will develop a general analytical framework drawing upon scholarly examination of more contemporary sequences of change occurring in the shifting relations between the state and market in modern industrial states over the last quarter of a century. These changes coalesce around the liberalisation of the post-war welfare state in industrialised democracies in pursuit of values and goals loosely associated with market competition, which has placed increasing pressure on the social democracy and citizenship aspirations fostered by the welfare state. These tensions, which one of us has described elsewhere as 'social citizenship in the shadow of competition', have been a central trope of regulatory politics since the mid to late 1970s (Morgan 2003). The politics of regulation in many different countries is pervaded by a broad sense that state intervention into the economy either bolsters markets or tempers their effects by adding a dimension of social inclusion. The growing trend towards indirect welfare provision (via the regulation of non-state providers and the consequent 'hollowing out of the state') is making the difference between regulatory intervention and direct state provision of welfare increasingly moot. Accordingly, the scope of 'regulatory politics' is now seen to encompass issues that are familiar as regulatory ones, such as environmental regulation, occupational health and safety regulation, financial services regulation and motor vehicle safety regulation, but also extends to state programmes for redistributing income to disadvantaged citizens, mandated health insurance for individuals in need, programmes for subsidising the cost of higher education for selected students or state intervention via statutory marketing collectives for the sale of agricultural products. But although these changes have led to an expansion of the resulting 'regulatory state', they should not mask the continuing importance of ideological battles over the basis and extent of justifiable state intervention into collective choices. It is in this dynamic socio-political context that regulation has emerged in academic literature as a distinct field of social inquiry.

In mapping this field, we select texts from a wide range of writing about regulation in law and social science, and intersperse extracts from these materials with our own commentary. The selection of text extracts is intended to illuminate the considerable variation in the focus and scope of intellectual inquiry ranging, for example, from close examination of regulatory sanctions and liability rules, through to broad questions of democratic legitimacy. In emphasising the breadth of regulation scholarship, our focus extends well beyond utility regulation with which the field it is often associated. We include extracts from the original texts, often at some length (rather than paraphrasing) to highlight the rich variety of texture in voice and discourse that characterises the field. These extracts illustrate the range of analytical frames used to explore regulation, drawing into sharper focus the differences between alternative perspectives on the regulatory endeavour and its multiple facets. There are, of course, tensions between some of the different disciplinary approaches, and one of the advantages of interleaving extracts from a range of disciplinary perspectives is that such tensions are revealed, and opened up for interrogation. The rather eclectic materials we have selected have been chosen primarily for their accessibility. Thus we have not necessarily selected seminal writings (not least because they can be somewhat inaccessible to the newcomer to the field). These extracts are linked by our commentary, with the latter also serving to highlight common ground and areas of divergence, and sometimes drawing out their wider implications. In particular, one of our aims is to explore the law's various roles in regulation. A discussion of the law's role provides a common thread running throughout the commentary. Taken together, the text and our commentary provide a wide overview of an immensely varied terrain held together by an exploration of the law's role and, to that extent, our commentary may be understood as offering a legal perspective on regulation.

A legal perspective on regulation

Regulation is a phenomenon that is notoriously difficult to define with clarity and precision, as its meaning and the scope of its inquiry are unsettled and contested. That said, a functional approach to regulation, often referred to as a cybernetics perspective, is widely used and accepted, explained by several leading social scientists as:

> ... any control system in art or nature must by definition contain a minimum of the three components ... There must be some capacity for *standard-setting*, to allow a distinction to be made between more or less preferred states of the system. There must also be some capacity for *information-gathering* or monitoring to produce knowledge about current or changing states of the system. On top of that must be some capacity for *behaviour-modification* to change the state of the system.
>
> (Hood *et al.* 2001: 23)

By focusing on a tripartite division between regulation's core functions, definitional contestation over the appropriate scope of the regulatory field is avoided. In contrast, attempts to define the proper scope of regulation provoke a much greater level of disagreement, often because of the political and ideological battles referred to above. At their narrowest, definitions of regulation tend to centre on deliberate attempts by the state to influence socially valuable behaviour which may have adverse side-effects by establishing, monitoring and enforcing legal rules. At its broadest, regulation is seen as encompassing all forms of social control, whether intentional or not, and whether imposed by the state or other social institutions. Lawyers have tended to focus on the narrower definitions, largely because of the state's monopoly over the coercive power of the law. From a traditional legal perspective, one might think of a statute promulgated by a sovereign legislature as the paradigmatic form of regulation. Regulatory scholarship is challenging three assumptions that are inherent in such a perspective.

The first assumption is that the state is the primary locus for articulating the collective goals of a community. Recent scholarship challenges this assumption by highlighting the emergence of non-state institutions, including commercial enterprise and non-governmental organisations, that operate as both a source of social influence and a forum in which public deliberation may occur. The second assumption is the hierarchical nature of the state's role: the idea that the state has final authority is increasingly challenged by the emergence of multiple levels and sites of governance that operate concurrently or in overlapping ways, rather than being vertically arranged. The third assumption is the centrality of rules as 'command' as the primary mode of shaping behaviour: the challenge here is twofold, not only encompassing empirically observed limitations to the effectiveness of legal rules, but also increasing recognition of the potential for alternative techniques of policy implementation.

The combined effect of these three pressures on state-centric and rule-centric notions of regulation is summed up in the notion of what Julia Black calls 'decentred regulation' (Black 2001). However, decentred regulation has not dislodged either the state or law, rather, it generates new questions about the *relationships between* the state and the range of other actors, institutions and techniques highlighted by a decentred approach. While finding answers to these questions will require lawyers to broaden their horizons beyond the vision of the state as a top-down rule-maker, they do not eliminate the relevance of law, nor a legal perspective on regulation.

This raises the question of what we mean by a legal perspective on regulation. It is a perspective that builds upon a dominant strand of regulatory scholarship that views the law as an instrument used by the state to achieve the community's chosen collective goals. Regulatory scholarship of this nature is concerned primarily with effective problem-solving. These approaches tend to downplay the non-instrumental values, institutions and ideals which lawyers often emphasise – the most obvious being the values and institutions encapsulated within the rule of law ideal.

Our legal approach builds on these more instrumentalist strands of regulatory scholarship, by bringing to the fore the political and constitutional context in which regulation is embedded. By political and constitutional context, we mean the social structures and institutions that allocate power at the macro-political level, rather than the more immediate context relevant to problem-solving within a particular policy sector. Our consideration of the macro-political linkages in which regulation occurs focuses upon the democratic market economy that characterises most Western industrialised countries, rather than considering other forms of political economy such as developing, socialist or Islamic states. Moreover, most of the book's exploration of regulation assumes that the nation-state is the primary forum for collective decision-making at the macro-political level. Whether the analytical framework we provide is capable of being applied in the context of more 'globalised' views of macro-political institutions is a question we address separately in the penultimate chapter.

Although our analytical framework encompasses a 'decentred' approach to regulation, the legal perspective which we adopt assumes, as the main context of analysis, a state-centric conception of law, that is, law as authoritative rules backed by coercive force, exercised by a legitimately constituted (democratic) nation-state. Our legal approach differs from traditional legal scholarship in so far as we do not focus on judicial interpretation of legal rules developed through case law. Rather, we emphasise the social context in which the law operates, thereby highlighting the law's instrumental role in shaping social behaviour. We also extend our examination beyond instrumental conceptions of law by considering the way in which law may give expression to particular values. Thus, we consider two related but distinct roles for law in regulation: the first is facilitative and the second expressive. We describe these roles in what follows in abstract, conceptual terms. They are not intended as philosophical claims about the nature of law, however, but rather as stylised concepts that summarise patterns of empirical variation.

In its *facilitative* role, law forms part of the infrastructure that links the state to the market, to the community and to individuals. For example, the state and the market can be thought of as influencing social and economic behaviour in contrasting ways. A highly simplified version of the contrast could view the state as providing benefits or imposing burdens in terms of the rule of law, in particular on an equal universal basis. By contrast, the market's invisible hand lets the price system dictate the burdens and benefits of exchange in a random, differentiated manner. For example, a community may decide that one of its collective goals is to sustain the quality of its waterways. It might achieve this by promulgating a binding legal rule prohibiting any person from dumping waste exceeding a specified quantity into its public waterways, and imposing a financial penalty on any person who violates this rule. However, the same collective goal might also be achieved by imposing a system of tradeable permits that allows certain amounts of waste to be dumped into public waterways upon payment of a specified sum. While there is a tendency to understand the first method as legal and the second as market-based, the law is in fact involved in both methods, albeit in different ways. In the first, the law's role is a familiar one which may be depicted by the image of *law as threat*. In the second, law facilitates the interaction of state and market, and thereby contributes to delineating the boundary between them. In so doing, law enables transactions to take place in the market just as

Law's role	Law's image	
	Law as *threat*	Law as *umpire*
Law's *facilitative* role: law as an instrument for shaping social behaviour	Proscribing conduct and threatening sanctions for violation to deter that conduct	Creating and policing the boundaries of a space for free and secure interaction between participants
Law's *expressive* role: law institutionalising values	Legitimating coercion	Reflecting shared or agreed morality of the community of players

Figure 1.1. Law's image.

much as it constitutes an expression of state command. We might depict this role for law with the image of *law as umpire*.

This brings to the fore the *expressive* facet of our depiction of the law's role, which also draws on the images of law as threat and as umpire, but to different effect. In providing the framework in which economic and social transactions take place, law interacts with morality and politics. As part of this interaction, the law constructs and constrains democratic institutions that articulate collective choice. In this role, the law has developed a range of ways to shape and constrain the power of institutions, particularly governmental institutions. Because governmental institutions may impose collective choices coercively, law acquires, at least in a democratic state, a normative dimension, for the state must legitimate its use of coercive force. Law may therefore be understood as institutionalising and giving expression to certain values that democracy itself presupposes and that cut across the political programme of particular governments. The law's embodiment of constitutional values represents one of several ways in which the law may have an expressive dimension. In this guise, constitutional values and principles (the separation of powers, the principle of legality, the requirements of due process, etc.) serve as constraints on the exercise of state power. For example, the law would not allow the imposition of a financial penalty upon the polluter of waterways unless due process had been respected: the image of *law as threat* is at play here by its legitimation of the burdensome consequences of violation by demanding conformity with due process requirements.

There might be other ways in which the law could be regarded as expressive. For example, legal standards promulgated by a democratically elected parliament may be thought of as giving expression to the community's general will, or to its shared values. Legal standards may also give expression to ethical principles. So, for example, if the legislative prohibited the dumping of waste into public waterways, imposing a sanction for violation, such a prohibition may be seen as expressing the community's shared commitment to environmental preservation and public condemnation of polluting behaviour. Others might claim that it is morally wrong to degrade the environment, and therefore the legal prohibition of such conduct may also be regarded as giving expression to this claimed moral principle. The law's expressive role is likely to be most familiar when regulation takes the classic form of rule-based proscription, particularly where legal prohibitions reflect strong condemnation of the prohibited conduct, thus reflecting the image of *law as threat*. Yet an expressive dimension may also be discernible when the law's role reflects the image of *law as umpire*. So, for example, the law would proscribe the issue of a tradeable pollution permit to an applicant who had not met the criteria for purchasing the permit: the image of law as umpire reflects the law's facilitative dimension in helping to create and maintain a structured framework for the free play of choice and creativity within the community of participants while also giving expression to the community's collective will concerning the appropriate conditions under which such interactions should occur.

Stated in summary form, our depiction of the law's facilitative and expressive roles in regulation are highly abstract, but we will elaborate further, locating them in more concrete contexts and providing detailed illustrations of these images as the chapters unfold. In Chapter 2's discussion of theories of regulation, the law's facilitative role will be explored at greater length, while in Chapter 3 the law's umpiring role will be considered alongside its facilitative function when considering regulatory instruments. The law's facilitative and expressive dimensions are both discussed in Chapters 4 to 6 when considering the law's respective roles in regulatory enforcement, legitimacy and accountability, and regulation within the supranational context. Although we will return to a discussion of the law's role in regulation in the concluding chapter, they may be usefully represented in schematic form in Figure 1.1.

Chapter overview

The idea of a legal perspective on regulation is relevant to the question of whether regulation has become more than a distinct and common object of scholarship, amounting to a methodology in itself. In presenting a legal perspective, this book offers a map of regulation scholarship which is ecumenical in outlook. While some scholars of regulation have begun to speak of a 'regulationist' approach (just as one refers to a criminological approach, a feminist approach or a socio-legal approach), we wish neither to construct nor to defend a single definitive vision of regulatory scholarship by bringing these sources together. The map of regulation which we draw in this book is structured around four core conceptual ideas which comprise Chapters 2 to 5, briefly outlined in the following discussion.

Theories of regulation

We begin by examining competing, and sometimes overlapping, theoretical frameworks that seek to explore the relationship between regulatory laws and the various social groups participating in, and affected by, the regulatory process. A theory (or model) of regulation is a set of propositions or hypotheses about why regulation emerges, which actors contribute to that emergence and typical patterns of interaction between regulatory actors. The theories discussed in Chapter 2 span a variety of disciplinary approaches, encompassing both explanatory and prescriptive outlooks. Theories of regulation can be broadly divided into three kinds: public interest, private interest and what may loosely be described as 'institutionalist' approaches. Public interest theories of regulation attribute to legislators and others responsible for the design and implementation of regulation a desire to pursue collective goals with the aim of promoting the general welfare of the community. Such theories are generally prescriptive in orientation, typically concerned to evaluate (often from an explicitly economic or political viewpoint) whether, and to what extent, a regulatory scheme fulfils particular collective goals.

Private interest theories, by contrast, are sceptical of the 'public interestedness' of legislators and policy-makers, recognising that regulation often benefits particular groups in society, and not always those it was ostensibly intended to benefit. Thus, private interest theories conceive of regulation as a contest between selfish 'rent-seeking' participants in the regulatory 'game', analysing the way in which political and law-making processes can be used by these participants to secure regulatory benefits for themselves. Private interest theories are largely explanatory in nature, concerned with explaining how and why regulation emerges and why regulatory processes and outcomes take a particular shape and form. Some private interest theories may also seek prescriptively to assess whether the resulting outcomes are economically efficient, typically observing that resources devoted to winning the regulation game often result in economic waste and are therefore socially unproductive (Ogus 2004: 73).

Unlike either public or private interest theories, which are more actor-centred, the array of approaches which we broadly label as 'institutionalist' tend to analyse regulatory interactions from a higher level of abstraction. Rather than focusing on the dynamics between individual actors, the focus of systems theory, for example, is on the dynamics of the 'legal system', the 'economic system' or the 'political system' — as well as, importantly, the interactions between these different systems. Although the classical version of systems theory, built by Luhmann (Brans and Rossbach 1997) and Teubner (Teubner 1986) on the basis of biological scientists' accounts of how living organisms self-regulate, defines the content and parameters of a system by referring to 'legal', 'economic' and 'political' systems, the contours of these so-called systems are fluid and contested. Moreover, discussions of exactly what is constituted by a 'system' operate at a very high level of abstraction.

So, for example, whereas private interest theorists exploring utilities regulation might investigate the ways in which a regulated industry lobbies regulatory agencies and legislative actors in order to secure regulatory benefits, systems theorists might focus on the way in which the economic and political systems communicate (or fail to communicate) with each other.

Network and 'regulatory space' approaches share with systems approaches a focus on institutional dynamics, and, for this reason, it may be helpful to view them contiguously. Unlike systems approaches, however, they operate from a less abstract base, building their accounts of regulatory dynamics from detailed observation of the patterns of interaction in a particular regulatory context. Accordingly, their unit of analysis tends to be a specific policy sector, such as public health, education or financial services. While these approaches, for those new to the study of regulation, may seem relatively amorphous, they are useful in highlighting complexity. In particular, they challenge divisions between public and private spheres, the existence of which may be too readily taken for granted in public and private interest approaches to regulation.

Regulatory instruments and techniques

While theories of regulation explore *why* regulation emerges, *which* actors contribute to that emergence and typical *patterns of interaction* between regulatory actors, Chapter 3 explores *how* the state attempts to influence social behaviour in pursuit of its policy goals. The discussion begins by exploring the wide array of instruments and techniques used to regulate social behaviour with the aim of understanding their mechanics. Although academics have sought to classify policy instruments in many different ways, no single classification system has emerged as definitive. Chapter 3 adopts a classification system which organises regulatory instruments according to the underlying 'modality' of control through which behaviour is intended to respond, identifying five such modalities: command, competition, communication, consensus and code (or 'architecture'). This schematic division is an oversimplification, adopted primarily as a heuristic device to illuminate the nature of tool-mechanics. As we shall see, many instruments are more accurately characterised as hybrid in nature, relying upon more than one mechanism in attempting to regulate behaviour. Indeed the general trend within literature concerning regulatory tools and techniques is to advocate combining techniques rather than relying upon any single instrument: an approach often referred to as a 'regulatory toolbox' approach.

As the toolbox metaphor implies, much of this literature assumes that questions concerning how to regulate are technocratic ones, driven by the quest to find effective solutions to problems. But one's choice of instrument has inescapable political dimensions, which Chapter 3 also seeks to unpack. So, for example, competition-based approaches that draw upon the competitive discipline of markets are typically seen as offering a greater degree of autonomy to citizens whose behaviour the state is seeking to influence. But in so doing, such approaches may convey implicit legitimation of that behaviour if the price is right. So, for example, attempts to reduce environmental pollution through a scheme of tradeable permits may imply that polluting activities are socially acceptable, unlike a scheme which prohibits environmental pollution and imposes penal sanctions on those who violate the legal prohibition. These normative dimensions are brought to the fore by examining law's expressive role in elaborating these techniques.

Enforcement and compliance

The exploration of compliance and enforcement undertaken in Chapter 4 focuses on the 'human face' of regulation. It is through the enforcement process that a set of legal standards designed to influence human and institutional behaviour is translated into social reality. Although enforcement action is necessary within all regulatory regimes, whatever modality of control is employed (with the possible exception of code), the literature on enforcement and compliance has focused primarily on enforcement taking place within a traditional command and control regime. Accordingly, this chapter begins with an examination of the problems associated with the interpretation, design and application of the law's command, where that command takes the form of legally enforceable rules. Many of these problems are ultimately attributable to the imprecise and indeterminate contours of human communication. But while the fallibility of human communication generates numerous difficulties, it also provides the creative potential for overcoming the limitations of rule-based control. It is the capacity for human interpretation and judgment exercised by regulatory enforcement officials that has formed the focus of a rich and well-developed literature documenting the findings of a varied range of ethnographic studies that have sought to investigate, understand and explain how regulatory enforcement officers seek to secure compliance. This literature has provided the springboard for further development in academic scholarship, albeit of a more normative kind, in developing prescriptive models intended to guide public officials in making enforcement decisions.

While much of the literature in this field has concerned variety in enforcement styles, there is also a related but distinct strand of literature concerned with variety in regulatory sanctions and the liability rules attaching to those sanctions. We examine these issues in the third part of the chapter, in the course of exploring the role of public and private actors in the enforcement process. The chapter closes by reflecting on the way the law contributes to regulatory enforcement and compliance. As we shall see, central to the study of regulatory enforcement is the width of discretion within regulatory systems (in the hands of both public and private actors), providing ample scope for human action, error, manipulation and creativity.

Legitimacy and accountability

The deeper evaluative questions of the kind touched on at the end of Chapter 4 are further explored in Chapter 5 by examining ideas of regulatory legitimacy and accountability. For this purpose, accountability is conceptualised as a set of mechanisms and processes that impose an obligation to reveal, to explain and to justify regulatory actions, and is therefore instrumental securing regulatory legitimacy. Treating accountability in this way initially involves a primarily functional analysis that identifies who is accountable, to whom, and for what in a particular regulatory arena. An important strand of the literature emphasises the increasing pluralism of actors implicated in accountability regimes, reflecting the general trend towards a decentred account of regulation. In so doing, it highlights not only the role of state institutions (legislatures, administrators, courts), but also the role of markets, consultation processes, third party auditing and accreditation mechanisms, private grievance procedures and so forth. From this perspective, accountability is secured by a complex array of interdependent and overlapping mechanisms rather than through a vertical hierarchy in which top-down state-centred mechanisms and institutions legitimate the activities of regulatory actors.

This approach raises a crucial challenge: identifying how and when to combine different mechanisms of accountability and to understand their interaction. In rising to this challenge, scholars have constructed various models or typologies of legitimacy which link different concrete mechanisms and strategies of accountability to particular sets of values that are considered essential preconditions to the establishment of regulatory legitimation. Legitimation here is a term that seeks to capture the extent to which a broad community acceptance of a regulatory regime subsists – that is, the extent to principal stakeholders and the general public are willing to give it allegiance. The range of these models and typologies is extensive, but they can be broadly organised around a key cleavage between pluralist and expertise models of legitimacy. While much of the literature in this field advocates nuanced combinations of a range of strategies and values, the desirability of any particular combination is ultimately a product of an underlying commitment to a particular political vision of governance. In particular, tensions between pluralism and expertise are concrete manifestations of disagreement over the commitments entailed by democratic governance. We therefore conclude the chapter by briefly considering the implications of contrasting visions of democracy for accountability and regulatory legitimation.

Regulation above and beyond the state

While the conceptual map developed in Chapters 2 through 5 are primarily developed through an exploration of regulation at the national level, Chapter 6 considers regulation occurring at the supranational level. Unlike the preceding four chapters, Chapter 6 has two aims: first, to consider the extent to which the analytic map developed in the first four chapters transposes to regulation in the supranational context, and second, to consider whether the shift to regulation above and beyond the state alters the role of law in regulation. Accordingly, Chapter 6 constructs an argument, supported by brief referenced examples, rather than interleaving commentary and extracts from academic literature in the manner of Chapters 2 to 5. As we shall see, in comparison to regulation at the national level, regulation above and beyond the state raises some common issues, whilst also posing different challenges or shifts in emphasis, from the parameters provided by scholarly examination of national regulation. In particular, when reflecting upon theories and techniques of regulation, compliance and legitimacy in the supranational context, the absence of an overarching authoritative institution equivalent to the nation-state that may legitimately exercise coercive power on the basis of its democratic underpinnings has a variety of implications. These can often be explored using the same theoretical resources already discussed in Chapters 2 to 5. At times, however, the supranational regulatory environment changes the prominence of particular facets of these frameworks. For example, network approaches to regulatory theory gain particular prominence as an inevitable consequence of the absence of an authoritative 'centre'. But the absence of an authoritative 'centre' also alters the context in which private interest theories of regulation operate and, as a result, the implications of their applicability. When exploring regulatory techniques, the range of command vs. competition-based approaches may be readily transposable in conceptual terms but, in practice, the absence of any overarching coercive source of authority seriously impedes their effective deployment. Thus voluntary or consensual-based techniques of regulation tend to be heavily relied upon, although these are often bolstered, albeit indirectly, by law's coercive reach through the harnessing of supranational regulatory programme to binding international trade commitments.

Sometimes the similarities are perhaps more striking than the shifts in emphasis. For example, dependence upon the exercise of discretion by regulatory enforcement officials in giving concrete expression to national regulatory norms resonates strongly with dependence upon the discretion of national legislatures and administrations to implement regulatory norms established at the supranational level in achieving global regulatory goals. Likewise, the monitoring function performed by non-state actors, be they private litigants or civil society groups, has been the focus of scholarly examination in both national and supranational contexts. The tension between pluralism and expertise as different sources of legitimacy in regulatory contexts also applies in a supranational context, as does the scope for participation by non-state actors and the complication of vertical hierarchies by networks of experts. However, the challenge to state sovereignty arising in the supranational context poses the questions of legitimacy that plague regulatory accountability within national contexts in a more intensely politicised way.

Conclusion

Before proceeding further, it may be helpful to identify how our approach relates to, yet differs from, approaches which other scholars of regulation have adopted. We are, as we stated earlier, hoping to reach both lawyers and non-lawyers, particularly those who are new to the field. However, we also seek to address readers who have some familiarity with the broad field of regulation. For lawyers with some exposure to the field, the idea of a 'legal perspective' on regulation may well evoke two particular strands of literature: the first about the administrative state, particularly analyses by public lawyers of the exercise of legal discretion by independent regulatory agencies; and the second concerning the role of courts and the growing juridification of regulation. While the insights of the first strand of literature are springboards to the approach we adopt in this book, the way we have constructed a map of the field adapts more readily to regulation involving non-state actors and extends more readily beyond the borders of the state. And while the juridification literature is incorporated within our exploration of regulatory legitimacy, our overall aim of incorporating multi-disciplinary material necessitates a more expansive focus. Thus both these literatures are complementary to our approach and, taken together, all contribute to enriched views of the law's relationship to regulation.

In addition, and especially in the context of broader social science approaches to regulation, there are three strands of literature that inhabit overlapping territory to that sketched out in this book. Among the most prominent is the rapidly expanding literature concerning risk, which inhabits even larger territory than that of regulation. The contours of its debates are equally contested and complex, but we consider one aspect of the risk literature – social scientific approaches to risk management – to share our concerns, albeit expressed in different language. The following edited quotation by a leading risk scholar reveals that, absent the detailed context and terminology of risk discourses, the issues raised in this literature are remarkably similar to those of regulation: indeed, the terms 'risk management' and 'regulation' could almost be used interchangeably, at least in this quotation:

> There is no commonly accepted definition for the term risk – neither in the sciences nor in public understanding . . . the term 'risk' is often associated with the possibility that an undesirable state of reality (adverse effects) may occur as a result of natural events or human activities . . . Risk is therefore both a descriptive and normative concept . . . [and] carries the implicit message to reduce undesirable effects through appropriate modification of the causes or, though less desirable, mitigation of the consequences . . . Risk management refers to the process of reducing the risks to a level deemed tolerable by society and to assure control, monitoring and public communication. (Renn 1998: 50–51)

This book overlaps with only one small part of the risk literature and adopts an approach that may differ in both methodological and philosophical fundamentals. The same is true of the literature on governmentality which draws on Foucauldian social theory. While scholars adopting a Foucauldian approach often focus on similar subject matter to that of scholars of regulation, the language they employ and worldview they adopt are radically different, and we have chosen not to explore the potential links or disconnects in this book.

Any attempt to classify theoretical materials is inevitably fraught with problems of boundary-drawing, and this problem is especially acute in an area such as regulation that has no natural disciplinary home. The framework that we offer does not purport to be fully comprehensive of all approaches: other people may draw the boundaries differently. For example, our framework is not structured around the role of various state organs, such as the legislature, executive and judiciary, although many of the issues surrounding their contribution to regulation are discussed in different parts of the book. The index can offer guidance to those interested in particular facets of regulation that are not immediately apparent from the chapter sub-headings. Moreover, with the exception of Chapter 6, each chapter, and sub-sections within chapters, can be read independently. In this way, the book may be a useful reference for those with a tangential interest in regulation, in addition to offering a map of the field to those interested in regulation as a whole. In setting out to construct a framework for thinking about regulation, we are not asserting that it is the best, let alone the only such framework. Grandiosity of this kind would be misplaced, particularly in a text which seeks to be introductory, and to enthuse the uninitiated. We hope that the approach offered here will serve this purpose.

References

Black, J. 2001. 'Decentring regulation: The role of regulation and self regulation in a "Post Regulatory" world', *Current Legal Problems* 54: 103–146.

Brans, M. and Rossbach, S. 1997. 'The autopoiesis of administrative systems : Niklas Luhmann on public administration and public policy', *Public Administration* 75: 417–439.

Hood, C., Rothstein, H. and Baldwin, R. 2001. *The Government of Risk*, Oxford: Oxford University Press.

Morgan, B. 2003. *Social Citizenship in the Shadow of Competition*, Law, Power and Justice Series, Aldershot: Ashgate.

Ogus, A. 2004. *Regulation: Legal Form and Economic Theory*, Oxford: Hart Publishing.

Renn, O. 1998. 'Three decades of risk research: Accomplishments and new challenges', *Journal of Risk Research* 1: 49–71.

Silbey, S. 1997. 'Let them eat cake': Globalisation, postmodern colonialism, and the possibilities of justice', *Law and Society Review* 31: 207–235.
Teubner, G. 1986. 'After legal instrumentalism? Strategic models of post - regulatory law', in Teubner, G. (ed.) *Dilemmas of Law in the welfare State*, Berlin: Walter de Gruyter.

Suggested further reading

Baldwin, R. and Cave, M. 1999. *Understanding Regulation: Theory, Strategy and Practice*, Oxford: Oxford University Press.
Baldwin, R., and McCrudden, C. 1987. *Regulation and Public Law*, London: Weidenfeld and Nicholson.
Baldwin, R., Scott, C. and Hood, C. (eds.) 1998. *A Reader on Regulation*, Oxford Readings in Socio-Legal Studies, Oxford: Oxford University Press.
Coglianese, C. and Kagan, R. 2006. *Regulation and Regulatory Processes*, Aldershot: Ashgate.
Daintith, T. 1997. 'Regulation', in Buxbaum, R. and Madl, F. (eds.) *International Encyclopedia of Comparative Law*, Volume XVII, 'State and Economy', Tübingen: J. C. B. Mohr (Paul Siebeck), New York: Oceana.
Derthick, M. and Quirk, P. 1985. *The Politics of Deregulation*, Washington DC: Brookings Institution.
Harlow, C. and Rawlings, R. 2004. *Law and Administration*, Law in Context Series, 2nd edition, Cambridge: Cambridge University Press.
Levy-Faur, D. and Jordana, J. (eds.) 2004. *The Politics of Regulation: Institutions and Regulatory Reforms for the Age of Governance*, Cheltenham: Edward Elgar.
Moran, M. 2002. 'Understanding the regulatory state', *British Journal of Political Science* 32: 391–413.
Nonet, P. and Selznick, P. 1978. *Law and Society in Transition: Toward Responsive Law*, New York: Harper & Row.
Scott, C. (ed.) 2003. *Regulation, The international library of essays in law and legal Theory Series*, Aldershot: Ashgate.
Wilson, J. Q. (ed.) 1982. *The Politics of Regulation*, New York: Basic Books.

2

Theories of regulation

2.1 Introduction

A theory of regulation is a set of propositions or hypotheses about *why* regulation emerges, *which actors* contribute to that emergence and typical *patterns of interaction* between regulatory actors. In answering the 'why' question, we range beyond law to other disciplines, and much of the material in this chapter draws upon the disciplines of politics, economics and sociology. In order to understand the academic literature on this topic, it is helpful to bear in mind two core ideas, which help to differentiate the focus of theories of regulation. Firstly, some theories assume a relatively clear dividing line between public and private actors and institutions while others view the line as blurred both in theory and practice. Secondly, some theories focus mainly on economically defined goals, factors and influences, while others supplement this focus with attention to more broadly defined political goals, factors and influences. Somewhat less attention has been paid to the kinds of values and concerns which lawyers tend to emphasise in exploring the patterned emergence of regulation. The aims of this chapter are therefore twofold. Firstly, to guide the reader through the different theories of regulation, drawing out the contrasts between the roles they give to public and private actors and institutions, and the degree to which they incorporate efficiency-enhancing, redistributive and other broader social objectives. Secondly, to consider the facilitative role of law in theories of regulation and to introduce (within that role) the image of law as umpire. Because existing literature on theories of regulation is largely inattentive to the role of law, this aim will be achieved by drawing out the implications of the text extracts in commentary.

We have divided theories of regulation into three main categories: public interest theories, private interest theories and institutionalist theories. All three categories have in common a concern to uncover the processes that lead to the adoption of a particular regulatory regime. Where regulation is understood essentially as state intervention into the economy by making and applying legal rules, theories of regulation can be seen as an explanation of how and why legislative standards come about. Public interest and private interest theories in particular can be approached as accounts of what happens to make government actors pass detailed rules that govern the conduct of private actors. But as Chapter 1 has emphasised, regulation scholarship is increasingly challenging the 'understanding' of regulation as state-enacted legal rules. As we shall see, private and other non-governmental actors play an increasingly important role in establishing and implementing regulation. Public interest theories of regulation attribute to legislators (and others responsible for the design and implementation of regulation) a desire to pursue collective goals with the aim of promoting the general welfare of the community. Private interest theories, by contrast, are skeptical of the so-called 'public interestedness' of legislators and policy-makers, recognising that regulation often benefits particular groups in society, and not always those it was ostensibly intended to benefit. Institutionalist theories tend to emphasise the interdependency of state and non-state actors in the pursuit of both public benefit and private gain within regulatory regimes. Although these theories originally focused on implementing regulation, they have powerful implications for uncovering the processes of how regulatory regimes emerge: implications which challenge divisions between public and private institutions or actors.

It is worth noting that theories of regulation often contain a mixture of explanatory and prescriptive elements, the former focusing on trying to *explain* why regulation emerges and the latter identifying the goal or goals which regulation *should* pursue. For example, some public interest theories of regulation may explain the emergence of regulation as a response to market failure, yet also *prescribe* regulation as the 'correct' response to market failure, because regulation should pursue the goal of achieving economic efficiency. By contrast, some private interest theories explain the emergence of regulation as a result of the pressure of private interest groups seeking to secure benefits for themselves. Some (but not all) private interest explanations may also be accompanied by a prescriptive assessment of whether the outcomes resulting from the processes they document are economically efficient. These examples suggest that we should not assume that public interest theories are prescriptive while private interest theories are explanatory. The inability to classify all public interest theories as prescriptive and all private interest theories as explanatory becomes more apparent once we examine theories of regulation that explicitly base their entire approach upon the potential fluidity of boundaries — both between public and private interest theories, and between explanatory and prescriptive motivations. Our third category of theory, which we loosely describe as 'institutionalist' approaches, highlights such fluidity. We will now proceed to explore these categories in more detail.

2.2   Public interest theories of regulation

Public interest theories of regulation, as stated above, attribute to legislators and others responsible for the design and implementation of regulation a desire to pursue collective goals with the aim of promoting the general welfare of the community. They can be further subdivided into those that articulate regulatory goals in terms of economic efficiency and those which include other political goals.

2.2.1   Welfare economics approaches

The 'economic version' of public interest theory is probably the most well known. In simple terms, it suggests that regulation is a response to imperfections in the market known as 'market failures'. Correction of market failures increases the community's general welfare and is thus in the public interest. Correlatively, those who press for regulation in response to market failures are agents of the public interest. Market failures can be typically defined by categories of monopoly (and other anti-competitive behaviour), externalities, public goods and information asymmetries. Ogus provides a clear explanation of these various market failures in the following extract.

Anthony Ogus, '*Regulation*' (2004)

We can see regulation as the necessary exercise of collective power through government in order to cure 'market failures' to protect the public from such evils as monopoly behavior, "destructive" competition, the abuse of private economic power, or the effects of externalities. Something like this account, explicitly or implicitly, underpins virtually all public-interest accounts of regulation. Regulation is justified because the regulatory regime can do what the market cannot. Where the regulatory regime works – produces market-correcting, general-interest policies – it should be left alone ... Any attempt to formulate a comprehensive list of public interest goals which may be used to justify regulation would be futile, since what constitutes the 'public interest' will vary according to time, place, and the specific values held by a particular society. In this [section], we shall nevertheless examine those [economic] goals which in modern Western societies have typically been asserted as reasons for collectivist measures, and which are derived from the perceived shortcomings of the market system. ... [We will] ... construe economic welfare in terms of allocative efficiency, a situation in which resources are put to their most valuable uses. ... [O]n certain key assumptions, the unrestricted interaction of market forces generates such efficiency. In the real world in many sets of circumstances these assumptions, notably adequate information, competition, and the absence of externalities, are not fulfilled – in short, there is 'market failure'. Many instances of market failure are remediable, in theory at least, by private law and thus by instrument which are compatible with the market system in the sense that collective action is not required. But ... private law cannot always provide an effective solution. Where, then, 'market failure' is accompanied by 'private law failure' ... there is a prima facie case for regulatory intervention in the public interest. It is important to stress that it is only a prima facie, and not a conclusive, case for such intervention. The reason is that either the regulatory solution may be no more successful in correcting the inefficiencies than the market or private law, or that any efficiency gains to which it does give rise may be outweighed by increased transaction costs of misallocations created in other sectors of the economy. In other words, 'market failure' and 'private law failure' have to be compared with 'regulatory failure'.

Monopolies and natural monopolies

Competition is a crucial assumption of the market model. Where it is seriously impaired by monopolies and anti-competitive practices there is market failure. Competition (or antitrust) law is the principle instrument for dealing with this problem ... A 'natural monopoly' is a special kind of monopoly which calls for very different treatment. While the undesirable consequences (that goods are overpriced and under produced relative to their true social value) arise equally in relation to natural monopolies, the remedy for the latter lies not in competition. Rather, the monopoly is allowed to prevail; and some form of (economic) regulation is necessary to control those consequences.

A natural monopoly occurs where it is less costly to society for production to be carried out by one firm, rather than by several or many. In most industries there are economies of scale; since part of a firm's costs are fixed, it is proportionally cheaper to increase output. But this is normally true only up to a certain point, beyond which the marginal costs of a firm's production tend to rise. The classic instance of a natural monopoly is where the marginal costs − and hence also average costs − of a single firm's production continue, in the long run, to decline. The monopoly tends to develop 'naturally' as it becomes apparent that a single firm can supply the total output of an industry more cheaply than more than one firm. Such a situation typically occurs when fixed costs, that is, those that are necessarily incurred whatever the level of output, are high relative to demand. Thus, for example, the supply of electricity requires an enormous initial investment in plant and cables and so forth before even the smallest demand can be met. On the assumption that these fixed costs constitute a high proportion of the total costs of supply, than once the initial investment has been made, the average costs of additional units declines as more are produced.

Even if the marginal costs of production begin to rise at a certain point, thus giving rise to what is sometimes called a 'temporary' natural monopoly, there may be features in the market which still make it cheaper for one firm to produce the total output of an industry. For example, demand may vary considerably according to time and season − there are peak consumption periods of electricity during certain winter hours − and yet the supplier must respond instantaneously to the demand. A second feature, which applies particularly to systems of communication, is interdependence of demand. If one person wishes to speak by telephone to another, and/or receive calls from him, both must subscribe to the same network; there is clearly an economy of scale in a single network. Intuitively, too, it would seem that the duplication of facilities, for example and laying of railway tracks or the construction of grid systems, is itself wasteful and therefore economically to be avoided. The essence of the problem is, however, not the duplication itself − there is such duplication in all competitive markets − but rather the ability, or inability, of the suppliers to achieve economies of scale through the use of a single set of facilities . . . .

Public goods

The second instance of market failure arises in relation to public goods. As its name would suggest, a public good is a commodity the benefit from which is shared by the public as a whole, or by some group within it. More specifically, it combines two characteristics: first, consumption by one person does not leave less for others to consume; and, a secondly, it is impossible or too costly for the supplier to exclude those who do not pay for the benefit. Take the often-cited example of a national defence system which provides collective security. That all citizens of Manchester will benefit from such a system will not diminish the benefit that will be enjoyed by citizens of Salford and it is not possible to prevent any citizens of Salford − say, one who does not pay his taxes − from the protection which the system provides. The example should make it obvious why the market method of allocation cannot be used to determine supply of a public good. Suppose a private firm offered to provide a community with protection according to the level of demand for such protection, as expressed by the willingness to pay. Each individual in the community would know that however much she was willing to pay for the protection would not affect the amount of protection actually supplied, because each would be able to benefit to the same degree however much she paid. If she paid nothing, she would still be able to 'free-ride'. Willingness to pay, in other words, cannot be used to measure demand and will thus fail to provide incentives for suppliers to produce.

National (or local) security is an example of a pure public good. Such goods are typically provided by suppliers which are publicly owned − in our example, the armed forces and the police. In fact this is not (economically) essential; a private firm could supply the good, but a public agency is required both to raise sufficient money to secure the supply and to make decisions determining the quantity and quality of the public good. The first of these functions must be carried out by a public institution because, to overcome the free-rider problem, it must have police power to impose taxes. The second requires the political authority to make decisions representing the will of the community, given that demand cannot be determined through individual preferences, as reflected in willingness to pay. However, that very inability to measure demand by reference to individual preferences makes it virtually impossible to devise 'rational' institutional structures for ascertaining the will of the community with any precision. If a policy-maker has to decide how much collective security to 'purchase', he should in theory ascertain the aggregate society demand by a summation of what all individuals within the community would be prepared, by way of taxes, to pay for it. Even if this information could be gathered at reasonable cost, it would be unreliable, since, given the free-rider problem referred to above, each individual would know that the amount which she stipulates that she is ready to pay would not affect the level of provision. Conventional democratic process cannot fare much better. Voting in a referendum cannot reflect the intensity of preferences – each voter can say only 'yes' or 'no' to a proposed programme – and electing representatives of a legislature invariably involves expressing preferences between different packages of policies.

There are many commodities which, though not pure public goods, nevertheless contain some public good dimension – they are sometimes referred to as 'impure' public goods. Such goods may be supplied and bought in the market but, unless corrected by regulatory interventions, they are subject to a degree of market failure. Education and training constitute examples. Clearly the person who receives this commodity is the primary beneficiary and the price that she is willing to pay for it should, in theory at least, reflect that benefit, principally the increase to her earning capacity. But other members of society also gain from the provision of education and training. For example, there are assumed to be material gains to present and future generations from a better-trained workforce; education may encourage socially responsible behaviour and political stability through a more informed electorate; and – though these may be difficult to define and to locate – 'cultural heritage' may be enriched.

Granted the existence of these consequences, a misallocation of resources will result from the unfettered operation of the market: the price which suppliers are able to obtain will not reflect the true social value of the education and training and, in consequence, there will be underproduction. The simplest regulatory corrective is for the payment of a public subsidy which will reflect this divergence between the private value of the product and its social value. But the public good hypothesis may also provide a justification for other forms of intervention. If society derives a benefit from education and training over and above that acquired by the immediate recipient, then it also has an interest in the quality of the product, and that may justify subjecting the contract between supplier and purchaser to the imposition of public quality standards.

Other externalities
Public goods constitute one type of externality, a form of market failure [in which] if a producer's activity imposes costs on third parties that are not reflected (or 'internalised') in the prices which he charges for his products a misallocation of resources results: purchasers of the product do not pay for its true social cost and hence more units of the products are supplied than is socially appropriate. [P]rivate law instruments may fail to correct [this] misallocation. We must now explore some aspects of externalities and the problems that are posed for effective regulation. Much traditional analysis tends to concentrate on relatively simple examples of externalities: an industrial polluter imposing costs on a neighbouring landowner should be made to 'internalise' that cost – the 'polluter-pay principle' – by means either of private law (for example, an action in nuisance) or of regulation (imposing environmental standards or taxing discharges). But externalities may have widespread effects, leading to considerable complexities for policy-makers concerned to devise appropriate legal corrections. Suppose that the pollution involves irreversible

ecological changes, which have a presumed adverse impact only on future generations. The misallocation cannot be corrected by private legal instruments because of
the time-lag in the private rights accruing. On public interest grounds, regulation
may be called for. But, 'rationally', how is the appropriate level of intervention to
be determined?

Take next the following example. A road bridge is poorly constructed and has to
be closed for two weeks for repairs to be effected. Traffic is diverted through
a peaceful village, causing disamenities to residents there; the congestion creates
delays to road users leading to productivity losses and inconvenience; and businesses
(e.g. a petrol station) adjacent to the bridge may lose custom during the two weeks.
On the face of it, we have here a series of externalities requiring some form
of correction. Typically when situations like this have generated private law claims
for compensation they have been rejected, and judges and academic commentators
have struggled in efforts to articulate policy and formulate principles justifying
such conclusions. Regulatory systems faced with similar problems have not reached
different solutions.

There are several reasons why it may be inappropriate to attempt to correct
apparent externalities, such as those described. In the first place, the third party on
whom the cost is imposed may have received *ex ante*, or will receive *ex post*, indirect
compensation for the loss. In these circumstances, no misallocation occurs. The facts
of the bridge case may be adapted to provide an illustration of *ex post* compensation.
If the petrol station suffers short-term losses while the bridge is being repaired
but gains in the long term from an increased traffic flow when improvements are
complete, no intervention is required: in a rough and ready way, the external cost has
been cancelled out by an external benefit. As regards *ex ante* compensation, suppose
that I purchase property in the knowledge that a firm nearby is engaged in a polluting
activity which will to some extent reduce the amenities attaching to my land.
Rationally, I will pay less for the property then would otherwise have been the
case. In such circumstances, the pollution does not constitute an externality, for
the capital value of my purchase has not been depreciated; through the reduced
price, the market has already taken account of the cost.

This pollution example also illustrates another problem in the definition
of externalities, and this leads us to the second reason why a corrective measure
may be inappropriate. We tend to envisage the externalities as unilaterally imposed
by one person (or firm) on another. In fact the causation issue is more subtle and
the policy implications, in consequence, more complex. It can be argued that the
cost, the disamenity attaching to my land, is as much the result of my presence there
as it is of the firm polluting the environment. No problem would, of course, arise
if the firm did not pollute; but equally no problem would arise if I (or someone else)
were not there to receive the pollution. Understood in this way, the language of
'externalities' disguises the basic nature of the problem, that there is a friction arising from the competing and conflicting claim of two parties (the firm and me) for
use of a single resource — the atmosphere. How should the conflict be resolved?
Applying the criterion of allocative efficiency, the economic answer is that the burden

of avoiding of eliminating the friction should be imposed on whichever of the parties can achieve this at lowest cost. If it costs the firm more to abate the pollution than for me not to locate my home in the vicinity, or to relocate if my purchase of the property predates the industrial activity, then economically it is inappropriate for the law, public or private, to restrain the pollution. Of course, for the purpose of this calculation, care must be taken to include all the costs arising from the avoidance or elimination of the friction. In the typical atmospheric pollution situation, large numbers (including possibly future generations) compete with the polluter for use of the environment, and, given the very high aggregate of their avoidance costs, abatement of the pollution will usually be the cheaper solution.

Thirdly, it is not appropriate on economic grounds to eliminate what are often referred to as 'pecuniary' externalities; these, unlike 'technological' externalities, do not give rise to a misallocation of resources. What we have hitherto considered as externalities are 'technological' externalities: they are harmful or beneficial effects on one party's productive activity or utility directly resulting from another party's behaviour. 'Pecuniary' externalities, on the other hand, are pure value (financial) changes borne by their parties which result from changes in technology or in consumer preferences. They involve indirect effects which alter the demand faced by the harmed or benefited third party. Pecuniary externalities are the result of the natural play of market forces. They involve wealth transfers which cancel out and not increases in the costs faced by society.

An example may help to clarify the important distinction. Alf is in the music-recording business; he sells tapes recorded in his studio. Celia, a neighbour, who manufactures widgets, installs new machinery which increases her productivity but is very noisy. Alf, as a result, has to add soundproofing to his studio. Bert markets a new recording device which is bought by some of Alf's competitors and enables them to sell tapes at a reduced price; in consequence, the demand for Alf's tapes drops dramatically. Alf purchases Bert's device to reduce his costs. Celia's noise is a technological externality since it increases social costs. Bert's device, on the other hand, while it may impose a loss on Alf, is a pecuniary externality: it does not add to social costs; rather, it enables resources to move to a more valuable use.

Finally, account must, of course, be taken of transaction costs. An externality may give rise to a misallocation but the administrative and other costs of correcting it may outweigh the social benefits arising from such action. It is for this reason that many trivial, or relatively trivial, externalities are ignored. However, what may lead to a trivial cost for each individual affected may in aggregate involve non-trivial and even substantial costs. The series of bomb hoaxes which at the time of writing are afflicting the operation of the main London railway termini illustrates the point well. If the time (opportunity) costs of all travellers are delayed and added to (i) their anxiety and hassle costs, (ii) the costs to travellers not directly involved but who in the light of the hoax choose a less preferred mode of transport, and (iii) the costs of security searches, the total must be considerable and would thus justify a substantial outlay in regulating the conduct.

Information deficits and bounded rationality

Consumer choice lies at the heart of the economic notion of allocative efficiency. To aim at a state in which resources move to their more highly valued uses implies that choices between sets of alternatives may be exercised; individuals prefer some commodities to others and such preferences are reflected in demand. The market system of allocation is fuelled by an infinite number of expressions of these preferences. However, the assertion that observed market behaviour in the form of expressed preferences leads to allocative efficiency depends crucially on two fundamental assumptions: that decision-makers have adequate information on the set of alternatives available, including the consequences to them of exercising choice in different ways; and that they are capable of processing that information and of 'rationally' behaving in a way that maximises their expected utility. A significant failure of either assumption may set up a prima facie case for regulatory intervention. Although traditional economic analysis of markets often assumes 'perfect' information, clearly the phenomenon never exists in the real world; some degree of uncertainty as to present or future facts must always be present. Equally clearly, from a public interest perspective, the absence of 'perfect' information cannot itself justify intervention. Given that information is costly to supply and to assimilate, the relevant policy question is rather whether the unregulated market generates 'optimal' information in relation to a particular area of decision-making, that is, where the marginal costs of supplying and processing the level and quality of information in question and approximately equal to the marginal benefits that are engendered. An analogy can usefully be drawn with the way in which an individual makes decisions on acquiring further information by means of comparative shopping. Suppose that I want to trade in the car I currently possess for a new car of a particular model. As I set out, I have no information on the likely price I will pay. The first dealer I visit offers me the new car for a certain sum . . . plus my car. Should I proceed to other dealers to obtain comparable information? Rationally, I should do so only if the benefit, the chance of obtaining a better price . . . exceeds my marginal cost . . . in terms of time and travel etc. in visiting the second dealer . . . . Indeed, I should go on obtaining further price quotations up to the point where the marginal cost of obtaining the last quotation equals the marginal benefit — I shall then have obtained the 'optimal' information for the transaction . . . [For a number of] reasons, precise estimation of 'optimal' information are unattainable, nevertheless it is possible to identify situations in which the information generated by the unregulated market is likely to be substantially sub-optional, thus locating areas of 'information failure' for possible interventionist measures.

The costs to consumers of acquiring adequate information on which to make purchasing decisions are often substantial. By means of advertising, sellers can typically provide this information more cheaply because economies of scale are involved and, in a competitive market, they have an incentive to do this, in order to distinguish their products from those of their competitors. There are, however, several factors which may blunt this incentive, or else lead to countervailing inefficiencies. First, the fact that information typically has a public good dimension — it is difficult at low cost to restrict its transmission to those who directly or indirectly pay for it and consumption by one user does not lower its value to other users – implies that there will be an under provision of such information in the unregulated market. Secondly, a seller's effort to distinguish his products from those of his competitors may lead to artificial product differentiation. This is a process in which potential buyers are led to believe that a particular commodity has special characteristics which either do not exist or are insignificant in relation to its use of consumption. The consequence is that the seller obtains a degree of monopolistic power over the product which is economically undesirable. Thirdly, the seller's incentive may extend to supplying false or misleading information, as well as accurate information, if he believes that that will enhance his profits. Such a practice may, of course, give rise to private law remedies for misrepresentation, and the prospect of a contract being held unenforceable, or damages being ordered, will reduce the incentive to cheat. For this purpose, it is important to appreciate that not all purchasers need to sue, or threaten to sue, for the private law sanction to be effective. The existence of a sufficient number of individuals at the margin – estimated to be about one-third of all customers – able to detect the deception and threaten effective action will ensure that competitive pressures are sufficient to discipline traders. Nevertheless, there may not be a sufficient number at the margin able to detect the deception, and for those who do the transaction costs incurred in taking steps to complain and threaten legal action may be high relative to their individual losses. To meet such contingencies, regulatory controls may be prima facie justifiable. Fourthly, competition may induce sellers to provide information as to a product's positive qualities, but what about negative qualities, that is, potential defects and risks? For obvious reasons, they are unlikely to be alluded to in advertising materials.

Another problem arises from the fact that information as to quality is more costly to supply and process then information as to price. Prices are calculated by reference to objective criteria (currency) and, in general, are easily communicated. Qualities are to some degree subjective and, particularly in the case of professional services and technologically more complex commodities, may not be discoverable by pre-purchase inspection. It follows that although consumers rationally trade price off against quality – they will be prepared to pay more for superior quality – if, on the information readily available to them, they can discriminate between prices but not between qualities, traders with higher-quality products will be driven out of the market, and there will be a general lowering of standards.

The assumption that individuals are capable of processing the information available to them and of making 'rational' utility-maximizing choices on the basis of it may be essential to the operation of the market model, but exploration of it lies largely outside the parameters of economic analysis. Most economists accept the notion that human behaviour is constrained by 'bounded rationality', that is, that the capacity of individuals to receive, store, and process information is limited. There has been some attempt to erect a model of decision-making based not on finding a utility-maximizing solution but rather on 'satisficing' that is, searching until the most satisfactory solution is found from among the limited perceived alternatives. But work of this kind has mainly been the province of psychologists, and mainstream economists have not refined their models of human behaviour to accommodate the problem.

The view of regulation portrayed in the preceding extract is essentially instrumental. Regulation is cast as a social practice that does or should function as a means to an end: that of maximising general welfare, conceived in terms of maximising allocative efficiency. Regulation may do this by correcting market failures, enhancing the efficiency of market-based ways of deciding what shall be produced, directing how resources shall be allocated in the production process and to whom the various products will be distributed. The instrumental nature of regulation from this perspective is linked to the facilitative role that law plays within regulation. Public interest theories of regulation tend to assume that regulation is embedded within legal rules enacted by legislatures, who may then delegate detailed rule creation to regulatory officials along with sometimes considerable discretion in developing such detailed rules. The legal rules in this picture are an instrument for shaping social behaviour, which regulatory officials will typically choose by evaluating whether using law in this way 'works'; i.e. whether it has the effect of securing the desired result, such as a correction of the identified market failure. Although this view of law's role may seem uncontroversial to non-lawyers, it differs considerably from the approach taken by legal academics concerned with analysing legal doctrine expounded by judges, who often focus on the internal coherence of judicial reasoning rather than on social outcomes. Public interest theories of the welfare economic kind adopt an instrumentalist view of the law, regarding it, as Tony Prosser puts it in a subsequent extract, 'as a tool used by state bodies to achieve their ends through the design of institutions'.

2.2.2   Substantive political approaches

Emphasis on the law's facilitative role in regulation may point to a possible limitation of economic conceptions of regulation, which do not explicitly incorporate values other than those concerned with achieving allocative efficiency. The underlying conception of the public interest underpinning welfare economic versions of theories of regulation is relatively narrow. They assume no more than that greater allocative efficiency in the use of society's scarce resources will reduce economic waste and allow more individuals to pursue whatever they personally consider to be their own version of the good life, expressed in terms of their ability to pay. In other words, the collective welfare is defined exclusively in terms of efficient resource use. By contrast, 'political versions' of public interest theory are more ambitious, in two important ways. Firstly, values such as social justice, redistribution or paternalism may also figure in the critical assessment of what justifies regulation. Secondly, they place greater emphasis on the *intrinsic* value of participation through a process of dialogue. From this perspective, regulation is justified when it establishes institutions that can foster collective learning through a process of participatory dialogue. Political versions of public interest theories of regulation therefore adopt a more multi-faceted conception of the public interest than economic theories; one arrived at by deliberation, mutual interchange, dialogue and collective processes.

The following two extracts illustrate these points. In the first, Sunstein discusses a range of non-economic substantive goals that justify regulatory intervention: public-interested redistribution, reducing social subordination, promoting diversity of experience, preventing harm to future generations, embodying collective desires and shaping endogenous preferences.

Cass Sunstein, '*After the rights revolution: Reconceiving the regulatory state*' (1990)

[Powerful] claims can be made, in principle, for social and economic regulation. In this respect, the relatively well-understood phenomenon of "market failure" is supplemented by a range of other defects in market ordering. A general regime of deliberate preference-shaping through governmental control of desires and beliefs is of course a central characteristic of totalitarian regimes. No one should deny that such a regime would be intolerable. But it would be most peculiar to take that point as a reason to deprive citizens in an electoral democracy of the power to implement collective aspirations through law, or to counteract, by providing information and opportunities, preferences and beliefs that have adapted to an unjust or otherwise objectionable status quo. [In fleshing out such goals], regulatory statutes . . . fall into recognizable patterns; they are often subject, at least in principle, to a powerful defence. [Such defences include redistribution, collective desires, diverse experiences, social subordination, endogenous preferences and the interests of future generations or nature].

Public-interested redistribution

Many statutes are designed to redistribute resources from one group to another. Some respond to a widely held or easily defended view that the benefited groups have a legitimate claim to the relevant resources. Statutes directly transferring resources to the poor or the disadvantaged . . . all fall in[to] this basic category.

Often redistributive measures do not directly transfer resources to disadvantaged people or to those whom we wish to subsidise, but instead attempt to deal with coordination or collective action problems faced by large groups. As we have seen, statutory protection of workers can be understood as efforts to overcome the difficulties of organization of many people in the employment market. Suppose, for example, that numerous employees prefer a nine-hour to a twelve-hour day. Suppose as well that many or most or all of them would prefer working twelve hours to not working at all. Workers may not be able to rely on the labor market to achieve their favored alternative. Individual workers will compete against each other to their collective harm. If their preferred solution is to be provided, it must be as a result of statutes that eliminate the option of unlimited working hours.

Because of the collective action problem, regulatory statutes must make the relevant rights inalienable. If workers are left free to trade these rights, the collective action problem will rematerialise. Labor markets create a prisoner's dilemma that is soluble only through governmental action. Ideas of this sort help justify minimum wage and maximum hour legislation and indeed [fair labour legislation] ... in general — though the distributional consequences here are complex, and there are many losers as well as winners, even within the group of workers. This kind of collective action problem produces a rationale for regulation that is based on redistribution rather than on economic efficiency. It is not at all clear that it is efficient to allow the creation of cartels among workers, even if it is in the interest of those thus authorised; and this latter point is not entirely clear in light of the fact that (for example) the minimum wage increases unemployment.

Regulation is often an attempt to redistribute resources to certain groups. Health and safety regulation is sometimes justified as a means of transferring resources to workers and consumers at the expense of employers and producers, whether or not there is a collective action problem. But redistributive rationales for regulation are heavily contested, and for good reason. In general, regulatory strategies are inferior to direct transfer payments as a means of redistributing wealth. One of the paradoxes of the regulatory state is that efforts to redistribute resources through regulation tend to hurt the least well-off, and in any case to have complex effects, many of them unintended and perverse. The market is extremely creative in overcoming efforts to transfer resources through regulation.

Consider, as particular examples, minimum price supports for farmers and rent control. It is by no means clear either that these regulations benefit a class with a strong claim to the public purse, or that the intended redistribution will really occur. Rent control, for example, has not served as a direct transfer of resources to the disadvantaged. On the contrary, it has discouraged new investment in housing, decreased the available housing stock, and benefited existing tenants, many of them financially well-off, at the expense of others, many of them poor.

There is a general lesson here. People often think that regulation produces a simple redistribution from one class to another, but the distributive effects of regulation are complex and sometimes unfortunate, in light of the flexibility of the market in ensuring ex ante adjustments to regulatory controls. Thus, for example, minimum wage legislation reduces employment, and some occupational health legislation decreases both salaries and employment. (To say this is not to say that such legislation should be repealed; it is necessary to know the magnitude of all of these effects in order to make such a judgment.) A related problem is that regulation sometimes benefits groups that might not deserve the help; it is not easy to argue that farmers as a class should receive the massive and varied subsidies embodied in federal law.

Collective desires and aspirations
Some statutes should be understood as an embodiment not of privately held preferences, but of what might be described as collective desires, including aspirations, "preferences about preferences", or considered judgments on the part of significant

segments of society. Laws of this sort are a product of deliberative processes on the part of citizens and representatives. They cannot be understood as an attempt to aggregate or trade off private preferences. This understanding of politics recalls Madison's belief in deliberative democracy.

Frequently, political choices cannot easily be understood as a process of aggregating prepolitical desires. Some people may, for example, want nonentertainment broadcasting on television, even though their own consumption patterns favor situation comedies; they may seek stringent environmental laws even though they do not use the public parks; they may approve of laws calling for social security and welfare even though they do not save or give to the poor; they may support antidiscrimination laws even though their own behavior is hardly race- or gender-neutral. The choices people make as political participants are different from those they make as consumers. Democracy thus calls for an intrusion on markets. The widespread disjunction between political and consumption choices presents something of a puzzle. Indeed, it sometimes leads to the view that market ordering is undemocratic and that choices made through the political process are a preferable basis for social ordering.

A generalization of this sort would be far too broad in light of the multiple breakdowns of the political process and the advantages of market ordering in many arenas. But it would also be a mistake to suggest, as some do, that markets always reflect individual choice more reliably than politics, or that political choices differ from consumption outcomes only because of confusion, as voters fail to realise that they must ultimately bear the costs of the programmes they favor. Undoubtedly consumer behavior is sometimes a better or more realistic reflection of actual preferences than is political behavior. But since preferences depend on context, the very notion of a "better reflection" of "actual" preferences is a confused one. Moreover, the difference might be explained by the fact that political behavior reflects a variety of influences that are distinctive to the context of politics. These include four closely related phenomena. First, citizens may seek to fulfil individual and collective aspirations in political behavior, not in private consumption. As citizens, people may seek the aid of the law to bring about a social state in some sense higher than what emerges from market ordering. Second, people may, in their capacity as political actors, attempt to satisfy altruistic or other-regarding desires, which diverge from the self-interested preferences characteristic of markets. Third, political decisions might vindicate what might be called meta-preferences or second-order preferences. A law protecting environmental diversity and opposing consumption behavior is an example. People have wishes about their wishes: and sometimes they try to vindicate those second-order wishes, or considered judgments about what is best, through law. Fourth, people may precommit themselves, with regulation, to a course of action that they consider to be in the general interest; the story of Ulysses and the Sirens is the model here. The adoption of a Constitution is itself an example of a precommitment strategy.

For all these reasons people seem to favor regulation designed to secure high-quality broadcasting even though their consumption patterns favor situation comedies — a phenomenon that helps justify certain controversial regulatory decisions by the Federal Communications Commission requiring nonentertainment broadcasting and presentations on issues of public importance. The same category of aspirations or public spiritedness includes measures designed to protect endangered species and natural preserves in the face of individual behavior that reflects little solicitude for them.

The collective character of politics, permitting a response to collective action problems, helps to explain these phenomena. People may not want to satisfy their meta-preferences, or to be altruistic, unless they are sure that others will be bound as well. More simply, people may prefer not to contribute to a collective benefit if donations are made individually, but their most favored system might be one in which they contribute if (but only if) there is assurance that others will do so. The collective character of politics might also overcome the problem, discussed below, of preferences and beliefs that have adapted to an unjust status quo or to limits in available opportunities. Without the possibility of collective action, the status quo may seem intractable, and private behavior will adapt accordingly. But if people can act in concert, preferences might take a quite different form; consider social movements involving the environment, labor, and race and sex discrimination. In addition, social and cultural norms might incline people to express aspirational or altruistic goals in political behavior but not in markets. Such norms may press people, in their capacity as citizens, distinctly in the direction of a concern for others or for the public interest. The deliberative aspects of politics, bringing additional information and perspectives to bear, may also bring out or affect preferences as expressed through governmental processes.

Government action is a necessary response here. Possible examples include recycling programmes, energy conservation programmes, and contributions to the arts, to the poor, and to environmental protection. The collective action problem interacts with aspirations, altruistic desires, second-order preferences, and precommitment strategies; all of these are most likely to be enacted into law in the face of a question of collective action. Moreover, consumption decisions are a product of the criterion of private willingness to pay, which contains distortions of its own. Willingness to pay is a function of ability to pay, and it is an extremely crude proxy for utility. Political behavior removes this distortion (which is not to say that it does not introduce distortions of its own).

These general considerations suggest that statutes are sometimes a response to a considered judgment on the part of the electorate that the choices reflected in consumption patterns ought to be overcome. A related but more narrow justification is that statutes safeguard noncommodity values that an unregulated market protects inadequately. Social ordering through markets may have long-term, world-transforming effects that reflect a kind of collective myopia in the form of an emphasis on short-term considerations at the expense of the future. Here regulation is a natural response. Examples include promoting high-quality programming in broadcasting, supporting the arts, and ensuring diversity through protection of the environment and of endangered species. In all of these respects, political choices are not made by consulting given or private desires, but instead reflect a deliberative process designed to shape and reflect values....

... The argument for regulation embodying collective desires is much weaker in three categories of cases. First, if the particular choice foreclosed has some special character − for instance, some forms of intimate sexual activity − it is appropriately considered a right, and the majority has not authority to intervene. Second, some collective desires might be objectionable or distorted. A social preference against racial intermarriage could not plausibly be justified as reflecting an aspiration or a precommitment strategy − though to explain why, it is necessary to offer an independent argument, challenging that preference and invoking a claim of justice. Third, some collective desires might reflect a special weakness on the part of the majority; consider a curfew law, or perhaps prohibition. In such circumstances, a legal remedy might remove desirable incentive for private self-control, have unintended side-effects resulting from "bottling up" desires, and prove unnecessary in light of the existence of alternative remedies. When any of these three concerns arise, the case for protection of collective desires is much less powerful. But in many cases these concerns are absent, and regulatory programmes initiated on these grounds are justified.

Diverse experiences and preference formation
Some regulatory programmes should be understood as an attempt to foster and promote diverse experiences, with a view toward providing broad opportunities for the formation of preferences and beliefs, and for distance from and critical scrutiny of existing desires. This rationale supports private ordering and freedom of contract as well. But it calls for regulatory safeguards when those forces push toward homogeneity and uniformity, as they often do in industrialised nations. For example, the Prevention of Significant Deterioration (PSD) programme of the Clean Air Act protests pristine areas from environmental degradation. The goal is to ensure that in a period of increasing urbanization and homogenisation, federal law ensures the preservation of unspoiled areas. This goal would be a worthy one even if private preferences, as expressed in markets, would not protect such areas. The Endangered Species Act is a similar effort to ensure that current and future generations will be able to explore diverse species of animals and plants.

Regulation of broadcasting − subsidizing public broadcasting, ensuring a range of disparate programming, or calling for high-quality programming largely unavailable in the marketplace − can be understood in similar terms. Indeed, the need to provide diverse opportunities for preference formation suggests reasons to be quite skeptical of unrestricted markets in communication and broadcasting. There is a firm theoretical justification for the much criticised and now largely abandoned "fairness doctrine", which required broadcasters to cover controversial issues and to ensure competing views. The fairness doctrine operated as an exceptionally mild corrective to a broadcasting market in which most viewers see shows that rarely deal with serious problems; are frequently sensationalistic, prurient, dehumanizing, or banal; reflect and perpetuate a bland, watered-down version of the most conventional views about politics and morality; are influenced excessively by the concerns of advertisers; and are sometimes riddled with violence, sexism, and racism. In view of the inevitable effects of such programming on character, beliefs, and even conduct, it is hardly clear that governmental "inaction" is always appropriate in a constitutional democracy; indeed the contrary seems true.

Social subordination

Some regulatory statutes attempt not simply to redistribute resources, but to elim- inate or reduce the social subordination of various social groups. Much of antidis- crimination law is designed as an attack on practices and beliefs that have adverse consequences for members of disadvantaged groups. Discriminatory attitudes and practices result in the social subordination of black, women, the handicapped, and gays and lesbians. Statutes designed to eliminate discrimination attempt to change both practices and attitudes. The motivating idea here is that differences that are irrelevant from the moral point of view ought not to be turned into social disad- vantages, and they certainly should not be permitted to do so if the disadvantage is systemic. In all of those cases, social practices turn differences into systemic harms for the relevant group....

... It is sometimes suggested that market pressures are sufficient to counteract social subordination, and that statutory intervention is therefore unnecessary. Businesses that discriminate will ultimately face economic pressure from those that do not. The refusal to hire qualified blacks and women will result in competitive injury to discriminators, who will therefore face higher costs and ultimately be driven from the marketplace. This process is said to make markets a good check on discrimination and on caste systems. Although such a process does occur in some settings, market pressures constitute, for several reasons, an inadequate constraint.

First, third parties might impose serious costs on those who agree to deal with members of disadvantaged groups; customers and others sometimes withdraw patronage or services. Consider, for example, the risks sometimes faced by firms that employ blacks, women, the disabled, and gays and lesbians. By their ability to impose costs, customers and others are well situated to prevent elimination of discriminatory practices. In these circumstances market pressures do not check discrimination, but instead guarantee that it will continue. A caste system of some sort is the predictable result. Undoubtedly such pressures have contributed to the perpetuation of discrimination in many settings.

Second, discriminatory behavior is sometimes a response to generalizations or stereotypes that, although quite overbroad and even invidious, provide an econom- ically rational basis for market decisions. Because the behavior is economically ratio- nal, not based on a competitively harmful racial animus, it will persist as long as markets do. For example, an employer might act discriminatorily not because he hates or devalues blacks or women, or has a general desire not to associate with them, or is "prejudiced" in the ordinary sense, but because he has found that the stereotypes have sufficient truth to be a basis for employment decisions. Of course it will be exceptionally difficult to disentangle these various attitudes, and they will frequently overlap; but in light of the history of discrimination against both blacks and women, it would hardly be shocking if stereotyping was sometimes economically rational.

This form of discrimination is objectionable not because it is a reflection of ordinary bigotry or even irrationality, but because it works to perpetuate the second-class citizenship of members of disadvantaged groups. Markets will do nothing about such discrimination; civil rights legislation reduces it. The example suggests that the line between antidiscrimination laws and affirmative action is far thinner than is generally believed.

Third, private preferences of both beneficiaries and victims of discrimination tend to adapt to existing injustice, and to do so in such a way as to make significant change hard to undertake. People often have a "taste" for discrimination, and one of the purposes of antidiscrimination law is to alter that taste. The beneficiaries of the status quo take advantage of strategies that reduce cognitive dissonance, such as blaming the victim. The victims also reduce dissonance by adapting their preferences to the available opportunities or by adapting their aspirations to fit their persistent belief that the world is just. Psychological mechanisms of this sort furnish a formidable barrier to social change.

In a closely related phenomenon, members of disadvantaged groups faced with widespread discrimination on the part of employers may well respond to the relevant signals by deciding to invest less than other people in the acquisition of the skills valued by the market. Individual and group productivity is a function of demand; it is not independent of it. Members of a group that is the object of discrimination may therefore end up less productive, not only because their skin color or gender is devalued, but also because the market sends signals that it is less worthwhile for them to develop the skills necessary to compete.

Fourth, and most fundamentally, markets incorporate the practices and norms of the advantaged group. Conspicuous examples include the multiple ways in which employment settings, requirements and expectations are structured for the able-bodied and for traditional male career patterns. In such cases, markets are the problem, not the solution. One goal of the advocates of antisubordination is to restructure market arrangements so as to put disadvantaged groups on a plane of equality − not by helping them to be "like" members of advantaged groups, but by changing the criteria themselves. A law cannot make it up to someone for being deaf or requiring a wheelchair; but it can aggravate or diminish the social consequences of deafness and lameness. Regulation requiring sign language and wheelchair ramps ensures that a difference is not turned into a systemic disadvantage. Here the conventional test of discrimination law − is the member of the disadvantaged group "similarly situated" to the member of the advantaged group? − itself reflects inequality, since it takes the norms and practices of the advantaged group as the baseline against which to measure inequality.

Statutes protecting the handicapped are the best example here. To say this is not to suggest the nature or degree of appropriate restructuring of the market − a difficult question in light of the sometimes enormous costs of adaptation to the norms and practices and disadvantaged groups. But it is to say that markets are far from a sufficient protection against social subordination.

Endogenous preferences
Some statutes interfere with market behavior when preferences are a function of, or endogenous to, legal rules, acts of consumption, or existing norms or practices. In these circumstances, the purpose of regulation is to affect the development of certain preferences. Regulation of addictive substances, of myopia, and of habits is a familiar example. For an addict, the costs of nonconsumption — of living without the good to which he is addicted — increase dramatically over time, as the benefits of consumption remain constant or fall sharply. The result is that the aggregate costs over time of consumption exceed the aggregate benefits, even if the initial consumption choice provides benefits that exceed costs. Behavior that is rational for each individual consumption choice may ultimately lead people into severely inferior social states. In such cases people would in all likelihood not want to become involved with the article of consumption in the first place. Regulation is a possible response.

Because of the effect of consumption, over time, on certain preferences, someone who is addicted to heroin is much worse off in the long-run — even though the original decision to consume was not irrational if one looks only at immediate costs and benefits. Statutes that regulate addictive substances respond to a social belief that the relevant preferences should not be formed in the first place.

We might describe this situation as involving an intrapersonal collective action problem, in which the costs and benefits of engaging in the relevant activity change dramatically over time for a particular individual. The central point is that consumption patterns induce a significant change in preferences. An addiction is the most obvious case, but it is part of a far broader category. Consider, for example, the sort of myopic behavior, defined as a refusal — because the short-term costs exceed the short-term benefits — to engage in activity having long-term benefits that dwarf long-term costs. Another kind of intrapersonal collective action problem is produced by habits people follow because of the subjectively high short-term costs of changing their behavior even when the long-term benefits exceed the short-term benefits . . . . For the most part, problems of this sort are best addressed at the individual level or through private associations, which minimise coercion; but social regulation is a possible response. Statutes that subsidise the arts or public broadcasting, or that discourage the formation of some habits and encourage the formation of others, are illustrations. So too are legal requirements to install seatbelts or have people buckle them. The subjective costs of buckling decrease over time. Once people are in the habit of buckling, the costs become minimal. The fact that the costs shrink rapidly after the habit of buckling has formed counts in favor of regulation, certainly on welfare grounds, and perhaps on autonomy grounds as well.

Moreover, market behavior is sometimes based on an effort to reduce cognitive dissonance by adjusting to current practices and opportunities. The point has large implications. For example, workers may underestimate the risks of hazardous activity partly in order to reduce the dissonance that would be produced by an understanding of the real dangers of the workplace.

Similar ideas help account for antidiscrimination principles. Most generally, the beliefs of both beneficiaries and victims of existing injustice are affected by dissonance-reducing strategies. The phenomenon of blaming the victim has distinct cognitive and motivational foundations. A central point here is that the strategy of blaming the victim, or assuming that an injury was deserved or inevitable, tends to permit nonvictims or members of advantaged groups to reduce dissonance by assuming that the world is just — a pervasive, insistent, and sometimes irrationally held belief. The reduction of cognitive dissonance is a powerful motivational force, and it operates as a significant obstacle to the recognition of social injustice or irrationality.

Irreversibility, future generations, animals and nature

Some statutes are a response to the problem of irreversibility — the fact that a certain course of conduct, if continued, will lead to an outcome from which current and future generations will be able to recover not at all, or only at very high cost. Since markets reflect the preferences of current consumers, they do not take account of the effect of transactions on future generations. The consequences of reliance on market ordering will sometimes be an irretrievable loss. The protection of endangered species stems in part from this fear. Much of the impetus behind laws protecting natural areas is that environmental degradation is sometimes final or extraordinarily expensive to repair. Protection of cultural relics stems from a similar rationale.

To a large degree, social and economic regulation of this sort is produced by a belief in obligations owed by the present to future generations. Current practices may produce losses that might be acceptable if no one else were affected, but that are intolerable in light of their consequences for those who will follow. Effects on future generations thus amount to a kind of externality. Such externalities might include limitations in the available range of experiences or the elimination of potential sources of medicines and pesticides; consider legislation protecting endangered species.

In more complex forms, arguments of this sort emphasise the multiple values of protecting species, animals, and nature. Some of these arguments are "anthrocentric", in the sense that they focus on the ultimate value of such protection to human beings. For example, many people enjoy seeing diversity in nature; and plants and animals furnish most of the raw materials for medicines, pesticides, and other substances with considerable instrumental worth to humanity. On this view, the loss or reduction of a species is a serious one for human beings. It is hard to monetise these values because of the difficulty of ascertaining, at any particular time, the many uses to which different species might be put.

A related but somewhat different argument emphasises the value of natural diversity for the transformation of human values and for deliberation about the good. On this view, the preservation of diverse species and of natural beauty serves to alter existing preferences and provides an occasion for critical scrutiny of current desires and beliefs. Aesthetic experiences play an important role in shaping ideas and desires, and regulation may be necessary to ensure the necessary diversity.

On a different account, the elimination of a species, particular animals, and perhaps of waters and streams is objectionable quite apart from its effects on human beings, and indeed for its own sake. This account itself takes various forms. Sometimes the argument is a democratic one: most people believe that obligations are owed to nonhuman objects, and the majority deserves to rule. Sometimes the invocation of the rights of nonhuman creatures and objects can best be understood as a rhetorical device designed to inculcate social norms that will overcome collective action problems in preserving the environment – problems that are ultimately harmful to human beings. In many hands, however, the argument, sounding in what is sometimes called "deep ecology", does not even refer to human desires. The idea here is that animals, species as such, and perhaps even natural objects warrant respect for their own sake, and quite apart from their interactions with human beings. Sometimes such arguments posit general rights held by living creatures (and natural objects) against human depredations. In especially powerful forms, these arguments are utilitarian in character, stressing the often extreme and unnecessary suffering of animals who are hurt or killed. Animal [welfare legislation] reflects these concerns.

2.2.3   Procedural political approaches

Sunstein's approach to justifying regulatory intervention is based on substantive values other than economic efficiency. His approach rests essentially on civic republican notions of 'virtue'. In other words, it relies on an implicit assumption that political systems define the content of collective agreement on certain ideas about what counts as 'good' in political, social and economic life. The extract from Sunstein above did not include any detail on the philosophical arguments underpinning his suggestions for the political goals and values that he argues justify regulation: we return to this briefly in Chapter 5. But the task of prescribing substantive visions of values that regulation can legitimately pursue is controversial, given the pervasiveness of moral disagreement and value pluralism that characterises modern societies.

Such controversy might be avoided by focusing on deliberative *processes* and attempting to avoid prescribing the substantive political goals or values which regulation should pursue. The extract that follows from Tony Prosser's work articulates this kind of procedural approach. Where a substantive public interest approach might suggest that the reduction of social subordination motivates and justifies (or should motivate) government intervention through law, a deliberative approach would instead ensure that a dialogue takes place between different actors in the regulatory regime about the relative desirability of pursuing such a goal. Prosser stresses, however, that if a dialogue is to approximate true deliberation, it must achieve more than simply bringing different groups together in a common forum. Rather, the procedures followed in such a dialogue should ideally enable or even encourage participants to reconsider and revise their views and interests as a result of the dialogue, and to so do without undue pressure from unequal power relations between the participants. In other words, there are certain constraints placed on regulatory procedures in this view of regulation, and these constraints, by minimising the effects of power inequalities, give regulation a 'public interest' flavour without specifying the substantive goals that justify regulation.

The following extract is taken from a book in which Prosser links an account of the structure and practice of utility regulation in the UK to certain theoretical aspects of the philosopher Habermas's work. Prosser makes this link by suggesting that a particular concept developed by Habermas, known as the 'ideal speech situation', provides a standard which can be used to criticise the processes provided within a regulatory regime. (The particular subject of his book considers the regulatory regimes established for the telecommunications, gas and electricity industries in the UK.) He emphasises two features of that 'ideal speech situation': firstly, that all participants have the same opportunities to initiate a dialogue, to engage in questioning and to give reasons for their claims and against the claims of others. Secondly, the discussion must be free from the constraints imposed by disparities in power between the participants.

Tony Prosser, *'Nationalised industries and public Control'* (1986)

My approach [to the role of law in relation to regulated utilities] would seem to reflect an instrumentalist concept of law; that is, seeing public law as a tool used by state bodies to achieve their ends through the design of institutions. In such a model, any assessment of the degree of success achieved could only refer to efficiency in achieving goals at the least possible cost: it would be concerned with the suitability of means rather than with specifying particular goals. However, law also contains a critical element ... Recent criticisms of a purely instrumental concept of law, such as those made by the Critical Legal Studies Movement in the United States, have stressed that law is *not* simply a means of achieving goals directly as it also has an ideological dimension in which the exercise of power is mediated and given justification.

[The essence of my approach is that] law is no longer seen as isolated from politics to form an outside constraint on political life: rather, law is a sub-branch of politics defined by its purpose of legitimation. Secondly, law is a purposive enterprise: rather than being defined as a set of authoritative materials it is a means of achieving social ends. These ends are not arbitrarily decided by the state but have an essential moral element in their definition.

How, then, can this critical element be applied...? One aspect of the critical approach is ... concerned with ... democratic ideals. Few concepts are in practice more controversial than that of democracy, and in practice it is impossible to draw clear institutional implications from this concept without highly controversial specification of its content. Specification here will occur through my drawing on the work of one critical theorist, work that has a special relevance to public lawyers — that of Jurgen Habermas. The particular conception of democracy in his work centres around the means of institutionalising a learning process, and Habermas has summarised it as follows:

I can imagine the attempt to arrange a society democratically only as a self-controlled learning process. It is a question of finding arrangements which can ground the presumption that the basic institutions of the society and the basic political decisions would meet with the unforced agreement of all those involved, if they could participate, as free and equal, in discursive will-formation. Democratization cannot mean an a priori preference for a specific type of organization.

A similar stress has also appeared in Freedman's account of arrangements in the United States for the regulation of industry: 'if statements concerning the nature of justice are themselves properly understood as questions inviting a continuing dialogue, then the discussion ... that follows is an invitation to renewed consideration of means for perfecting the procedural arrangements that prevail for the moment'. Together, these approaches suggest that the central concern will be the development of institutions that can foster the means for learning through a process of participatory dialogue, and that this will be a matter of devising suitable procedures. [As] I argued earlier, ... the design of institutions is a legal matter: we now have the beginnings of criteria we can draw on in developing legitimate institutions.

I have treated this as a particular conception of democracy. However, why is this the one we should adopt in preference to its many competitors? First, it could be argued that participatory claims are implicit in current arrangements but are not given practical implementation. For example, the very existence of consumer councils for ... nationalised industries [delivering public utility services such as telecommunications] implies that they are there to provide a means of outside influence on decision-making by the industries and to widen the range of information and viewpoints considered in policy-making. I will compare this with actual practice, however, which to a large extent negatives such claims. Similarly, [as I have argued elsewhere], ... legal systems in liberal societies ultimately justify themselves by reference to particular ideals which can be compared with existing practices, the disparity [can be] ... a source of criticism and possible political change. A similar approach could be adopted where it can be established that there are decision-making arrangements justified by appeals to the ideal of participatory decision-making. There is a further sense in which Habermas's work produces criteria against which the legitimacy of institutional design can be assessed, a sense independent of the claims made in a particular society. This is a highly complex argument which I can only summarise in a simplified manner here. In brief, the argument is that certain human interests transcend ideology and so are, in effect, necessary conditions of social existence. One of these is communication; this is necessary in the strong sense that if the norms of rational communication can be established successfully, any attempt to deny them must in fact be an implicit endorsement instead, since even such attempted denial can only be expressed through communication. Habermas argues that any smoothly functioning communicative interaction rests on an implicit consensus in which various claims are mutually accepted; the claims include the truth of assertions and the correctness of norms referred to in speech. If the consensus breaks down through challenge to the claims, it can only be restored through testing their truth or correctness through discourse, a special form of communication shaped only by the force of the better argument. Thus any act of communication rests on the assumption that the participants will be able to justify the beliefs and norms they uphold through the giving of reasons: an assumption of accountability. In practice this will usually be a fiction because ruling norms and beliefs will be imposed through the exercise of power rather than on rational grounds, but nevertheless communication must proceed as if the assumption were true.

This raises the question of how we could distinguish such 'systematically distorted communication' imposed by force and producing a mere pretence of agreement from a truly discursively justifiable agreement. Habermas resolves this by pointing to the conditions under which a discursively reached agreement could occur: these comprise his central concept of the ideal speech situation. This is characterised in that all participants have the same chances to initiate discourse and to engage in questioning and giving reasons for and against claims made. Thus all assertions and norms are potentially subject to discursive examination. Moreover, as well as there being the opportunity for unlimited discussion, the discussion must be free from the constraints imposed by domination, by disparities in power between the participants. This will ensure that beliefs and norms will only be found to be justified if they are based on generalisable interests rather than being imposed by the powerful. Of course, such a consensus is not achieved in social interaction in practice, but it is presupposed and anticipated in debate, for in justifying belief we have to assume that the outcome of the debate will be shaped by the force of the better argument rather than through the exercise of power as a constraint on discussion. A key point is that the attainment of a justified consensus (truth) can be divorced from the ideal of a particular form of social organisation enabling its attainment.

Readers impatient of philosophical discussion will be wondering why this [might be] . . . relevant to [discussions] about [regulatory issues such as] public law and nationalised industries. The answer is that the assumed consensus of the ideal speech situation provides a standard against which to assess institutions in terms of the possibility of attaining such consensus through them: it provides, if the argument is valid, an objective base for the critical assessment of institutional legitimacy. Thus the irrationality of domination which today has become a collective peril to life, could be mastered only by the development of a political decision-making process tied to the principle of general discussion free from domination. Our only hope for the rationalization of the power structure lies in conditions that favour political power for thought developing through dialogue. Truth is thus inseparable from the institutional arrangements for its attainment.

In fact, it is possible to translate the criteria of the ideal speech situation directly into concepts familiar to political scientists and, to a lesser extent, to public lawyers.

The first of these is *participation*. However deficient implementation in practice might be, this implies reference to the ideal of the creation of opportunities for widening debate to encompass a range of affected interests and a fuller range of information, and so invokes the ideal of discussion free from domination with equal power to shape the outcome given to all affected. In practice it forms a major legal concern in parts of land-use planning through the public local inquiry and also in the limited areas covered by the principles of natural justice, but has not attracted legal attention elsewhere. In [the context of utility regulation, it is relevant to] ... the corporate planning process of the nationalised industries, and in ... the degree to which workers in the industries and bodies acting for consumers have been able to participate in the planning process. . . . .

The second concept is that of *accountability*: in a sense it is the *ex post facto* equivalent of participation. Accountability demands the giving of reasons for actions, and (particularly in relation to the institutions under examination here) the development of procedures and fora through which reasons and explanations for action can be demanded, assessed and lessons learned for the future. Its essence was captured in the Webbs' advocacy of 'measurement and publicity' referring to the establishment of scrutinising machinery based on as free a flow of information as possible . . . .[In the context of utility regulation, it arises in] ... the arrangements for the accountability of nationalised industries towards consumer bodies, and [in] . . . . Parliamentary accountability through the use of Parliamentary Questions, the work of Select Committees and through audit, together with other forms of scrutiny such as that by the Monopolies and Mergers Commission.

It should be apparent by now that the achievement of any progress towards the criteria of legitimacy is dependent on a relatively free flow of information so that participation can be addressed to a realistic set of choices and so that adequate explanations can be gained for accountability. It is now accepted wisdom that Britain has a highly secretive political culture and the nationalised industries have been no exception to this: concern with the degree of openness [is also central to my argument] . . . .

Legitimacy in practice

The criteria I have set out above have been portrayed as a means of implementing a particular conception of democracy. It should not be thought, however, that they represent some sort of luxury quite independent of the practical effectiveness and efficiency of the institutions being studied; or (even worse) that participation and accountability inherently reduce effectiveness and efficiency, for example through distracting the attention of those who should be getting on with the job in hand. Rather, I [would] argue, that effective planning *implies* participation and accountability, for participation is the only means by which input from the changing environment can reach planners and the only way in which representation can take place of other interests on whom implementation depends. Similarly, it is only through accountability that it is possible to bring different viewpoints to bear on experience and so increase the opportunities for learning from it. This is particularly so in a political culture of 'elite consensus' with limited opportunity for self-correction ... Thus 'institutional legitimacy is an indispensable condition for institutional effectiveness', as Freedman argues.

It should not be assumed that the criteria I have set out dictate any *particular* institutional or procedural arrangements: they are ideals and their embodiment will be shaped by their context. It would, of course, be wrong to assume that a nationalised industry should be subject to the same procedural constraints as, for example, a central government department. In particular, the fact that some nationalised industries have to operate in competitive markets will have an important effect in shaping the scope for the application of the criteria. The implications of this should not, however, be exaggerated ... the extension of market principles to all economic activity is impossible, both in theoretical and practical terms; and ..., appeals to market legitimation have all too often served simply to disguise lack of accountability for action involving an inevitable political element. [The nub of my argument is] that ... the issue ... is one of how is democracy to be combined with autonomy ... [i.e. one] of the design and interrelation of institutions. It has been argued ... that in complex, differentiated modern societies law is suited not so much to direct intervention to shape social processes as to installing and defining the bounds of autonomous institutions within which learning processes can take place. Law thus provides an 'external constitution' within which processes of social development and interaction with the environment can take place. Market conditions do not do away with the need to create and define institutions, but rather mean that in particular circumstances justifications exist for permitting a considerable degree of autonomy.

2.2.4 The role of law in public interest theories of regulation

The three approaches surveyed above, which we could conveniently label 'welfare economics', 'substantive political' and 'procedural political', respectively, may all be seen as examples of public interest theories of regulation, despite differences between their conceptions of the public interest. While political and welfare economic approaches use very different languages to define the content of the public interest, there is some overlap between the substantive goals advanced by the different theories. This is especially so if one considers 'translating' the public interest goals of the substantive political approach into the language and conceptual framework of the welfare economic approach. For example, the ways in which Sunstein discusses regulation as giving effect to collective desires and aspirations may overlap substantially with the goal of correcting the market failure of information asymmetry that Ogus discusses. Another thread of commonality between the various approaches to public interest theory is the facilitative role that law plays: functioning as an instrument for achieving the chosen public interest objectives. Theories that specify substantive objectives, such as reducing social subordination or improving market efficiency, in many ways treat positive legal commands as an assumed vehicle for the achievement of these objectives. One might almost view them in this sense as theories of the law-making process,

specifying the goals which explain and justify the action of law-makers in formulating legal commands embodied in regulatory regimes that are intended to
achieve those substantive goals.

The procedural version of public interest theory offered by Prosser also
gives law a facilitative role, albeit with slight differences. In this theory, law
(including judicial and regulatory institutions) has the task of devising
suitable procedures that will foster participatory dialogue. Law's role here resembles the image of umpire briefly introduced in Chapter 1: establishing and maintaining the boundaries of a space for free and secure interaction between
regulatory participants. In so doing, the law is still functioning as a vehicle
for achieving the public interest, although what constitutes that public
interest will emerge from dialogue between the players. In short, we use
Prosser's approach here to illustrate the umpiring facet of law's facilitative role,
although it may have additional resonance which we will consider in Chapter 5.
As we shall see in the next section, private interest theories of regulation also have
strong procedural dimensions, but with rather different implications for the role
of law.

2.2.5   Discussion questions

1. Is the relationship between welfare economic approaches to regulation and
    political public interest approaches complementary, exclusive or interdepen-
    dent? In particular, can welfare economic approaches take account of values
    other than economic efficiency by 'translating' or 'reconceiving' them as eco-
    nomic concepts?
2. Might welfare economic approaches be appropriate for some issues, and
    political approaches for others? – Consider, for example, price regulation
    in utilities, environmental regulation and public service broadcasting regula-
    tion. Identify the harm addressed by regulation, and consider whether it
    is equally well addressed by welfare economic or political (substantive or
    procedural) approaches.
3. In thinking about the relationship between political and welfare economic
    approaches, consider the tension between efficiency and non-efficiency-based
    goals of regulation, and the extent to which regulation can feasibly serve both.
    Are there inevitable trade-offs? If trade-offs are inevitable, are they concep-
    tually incommensurable and what implications does this have for how they
    should be made?
4. Do public interest theories of regulation have any implications for how orga-
    nisations (such as regulatory agencies, or firms subject to regulation) should
    order their internal affairs? Consider particularly with respect to the proce-
    dural approach outline by Prosser.
5. What difference would it make to consider a regulatory problem such as
    safety standards for the medical profession if one interprets the public interest
    justifying regulation on the one hand as a problem of information asymmetry,

or on the other hand as a question of expressing collective desires and aspirations?

6. What are the boundaries of 'public interest' — i.e. when is a group representing a 'public interest' and when is a group representing the interests of its (collective) members? Is the endorsement of group interests by the state a necessary component of a claim to represent the public interest?

2.3   Private interest theories of regulation

Private interest theories of regulation are premised on an assumption that regulation emerges from the actions of individuals or groups motivated to maximise their self-interest. On this view, regulation may or may not promote the public interest, but if it does, it is a coincidence. This is a central aspect of private interest theories, and means that any connection between regulatory intervention and the public interest is a *contingent* one, demonstrable through empirical and context-specific enquiry only. Although this is strictly true of public interest theories as well, it is probably fair to say that public interest theories are often underpinned by an implicit optimism about the capacity of regulation to promote some form of public interest. By contrast, many advocates of a private interest approach to regulation are fairly skeptical about this capacity. Economic versions of private interest theory are especially inclined to challenge public interest justifications offered in support of regulation. Other approaches, especially political ones, hold varying perceptions of the degree to which they consider the public interest to be a meaningful concept at all, or on how likely it is to emerge.

These varying degrees of skepticism can colour the accounts of regulation given by these writers in a manner which may suggest that they are politically opposed to regulation. Any such political judgements are, at least conceptually, neither necessary nor logical aspects of private interest theories. But it is nonetheless true that private interest theories of regulation gained particular prominence in conjunction with the rise of political ideologies in favour of deregulation. Private interest theories have tended to stress the ease with which 'regulatory failure' and 'regulatory capture' occur. Regulatory capture happens when officials within regulatory institutions who are charged with promoting collective welfare develop such close relationships with those they regulate that they promote the narrow interests of this group instead of the public interest of the broader community. It is an important way in which regulatory failure can happen, i.e. when the collective costs of regulation outweigh the benefits it brings.

Thus, there is a kind of mirror-image relationship between the assumptions underpinning public and private interest theories. Public interest theories stress market failure and the capacity of regulation to correct such failures. Private interest theories stress regulatory failure and the tendency of regulation to benefit narrow special interests rather than to promote collective welfare.

2.3.1   Political private interest approaches

Many variants of private interest theory exist, ranging from public choice theory, to principal-agent theory to what is sometimes called 'positive political economy' approaches. We will not delve here into the intricacies of each of these variants, but aim instead to capture some general aspects that are true of all of them. As with public interest approaches, a politically inflected version of the private interest approach can be distinguished from an economically grounded version. The political version might be thought of as a more 'hard-headed' version of the procedural version of political public interest theory represented by Prosser's extract above. The vision here is one of regulation emerging from the cumulative results of various interest groups pressing their views to regulatory agencies and legislators. The emphasis is on regulation emerging from the actual process of this exchange of views, a perspective linked to political science ideas of 'interest group pluralism'.

In political versions of private interest theory, political outcomes, and the regulatory rules in which they are embedded, are the aggregate result of different groups pursuing their own versions of the public interest without any overall umpire imposing constraints on the content of those versions. The 'private' nature of the theory arises because of the absence of any strong sense of a referee: the regulatory arena is shaped, from this perspective, by a political process in which inequality of resources will inevitably give some groups advantages over others. Thus, unlike public interest theories of a political proceduralist kind, there is less emphasis on correcting procedural defects in the regulatory process. Sometimes skewed participation is compensated by a more corporatist process, that is, where the state steps in to legitimate certain groups over others. But even if the state does intervene, interest group pluralism can be contrasted with public interest theories in two ways: it rejects any advocacy of specific substantive goals, and it also rejects the notion that the resulting process is capable of transforming or transcending individual private goals and generating a shared consensus. Instead, the public interest is the aggregate result of the diverse individual and group pressures that have influenced the regulatory process. Private interest theorists are, as stressed, skeptical about the 'thicker' conceptions of collective welfare endorsed by public interest theorists of various stripes. The following extract from Croley captures these features of what he calls 'neo-pluralism', which for our purposes represents a politically inflected version private interest theory of regulation.

Stephen Croley, '*Theories of regulation: Incorporating the administrative process*' (1998)

> The neopluralist takes group interests as central to determining regulatory outcomes. One strand ... represented by Gary Becker ... assumes that organised interest groups

compete with one another (using votes and other political resources) to obtain state-provided goods, including favorable regulation. In his model ... a given group will calculate how many resources it should spend in pursuit of that good, given the value of the political good to its members and the countervailing efforts of other groups. Furthermore, regulatory outcomes are not all-or-nothing propositions ... but rather reflect the zero-sum equilibrium of countervailing group forces: A "winning" group will gain only up to the point where an opposing group will exert enough resistance to limit the "winner's" gains. The implication of Becker's model is that only the most efficient groups — that is, those that demand political benefits the most as measured by their ability to invest in them — will be able to acquire them, and only insofar as it is worth no other group's cost to resist ... Another, related strand of the neopluralist theory also takes a benign, though guarded, view of interest-group competition. According to this view too, regulatory outcomes are the result of interest-group pressures, in a regime in which many different groups press their many different interests and concerns upon regulators. Regulators are central to this strand of neopluralist theory, but ... they function largely as conduits and aggregators for the preferences and demands of private groups.

This is not to say, however, that interest groups always get the regulatory outcomes they want. To the contrary, group success is constrained in two ways. First, groups' abilities to influence regulatory decisions are limited by the costs of mobilizing, communicating their cause to regulators, and providing legislators with electoral resources. Such costs can be considerable. Second, groups face competition from rival groups with incompatible regulatory preferences. Any given group will enjoy the regulatory outcomes it favors only if it can prevail over other groups that favor other outcomes.

Regulators too, then, are constrained by group rivalry. Legislators, for their part, would like to curry the favor of all potential providers of electoral resources. Because not all interest groups want the same policies, legislators will seek to find compromises and to form coalitions among potentially supporting groups whose interests partially overlap. Legislators, in other words, will function as entrepreneurs in putting together prevailing coalitions. Acting in their own interests, they will broker compromises, rewarding the electorally powerful and those whose regulatory goals are compatible with other groups. Consequently, those most able to command electoral resources and those whose interests overlap with other groups' will tend to prevail; those with fewer resources and more unique interests will tend not to prevail. Again, regulatory outcomes in the end reflect a competitive equilibrium among rival groups.

In partial contrast to Becker, however, this more familiar strand of neopluralist theory is ambivalent towards the consequences of interest-group behavior. According to it, interest-group competition can and often does produce lopsided results. But ... the neopluralist theory is unprepared to conclude that regulatory government inevitably spells domination of the undetecting many by the organised few. The neopluralist theory's main descriptive claim holds instead that interest-group competition is sufficiently pluralistic, especially given the presence of many "public" interest groups apparently representing broad interests, to undermine the public choice theory's claims and predictions. On this view, regulatory decisionmaking is ... complicated ...: while some interest groups may very well enjoy excessive influence with public decisionmakers ... the problem of illicit interest-group influence is not intractable, but may be solved by adjusting the regulatory decisionmaking apparatus ... For example, ... new methods of statutory interpretation that seek to protect underrepresented interests or that force explicit deliberation and disclosure of statutory goals by legislatures .... [or] reforms facilitating participation in regulatory decisionmaking, including more robust standing rights for interest groups representing underrepresented interests [or] greater reliance on governmental decisionmaking bodies (such as independent agencies ...) who might be less susceptible to uneven interest-group pressures. ... [W]hatever the specific policy reforms advocated, they share a common premise: Such reforms all seek to correct imbalances in the interest-group competition — to level the interest-group playing field. They [have] a favorable view of interest-group competition, so long as that competition is fair. To the extent that many interests are adequately represented by organised groups, the theory endorses group competition. Where, on the other hand, some interests are systematically underrepresented and regulatory outcomes are therefore biased, the theory calls for reforms that in one way or another reproduce the results that would be generated in an environment of healthy interest-group competition.

. . .

A question arises: [can] the neopluralist theory appeal to actual examples of regulatory policies reflecting a benign compromise among many competing interest groups: Do regulatory outcomes lend strength to the theory's commitment to regulation? Although some questioned the importance of interest-group influence, most scholars studying group politics in the 1960s reached the conclusion that narrow business interests typically prevail in policymaking processes over relatively diffuse public interests. These scholars agreed with the pluralists that interest-group activity is central to explaining policy outcomes, but argued that such activity is characterised much less by competition among heterogeneous interest groups than it is by business-interest domination. This view ... has largely prevailed over the competing view that interest-group influence on policy outcomes is quite modest.

Still, interest group theorists might respond that even if the public interest movement does not defy the public choice theory, it should give one pause about strong versions of that theory. On this view, although the consumer and environmental movements of the early 1970s occurred too late to rescue pluralism, they at least complicate the public choice theory's story. The proliferation of consumer and environmental groups certainly increased interest-group competition in regulatory politics and made regulatory rent-seeking by business groups and trade associations more difficult. But the available empirical evidence does not necessarily provide strong support for even this qualified view. For example...[studies] of interest-group competition following the consumer and environmental movements find that an increase in the number of interest groups does not automatically translate to greater interest-group competition . . . [W]hile more groups are active in recent years in certain policy domains, there is little interest-group competition on particular policy issues within them. Instead, individual groups tend to create and occupy narrow policy-issue niches in which they face no competition from other groups. By developing policy niches, individual groups enjoy dominance on the specific issues in which they have developed expertise. To be sure, groups may initially compete over the occupation of a policy niche, which provides some support for the neopluralist vision, but the point remains that an increase in the number of interest groups active in regulatory decisionmaking does not necessarily mean more interest-group competition. Taken on its own terms, then, the neopluralist theory of regulation . . . has little to say about such matters as how groups purportedly representing the average voter emerge, whether they are truly representative, and whether their resources are sufficient to allow them to impede rent-seeking by other interest groups. This is not to say that interest group theorists are wrong to believe that on the whole regulatory outcomes do reflect many competing interests. Nor is it to say that their policy reforms aimed at correcting for interest-group imbalances are ultimately misguided. But if the neopluralist theory's commitment to regulation is well placed, it is so for reasons the underdeveloped theory itself has not yet supplied.

2.3.2   Economic private interest approaches

We turn now to the economically grounded version of private interest theories of regulation. This approach is the most skeptical of all of the viability of public interest effects of regulation. This skepticism arises because these theories view the political process itself through the lens of economic theory. This is why some private interest approaches are given the label of 'public choice'; they focus on how individual citizens collectively choose the rules that govern their affairs. Although this conceptualises the provision of regulation itself as if it were a good or service provided at the intersection of forces of supply and demand in the political arena, the word 'public' still recognises the collective and political nature of the outcomes. Economic versions of private interest theory use an analysis of the cost-benefit structure of collective action to conclude that regulation is more likely to reflect the policy preferences of powerful and narrowly focused interest groups and as a consequence to generate net social loss. Croley's summary of public choice theory, the most well-known variant of private interest approaches, nicely summarises the logic underpinning this vision of why regulation emerges.

Stephen Croley, *'Theories of regulation : Incorporating the administrative approach'* (1998)

The public choice theory of regulation analogises regulatory decisionmaking to market decisionmaking. Specifically, it treats legislative, regulatory, and electoral institutions as an economy in which the relevant actors — including ordinary citizens, legislators, agencies, and organised interest groups most affected by regulatory policies — exchange regulatory "goods," which are "demanded" and "supplied" according to the same basic principles governing the demand and supply of ordinary economic goods. Such regulatory goods include, for example, direct cash subsidies, controls over entry into a market, such as tariffs, controls over the substitutes and complements of economic goods, and price controls. These regulatory goods are demanded by those who stand to gain from them. A producer of a given good, for example, would enjoy great economic benefit from regulations that made substitute goods more expensive and complementary goods cheaper. As the sole supplier of regulation, only the state can supply demanded regulatory goods, which legislators, organised and disciplined by political parties, are willing to do in exchange for the political support they need to stay in office. Regulatory trades take place, then, because they further the (private) economic interests of those on the demand side and the (private) political interests of those on the supply side. The resources necessary to meet suppliers' political needs constitute the "price" of regulatory goods.

Naturally, the outcome of these forces of supply and demand is a function of the constraints under which the participants in the regulatory marketplace operate. These constraints are determined, according to the public choice theory, by the general rules through which democratic political decisions are made. And therein lies the trouble, for democratic decisionmaking results in regulatory policies that benefit narrow interests at the expense of broad interests, for reasons now familiar.

Simply stated, the regulatory interests of the individual voter (or the consumer) are dominated by the regulatory interests of organised subgroups of the citizenry because the latter have incentives to influence regulatory decisionmaking which the former lacks. The individual voter lacks such incentives given the benefit-cost trade-off of pursuing her regulatory interests: The benefits are low; the costs relatively high. In Stigler's words:

What is the consumer's recourse if he is being exploited by a federal marketing order which either neglects his interest or, as is the case at present in the United States, positively arms and protects a cartel in exploiting this consumer? His sole defense is to organise a political campaign to change or eliminate that marketing scheme. For the individual consumer this is a bleak prospect. The costs—in time, effort, and money — to change legislation are large; the reward to any one consumer from joining a consumer lobby is negligible.

As this example suggests, collective action barriers constitute the individual voter's main obstacle to organizing to further her regulatory interests; the individual consumer's "rewards" from her own contribution would be "negligible"...[F]or reasons deeply rooted in the logic of collective action, most citizens lack any real incentive to try to influence regulatory outcomes.

Thus, while the public choice theory analogises regulatory behavior to market behavior, it also holds that the analogy ultimately breaks down. From the vantage point of ordinary citizens, the crucial differences between regulatory decisions and market decisions are threefold. First, regulatory decisions are "all-or-nothing" propositions: Whereas in the economic marketplace citizens can decide to patronise airlines or rail lines, or neither, as their individual needs require, a regulatory decision about whether to provide favorable regulation to either affects all citizens, whether they fly, ride the rails, or neither. The scope of regulatory decisions extends across virtually all citizens, who are affected by those decisions at least on the financing side. And once the state makes a decision about which package of regulatory goods to supply, individual voters have no opportunity to "exit" the regulatory market. Second, regulatory decisions are more permanent than marketplace decisions. Whereas a citizen could elect to fly one week, and then ride a train the next, the collective decision to provide a federal subsidy to the airlines or to the railroads will not be frequently reexamined once made. Finally, regulatory decisions are collective decisions, and, as such, must be made simultaneously. Where some decision depends on whether its supporters outnumber its detractors, those supporters and detractors must, at some discrete point and time, be counted.

Because regulatory decisions are, relative to market decisions, infrequent, simultaneous, and global, regulatory outcomes are undisciplined: Individual citizens have little or no occasion for registering their regulatory interests, including their interests against regulatory policies that bring them no benefits. ... Direct citizen participation in regulatory decisionmaking is ... rare — taking place only as often as elections for political representatives — and very crude — citizens vote for political candidates with very little information about those candidates' positions on regulatory issues, and must moreover vote for a mixed bundle of such policies at once. Citizens ... [therefore delegate] regulatory decisionmaking power to representatives with wide discretion thus creat[ing] significant principal-agent slack, with regrettable consequences. Because most citizens are largely uninformed about most regulatory decisions, and because they moreover lack incentives to become sufficiently informed to reward legislators who do not shirk, legislators do not — cannot — protect the broad regulatory interests of their constituencies. This is true because organised interest groups — industry groups, occupational groups, and trade associations — who are informed because they have an especially high demand for regulatory goods do monitor legislators, punishing those who consistently fail to provide such goods and rewarding those who provide favorable regulation. Thus interest groups capitalise on the opportunities created by principal-agent slack, made worse by most voters' collective action problems, in order to buy regulatory goods that advantage them. For their part, interest groups pursue regulatory goods, like any other goods, up to the point where the marginal costs equal the marginal benefits of doing so. And in contrast to the benefits for the individual voter, the benefits for groups of pursuing favorable regulatory outcomes are often worth the costs. This is true given the concentrated distribution of those benefits. In the context of a federal milk marketing order, the "farmers, milk companies, and laborers in the industry have much larger stakes, and they can and do" undertake the effort necessary to generate marketing orders that favor them. Given that the benefits of regulatory goods are higher for organised groups than for individual voters, the former enjoy much more influence — offer higher bids — in regulatory decisionmaking relative to the latter.

Not that the price of favorable regulation is cheap. . . . Regulation-seeking groups must front the costs of communicating with politicians and participating in political decisionmaking, including the costs of consultants, lawyers, and lobbyists. Second, groups must also cover the costs of earning the support of legislators, which is to say, the costs of providing legislators with political benefits — votes and financial resources. This second cost implies another: Regulation-seeking groups must also pay the costs of "regulatory competition." That is, they must outbid competitor groups, which means that they must not only supply legislators with resources that translate into political benefits, but with more of such resources than competing groups. Thus, no given interest group will enjoy all of the regulatory goods it desires; scarcity constrains any group's buying power.

Even so, the regulatory market works, on the whole, to the advantage of organised groups with narrow interests. Interest groups with the most at stake in a particular regulatory decision, who spend the most to buy that decision, typically see their demand for regulation met by legislators who acquiesce in order to enjoy continued electoral success and the benefits that holding office brings. In the process, ordinary citizens lose, though they rarely feel their loss in any particular case. Nor is the end result purely distributional. The regulatory goods that organised groups obtain often come at a price not worth their costs; concentrated group gains usually "fall short of the [diffuse] damage to the rest of the community." Thus are regulatory policies typically inefficient. As regulatory goods are sold to groups representing concentrated interests, the few gain, and the many lose by more.

The public choice theory's description of regulation carries with it a reform agenda: The view that the fundamental differences between regulatory and market decisionmaking explain the problem with regulation strongly suggests that market outcomes are preferable to regulatory outcomes. And in fact, public choice theorists often argue for increased reliance on markets rather than on government regulation. Limiting regulators' power, and thus their ability to advance the interests of small groups at the greater expense of general interests, would enhance social welfare. Market outcomes, however imperfect, are better than the regulatory products of an intractable regulatory regime.

. . .

A Critical Assessment — The public choice theory constitutes a powerful challenge to those who would preserve the regulatory regime, a challenge which has enjoyed considerable influence. . . . And yet, its case against regulation is by no means entirely compelling.

One problem with the public choice theory concerns the enormous weight it implicitly attaches to legislators' electoral goals. While its premise that legislators supply demanded regulatory goods to groups in exchange for resources that secure their positions in office may be plausible on a general level, the difficulty is that the theory seems to contemplate that legislators are always very worried about the next election — that fear of electoral defeat consistently renders legislators ever willing to meet the highest bidder's regulatory demands. This vision is problematic . . . . Simply knowing that a legislator seeks security of office does not, without more, imply anything specific about how that legislator will behave or, more particularly, how that legislator will satisfy the regulatory preferences of competing interest groups. [Further] ... it seems implausible to assume that job security constitutes legislators' only goal − that legislators seek office solely to maintain it.

A second general problem with the public choice theory's conceptual apparatus, and its specific focus on legislator motivation in particular, is ... that almost all administrators are fairly well insulated from electoral political pressures. Such insulation may give them room to pursue general-interest regulation, subject only to legislative supervision that pulls in the opposite direction ....

... [P]ublic choice theorists have suggested that their theory is in fact testable; its expectations can be measured against real-world events ... Unfortunately for the theory, however, the empirical evidence is far from overwhelming. First, specific examples of policies that public choice theorists have offered to provide affirmative support for the theory are fairly rare ... Public choice theorists have identified regulatory policies in the airlines, securities, telecommunications, television, and trucking industries as their main examples lending credence to the public choice theory's predictions ... But while these examples may have corroborated the public choice theory at one time, they no longer do so. For regulatory policies in precisely these same areas constitute the examples that the public interest theory invokes on its behalf... [P]ublic interest theorists point to deregulation, especially of the airlines, but also of the securities, telecommunications, and trucking industries. At least according to public interest theorists, regulatory policymaking in each of these cases suggests that, at least on important occasions, the concentrated interests of powerful organised groups lose out to the diffuse interests of the mostly unorganised citizenry. Interestingly enough, then, the public choice theory points largely to the same set of facts that other theories identify in support of their (different) predictions. To that extent, these policies are incompatible with the public choice theory's prediction that the average voter/consumer will routinely see her regulatory interests sacrificed to those who are better able to pay the price of favorable regulation. The public choice theory holds that such instances will not occur.

2.3.3 The role of law in private interest theories

In private interest theories as a whole, the role of law has both commonalities with and differences from its role in public interest theories. In terms of commonality, both public and private interest theories tend to assume that law, in the sense of public and democratically enacted rules, is a vehicle for securing collective outcomes. In other words, law continues to play a facilitative role in private interest theories in so far as that role has an instrumental dimension. But unlike public interest theories, private interest theories pose a much more sustained challenge to the idea that these outcomes promote collective *welfare*. This is because they tend to be pessimistic about the possibilities for 'welfare maximising' production of a regulated good. This gives an additional gloss to assumptions about the role of law, warning that the law is likely to be a means to ends that undermine community welfare. This is a contingent implication that has to be proved empirically in any particular case, as we have already stressed.

A further difference arises from our earlier discussion about how private interest theories conceive of the law as a regulatory good: i.e. the 'product' of a political market, produced at the intersection of the supply and demand of domestic electoral support. That intersection is still an arena of political contestation, but, at least in the national context, law is a monopoly good since the law-making arena is the only place where the good can be produced. This gives law the quality of a passive object that regulatory actors compete for. This is consistent with the idea that once secured, law will act as a vehicle for securing collective outcomes, but the emphasis is on the struggle from which regulatory law emerges. This reflects in part the observation made in Chapter 1 that private interest theories tend to give causal accounts of the emergence of regulatory regimes while public interest theories are more prescriptive, highlighting the regulatory goals that the law should ideally facilitate.

The difference is also linked to diametrically different assumptions about intrinsic human nature underpinning public and private interest theories of regulation. Niskanen, a well-known adherent of a private interest approach to bureaucracy, quotes a British Labour MP in the 1970s in terms which give a vivid flavour to these differences. Countering the suggestion that contracting-out or productivity bonuses might enhance the efficiency of the British civil service, the unnamed politician responds:

> Efficiency in administration lies in service to the people, in understanding, compassion, patience with the weak and ignorant, in being scrupulously fair between one citizen and the other ... Where do we recruit all these saints? I reply that we already have them in the British Civil Service ... A good bureaucracy does not need and should not have, the lubricants which make the wheels go round in the world of private enterprise ....

That this view now sounds anachronistic need hardly be said, yet few are willing to sacrifice entirely the notion that regulation can harness public-spirited desires to pursue the public interest. It may be that private interest approaches to regulation have provided a necessary corrective to the excessive optimism or even naïveté of public interest theories, pointing to the desirability of a judicious mix of the two, combined with an appreciation of when and why limits to either approach emerge. At least some versions of what could loosely be called institutionalist theories of regulation, which we explore in the next section, seek to achieve just such a mix.

2.3.4   Discussion questions

1. Are economic private interest approaches to regulation complementary to, exclusive of, or interdependent with political private interest approaches? One way of approaching this question is to consider whether economic

approaches are more appropriate for some policy sectors and political approaches for others.

2. What difference would it make to consider a regulatory problem such as safety standards for the medical profession through the lens of regulatory capture on the one hand, the lens of interest group pluralism on the other hand?

3. How does the economic version of private interest theory deal with the problem that some interest groups are more powerful than others?

4. Do private interest theories of regulation have any implications for how organisations (such as regulatory agencies, or companies subject to regulation) should order their internal affairs?

5. In analysing a regulatory regime, is it appropriate to use political public interest approaches to set substantive goals for a regulatory regime and economic private interest approaches for the design of that regime?

2.4 Institutionalist theories of regulation

Our third category of theories of regulation is to some extent a 'grab-bag', grouping otherwise very different theories under one heading for two reasons detailed below. The label 'institutionalist' is intended to capture any theory where rule-based spheres, or the relationship between different rule-based spheres, play an important role in explaining why or how regulation emerges. By 'rule-based spheres' we mean formal organisations (e.g. regulatory agencies, corporations, states), embedded norms and routines (e.g. risk analysis, cost-benefit accounting, precedent, advocacy norms) or 'systems' as understood by system theory (e.g. legal systems, economic systems, political systems). The intent of this section is to present three approaches in sequence, which each give increasing prominence to the role of organisations, institutions and systems in regulatory dynamics. Common to these approaches, which differ from each other in many respects, is that they consider institutional dynamics to have, in a sense, a 'life of their own' in regulatory regimes, such that they will often shape the outcomes of regulation in surprising ways, given the preferences and interests of regulatory participants. A second common factor uniting the approaches grouped under this label is that they increasingly blur the differences between public and private actors, and between public and private interests, differences that have been central to our survey so far.

2.4.1 Tripartism

The first approach, the highly influential one of Ayres and Braithwaite, provides a bridge between the 'actor-centred' approaches discussed so far and more 'systems-focused' approaches that operate at a higher level of abstraction. Ayres and Braithwaite do not take a systems approach, but blend public and private interest approaches in a manner that highlights institutional dynamics. Yet they retain a very concrete focus on actors, focusing on how an analysis of the costs and benefits that typically accrue to players in the regulation game − redolent of the private interest approach − can, under certain conditions, produce public interest outcomes that are compatible with, and even heightened by, deliberation, dialogue and trust-building empowerment. Ayres and Braithwaite reject the idea that deliberative processes, in the sense used by Prosser in the earlier extract, are incompatible with calculations of cost-benefit payoffs. Instead they argue that the two are compatible, at least *when cooperation pays*. The point at which this occurs is known as the point of 'efficient capture', explained in the following extract.

Ayres and Braithwaite, '*Responsive regulation*' (1992)

In this chapter we argue that features of regulatory encounters that foster the evolution of cooperation also encourage the evolution of capture and corruption. Solutions to the problems of capture and corruption − limiting discretion, multiple-industry rather than single-industry agency jurisdiction, and rotating personnel − inhibit the evolution of cooperation. Tripartism − empowering public interest groups − is advanced as a way to solve this policy dilemma. A game-theoretic analysis of capture and tripartism is juxtaposed against an empowerment theory of republican tripartism. Surprisingly, both formulations lead to the conclusion that some forms of capture are desirable. The strengths from converging the weaknesses of these two formulations show how certain forms of tripartism might prevent harmful capture, identify and encourage efficient capture, enhance the attainment of regulatory goals, and strengthen democracy. Although the case we make for tripartism is purely theoretical and general in its application to all domains of business regulation, our conclusion is a call for praxis to flesh out the contexts in which the theory is true and false.

The problem: Business regulation is often modelled as a game between two players − the regulatory agency and the firm. Naturally the world is more complicated than this. On the state side there are other players like prosecutors and oversight committees of legislators, whereas on the business side there are other players like industry associations. On both sides, individual actors wear many hats. Therefore it is a rash simplification to interpret individual actions as those of the faithful fiduciary of the profitability interests of the firm on the one hand, and the fiduciary of agency interests in securing compliance with its statute, on the other.

This chapter seeks to problematise somewhat this simplification by modelling the idea of capture. Capture is a notion that has enjoyed political appeal among critics of regulation from both the right and the left. Among economists, models of regulatory capture have gained wide acceptance. Yet capture has not seemed to be theoretically or empirically fertile to many sociologists and political scientists working in the regulation literature. Here we will consider whether capture has proved analytically barren for those social scientists because of a failure to disaggregate different forms of capture. Ironically it is an economic analysis that clarifies the disaggregation needed to enable a more fertile social analysis of capture.

The Evolution of cooperation, corruption, and capture: Although the simplifications involved in modelling regulation as a game between two players with unproblematic interests are transparent, such simple models, with their elegance and clarity, can be the foundations on which we build more subtle and complex accounts. Moreover, simple prisoner's dilemma models of regulation do have some capacity to explain regularities in regulatory outcomes. These are models that construe regulation as a game between two players, each of which can choose between cooperating or defecting from cooperation with the other player. For the firm, defection means law evasion; for the regulator, defection means punitive enforcement. Whatever the other player does, defection results in a higher payoff than cooperation. The dilemma is that if both defect, both do worse that their joint cooperation payoff.

Let us illustrate this explanatory capability and in doing so go to the nub of the theoretical concern of this chapter. Grabosky and Braithwaite's (1986) study of ninety-six Australian business regulatory agencies found that agencies were more likely to have a cooperative (nonprosecutorial) regulatory practice when they regulated: (1) smaller numbers of client companies; (2) a single industry rather than diverse industries; (3) where the same inspectors were in regular contact with the same client companies; and (4) where the proportion of inspectors with a background in the regulated industry was high.

Grabosky and Braithwaite interpreted these findings as support for [the] notion of ... formal law increasing as relational distance between regulator and regulatee increases, and more ambiguously as support for capture theory. But equally these findings are just what would be predicted from ... theor[ies about cooperation] ... [that] ... show that the evolution of cooperation should occur only when regulator and firm are in a *multiperiod* prisoner's dilemma game. Repeated encounters are required for cooperation to evolve ... Thus, cooperation should be more likely when the same inspector is repeatedly dealing with the same firm. Similarly, when an agency regulates a small number of firms in a single industry the chances of repeated regular encounters are greater than with an agency that regulates all firms in the economy. And indeed inspectorates recruited from the industry may be in a better position to secure an evolution of cooperation because they are enmeshed in professional networks that give more of an ongoing quality to their relationship.

Yet the fact that such findings can be interpreted in either capture or evolution of cooperation terms goes to the heart of our dilemma. The very conditions that foster the evolution of cooperation are also the conditions that promote the evolution of capture and indeed corruption. A revolving door simultaneously improves the prospects of productive cooperation and counterproductive capture. Where relationships are ongoing, where encounters are regularly repeated with the same regulator, corruption is more rewarding for both parties: the regulator can collect recurring bribe payments and the firm can benefit from repeated purchases of lower standards. Moreover, ongoing relationships permit the slow sounding out of the corruptibility and trustworthiness of the other to stand by corrupt bargains (and at minimum risk because an identical small number of players are involved each time).

This is why if you are looking for corruption in a police force, you look at those areas where there is regular contact between police in a particular squad and long-term repeat lawbreakers — prostitution, illegal gambling, other vice squad targets, and organised drug trafficking. You are less likely to find it in police dealings with robbers, burglars, and murderers. The ninety-six-agency Australian regulation study found (via highly speculative data) that corruption was more likely in agencies that had two qualities: they maintained close cooperative relationships with the industry, and engaged in regular sanctioning of the industry. Cooperation corrupts; cooperation qualified by the possibility of defection corrupts absolutely!

Classically, enforcement agencies deal with the risks of corruption and capture by regular rotation of personnel. Contrary to the policy prescription required for the evolution of cooperation, the anticorruption policy is to ensure that the suspect confronts different law enforcers on each contact. Officers are rotated between regions and among sites within regions.

Another variant of the same policy dilemma arises with discretion. Wide discretion "presents a real danger of corruption and capture". But narrow discretion results in rulebook-oriented regulation that thwarts the search for the most efficient solutions to problems like pollution control. When the reward payoff for cooperation is low as a result of such confining discretion, then the evolution of cooperation is unlikely. Might it be possible, however, to allow discretion to be wide, but to replace narrow rule-writing to control capture with control by innovative accountability for the exercise of wide discretion?

This then is the policy nut we seek to crack. How do we secure the advantages of the evolution of cooperation while averting the evolution of capture and corruption? Our answer lies in a republican form of tripartism. Tripartism is a process in which relevant public interest groups (PIGs) become the fully fledged third player in the game. As a third player in the game, the PIG can directly punish the firm. PIGs can also do much to prevent capture and corruption by enforcing ... a norm of punishing regulators who fail to punish noncompliance. Here the effect of the PIG on the firm is mediated by the PIG's effect on the regulator — instead of directly punishing firms, it punishes regulators who fail to punish firms. [This] ... can dramatically increase the prospects of stable compliance. The fully fledged tripartism we consider, where PIGs are empowered to punish firms directly, is a more radical option that has been conspicuously unanalysed, in spite of incipient instances of its implementation in many countries.

Who guards the guardians? In another sense this chapter is about who guards the guardians. The problem of guardianship ... is that we tend to deal with failures of trust by accumulating more and more layers of guardianship. The untrustworthiness of nth order guardians is monitored by $n + 1$th order guardians, and so on in infinite regress. In the present case, who will guard the PIGs? PIGs can be captured and corrupted; history is littered with cases of PIGs caught with their snouts in the trough.

We hope to show that this way of setting up the problem entails a rather too mechanistic conception of guardianship. What we put in its place is a notion of contestable guardianship. The idea of contestable markets arises where there is such a small number of producers in a market as to provide little direct guarantee that they will vigorously compete to hold each other's prices down. According to the theory, firms will nevertheless hold prices down because, as long as there are not formidable barriers to entry, they will fear that high prices will cause the entry of a new competitor who will seize their market share with lower prices.

The trick of institutional design to deal with the problem of regulatory capture, we suggest, is to make guardianship contestable. This is no easy matter, just as it is no easy matter to render economic markets contestable. Of course, the fact that economic markets rarely fit the theory of contestability says nothing about the possibilities for rendering political influence contestable in a democracy. To secure contestability, what is required is a regulatory culture where information on regulatory deals is freely available to all individual members of a multitude of PIGs. Also required is a vital democracy where PIG politicians are always vulnerable to accusations of capture by competing PIG political aspirants who stand ready to replace them. If talk of competition for PIG influence seems unreal, it is only because we are thinking of arenas where PIGS are powerless; where PIGs are empowered, aspirants emerge to contest the incumbency of PIG politicians.

Contestability can mean more than simply competition within the PIG sector for seats at the bargaining table. It can also mean, in a manner more directly analogous to contestable markets, pro-consumer discipline exercised by the potential of PIG entry into a regulatory domain that PIGS have decided not to enter. In a regulatory culture characterised by consumer groups becoming politically active whenever major consumer interests are threatened, the mainstream players of the regulatory game may guard against such consumerist assault by being mindful of consumer interests.

What Is Tripartism? Tripatism is defined as a regulatory policy that fosters the participation of PIGs in the regulatory process in three ways. First, it grants the PIG and all its members access to all the information that is available to the regulator. Second, it gives the PIG a seat at the negotiating table with the firm and the agency when deals are done. Third, the policy grants the PIG the same standing to sue or prosecute under the regulatory statute as the regulator. Tripartism means both unlocking to PIGs the smoke-filled rooms where the real business of regulation is transacted and allowing the PIG to operate as a private attorney general.

Generally in this book we refer to the simplest model of tripartism where a single PIG is selected by the state (or by a peak council of PIGs) as the most appropriate PIG to counterbalance the regulated actors. That PIG then elects its representative to participate in that regulatory negotiation. Contestability in this simple model is, therefore, accomplished by (1) different PIGs competing for the privilege of acting as the third player in the regulatory negotiation; and (2) different PIG politicians within each PIG competing for election to the negotiating role. The simplest model will not always be the most appropriate — the appropriate model of tripartism will be an historically and institutionally contingent matter. However, the simplest model has definite attractions: it should delay minimally decision making in arenas where no decision is the worst possible decision. And it should maximise the prospects of genuine dialogue around the table leading to a discovery of win-win solutions, instead of a babble of many conflicting voices talking past each other. In this book, tripartism is considered as a strategy for implementing laws and regulations that have already been settled. If one wanted to extend its application to the rule-making process itself, an extension that may have merit, then clearly the simple tripartism model would provide too narrow a basis for PIG participation.

But who are the PIGs? Here it is best to resist pleas for a clear definition of the public interest and who represents it. One reason is that what we ultimately favour is a contested, democratic theory of the public interest rather than an account that can be neatly packaged in advance of the operation of democratic process. Second, what we urge democratic polities to do is identify, on an arena-by-arena basis, the group best able to contest (rather than "represent") that public interest embodied in a particular regulatory statute. These groups are thrust into the breach to fight for the public interest the legislature intended to be protected by a regulatory statute; but, in fact, they will more often than not be private interest groups.

An environmental group empowered as the third party in environmental regula-tion may be a PIG largely devoid of private interest. But we include as PIGs trade unions empowered to defend the interests of their members in occupational health and safety regulation. Indeed, it could even be that a suitable group to contest the public interest in a consumer protection statute to guarantee the quality of auto-mobiles could be the industry association of car rental firms. The most knowledge-able group to intervene in a cozy regulatory arrangement that maintains oligopolistic prices for wheat may be the industry association of flour millers.

... The simplest arena to understand how tripartite regulation would work is with occupational health and safety. In a unionised workplace, elected union health and safety representatives would have the same rights to accompany the inspector in the workplace as the company safety officer. They would have the right to sit in on and ask questions at any exit conference at the end of the inspection and at any subse-quent conference. They would receive copies of the inspection report and of any subsequent correspondence between the parties. If they perceived an unwarranted failure to prosecute, to shut down a machine or to take any other enforcement action, they would have the same standing as the government inspector to pursue that enforcement action...

As Meidinger (1987) cogently argues, there is no touchstone, no objective stan-dard, by which we can separate the public interest from private interests. Social life seems "almost always to involve a combination of pecuniary interest-pursuit and citizenship" In practical terms, citizen concerns about themselves motivate their identification of public concerns: "reason is mostly likely to be applied by passion — in the form of interests". This is not to support the crude "deals thesis" that one sometimes sees in law-and-economics writing. Regulation is largely contested in a public-regarding discourse; it is a shallow analysis to view interest groups as unashamedly using the state regulatory apparatus as no more than a vehicle for advancing their private interests. Certainly, our conclusion will be that this latter form of discourse should be discouraged by our regulatory institutions. Public-regarding discourse, which is already encouraged in many ways by regulatory agencies and the courts, should be further encouraged ... Achieving regulatory effectiveness through a balance of control is not about simply striking a compromise of interests. It is about understanding each other's needs and then sharing ideas in the pursuit of risk management strategies that deliver acceptable protection at acceptable cost. As the negotiation experts have instructed us, we will all do better if we focus less on positions and more on designing new solutions that are responsive to mutually understood needs, new solutions that may bear no relation to initial bargaining position ...

As the last paragraph of the above extract shows, the approach of Ayres and Braithwaite explicitly aims to blend both public and private interest assumptions about human nature. They do so by arguing that a particular institutional design — tripartism — can create a system of checks and balances that harness private interests to work in favour of the public interest. Although they caution that their strategy applies more clearly to the implementation of existing regulatory regimes, their approach has been so influential in regulation scholarship as a whole that it is presented here as one that could apply to explaining the emergence of a regulatory regime. The discussion questions encourage further reflection on whether this extension of the original scope of their theory is workable.

2.4.2 Regulatory space

Our second example of an institutionalist approach is known as a 'regulatory space' approach and moves further away from delineating 'public' and 'private' interests and casting them in opposition to, or tension with, each other. Instead, the idea of regulatory space emphasises a place where regulation occurs, almost a kind of physical arena which influences the practices that happen within it. In so doing, less emphasis is placed on individuals and groups and the outcomes they pursue or aspire to. Indeed, Hancher and Moran in the next extract go so far as to say that 'little can be gained by depicting [regulation] in the dichotomous language of public authority versus private interests'. Instead, a regulatory space approach examines how the actions and intentions of regulatory actors are embedded in larger systems and institutional dynamics. For example, utilities regulation may involve very similar actors in different countries and yet different national political contexts would shape the preferences of these actors in different ways, leading to the emergence of different regulatory regimes. The extract from Hancher and Moran includes some discussion of how such different national political contexts shape regulation, a discussion that is taken up again in Chapter 4 in relation to how different national contexts shape regulatory enforcement. More generally, they emphasise 'system dynamics' over the specific preferences and interests of individual groups or actors. 'Regulatory space' contains not only state actors and formal public authority, but also non-state actors and sources of authority over which the state may not have a monopoly such as information, wealth and organisational capacity. Two important ideas emerge from this approach. The first is the limited relevance of law and formal public authority within a regulatory space. The second is that regulatory outcomes might not align with the predictions of private interest theory, because history, national culture and organisational dynamics (such as the standard operating procedures of large institutions) may shape the regulatory dynamics of a particular policy sector in ways that the combined interests of the different actors would not.

Hancher and Moran, 'Organizing regulatory space' (1989)

Regulation is virtually a defining feature of any system of social organization, for we recognise the existence of a social order by the presence of rules, and by the attempt to enforce those rules. ... Within the broad field of regulation, however, a special place is occupied by ... the regulation of economic activity in Western capitalist societies, where organization on market principles is combined with a high level of industrial development. Economic regulation under advanced capitalism has several distinctive features, and these features in turn shape the character of regulatory activity ... The most striking single feature of economic regulation is that it is dominated by relations between large, sophisticated, and administratively complex organizations performing wide-ranging economic and social tasks. Such bodies obviously include the various agencies of the state – government departments, quangos, and specialised regulatory bodies – but they also encompass organised interest groups, trade unions, and firms. The importance of the large firm in the regulatory process is particularly notable. Indeed an important theme is the central place of the large, often multinationally organised, enterprise as a locus of power, a reservoir of expertise, a bearer of economic change, and an agent of enforcement in the implementation process. Understanding economic regulation, then, means understanding a process of intermediation and bargaining between large and powerful organizations spanning what are conventionally termed the public and private domains of decision-making. But this understanding points to an important, related, feature. The economies of advanced capitalist societies have been universally marked by a high level of state intervention. Regulation is embedded in the practices of the interventionist state. The aims of regulation are commonly only explicable by reference to the wider structures and more general aims of the interventionist system. Economic regulation under advanced capitalism – its formation as much as its implementation – invariably involves interdependence and bargaining between powerful and sophisticated actors against a background of extensive state involvement. But the particular character of an individual nation-state adds two other distinctive features, the first to do with the role of law, the second with the allocation of sovereign authority. Nations with advanced capitalist economies are almost universally governed, or claim to be governed, according to some principles of constitutional democracy. The exercise of public power, in other words, rests on legal authority, and this legal authority is made legitimate in turn by appeal to popular will. Of course by no means all economic regulation is cast in the form of legal rules, but the central importance of the principle of constitutionalism means that the range and form of regulation is deeply influenced by the particular conception of the scope and purpose of law which prevails in any particular community at any particular time. To put the point more technically, the purpose and character of economic regulation is in part a function of the nature of the surrounding legal culture.

Conceptions of the proper role of law are in turn intimately connected with notions about the appropriate allocation of sovereign authority. Economic regulation is practised in a highly developed form in societies combining organization on market principles, domination of many sectors by giant firms, and political rule according to formally democratic principles. The combination of these three features sets up great tensions in the regulatory process, a tension reflected in much of the literature on the subject. Democracy, especially in the Anglo-Saxon tradition, is closely associated with parliamentarianism: that is, with the assumption that a monopoly of legitimate authority flows from the command of popular and legislative majorities. Regulation, on this conception, is a process by which popular and public control is exercised over the workings of private power in the market-place. The idea was well expressed by Gabriel Kolko, one of the most eloquent defenders of American regulation under the New Deal, when he spoke of the regulatory agencies created in that period as 'the outposts of capitalism' designed to control the market-place 'lest capitalism by its own greed, fear, avarice and myopia destroy itself.'

The notion that economic regulation is a process by which sovereign public authority disciplines and controls private interests has exercised a particularly strong influence over American thinking about the subject. Since the literature on regulation, in the English language at least, is largely American inspired, the notion has in turn deeply influenced debates about the historical development of economic regulation and about its proper place in modern democratic systems. The most important consequence has been an instinctive belief that 'private' influence over the regulatory process is illegitimate. If regulation is assumed to be an activity in which some ideal of the public interest is pursued at the expense of the private, then evidence that private interests benefit from regulation, or that they exercise a strong influence over the regulatory process, is naturally treated as a sign that the purpose of the activity has been distorted.

These notions are particularly marked in the long-running debate about 'capture' in regulation. The very idea of 'capture' betrays an assumption that there is a sphere of public regulatory authority which ought to be inviolate from private influence. Both Kolko's historical interpretation of regulation as a response to the needs of powerful corporate interests, and the vast literature 'exposing' particular instances of regulatory capture, are united by the belief that the practise of regulation has involved the subordination of public authority to sectional interest. Likewise the most influential critique of the interventionist regulatory state produced by a political scientist — Lowi's *End of Liberalism* — rests on the argument that there once existed, and should exist again, a liberal constitution possessing an inviolable public core, bounded by law, and clearly distinct from the private sphere. Even observers sceptical of 'capture' theories have shared the assumptions of their opponents: debate has typically turned on attempts to rebut the empirical accuracy of capture theory, rather than on attempts to question the assumption that there should indeed exist an inviolable public sphere.

It is undoubtedly the case that arguments about the capture or otherwise of the regulatory process raise important issues of both constitutional principle and substantive outcome. Questions about who benefits from regulation, and who is allowed to shape the decisions made by regulatory agencies, are plainly central to understanding and evaluation. Yet to couch the discussion in terms suggesting the necessity of identifying and defending a clearly delimited sphere of public authority is unhelpful. It rests on the culturally restricted constitutional assumption that the roles of 'public' and 'private' in the regulatory process can be authoritatively distinguished. But as we explore below, there actually exist significant national variations in how the public-private divide is conventionally drawn. More seriously, the 'capture' debate obscures perhaps the single most important feature of economic regulation under advanced capitalism: that the most important actors in the process are organizations, and organizations which, regardless of their formal status, have acquired important attributes of public status. Of the formally 'private'organizations with public status, none is more important that the large firm.

The role of the large firm is unique. Whereas the regulation of the behaviour of individual 'private' actors is concerned with the imposition of a public or general will on private citizens, large firms cannot be described as private 'takers' of regulation in this sense. They have acquired the status of 'governing institutions'. As Lindblom has argued, in a market economy firms carry out functions of an essentially public character. Their decisions on investment, employment, and output have important allocational and distributional implications which resonate in the 'public' sphere. The corporate strategy of individual firms is a major determinant of the direction of the regulatory process. Public governmental agencies do not merely act upon firms as, so to speak, external agents. Corporations are major centres of expertise, and they constitute a significant independent social and administrative hierarchies. Their integration into the implementation of regulation is very often a precondition to success. This is so even where the ownership structure of a firm is independent of a (state) public agency; but the fusion of private and public ownership is actually now a common feature of advanced capitalist economies.

Economic regulation of markets under advanced capitalism can thus be portrayed as an activity shaped by the *interdependence* of powerful organizations who share major public characteristics. In the economic sphere no clear dividing line can be drawn between organizations of a private nature and those entitled to the exclusive exercise of public authority. The fusion is made more complete by one of the features remarked on earlier: economic regulation is an integral part of the activities of the modern interventionist state. While much economic regulation does indeed involve the making of rules and the enforcement of standards, this occurs within a framework of much more diffuse intervention, concerned with a wide range of often unstated and even contradictory objectives. Economic rule-based regulation is not a distinct activity; it is woven into a larger fabric of intervention. The overall pattern is marked by a high level of social and administrative complexity. In regulation much of the most important activity consists in the routinised application of general principles, which may be devised by the regulatory authority or alternatively may be little more than the company's standard operating procedures, officially endorsed as general principles. Hence we say that certain ways of doing things become 'institutionalised'. At the same time, however, organizational alliances are constantly forming and reforming without any reference to a conventional public-private divide. Parties bargain, co-operate, threaten, or act according to semi-articulated customary assumptions. The allocation of roles between rule makers, enforcers, and bearers of sectional interests constantly shifts, again obeying no obvious public-private dichotomy. In such a world firms are not bearers of some distinct private interest which is subject to public control; they are actors in a common sphere with other institutions conventionally given the 'public' label.

Economic regulation under advanced capitalism is therefore best conceived as an activity occurring in economies where the public and private are characteristically mixed, where the dominant actors are powerful and sophisticated organizations, and where the biggest firms have taken on many of the features of governing institutions. In this world the language of regulatory capture is largely devoid of meaning. Questions about who participates in and benefits-from regulation are certainly important: explaining the complex and shifting relationships between and within organizations at the heart of economic regulation is the key to understanding the nature of the activity. But little can be gained by depicting the relationship in the dichotomous language of public authority versus private interests. On the basis of the evidence collected in this volume we can see that different institutions have come to inhabit a common regulatory space. The central question for the analyst of the European regulatory scene is not to assume 'capture', but rather to understand the nature of this shared space: the rules of admission, the relations between occupants, and the variations introduced by differences in markets and issue arenas. The character of regulatory space is our next theme . . . .

The concept of 'regulatory space' is an analytical construct. It is defined . . . by the range of regulatory issues subject to public decision. A number of obvious consequences follow from this. First, precisely because it is a space it is available for occupation. Secondly, because it is a space it can be unevenly divided between actors: there will, in other words, be major and minor participants in the regulatory process. Thirdly, just as we can identify a general concept of regulatory space in operation in a particular community we can also speak of specific concepts of regulatory space at work in individual sectors: in pharmaceuticals, for instance, issues of safety and price control are subjects, or potential subjects, of regulatory activity, whereas in the automobile sector only the former set of issues are included. Fourthly, because 'regulatory space' is an image being used to convey a concept, it can be augmented by similar images: thus because an arena is delineated space we sometimes speak of a 'regulatory arena'. The boundaries which demarcate regulatory space in turn by a range of issues, so it is sensible to speak of regulatory space as encompassing a range of regulatory issues in a community. In these terms regulatory space may be furiously contested. Its occupants are involved in an often ferocious struggle for advantage. Any investigation of the concept involves examining the outcomes of competitive struggles, the resources used in those struggles, and the distribution of those resources between the different institutions involved. In other words, the play of power is at the centre of this process.

Discovering who has power in regulation involves paying close attention to the relations between the organizations which at any one time occupy regulatory space. But the idea of a space also directs us to a far more important aspect of power. It encourages us not only to examine relations between those who enjoy inclusion, but also to examine the characteristics of the excluded. That the structure of power is shaped by modes of exclusion from any political process is an elementary truth. In the case of economic regulation, however, the observation has a particularly sharp point. When we speak of the politics of economic regulation under advanced capitalism we are speaking of a set of power relationships dominated by large organizations. These complex organizations — the biggest firms, representative associations, regulatory agencies, central departments of state — are organised in administrative hierarchies whose method of doing business is shaped by standard operating procedures. Institutional procedure, that is, the routine application of established practices, rather than individual choice, is the dominant influence in deciding who is taken into, or kept out of, regulatory space. Since the rules of organizational life have a routinised character, exclusions tend to be systematic. Understanding who is in, and who is out, is therefore particularly vital, and depends crucially on analysing the customary patterns of organizational relationships in any particular regulatory space.

If groups can be organised into, or organised out of, regulatory space, the same can be said of issues. There are no obvious natural limits of boundaries to regulation. Notions of what is 'regulatable' are plainly shaped by the experience of history, the filter of culture, and the availability of existing resources. The fact that economic regulation is predominantly regulation by and of large organizations means, however, that notions about appropriate scope are routinised, and are embedded in organizational procedures. Understanding why some issues are prioritised, included, or excluded, at different times and in different places, thus demands an exploration of how organizations become committed to, and maintain a commitment to, particular definitions of the scope of regulatory space. Likewise, understanding changes in the notion of what issues should be included demands attention to the shifting balance of power within and between institutional actors inside the common regulatory space.

The factors determining the shape of this space, and the relative position of its occupants, are many and complex. But the gist of understanding lies in one simple observation: the most important relationships in economic regulation are relationships between organizations. ... Here only a sketch of the main influences can be offered [which are place, timing and organisational structure.] ...

National Peculiarities: ... Regulation occurs, it is a truism to observe, in particular places, and therefore place matters. The most important delineation of place is provided by the boundaries of the nation-state. Nations arrange their regulatory spaces in distinctive ways . . . [A]lthough the economies of advanced capitalist nations exhibit similar patterns of extensive regulation dominated by a small number of large organizations, there exist significant national variations in the political and constitutional responses to these similarities. Different national traditions conceive of the public-private authority in different ways; and different national traditions likewise allow access to regulatory space to different constellations of actors. The differences are summed up in the importance given to concepts of legal and political culture. Though some argument exists about the independent explanatory power of cultural variables, there can be no doubt that they are at the very least important in mediating the influence of historical experiences ... In regulation, culturally formed assumptions about the purpose and role of law are particularly significant. These assumptions can determine whether regulation happens at all, its scope, how far it is embodied in statute or formal rules, and how far the struggles for competitive advantage which are a part of the regulatory process spill over into the Courts . . . .

One of the most striking illustrations of the significance of these kinds of variables is provided by a comparison of Anglo-American and European conceptions of public law. In the Anglo-American tradition, where a legal concept of the state is either absent or only weakly present, public law been essentially concerned with the pragmatic control of public power, especially of the kind of discretionary power which is embedded in the process of economic regulation. In the UK especially, law has not been viewed as the great interpreter of politics. The continental European tradition, more firmly rooted in Roman law, by contrast assigns a central place to the state both as idea and as institution. This establishes the unique character of public authority in terms of sovereignty and/or function.The jurisprudence of public law, enforced through a distinct and specialised court structure in France and West Germany, is developed independently of private law norms, whereas in the United Kingdom and United States the control of public authority has been characteristically secured through the ordinary courts.

Within these broad traditions, distinct national configurations abound. Vogel has recently explored the striking differences produced by British and American attitudes to the relevance of litigation in the regulatory process, contrasting the detailed rules and adversarial enforcement common in the United States with the discretionary guidelines and co-operative implementation characteristic of so much British regulation. Within the European tradition very different national patterns also exist. In France the ideal of a unitary state and the 'paternalistic conception of a prerogative police power, conceived as the general regulation of French society for the public good' still permeates public law theory and practice. The constitution is viewed, not so much as a source of legitimate authority, but rather as an expression of the idea of the unity of the state. In such circumstances, especially in the sphere of economic regulation, administrative courts are considered to be of relatively limited value in challenging the rulings of administrations 'addicted to discretionary adaptation of the rules to suit the political convenience of governments'. This truncated approach to constitutional values is reflected in public law procedures and norms. The administrative courts may review the legality of a decision but will not, except in very unusual circumstances, substitute their own evaluation of the facts for that of an administration. The Council of State — the highest administrative 'court' — has indeed consistently refused to interfere in economic decisions involving the exercise of discretion,

The place of the constitution and constitutional values in shaping the practice of regulation in West Germany stands out in sharp contrast. The Basic Law of 1949 is viewed as embodying a juristic idea of the state. When combined with Roman law traditions of deductive legal reasoning from a unified set of principles, this has meant that the 'constitution has acquired an imperative character and policy has become highly judicialised'. The West German Constitution is seen 'not just as a general framework establishing a minimum consensus about certain principles' — in the manner of, for instance, the American Constitution — but as a 'political programme containing particular substantive goals'. This commitment to legalism and formalism has limited the exercise of executive power and given the Courts a prominent role in controlling the scope of regulatory activity and the range of regulatory discretion. Equipped with highly generalised constitutional principles such as the right to equal treatment the freedom to own property, and the freedom to pursue a profession, the German Courts have not hesitated to invalidate both administrative regulation and legalisation.

This sketch illustrates some of the important ways in which the character of a legal culture mediates the regulatory process, fixing the scope of regulatory space and influencing who gains entry and on what terms. Variables attributable to distinctive legal cultures may also determine the ability of 'excluded' interests to challenge the existing distribution of power within the common regulatory space. Legal culture may further operate as an important variable in determining the way in which the different rules interact to create a regulatory framework. For instance, the interplay of rules established by statute or collective bargaining and the rules established by statute or common law in the regulation of labour markets, varies considerably between the large European democracies. Similar variations exist in financial regulation: some disclosure practices which are simply the standard operating procedures of large firms in the UK have become 'juridified', or expressed as legally binding rules, in the USA...

Historical timing: ... Regulation is practised in time as well in space. The historical timing of regulatory initiatives and development can thus be critical. ... The significance of timing arises from an elementary characteristic of regulation as an activity: it has to be organised. Without appropriate institutional arrangements implementation simply does not take place. The act of organization in turn demands resources: the knowledge to create or to copy regulatory institutions; the money and people to run those institutions; the expertise to devise rules, and to monitor and police their enforcement. The organization that controls these resources will dominate regulatory space; and the organization that commands the necessary resources at the historical moment when regulation is initiated has a good chance of exercising a continuing dominant influence....The significance of timing is emphasised by the nature of regulation itself. Regulation is largely a matter of organizational routine, of institutionalised procedures punctuated by occasional crises, economic or political. Such crises serve the function of inducing change, or at least initiating a search for alternative institutional arrangements. In between periods of crisis, the more dominant organizations can retain and consolidate their position of superiority, so that alternative mechanisms of regulation are ignored or suppressed. The moment of historical origin of regulation can thus be of the utmost significance ... Regulation almost always happens because some sense of crisis is precipitated, but the crisis can occur at very different historical moments. . . . The balance of institutional forces at the moment of crisis is plainly of enduring importance. In some sectors at the crucial initial moment the state command the necessary regulatory resources, and its own agencies or actors dominate the process. . . . The key analytical point is that understanding regulatory arrangements in the present depends on understanding the historical configuration out of which they developed. . . .

Organizational structure: Economic regulation is predominantly regulation by and through organizations. In any particular arena the character of these organizations will vary; the variations in turn influence the nature of the activity. The most fundamental effect governs who or what exercises any power in the regulatory process. The everyday practice of regulation of course involves dealings between individuals. But these individuals characteristically only enjoy access to regulatory space because they have some organizational role: as employees of firms, as the voice of an organised interest, as servants of the state. Private citizens rarely have a significant legitimate role in the formulation and implementation of regulatory policy. Intellectuals may occasionally contribute to the shaping of regulatory ideologies, though even in such cases their influence depends heavily on their identification with the organizational bearers of scholarly knowledge, such as universities and professional associations. Individual political entrepreneurs like Nader in the United States can likewise periodically intervene, though as the history of Nader's campaigns indicates continuing influence depends heavily on the ability to embody activity in organizational form.

Organizational status is thus the most important condition governing access to regulatory space. Private individuals who do not perform organizational roles, or who are not bearers of organizational interests, enjoy limited and usually temporary success in any attempt to intervene. Citizens are 'takers' of regulation; organizations are makers and shapers. Very occasionally private citizens may succeed in mounting a successful legal challenge to a regulatory programme, but sustained or permanent participation is precluded.

The organizations typically dominant in regulatory space, whether they are conventionally labelled 'private' or 'public', share important characteristics. They are usually big − in the case of the state and the largest firms very big indeed — and are marked by the elaborate internal division of administrative labour and extended administrative hierarchies. These features impose both co-operative and conflictual elements on the practice of regulation. When regulatory space is dominated by large, hierarchical bodies regulation inevitably becomes a co-operative matter, because only such a means can it be accomplished. Almost nothing of significance is done in regulation as the result of the actions of any single individual or simple organizational entity. The regulatory task is subjected to an elaborate and elongated division of labour. Even the design and implementation of comparatively simple standards (like the introduction of transparency guidelines to advise doctors on prescribing) depends on co-operation between large numbers of individuals occupying very different roles in the hierarchies of different organizations. This observation merely serves to reinforce one of our earlier points: that the big firms who are major occupiers of regulatory space can in no sense be pictured as mere 'takers' of regulation. Even if they are not explicitly involved in the formal process of rule-making, nothing would happen to promulgated rules without their extensive co-operation.

In economic regulation, therefore, the most important parties are bound together in relations of exchange and interdependence. But, the co-operation enforced by the division of administrative labour should not conceal the way the organizations who inhabit regulatory space are riven by competition and conflict. Indeed the essence of regulatory politics is the pursuit of institutional advantage: the pursuit of advantage in the market-place, measured by indices like market share and profit; and the pursuit of command over the regulatory process itself, as measured by the right to make rules and to command their means of implementation. Regulation — and the rules and distribution of power through which it operates — is always a 'stake' of industrial or political struggle.

Organizational status as a condition of access to regulatory space; large-scale, extended hierarchies; a refined division of administrative labour; enforced co-operation in the implementation of regulation; the relentless pursuit of institutional advantage: these are the most important consequences of the organizational character of economic regulation under advanced capitalism. But of course these shared institutional characteristics still allow for considerable diversity, and this diversity influences not only the allocation of power within the regulatory space but also perceptions of what should be regulated, and how the necessary tasks should be accomplished. Four influences are particularly important: the way organizational procedures impose different views about the substance of regulation; the variations introduced by governmental structure and structure of ownership; variations in the internal cohesion of firms; and variations in the social and cultural cohesion and economic strength of industries and sectors.

[**Overall then**], understanding the nature of the regulatory process in advanced capitalist economies involves, above all, understanding the character of the organizational forms dominant in regulatory arenas. Our sketch shows that the allocation of power and influence within regulatory space is influenced both by legal tradition and by a wide range of social, economic, and cultural factors.

2.4.3 Systems theory

While Hancher and Moran's regulatory space approach tends to emphasise the complexity and contingency of how regulation emerges, it is still very concrete, grounded in history, formal institutions and detailed attention to power dynamics. 'Systems theory', however, is the most abstract of what we are calling institutionalist approaches to regulation. Discussions of exactly what is constituted by a 'system' operate at a very high level of abstraction. So, for example, whereas public choice theorists exploring utilities regulation might investigate the ways in which the regulated industry lobbies regulatory agencies and the legislature in order to secure regulatory benefits, systems theorists might focus on the way in which the economic and political systems communicate (or fail to communicate) with each other.

But although this example gives a regulatory context for applying systems theory, systems theory is more than a theory of regulation. It is rather a theory of society, which builds on biological scientists' accounts of how living organisms self-regulate, and particularly of how they relate to their environment in so doing. The influence of biology may seem arcane, but the important point to take from it is the notion that self-regulation is the starting-point for understanding how systems create order. While this has sometimes been interpreted as veiled prejudice against regulation, it is not intended as such. Rather, it is a descriptive consequence of applying empirical observations about biological systems to social settings.

One of the central findings of systems theory is that systems tend to be closed, self-referential 'spaces' that perpetuate their own existence by a series of operations and a system of language that is only comprehensible internally to those who speak the language of the system and understand its workings. The legal system, for example, uses the language of doctrinal analysis and legal precedent to analyse situations by reference to a code that labels outcomes as either 'legal' or 'illegal', whereas the economic system uses economic analysis and evaluations of efficiency or inefficiency. Legality and efficiency are systemically incommensurable, because the legal and economic systems operate at least partially autonomously from each, and most crucially, can only influence each other *indirectly*. Many traditional approaches to regulation are based on the assumption that legal commands will shape the behaviour of economic and political actors to produce certain outcomes. Systems theory is much more skeptical about this. It views hierarchical legal authority as an external irritant to the economic system: one to which it will respond if it can translate its meaning into terms that make sense within the internal logic of its own system. If we think of a 'system' as something less encompassing than the 'economic system' — say, the health and safety system of the oil and gas industry — this approach may come close to a regulatory space approach, but it is more inclined to focus on systemic logics than on the actions or intentions of individuals or groups. In the following extract from Teubner's early work, he presents law as inherently self-restraining: as a social practice that regulates self-regulatory mechanisms, rather than regulating the substance of a particular issue, such as health and safety.

Gunther Teubner, '*Dilemmas of law in the welfare state*' (1986)

Why make use of the theory of self-referential systems? ... What follows for our problematic law and society relation if we reformulate them in terms of self-referentiality? What hypotheses, what recommendations for political-legal action are implied?

The message of self-reference can be clearly distinguished from older versions of systems theory. While classical notions of system concentrated on the internal relations of the elements, searching for emerging properties of the system ("the whole is more than the parts"), modern theories of "open systems" reject the "closed systems approach" and stress the exchange relations between system and environment ... [The guiding questions of the open system approach are:] How can the system cope with an over-complex environment? ... How can we explain internal structures as a result of environmental demands? ... In what way are inputs processed into outputs through an internal conversion process? ...

In a sense, the theory of self-referential systems seems to return to the concept of a closed system, even to a radical concept of closure. *A system produces and reproduces its own elements through the interaction of its elements* — by definition, a self-referential system is a closed system. However, what makes the theory more promising than both its forerunners is the inherent relation of self-referentiality to the environment.

Self-referential systems, being closed systems of self-producing interactions, are, necessarily at the same time, open systems with boundary trespassing processes. And it is precisely the linkage between internalizing self-referential mechanisms and externalizing environment exchange mechanisms which makes the concept of self-reference more fruitful and more complex than its predecessors with their somewhat sterile alternative of closed versus open systems.

If we are using self-referentiality as the criterion to judge competing strategic models of post-instrumental law, two directions of analysis seem to be fruitful. One concerns the question about what effective *limits* the self-referential structure of social systems sets to legal intervention. The second direction of analysis concerns the *social knowledge* which is necessary if law acting within those limits seeks to cope with self-referential structures of the regulated areas. Thus, we arrive at the following theses if we reformulate the premises of the competing strategic models in terms of that theory:

1. *The Regulatory Trilemma*: The implementation strategy will ultimately run aground on the internal dynamics of self-referential structures of both the regulating and the regulated system. Without taking into account the limits of "structural coupling", it inevitably ends in a trilemma: it leads to either "incongruence" of law and society, or "over-legalization" of society, or "over-socialization" of law. Moreover, the models of causal linearity which the implementation strategy uses seem to be insufficient for the social knowledge that is required for the "regulation" of autopoietic systems.

2. *Social Self-Closure*: The re-formulization strategy neglecting in its turn the need of self-referential systems to externalise, develops no obstacles against the dynamics of social self-closure. An increase in subsystem rationality may be the result, but with possibly disastrous effects with regard to the coordination with the system's environment.

3. *Response to Self-Referentiality*: In contrast, the third strategic model seems to be compatible with the self-referentiality. As we have seen, for the control of self-regulation, theorists have developed a broad range of rather diverse recommendations about the way to "proceduralise" the law. Now, in the light of self-referentiality, what seem to be obviously heterogeneous recommendations can be interpreted as complementary strategies. The maintenance of a self-reproductive organization needs societal support. The recommendations can be read as strategies to make compatible the self-referentiality of various social sub-systems. "Proceduralization" represents society's response to the needs of self-referentiality: "autonomy", "externalization", and "coordination".

If we translate our problem of legal regulation into the language of self-reference, a decisive difference becomes apparent. Models of regulation and of implementation, even if they are developed in the open system framework, deal with the implicit assumption of basal linearity. This means, that they see the relation between the regulating systems (politics and law) and the regulated system (functional subsystems, organization, interaction) as a relation between environment and system in which the regulating systems maintain and control the goals and the processes of the regulated systems ... While it is true that they abandon a purely instrumentalist model and take into account autonomy in the regulated area and complicated interaction processes in the implementation field, they still have no adequate concept of what constitutes the autonomy of the regulated system. They still conceive of the regulated system as "allopoietic", as dependent on the actions of the regulating system.

In contrast, a theory of self-reference would define the regulated area as a system consisting of elements which interact with each other in such a way that they maintain themselves and reproduce elements having the same properties as a result of repeating the self-producing interaction. They are systems that keep their reproductive organization constant. To be sure, their concrete structures can be influenced and changed by regulation, but only within the limits of that reproductive organization ... [R]egulations do not at all change social institutions, they produce only a new challenge for their autopoietic adaptation. Any external regulatory influence which leads to a new internal interaction of elements not maintaining its self-reproductive organization, is either irrelevant or leads to the disintegration of the regulated system.

The picture becomes more complicated if we take into account that the regulating systems, politics and law, are themselves reproductive systems. We have then to reformulate the hierarchical relation of regulation into a circular interaction between three self-referential systems (law, politics, regulated subsystems). The limits of regulation are then defined by the threefold limits of self-reproduction. *A regulatory action is successful only to the degree that it maintains a self-producing internal interaction of the elements in the regulating systems, law and politics, which is at the same time compatible with self-producing internal interactions in the regulated system.* This threefold compatibility relation may be called "structural coupling". Thus, we can formulate the *regulatory trilemma*: If regulation does not conform to the conditions of "structural coupling" of law, politics and society, it is bound to end up in regulatory failure. There are three ways regulation can fail:

(a) *"incongruence" of law, politics and society*
The regulatory action is incompatible with the self-producing interactions of the regulated system — the regulated system reacts by not reacting. Since the regulatory action does not comply with the relevance criteria of the regulated system, it is simply irrelevant for the elements' interactions. The law is ineffective because it creates no change in behaviour. However, the self-producing organization remains intact, in law as well as in society. This is what one might call the "symbolic use" of politics and law.

(b) *"Over-Legalization" of society*
Again, the concrete self-producing interactions within law, politics and within society are not compatible with each other. In this case, however, the regulatory action influences the internal interaction of elements in the regulated field so strongly that their self-production is endangered. This leads to disintegrating effects in the regulated field ... The regulatory programmes obey a functional logic and follow criteria of rationality which are poorly suited to the internal social structure of the regulated spheres of life. Law as a medium of the welfare state works efficiently, but at the price of destroying the reproduction of traditional patterns of social life.

(c) *"Over-Socialization" of Law*
A third type of regulatory failure should be taken into account. Once again incompatibility of self-production is the result of regulation, but in this case with the difference that the self-producing organization of the regulated area remains intact while the self-producing organization of the law is endangered. The law is "captured" by politics or by the regulated subsystem, the law is "politicised", "economised", "pedagogised" etc. with the result that the self-production of its normative elements becomes overstrained. Overstrain of the law in the welfare state may be the effect of its political instrumentalization, but it may also be the law's "surrender" to other sub-systems of society at the cost of its own reproduction. The "over-socialization" of law may take on many forms.

All in all, these three types of regulatory failure which each show very distinctive features have one thing in common. In each case, regulatory law turns out to be ineffective because it overreaches the limitations which are built into the regulatory process: the self-referential organization of these systems, of either the regulated field, or politics or the law itself. The effects are likewise problematic, being either irrelevance of regulation or disintegrating effects in the self-reproductive organization of law, politics or society.

. . .

Up to this point, we have discussed how law reflects two basic needs of self-referential subsystems: the need for autonomy and the need for externalization. A third dimension becomes apparent if one takes into account that not only social subsystems but also the encompassing society as a whole constitutes a self-referential system. The interaction of the functional subsystems, politics, economy, law, education, religion, family etc. can be seen as a self-producing interaction between elements of a larger system. Each of these subsystems contributes to the maintenance of societal self-reference. The law's contribution in this respect is the resolution of inter-system-conflicts by a specific "procedural regulation". Helmut Willke has developed a concept of a legal programme aiming at this function: the "relational programme". As opposed to the typical programmes of formal law (conditional programme) and of instrumental law (purposive programme), the function of relational programmes is to make compatible different purposes and rationalities of social sub-systems by committing political and social actors to discursive procedures of decision-making. He identifies the emergence of this new type of legal programme in diverse inter-system-coordination mechanisms, such as the ... Science Council in the Federal Republic of Germany. As Mayntz puts it: "It is in fact an aim of procedural regulation at the supra-organizational level to set up such networks or to provide platforms for such coordination which, where no hierarchical relationships of dependence are involved, will mainly proceed through bargaining".

One promising mode of understanding the working of such "relational programmes" can be found in the theory of "black-boxes" developed in the context of cybernetics. Self-referential systems − social systems like law, politics and regulated subsystems − are like "black boxes" in the sense of being mutually inaccessible to each other. One knows the input and output; the conversion, however, remains obscure. Now, black-box-techniques do not aim at shedding light onto this obscure internal conversion process, but circumvent the problem by an indirect "procedural" activity. They concentrate, not on the internal relations within the black box, but on the interrelation between the black boxes. Black boxes become "whitened" in the sense that an interaction relation develops among them which is transparent for them in its regularities. So law still cannot intervene directly into the economy; legal access consists in the relation between law and economy. It is the peculiarity of relational programmes that they regulate internal processes in systems indirectly so that they concentrate on the relations between the systems. That means again to drastically decrease the requirements of cognitive capacities of law and politics, since they no longer attempt to directly influence economic action but to influence only the "concerned action", whose internal structure is for them much more transparent. It is crucial that between the interaction relation and the regulated system (in our example, between concerted action and economy) consists a dense connection which is the course for guidance effects. This is to be expected from two mechanisms. One is the commitment of economic actors in the concerted action and the other is that the concerted action as such develops cognitive modes of the economy which may be more adequate than those of politics and law. This whole way of thinking ... [suggests that] one has to give up concepts of comprehensive social planning since they are utopian and unrealistic and replace them by more realistic models in which limited strategic knowledge is combined with social interaction, that is in our concept the interaction between the two black-boxes in order to reach guidance effects within one of the black-boxes.

Autonomy, externalization and coordination — these are three dimensions in which reflexive law responds to the basic needs of self-referential systems. These dimensions have been analyzed by different legal theorists with the intention of pointing out the developmental tendencies of post-instrumental law. With the concept of self-referentiality I have tried to demonstrate that they represent complementary rather than competing approaches.

. . .

[This approach] stress[es] the aspect of enhancing specific learning capacities in decentralised social subsystems. These learning capacities should be oriented toward re-introducing the consequences of actions of social sub-systems into their own reflexion structure.

2.4.4   The role of law in institutionalist approaches

Law once again continues to play a facilitative role in institutionalist theories of regulation and, in all the approaches surveyed here, this role takes on a proceduralist dimension. In Ayres and Braithwaite, law might help to create and maintain the tripartite structure that brings together public and private actors, for example by mandating third-party participation in regulatory rule-making. Hancher and Moran, in their own words, argue that, 'the character of a legal culture mediates the regulatory process, fixing the scope of regulatory space and influencing who gains entry and on what terms'. For Teubner, 'the law's contribution ... is the resolution of inter-system conflicts by procedural regulation', which he stresses is not only a matter of fostering a dialogue between regulatory actors, but also of understanding that regulatory actors operate in semi-autonomous social sub-systems. Despite the very different background theoretical assumptions of our 'grab-bag' of approaches, they can all be seen as fleshing out the image of law as umpire. This image was briefly introduced in relation to procedural political approaches such as Prosser's but is arguably central to institutionalist theories of regulation.

2.4.5   Discussion questions

1. Is Ayres and Braithwaite's approach helpful for understanding how and why regulation emerges? Or is it more applicable to compliance with already existing regulatory regimes?

2. Ayres and Braithwaite could be thought of as trying to blend public and private interest approaches while keeping them less complex than other institutionalist approaches. They do this in particular by creating a 'triangle/pyramid' image of the regulatory space rather than a network. How would we decide which actors should legitimately represent the apex of the triangle?

3. What would Ayres and Braithwaite advise where there is no overlap between mutual empowerment and individual gain? (i.e. when the conditions of 'efficient capture' do not prevail?)

4. Since a regulatory space approach de-emphasises the state, does this make it particularly suitable for exploring regulation in an international context where there is no global government?

5. Can you think of concrete ways in which the design of a regulatory regime could achieve what Teubner calls 're-introducing the consequences of actions of social sub-systems into their own reflexion structure'?

6. Does systems theory tell us anything about regulation that regulatory space approaches do not?

7. Consider political debates about regulation of smoking in public places, gambling and drug legalisation from the perspective of public interest, private interest and institutionalist theories. Do they help in deciding whether regulation is a good idea?

2.5   Conclusion

The relationship between the three broad categories of theories of regulation surveyed in this chapter could take many forms. For example, one could argue that public interest theories place an emphasis on the goals, functions and values that justify regulation; private interest theories are concerned with explaining why regulation emerges and why it takes the forms it does; and institutionalist theories focus on the process of how regulatory institutions work, drawn from an understanding of implementation dynamics but with considerable implications for explaining how regulation emerges in the first place. Alternatively, the literature surveyed in the chapter could be viewed as a series of assertions by public interest theorists, counter-assertions by private interest theorists backed by explanatory models, and attempts (that we have collectively labelled 'institutionalist' theories) to blend the best of these traditions in hybrid forms that reflect current empirical complexities. The relationship between the theories may take multiple forms, depending on the purpose of the enquiry, and the discussion questions have attempted to point readers to some lines of enquiry that would help explore the possible relationships.

The role of the law underpinning each class of theory differs according to the chosen theory. The role of law as authoritative rules backed by coercive force, exercised by a legitimately constituted nation (democratic) state, has been introduced here primarily as a facilitative one, instrumental to achieving collective public purposes. Both public and private interest theories accord at least a thin role to law in facilitative terms, by constituting the framework within which the collective goals of a regulatory regime are pursued. Private interest theory, however, evinces a considerable degree of skepticism about the likelihood that law's facilitative role will be beneficial if it extends *beyond* a role of constituting a market. Some public interest theories are more optimistic about regulation's capacity to promote collective welfare and link that capacity, at least implicitly, to *law's* ability to facilitate the achievement of those goals. Procedural political approaches — exemplified by Prosser in this chapter — the weight of responsibility placed on law's facilitative role, by limiting it to a procedurally focused contribution.

Institutionalist approaches, our third category of theories, tend to downplay law's role in directly controlling the pursuit of regulatory goals, emphasising non-legal organisational and systemic dynamics as crucial to regulatory trajectories. In the context of densely interwoven networks of public and private actors, the state's role shifts away from that of interventionist controller (whether benignly or malignly viewed) to one of moderating private and public policy interests. Law's role in this context is to structure the interactions between regulatory participants rather than directly to shape the substance of the regulatory issue. Law performs a coordinating function, one element in a reflexive process of influence and change within a regulatory space, system or network. Throughout this chapter, we have explored the facilitative dimension of law's role in regulation and introduced the notion that an umpiring image is one important aspect of that dimension. The facilitative dimension of law's role may, however, produce a rather different image — that of law as threat. It is this image of law as threat to which we turn in the following chapter, in the course of examining regulatory instruments and techniques.

References

Ayres, I. and Braithwaite, J. 1992. *Responsive Regulation: Transcending the Deregulation Debate*, Oxford: Oxford University Press.

Becker, G. S. 1983. 'A theory of competition among pressure groups of political influence', *Quarterly Journal of Economics* 98: 371–400.

Croley, S. 1998. 'Theories of regulation: Incorporating the administrative process', *Columbia Law Review* 1: 56–65.

Freedman, J. O. 1978. *Crisis and Legitimacy*, Cambridge: Cambridge University Press.

Habermas, J. 1979. *Communication and the Evolution of Society*, Oxford: Heinemann.

Hancher, L. and Moran, M. 1989. 'Organizing regulatory space', in Hancher, L. and Moran, M. (eds.), *Capitalism, Culture and Regulation*, Oxford: Clarendon Press.

Kolko, G. 1967. *The Triumph of Conservatism*, Chicago: Quadrangle Books.

Lowi, T. J. 1969. *The End of Liberalism: Ideology, Policy, and the Crisis of Public Authority*, New York: Norton.

Mayntz, R. 1983a. *Implementation Politischer Programme II*, Opladen: Westdeutscher Verlag.

    1983b. 'The changing conditions of effective public policy – A new challenge for policy analysis', *Policy and Politics* 11: 123–143.

Meidinger, E. 1987. 'Regulatory culture: A theoretical outline', *Law and Policy* 9(3): 355–386.

Niskanen, W. 1998. *Bureaucracy: Servant or Master? Lessons from America*, London: Institute of Economic Affairs.

Ogus, A. 2004. *Regulation: Legal, Form and Economic Theroy*, Oxford: Hart Publishing.

Prosser, T. 1986. *Nationalised Industry and Public Control: Legal, Constitutional and Political Issues*, Oxford: Blackwell.

Sunstein, C. 1990. *After the rights revolution: reconceiving the regulatory state*, Cambridge (MA): Harvard University Press.

Teubner, G. (ed.) 1986. *Dilemmas of Law in the Welfare State*, Berlin: Walter de Gruyter.

Willke, H. 1983. *Entzauberung des Staates*, Königstein: Athenäum.

Suggested further reading

Black, J. 2000. 'Proceduralizing regulation Part I', *Oxford Journal of Legal Studies* 20: 597–614.

    2001. 'Proceduralizing regulation Part II', *Oxford Journal of Legal Studies* 21: 33–58.

Brans, M. and Rossbach, S. 1997. 'The autopoiesis of administrative Systems: Niklas Luhmann on public administration and public policy', *Public Administration* 75: 417–439.

Dunsire, A. 1996. 'Tipping the balance: Autopoiesis and governance', *Administration and Society* 28(3): 299–334.

Dyson, K. 1980. *The State Tradition in Western Europe*, Oxford: Martin Robertson.

Farber, D. and Frickey, P. 1991. *Law and Public Choice: A Critical Introduction*, Chicago: University of Chicago Press.

Fels, A. 1982. 'The political economy of regulation', *University of New South Wales Law Journal* 5: 29–60.

Freeman, J. 1999. 'Private parties, public function and the real democracy problem in the new administrative law', in Dyzenhaus, D. (ed.), *Recrafting the Rule of Law*, Oxford: Hart Publishing, 331–370.

Grabosky, P. and Braithwaite, J. 1986. *Of Manners Gentle: Enforcement Strategies of Australian Business Regulatory Agencies*, Melbourne: Oxford University Press.

James, O. 2000. 'Regulation inside government: Public interest justifications and regulatory failures', *Public Administration* 78: 327–343.

King, M. and Schutz, A. 1994. 'The ambitious modesty of Niklas Luhmann', *Journal of Law and Society* 23: 261–287.

Lange, B., Haines, F. and Campbell, D. (eds.) 2003. 'Regulatory spaces and interactions', Special Issue, *Social and Legal Studies* 12(4): 411–545.

Nelken, D. (ed.) 2001. *Law's New Boundaries: Consequences of Legal Autopoiesis*, Aldershot: Ashgate.

Noll, R. and Owen, B. 1983. *The Political Economy of Deregulation: Interest Groups in the Regulatory Process*, Washington DC: American Enterprise Institute.

Picciotto, S. and Campbell, D. (eds.) 2002. *New Directions in Regulatory Theory*, Oxford: Blackwell Publishing.

Prosser, T. 1999. 'Theorising utility regulation', *Modern Law Review* 62: 196–217.

Scott, C. 2001. 'Analysing regulatory space: Fragmented resources and institutional design', *Public Law* 283–305.

Stewart, R. B. 1975. 'The reformation of American administrative law', *Harvard Law Review* 88: 1669–1813.

Stigler, G. 1971. 'The theory of economic regulation', *Bell Journal of Economics and Management Science* 2: 3–21.

3

Regulatory instruments and techniques

3.1 Introduction

One of the core concerns of the previous chapter involved attempts to explain *why* regulation emerges. In this chapter, we turn away from considering attempts to *explain* regulation, towards questions of mechanics, in responding to questions concerning *how* to regulate. In so doing, we will assume that the collective goals of a regulatory regime have been identified and defer consideration to whether those goals may be regarded as legitimate to the discussion in Chapter 5. By turning our attention to the mechanics of control, the scope of this academic inquiry may seem more concrete and less abstract than the previous chapter's discussion of theories of regulation. Yet the ground may not be quite as firm as it initially appears, for, as we shall see, the literature in this field is rich and fertile, having been ploughed by scholars from a range of social scientific disciplines and sub-disciplines, including law, economics, public administration, public policy, comparative government and self-confessed 'regulationists'. Despite the breadth of its variation, this literature is united by a common enterprise: to understand and explore the instruments and techniques by and through which social behaviour may be regulated, and the relationship between those techniques and their context.

Our discussion begins by exploring the wide array of tools and techniques that are used in regulating social behaviour in order to acquire an understanding of their mechanics. This exploration proceeds by classifying instruments into broad categories, based upon their underlying technique or 'modality' of control. It is important to acknowledge, however, that scholars have sought to classify regulatory instruments in many ways, none of which can claim pre-eminence. No scheme of classification is watertight, including the system adopted here. Accordingly, the classification scheme that follows is intended as a heuristic device, providing a vantage point from which to begin our exploration of the mechanics of regulatory control. As we shall see, many instruments display a hybrid character, drawing upon an amalgam of mechanisms in seeking to elicit behavioural change, and the permeable, overlapping nature of the these categories draws into sharper focus once we consider the law's contribution to tool mechanics.

Having examined the *mechanics* of regulatory instruments, the discussion then turns to questions of concerning the *choice* of regulatory instruments. These questions may arise at many different levels. Even if policy-makers can agree upon the class of instrument to use in any given context, further choices must be made concerning the preferred tool within that class and choices may also need to be made amongst different legal forms. In order to assist those involved in the regulatory process to navigate this potentially fraught territory, scholars have sought to illuminate a range of concerns that may bear upon instrument choice. These analyses can be broadly divided into those concerned with issues of tool effectiveness and those focusing on issues of legitimacy, the latter encompassing a range of non-instrumental matters, including the institutional, cultural and political context in which regulation takes place. As the discussion proceeds, attention is drawn to the law's relevance and influence both upon tool-mechanics and tool-choice. The concluding discussion draws together the threads of this discussion, seeking to illuminate the breadth and depth of the law's influence on the efficacy and legitimacy of regulatory instruments.

3.2   Understanding regulatory instruments

In exploring regulatory instruments, scholars have organised or classified them in many different ways, utilising a variety of tool dimensions as the basis for classification. Although no classification system has yet emerged from the multiplicity of available schemes as definitive, such pluralism is a source of strength rather than a cause for concern, for it allows for a critical comparison between different instruments, depending upon the particular question and context in which such a comparison arises. The scheme around which this chapter is constructed classifies instruments according to the underlying 'modality' through which behaviour is sought to be controlled, identifying five classes: command, competition, consensus, communication and code (or architecture). Although the law's role within each class is highlighted as the discussion proceeds, it must be borne in mind that, because a variety of classification systems have been adopted within scholarly analyses, the various extracts set out in this chapter may utilise different classification schemes and nomenclature in referring to a particular class or kind of instrument.

3.2.1   Command

The typical starting point for understanding regulatory instruments, and the one with which lawyers are most familiar, begins with an examination of command-based mechanisms for regulating behaviour. These mechanisms involve the state promulgation of legal rules prohibiting specified conduct, underpinned by coercive sanctions (either civil or criminal in nature) if the prohibition is violated.

In this way, the law operates in its classical form — through rule-based coercion, and such mechanisms are therefore often referred to as 'classical' regulation or 'command and control' regulation in policy and academic literature. But although both lawyers and non-lawyers tend to associate regulation with classical command-based mechanisms, they are neither easy nor straightforward to establish. The following extract by Daintith illustrates how command works by presenting its features in critical context, contrasting the costs to central government associated with relying upon the command of law (which he terms 'imperium') with those associated with the government's deployment of wealth (which he terms 'dominium'):

T.   Daintith, '*The techniques of government*' (1994)
Policy and its implementation
... Central government can seldom solve problems simply by changing its own behaviour. ... If there is to be real action — as opposed to a disguised 'do-nothing' approach—this must mean that some people at least are led to behave differently from the way they would have behaved in the absence of governmental intervention.
   ... I use the term *imperium* to describe the government's use of the command of law in aid of its policy objectives, and the term *dominium* to describe the employment of the wealth of government for this purpose. The point of choosing a special terminology to mark this distinction is that different constitutional frameworks exist, as we shall see, for the deployment of these two kinds of resources.

Imperium and dominimum
At their simplest, *imperium* laws involve setting a standard or rule for the behaviour of the relevant persons and providing sanctions for non-compliance. Examples from 1992 include the Timeshare Act, changing general contract rules to protect incautious purchasers of 'timeshares', especially in overseas property; the Competition and Service (Utilities) Act, supplementing the regulation of the privatized telecommunications, gas, water, and electricity industries; and the Seafish (Conservation) Act, making new provisions for the control of sea-fishing. Such legislation, while more sophisticated in drafting, differs little in character from statutes like the Artificers and Apprentices Act of 1562 (fixing rules for apprenticeships and levels of wages), the Act to Regulate the Price and Assize of Bread of 1709 (requiring observance of bread prices fixed by the magistrates) or, indeed, from the distant ancestor of the Seafish (Conservation) Act 1992, the Act for the Better Preservation of Sea Fish of 1605 (which likewise imposed catch restrictions).
   In earlier centuries, however, regulatory laws, with some rather haphazard enforcement mechanisms, were about the only resource for economic management available to government for influencing private behaviour. Today government has available, in addition to a much greater enforcement capacity, enormous resources of public funds and public property, accumulated through taxation, borrowing, and purchase. The public today tolerates high levels of taxation and government spending; the level of total public expenditure in 1991–2 was

£244bn., representing 42 per cent of gross domestic product. While this represents a decline from its highest-ever share of 49.25 per cent in 1975–6, and while the fastest-growing areas of expenditure are those, like social security, which are in the nature of fixed commitments, government still has plenty of scope for *buying* compliance with policy by offering such incentives as grants, soft loans, tax concessions, free or cheap public services, and like inducements, to those who act consistently with its plans. Normally, therefore, the policy-maker can at least consider the use of *dominium* as a possible solution to all or part of his problem.

Financial and compliance costs

At first sight, however, simple considerations of cost would seem to militate against a switch from *imperium*. Economic incentives for compliance with policy may not form a major fraction of public expenditure, but they still cost the State (and hence the taxpayer) money, in a period when there is chronic concern about whether democratic States have reached the limit of their revenue-raising capacity. Moreover, such costs may be hard to control and to measure in advance, for reasons we consider later. *Imperium*, by contrast, seems to come cheap. While enforcement costs need to be reckoned with, costs of compliance with policy are placed wholly on those whose behaviour is to be affected. Taxing undesired activities may even bring the exchequer a net return, after collection costs, and consequential losses of other forms of revenue such as income tax, are taken into account. Attitudes to compliance costs are however changing. It has long been understood that there is no point in imposing compliance costs on those who simply cannot afford to pay them. If government wants to improve the standard of insulation in existing houses, it will do far better to offer grants than to impose a duty to insulate: poorer householders may simply be unable to afford insulation, and imposing fines for breach of the duty will make them poorer still. Thanks to work by American economists, it is now also well understood that even where these costs can be absorbed, they may if excessive significantly diminish national economic welfare. They may involve wholly unproductive activities, such as form-filling; they may also diminish industrial competitiveness in international trade. Quantification remains difficult, but consciousness of the issue is clearly manifest in repeated attempts at elimination of unnecessary *imperium-type* regulations, and in caution about the adoption of new ones.

Legislative costs

Such caution is likely to be reinforced by the important non-financial costs carried by *imperium*, chief among which are the political costs of securing the passage of legislation. It is a fundamental principle of our constitutional law, established in the *Case of Proclamations*, that the government cannot, otherwise than through parliamentary legislation, exercise regulatory power, that is to say, alter the existing legal rights of its subjects. If, therefore, government wants to use the technique of *imperium* for the achievement of a policy, it must either find existing legislative powers which are suitable for the purpose, or undertake the burden of new legislation. Such a burden will be substantial. The legislation is quite likely to be lengthy and complex. The function, after all, of the constitutional rules requiring parliamentary legislation in such cases in to protect the interests of the individuals whose pre-existent legal rights and freedoms are affected. While Parliament regularly delegates to ministers the power to make detailed regulations, it tends to spell out in the statute itself both the general scope of the regulations and the precise sanctions or other effects that may attach to them . . . .

To secure the passage of such legislation, even if it is politically uncontroversial, requires heavy investments of scarce governmental resources. Government must draw on its stores of influence (over its own back-benchers and perhaps other Members of Parliament) and of time (within an always crowded parliamentary calendar). Even greater efforts may be required to pass legislation which divides Parliament deeply along party or (perhaps worse) other lines. Government may be ready to pay such costs for a variety of reasons. They may produce an immediate political dividend, as where the restriction of the rights of a particular group operates to enlarge the opportunities of a larger constituency – of consumers as against manufacturers, for example, or of tenants as against private landlords. They may be necessary in order to comply with international obligations already entered into. They may be seen as the only way of quickly awakening the public to what government regards as an emergency situation: the short-term price- and wage-freezes contained in the Prices and Incomes Act 1966 and the Counter-Inflation Act 1972 perhaps served this function.

In some cases, however, these legislative costs can be cut by switching to *dominium*, whose legitimate exercise may involve much lower political costs. The reason is that while the spending of funds by central government, no less than the exercise of force, requires legislative authorization, that requirement rests not on the idea that individuals need protection against the oppressive use of funds, but that the public collective interest in the proper disposition of those funds should be safeguarded. The distinction is reflected both in the juridical nature of the requirement and the nature of the legislation that results from it. Whereas the requirement of legislative authorization for regulatory measures was pronounced in clear terms by a court on the basis of the common law, that of legislative approval for, and appropriation of, public spending (as opposed to the raising of revenue by taxation) developed gradually over time, as the system of legislative appropriation of public funds developed from being partial and occasional to being regular and comprehensive.

Enforcement of legislative control over spending has been very largely a matter for the Public Accounts Committee of the House of Commons (aided by the Comptroller and Auditor-General), rather than for the courts. In consequence, authoritative judicial statements of principle are lacking, and it remains unclear to what extent, as a matter of law, government remains free to spend public funds in advance of, or independently of, their appropriation. As a practical matter, the need to obtain an appropriation in due form can rarely be avoided for long, but it should be noted that the form of the annual Appropriation Act imposes few constraints on the way in which government spends the sums granted by reference to the areas of departmental activity listed in the Act. As long as the expenditure falls within the functional description and the amount mentioned in the Act, government may apply that expenditure in pursuance of whatever policy it thinks fit. Systematic exploitation of this freedom, especially by way of attaching conditions to eligibility for, and terms and conditions of, government contracts, has in the past enabled governments to enforce policies which have not received legislative sanction. Examples are the minimum-wage policies pursued consistently for a hundred years before 1983 (which were sanctioned by a series of 'Fair Wages Resolutions' of the House of Commons), and the pay-restraint policy operated from 1977—8, whose only link with Parliament was a White Paper presented to — but never expressly approved by — the House of Commons.

Despite the latitude it affords for such collateral, non-statutory policies, this form of legislative authorization for spending is the only one required, as a matter of law, by our constitution. As a matter of convention, however, government is expected to seek from Parliament continuing authority, in the form of a specific statute, for programmes of expenditure which may be expected to extend over a number of years. The convention remains vague, and exceptions are admitted: the current system of government funding of the universities, initiated in 1919, continued on an 'Appropriation Act only' basis until 1988. Till then it was thought that the demands of academic freedom warranted this exceptional treatment. The Criminal Injuries Compensation Scheme, initiated in 1964 on an 'experimental' basis, was not placed on a statutory footing until 1988.

Even where, as is normal, specific legislation is procured, the process may be less burdensome and constricting for government than is the case with *imperium* legislation. With the major exception of social-security legislation, where the clear definition of individual rights to receive benefit is of paramount importance, *dominium* legislation pays little attention to the position of the recipient, or would-be recipient, of the public funds dispensed. Its concern is rather with establishing substantive criteria for expenditure and mechanisms for ensuring that they are respected and the aims of the expenditure achieved. Often this can be done through fairly skeletal provisions which leave a very broad discretion to ministers and other funding agencies, even to the point of choosing which industries are to receive financial support and under what conditions. Procedures for the protection of individual interests, such as rights to make representations or to appeal against unfavourable decisions, are rare. *Dominium* statutes thus tend to be shorter and less complex, with much important detail being relegated to delegated legislation or, increasingly often, to wholly informal 'schemes' for the distribution of funds. In all these questions of style there is a clear contrast with *imperium* legislation. Other things being equal, therefore, the less onerous legislative requirements attaching to *dominium* may certainly weigh with the policy-maker in his choice of implementing mechanisms. *Dominium* can thus offer great flexibility, which may be sufficient to accommodate even major changes in policy or its implementation. ... A further advantage of *dominium* is the possibility of running a policy on a short-term, experimental basis, without the need for special legislative authority, until its effectiveness has been demonstrated, an option which the formal and unilateral employment of *imperium*, such as I have already described, simply does not admit.

The problem of uncertainty

This idea of experimentation in policy responds to a problem of executive government which goes far to explain the often disappointing or even perverse results of policy initiatives. This is the problem of uncertainty, or more precisely, of the lack of reliable information. To operate efficient policies which seek to change people's behaviour, government needs adequate information first about how they should behave – that is, what standard or target it should set; secondly, about how they are behaving now, and why; and thirdly, about what sanctions or incentives will align their behaviour with the desired standard or target. None of this information is easy to come by, but getting any of these answers wrong is liable to vitiate the policy. Consider the third question, with an example from the field of *dominium*. Suppose government decides that one answer to part of the unemployment problem is to offer grants to encourage people to retrain for different jobs. If the grants are too low, hardly anyone retrains, and the policy does not work. If the grants are too high, far more people may opt for retraining than was expected, which may strain government budgets; and they may retrain out of useful and employable occupations, so that the government ends up paying public funds to create a shortage of skills. The problem is one of knowing how very large numbers of individuals will react to financial incentives. The same is true of reactions to taxes and, less obviously, to regulatory measures, even those with criminal penalties. Not everyone obeys. People will calculate the costs and benefits of compliance or non-compliance with regulations much as they calculate the incidence of taxes: such factors as rigour of enforcement, stigma of conviction, and severity of penalties may all play a role. . . . Overcoming these information difficulties thus remains vital to effective government, whatever its dominant ideology. Information requirements furnish a valuable key to the understanding of government choices among instruments available for the implementation of its policies.

3.2.2   Competition

The drawbacks associated with using command-based techniques are often claimed to be so extensive that, at least in terms of policy rhetoric if not in political practice, such mechanisms appear to have fallen out of favour. These shortcomings, elaborated on below in the following extract by Ogus, help to explain the turn towards regulatory tools that harness the competitive forces arising from rivalry between competing units as a means for regulating social behaviour. A wide variety of such tools are available, often referred to as economic instruments, including charges, taxes, subsidies (which Daintith refers to in the preceding extract as a form of 'dominium' intervention), tradeable emission/property rights and changes in liability rules. These tools are briefly described and explained in the following two extracts.

A. Ogus, 'Regulation' (1994)

The general disenchantment with . . . traditional regulatory forms which has emerged in the last two decades has led to pressure not only to deregulate but also to experiment with other regulatory forms which encourage the desired behaviour by financial incentives rather than by legal compulsion. Such incentives can be either negative (conduct is legally unconstrained but if a firm chooses to act in an undesired way it must pay a charge) or positive (if a firm chooses to act in a desired way it is awarded a subsidy).

Although the idea has recently gained considerable currency as a method of dealing with externalities, particularly those arising from environmental pollution, it is far from new. Governments have sometimes sought to finance and determine the supply of public goods (for example, highways and public broadcasting services) by imposing charges on users. As regards negative externalities, economists have long recognized that the misallocation of resources can be corrected by imposing a tax on the firms responsible, thereby ensuring that the external cost of a product or service is 'internalized' in its price.

Those advocating the use of economic instruments (EIs) have argued that they overcome many of the perceived deficiencies of traditional 'command-and-control' regulation (CAC). First, while CAC often gives rise to a complex and detailed set of centrally formulated standards, EIs can function on the basis of broad target goals, with a reduction of information and administrative costs for both the regulators and the firms. Secondly, the greater freedom conferred by EIs on firms creates incentives for technological development. Thirdly, whereas the enforcement of CAC is subject to considerable uncertainty as regards apprehension, prosecution and the level of sanctions, EIs entail the certain payment of specific sums. Fourthly, negative EIs (i.e. charges) generate funds which can be used to compensate the victims of externalities; CAC regimes rarely allow victims to be compensated. . . .

2. Forms of economic instruments

(a) Charges and taxes

The most widely used EI form involves the imposition of a charge or tax on individuals or firms. To correct misallocations arising from externalities, the amount set should be equal to the marginal damage which the individual or firm inflicts on others. Because the external cost of the activity is thereby borne by the actor, this should, if the activity takes place within a competitive market, ensure an allocatively efficient level of production and consumption.

From an economic perspective, the principal function of the fiscal instrument is thus to induce a behavioural response. But, of course, taxes are more frequently used simply to produce revenue for general governmental purposes and in such contexts the amounts levied tend to be determined by distributional criteria, notably the ability to pay, rather than by reference to allocational considerations. In consequence, there are difficulties in locating 'genuine' EIs within the mass of fiscal provisions: some instruments may have been intended as revenue taxes, or charges to cover administrative expenditure, but have important incentive effects; others may have been intended as EIs but in practice are dominated by revenue or administrative considerations.

Subject to these difficulties, we may identify three main categories of charges or taxes which have, or may have, important incentive functions, and thus be treated as EIs. They represent interventions at different points in the causal relationship between a given activity and the external costs which it generates. . . .

The first is imposed on the use of a product which gives rise to an external cost. . . [T]he relationship between use of a product and its external cost is inevitably imprecise, and the amount levied may be arbitrary relative to the harm actually caused. This is particularly likely where, as in the case of pollution, the harm varies over time and in relation to the impact of other causes. . . .

The second category . . . attaches to the quality and/or quantity of harmful substances emanating from a given activity; hence, in relation to pollution, it is often called an 'effluent charge'. While evaluation of the external costs may remain highly problematic, the scaling of the payments to the harmfulness of the discharge as it enters the environment allows for a greater focus on the marginal impact of an activity . . . .

Under the third category . . . the amount payable is directly related to the harm caused. Clearly, this approach is feasible only where there is a definite and immediate causal relationship between the activity and the harm and where the latter is easily quantifiable. In practice, therefore, it has been adopted predominantly in situations where specific measures have been taken to eliminate the harm and the tax represents the cost of those measures. Reimbursement of the costs incurred by public authorities in the disposal of waste constitutes a frequently adopted example.

(b) Subsidies

Subsidies represent the symmetrical opposite of charges and taxes: payments are made to individuals or firms to induce them to reduce undesirable activity. Economically, they can have the same effect as charges and taxes: if the payment reflects the marginal cost of eliminating the externality, an efficient allocation of resources should ensue. However, a subsidy may encourage output to grow to a larger size than that which would prevail under a perfect-internalising charge and in the long run may therefore generate inefficiency. And, of course, the distributional consequences are profoundly different. A tax on a firm increases its costs of production and also generates revenue which can be used to compensate those adversely affected, while the burden of a subsidy scheme falls on general taxpayers. Moreover, such a scheme may create perverse incentives, for example, by inducing firms to increase externalities in order to attract further subsidies. For these, as well as political-ideological reasons, there has been a decline in the use of subsidies, most notably in the field of environmental protection, where the 'polluter-pays-principle' has become accepted dogma. Even when subsidies were more generally available, there was a problem, as with taxes, in distinguishing those which were intended to operate as EIs from those designed primarily for redistributional purposes, hence to increase the wealth or income of specific groups of industries or households.

Nevertheless, examples can be given of current subsidies used for EI purposes. They may take the form of a grant (or an interest-free loan) to assist in the purchase of a particular product or equipment – e.g. home thermal insulation grants to limit energy consumption – or the preservation of some public good – e.g. wildlife habitats. Compensation may be offered for a loss of profits resulting from a voluntary restriction on the use of harmful products or processes. Finally, subsidies may operate indirectly through a reduction of tax liability; for example, an accelerated depreciation allowance may be granted for capital expenditure on pollution abatement equipment.

(c) Tradeable emission rights

An EI much discussed in the context of environmental protection is based on the idea that allocative efficiency can be achieved by allowing pollution rights to be traded. Under a 'pure' form of such a system, a public agency would set an absolute limit to the amounts to be discharged into a given airshed or watershed, derived from its perception of optimal ambient quality, and through an auction process sell rights to emit portions of that total to the firms which bid the highest price for them. Once acquired, the rights would be freely tradeable between firms, so that eventually they would be owned by the firms which would value them the most, because they have the highest costs of pollution abatement. Allocative efficiency will be achieved since the lower-cost abaters will find it cheaper to abate than to acquire the pollution rights. No jurisdiction has yet adopted tradeable emission rights in this form. The nearest to it can be located in the American regime for sulphur dioxide emissions which was introduced in 1990. Firms making such emissions are granted allowances which they may trade among themselves. No provision is, however, made for the auctioning of the allowances. The absence of such provision has been criticized both because efficiency is impaired, the transaction costs of ordinary trading being higher than those of auction-trading, and on the distributional basis that the system will not generate resources to compensate pollution victims.

The economic instruments referred to by Ogus in the preceding extract all rely on some kind of direct payment, either to or from the regulated entity, depending on the form of instrument in question. Such instruments are intended to bring about the desired behavioural change through the operation of the competitive forces of the market. In this respect, attempts to shape social behaviour by altering the legal liability associated with particular conduct can be seen as ultimately based on the competitive force of markets, discussed by Breyer in the following extract.

S. Breyer, 'Regulation and its reform' (1982)

Changes in liability rules

Scholars have sometimes advocated reliance upon (or changing) the law of torts to mitigate the harm caused by several market defects. For many years, the only effective course of action open to pollution victims was to sue the polluter for "trespass" or "nuisance". These suits, asking for an injunction or damages, discouraged or prevented pollution to a limited degree. Similarly, tort law has been used to prevent or discourage accident-causing activity. In both cases, market defects arguably are present. Pollution often represents a spillover cost of producing a product. Accidents also impose spillover costs. A power lawnmower may injure not only its purchaser, but also innocent bystanders, the victim's family, and the general public which pays for his medical care. Accidents may also result in part from informational defects. If the buyer of the lawnmower does not understand the risk he runs in purchasing it, he may not buy a higher-priced, safer product. Is it possible to mitigate these problems by changing the law of torts? By creating class actions, for example, or by liberalizing standing rules to allow more pollution victims to sue? Will the number of accidents or their costs decline if producers are held strictly liable for the accidents caused by their products instead of being held liable only for negligence?

The accident problem illustrates the potential uses and pitfalls of changing liability rules. In principle, consumers are willing to take some risk. How safe the product ought to be depends upon the amount of harm its users are likely to suffer, and upon the cost of reducing that harm by making the product safer. Ideally, if all potential victims know the precise risks of harm from using a product and the precise costs of making the use of that product safer, they might bargain with producers (for example, by purchasing safer products and thus forcing manufacturers of more hazardous products to improve the safety of their products or risk going out of business). Ideally, such a bargaining process would result in production of goods exhibiting just the right amount of safety characteristics. Yet, arguably, buyers do not have adequate information about safety and may be unable to understand the information they are given. Indeed, the government for paternalistic reasons may wish to require more safety than users would otherwise purchase. Thus, power lawnmower buyers may not shop around sufficiently to find safer mowers, and producers may make mowers that are less safe than is desirable. At this point, one might ask whether rearranging liability rules will reduce the cost of accidents by encouraging manufacturers to make safer products.

In the past few years the law governing product liability has indeed changed. Previously, producers were liable only for accidents caused by their negligence. Now they are "strictly liable" for any accident caused by a defect in the product, whether or not it was negligently produced. The change has helped overcome the market defects. Previously, buyers of dangerous products may have been unaware of the risk or had inadequate opportunity to buy, say, power lawnmowers that were safer but slightly more expensive. If so, the lawn-mower producer had no direct financial incentive to look for ways to make the mower safer. A shift to strict liability forces the manufacturer to pay compensation for many more of the accidents caused by the mower. Moreover, the larger the number of accidents, the more he must raise the price of the mower, deterring purchases of a dangerous product. Where insurance companies charge lower premiums to manufacturers with better safety records, each firm will also find that increased safety saves it premium money and thereby may allow it to charge lower prices, giving the safer machine a competitive edge.

Calabresi and Melamud suggest that to structure liability rules one should begin by using the following principle: when it is uncertain whether a benefit (such as a lawnmower with a certain risk) is worth the potential costs (such as the harm of related accidents), one should construct liability rules such that the costs (of the harm) are placed on the party best able to weigh the costs against the benefits. This principle is likely to place costs upon the party best able to avoid them, or, where this is unknown, on the party best able to induce others to act more safely. This principle seems to argue for making the lawnmower manufacturer strictly liable if he is best able to weigh the benefits, risks, and avoidance costs involved. Similarly, in the case of pollution, the rule would place liability on the factory owner, for he is in the best position to determine whether it is more efficient to curtail pollution or to compensate the victims of his noisome emissions.

The decision to shift liability rules is difficult to make in practice. First, all liability rules embody a complex system of incentives. It is difficult to obtain enough empirical information to know just how the incentives created by a new rule will work . . . .

Second, the court system itself functions imperfectly. Many injured persons may be unaware of their rights or reluctant to sue for other reasons. Or they may find it too expensive to sue. The courts are plagued by delay, with plaintiffs often waiting years for trial. Moreover, the damage verdict may bear little relation to the actual harm — juries may be swayed by sympathy for a plaintiff or they may feel that a defendant has a deep pocket. The resulting award may exceed any compensation for which the victim would have been willing to insure before the accident. At a minimum, verdicts will differ widely in amount from one court and case to another. Further, the courts will have to draw fine legal lines . . . [which] will also vary from one court or region to another, and can result in an ever-changing standard of liability. Also, the common law, as administered by the courts, may reflect certain noneconomic or moral factors that will make it difficult to use shifts in common-law liability to achieve basically economic ends. No rearrangement of property rights that makes a drug manufacturer liable *for failure* to produce a drug, for example, is likely to prove acceptable. Some have argued for the existence of other moral constraints as well.

Third, the shift of liability rules will affect the relative wealth of the parties. If, for example, liability rules are changed so that airports emitting noise must pay those living nearby, the value of homes in the nearby area will rise and the wealth of those who must pay increased airfares (which pay the cost of compensating the homeowners) will fall. Similarly, a system that shifts the allocation of rights between firms emitting smoke and nearby residents or between manufacturers and accident victims affects the income or wealth of the parties. This shift will affect the desirability of the change and certainly will determine the strength of support for or opposition to it.

Fourth, the process of changing a liability rule may have other, broad social consequences that affect its desirability. For example, if appellate courts change the rule, will they do so prospectively or retroactively? What is the precedental effect of their decision on the general power of the courts to change prior case law? How does this precedent affect the relation between courts and legislatures? If new rights are suddenly created, but the courts lack the resources to enforce them or to satisfy them, what are the consequences? Will the public lose faith in the courts? Will Congress be forced to double or triple the number of federal judges? Such questions can be multiplied. But they are clearly relevant to a decision to overcome a market defect through shifts in liability rules.

As indicated in [an earlier chapter], reliance upon court-enforced liability rules has not proven adequate to deal with the problem of pollution. Determining the extent of the damage and providing a standard of conduct for manufacturers, developing criteria that might apply uniformly and independent of the court, over-coming the problem of inadequate access to the court − all have made recourse to some form of administrative process seem desirable. The efforts to change liability rules governing accidents have proved more successful. Thus, the changing of liability rules remains, in some instances, a possible substitute for (or supplement to) a classical system of regulation.

Because competition-based tools aim to enrol the competitive force of markets to elicit behavioural change, rather than relying directly on the coercive threat of legal sanctions, the influence of the law is much less visible when contrasted with command-based tools. But it does not follow that the law is absent, for the law plays a vital *facilitative* role. It provides a stable institutional framework that ensures the freedom and security of economic transactions in the market. Nor are the law's coercive demands necessarily avoided, for some competition-based techniques (such as taxes and charges) are directly underpinned by coercive legal sanctions operating at a secondary level generating the legal obligation to pay. These sanctions may be brought to bear in the event of evasion or non-payment of amounts due. Even in cases where the obligation to discharge payment arises from a voluntary market transaction between private parties (rather than as lia-bility for a tax or charge due to the state), the law's coercive force may eventually be enlisted to ensure payment. Thus, even within competition-based approaches, the law's command may exert an indirect influence, in which behaviour is shaped through a combination of competition, operating strongly in the foreground yet backed by command, hiding − to a greater or lesser extent depending upon the tool under consideration − in the background.

It is worth noting, however, that competition-based mechanisms may be used to regulate the behaviour of individuals and organisational units *within* a discrete subset of the general community, rather than applying to the public at large. Bureaucracies can be thought of as constituting a form of bounded community which may be regulated through competition, a technique which has grown in popularity as means for regulating British public services in recent decades. For example, perhaps the most well-known use of rivalry between organisational units competing for resources has taken place through the use of 'quasi-markets' within the National Health Service (NHS) which operated throughout the 1990s. Although competitive rivalry was employed to regulate public service providers across a broad range of policy sectors in addition to public health, the term 'quasi' was used to describe markets established within the NHS because the contractual agreements upon which they were based were not legally enforceable so that the resulting market framework was of a partial and incomplete kind. Similar competitive techniques may also be used within a private sector organisation, as a means by which senior management seeks to exert control over the organisation's operational units.

When competitive mechanisms of this nature are deployed as a means for internal organisation, within either public or private bureaucracies, the law's influence recedes to the level of *permission*, rather than active facilitation. In these contexts, the role of the law is merely to provide a permissive framework which allows both public and private organisations the freedom to arrange their internal affairs as they wish, provided that legal requirements (and constitutional requirements applicable to the public sector) for ensuring external accountability are complied with. The most obvious of these are financial reporting obligations that apply to both public and private sector organisations. The context in which such mechanisms have been employed appears to have lead to a rather sharp disciplinary and sub-disciplinary divide — the study of mechanisms of internal organisation (including the use of quasi-markets) within the public sector has typically been the preserve of scholars of government, political science and public lawyers, while the study of mechanisms of internal organisation within the private sector has hitherto been the preserve of scholars in management studies, accounting, finance, economics and (to a lesser extent) corporate law.

3.2.3 Consensus

The law's facilitative role also underpins a third class of regulatory instruments: those reliant upon consensus and co-operation as the means through which behaviour is regulated. This class spans an exceptionally broad spectrum of regulatory arrangements. It may include regulatory tools and techniques typically referred to as forms of 'self-regulation', through to those involving various forms of co-operative partnerships between state and non-state actors in seeking to regulate social behaviour. Despite the myriad of tools falling within this group, they can be distinguished from other classes of instrument on the basis that the mechanism through which behaviour is influenced and constrained rests primarily on the *consent* of its participants. As we shall see, the consensual basis of these regulatory arrangements may derive their force from the legal support offered by contract law, or from social consensus in which the community, rather than coercive legal institutions, provides the primary mechanism through which control is exerted.

One of the most well-known consensual forms of regulation is typically referred to as 'self-regulation'. This term is used throughout academic literature to encompass a broad array of regulatory arrangements that may vary along a number of dimensions, including the character and level of state involvement, the degree of formality with which those arrangements are established and enforced, the extent to which the self-regulatory body exerts exclusive or monopoly control over the regulated activity and the level at which behaviour is regulated. Despite this variation, there are a number of claims frequently made in favour of self-regulatory mechanisms that are often invoked to support its use. In particular, where the regulated activity is thought to require a high level of technical or expert knowledge, it is often claimed that the industry has superior informational capacities to the state so that industry self-regulation is more likely to be efficacious. Others are highly sceptical of these claims, observing that they are typically invoked by members of the so-called elite professions (doctors, lawyers, academics and so forth), viewing such claims as self-serving attempts by members of such communities to stave off unwanted state intervention. These claims are elaborated upon by Ogus in the following extract:

A. Ogus, '*Rethinking self-regulation*' (1995)
I Justifications and explanations for self-regulation

... What then are the advantages traditionally claimed for self-regulation over public regulation? First, since self-regulatory agencies (hereafter SRAs) can normally command a greater degree of expertise and technical knowledge of practices and innovatory possibilities within the relevant area than independent agencies, information costs for the formulation and interpretation of standards are lower. Secondly, for the same reasons, monitoring and enforcement costs are also reduced, as are the costs to practitioners of dealing with regulators, given that such interaction is likely to be fostered by mutual trust. Thirdly, to the extent that the processes of, and rules issued by, SRAs are less formalized than those of public regulatory regimes, there are savings in the costs (including those attributable to delay) of amending standards. Fourthly, the administrative costs of the regime are normally internalized in the trade or activity which is subject to regulation; in the case of independent, public agencies, they are typically borne by taxpayers.

It would, however, be naive to assume that public interest justifications provide an exclusive explanation for the existence of self-regulatory regimes. Obviously, private interests that are threatened by regulation may gain considerable benefits if they are allowed themselves to formulate and enforce the relevant controls. From the abundant literature on public choice theory which treats legislation as a response to the competing demands of interest groups, there emerges the hypothesis that regulation serves mainly to confer rents (supra-competitive profits) on the regulated firms. If regulatory rule-making remains with the legislature or an independent agency, groups representing such firms have the task of exerting influence on those institutions and diverting them away from public interest goals or other, competing, private interest claims. Of course, delegation of the regulatory powers to SRAs relieves the groups of this task and the relative absence of accountability and external constraints maximizes the possibilities of rent-seeking — 'with self-regulation, regulatory capture is there from the outset'.

II Traditional criticisms of self-regulation

Lawyers and economists have been equally scathing in their criticisms of self-regulation. From a legal perspective, it is seen as an example of modern 'corporatism', the acquisition of power by groups which are not accountable to the body politic through the conventional constitutional channels. The capacity of an SRA to make rules governing the activities of an association or profession may itself constitute an abuse if it lacks democratic legitimacy in relation to members of the association or profession. The potential for abuse becomes intolerable if, and to the extent that, the rules affect third parties. Further, if — as often occurs — the SRA's functions cover policy formulation, interpretation of the rules, adjudication and enforcement (including the imposition of sanctions) as well as rule-making, there is a fundamental breach of the separation of powers doctrine. Finally, irrespective of theoretical considerations, SRAs are claimed to have a poor record of enforcing their standards against recalcitrant members.

In line with the rent-seeking hypothesis described in the last section, economists have developed models to predict how firms will benefit from self-regulatory regimes; and numerous studies have been published which purport to validate empirically the prediction. Thus SRAs with exclusive power to issue licences authorizing the practice of a profession or occupation have used that power to restrict entry and thereby to enable incumbent practitioners to earn supra-competitive profits. So also their formulation of ongoing quality standards has enabled them to protect anti-competitive practices: for example, fee regulation and restrictions on advertising which limit price competition; and 'professional ethics' which may serve the well-being of practitioners rather than their clients and mask prohibitions on cost-saving innovation.

III The nature of self-regulation

One problem with the traditional criticisms of self-regulation is that they are based on a narrow, stereotyped conception of the phenomenon. There is, in fact, a multitude of institutional arrangements which can properly be described as 'self-regulation' and ... it is wrong to tar them all with the same brush.

To appreciate the range of possibilities, it may be helpful to identify some key variables. Take, first, the question of autonomy. There is no clear dichotomy in this respect between 'self-regulation' and 'public regulation', but rather a spectrum containing different degrees of legislative constraints, outsider participation in relation to rule formulation or enforcement (or both), and external control and accountability. Thus, at one extreme, rules may be private to a firm, association or organization; at the other, they may have to be approved by a government minister or some independent public authority. Secondly, the rules or standards issued by the SRA may have varying degrees of legal force: they may be formally binding, codes of practice which presumptively apply unless an alleged offender can show that some alternative conduct was capable of satisfactorily meeting the regulatory goals, or purely voluntary. Thirdly, regimes may differ according to their degree of monopolistic power. They may apply to all those supplying a relevant market; alternatively they may be adopted only by a group of suppliers (or even a single supplier) who compete with others in the market . . . .

As Ogus points out, the term 'self-regulation' may be used to encompass a wide variety of institutional arrangements. The stereotypical or 'classical' form of self-regulation is generally understood as agreement between those involved in the relevant activity to regulate their own behaviour through the creation of some kind of regulatory body (such as an industry or sports association) entrusted with the task of promulgating and enforcing a code of conduct governing the behaviour of its members. The power of such a body to develop, apply and enforce such a code of conduct derives from the agreement of its members in which the ultimate sanction for violation is typically expulsion from membership. While the underpinning contractual arrangements are likely to include specific mechanisms for dealing with disputes arising between the regulatory body and one or more of its members, the law operates as a fall-back mechanism, enabling the parties to have recourse to the courts to interpret and enforce the terms of the agreement if they cannot resolve disputes extra-judicially. Seen in this light, the law's role is essentially facilitative: it respects citizen's freedom of contract, enabling them to enlist its coercive force to safeguard the security of agreements to which they have freely consented.

In so far as consent-based tools of this nature rely upon the law's facilitative capacity to provide a stable institutional framework within which the security of agreements is ensured, they resemble competition-based tools. Some self-regulatory regimes may, however, enlist the law's coercive power more extensively, and thus reduce the autonomy of the self-regulatory body to operate independently of state control. So, for example, the state may 'delegate' the task of regulating a particular sector or profession to a self-regulatory industry body or professional association, while retaining a residual oversight role, perhaps by imposing periodic reporting requirements on the self-regulatory body and by retaining legal power to issue guidance or directions to it concerning the way in which it is to carry out its regulatory functions. Regimes of this kind can be understood as a form of 'hybrid' technique, relying upon both command and consent, discussed more fully in section 3.2.6. However, it is also possible for the law to operate in a much more limited fashion. In these circumstances, the consensual character and basis of self-regulatory arrangements may be informal in nature, deriving their force from social norms and consensus, rather than from legally enforceable agreement. In such cases, the sanctions for violating behavioural norms take the form of social disapproval or ostracism, rather than a legally coercive response. Here, the law operates at its most remote, respecting the freedom of association enjoyed by citizens, subject only to a potential and typically implicit threat that state (i.e. legal) intervention will be introduced if community-based controls are inadequate to protect the public from harm. In other words, the law's threat recedes into the background, although it does not disappear entirely.

3.2.4 Communication

The force of social norms and consensus provides the underlying mechanism for another class of regulatory instruments, those resting upon *communication*. Simple communication-based techniques include attempts to persuade and educate members of the regulated community, or those affected by the regulated activity, to act in a manner that will facilitate the achievement of regulatory goals. Communication-based tools regulate behaviour by enriching the information available to the targeted audience, thereby enabling them to make more informed choices about their behaviour and, it is hoped, to choose to act in a manner that facilitates the attainment of regulatory objectives. The aim is therefore to bring some kind of indirect social pressure to bear on individual decision-making in the hope that it will lead to behavioural change. Although government-backed public education campaigns are the most familiar form of communication-based instrument, the following extract demonstrates that such techniques are often combined with other techniques of control.

K. Yeung, '*Government by publicity management: Sunlight or spin?*' (2005)
(a) Regulation by mandatory disclosure
> ... Rather than attempting to regulate production processes, product composition, quality or price, the state might instead mandate the disclosure of information relating to the composition, its side-effects and/or its process of production, with the aim of facilitating more informed decision-making by citizens in their purchasing and consumption decisions. Such mandatory disclosure regimes may be valuable in responding to "market failures" arising from circumstances in which the market fails to generate the "optimal" amount of information ("information deficits"), or in responding to circumstances in which a regulated activity generates external costs ("externalities") which may be efficiently dealt with by informing third parties about the externality to enable them to take steps to avoid it, rather than prohibiting or otherwise restricting the regulated activity. The control mechanism through which mandatory disclosure is designed to work operates in two directions. From the purchasers' perspective, the mandatory disclosure of product information enables them to make more informed decisions concerning the acceptability and desirability of the product. In addition, suppliers may also be expected to adjust their production decisions and processes in the face of mandatory disclosure, not only in response to shifts in purchaser behaviour, but the obligation to disclose certain kinds of information may act as a deterrent against fraud or misrepresentation, reflecting the well-known claim by Louis Brandeis that "sunlight is the best disinfectant".

Managers naturally have incentives to suppress unfavourable information concerning product quality, so that a scheme in which the disclosure of such information is compelled may be expected to discourage the production of goods and services of such quality. The extent to which any particular scheme of mandatory disclosure relies upon adjustments to purchaser or producer behaviour will vary, depending upon the nature of the risk which the regulatory regime seeks to address, and the kind of information compelled for public disclosure.

Mandatory disclosure regimes may therefore be thought to combine both command and control regulation with market-based mechanisms. To the extent that the state compels disclosure from producers, backed by some form of criminal or civil sanction for non-compliance (possibly supplemented by the conferral of private rights on those who rely on information supplied which fails to meet the mandated standards), mandatory disclosure regimes may be seen as a form of command and control regulation. On the other hand, to the extent that such regimes rely on consumers to decide for themselves whether or not to purchase the product in question, rather than directly controlling the production process or output, they may be seen as a form of "market-based" form of control, creating a scheme of incentives that may be expected to influence the behaviour of both suppliers and purchasers. In other words, identifying the character of mandatory disclosure regimes serves to highlight the need to approach rigid typologies of regulatory tools and techniques with care, illustrating how particular facets of so-called conventional regulatory techniques of command and control may be creatively combined with market-based techniques to form a potentially valuable hybrid policy instrument.

While economists often favour disclosure-based techniques over what they regard as more interventionist command and control approaches, regarding the former as more responsive to market forces, mandatory disclosure regimes have not been without their own problems. For example, the principle of transparency that may be seen as underpinning disclosure regimes may clash with values of confidentiality and privacy, in circumstances where the latter values may have a plausible claim to priority. Yet appeals to confidentiality may often be invoked by participants in the regulatory process to promote self-serving ends, thereby undermining the effective implementation of regulatory policy objectives. Assessing the overall costs associated with disclosure-based regimes may also be a formidable task, particularly given the difficulties of identifying and quantifying the costs imposed on the regulated entities associated with generating, collating and reporting the information mandated for disclosure, let alone the costs to the authority responsible for administering and enforcing a disclosure regime. In addition, mandatory disclosure systems may, like many other forms of regulation, be unresponsive to the dynamic context in which they operate, locking in behavioural incentives that may become unhelpful, redundant or even counter-productive. Finally, disclosure-based schemes assume that consumers are not only rational decision-makers, who make their purchasing decisions following a reasoned evaluation of product and price information, but that they are capable of accurately understanding and evaluating the information provided. Various empirical studies indicate that the impact of information on individual behaviour is highly context sensitive. For example, in relation to the regulation of financial and investment products, where mandatory disclosure regimes have been a central means of regulation, there is evidence to suggest that the information disclosed may have very little effect on consumer investment decisions, either because they are unaware of the information, fail to appreciate its significance, or choose rationally to disregard such information in their decision-making processes. In other words, regulation by information disclosure assumes that consumers are not only rational decision-makers who make their purchasing decisions based following a reasoned evaluation of the product and price information, but that they are capable of accurately understanding and evaluating the information provided. Yet these assumptions may not accurately reflect the reality of individual behaviour.

(b) Voluntary disclosure regimes

Although scholarly analyses of disclosure-based regimes tend to focus on those mandated by the state, such regimes may also (although perhaps less commonly) be "voluntary" in nature. Within a capitalist economy, producers face powerful incentives voluntarily to disclose information concerning production processes and/or product quality in order to attract purchasers. Rising consumer awareness of the ethical implications of certain production processes has been accompanied by the emergence of voluntary certification systems, or what cynics might describe as "ethical branding" — in which producers publicly and voluntarily disclose the ethical integrity of their production processes (e.g. tuna fish may be labelled as "dolphin friendly", cosmetic products labelled as "not tested on animals", and coffee labelled as compliant with "fair trade" policies). Whether or not one regards voluntary disclosures of this nature cynically as a mere commercial marketing ploy, or more optimistically as an attempt by individual firms genuinely seeking to "ratchet up" ethical standards of production in circumstances where multiple producers voluntarily agree to adopt a uniform system through which they endeavour to signal to the consuming public the quality of their product or production processes, such initiatives may be regarded as a regime of voluntary self-regulation by participating producers. The signalling of product quality information may be binary in nature, for example, signifying whether a product meets certain standard specifications, such as the use of the "FAIRTRADE" logo in conformity with the standards set by the Fairtrade Labelling Organizations International ("FLO"), or might involve a graded quality system, such as the use of "star" ratings adopted by the Automobile Association ("AA") to indicate the quality of service and facilities offered by approved AA accommodation providers. The information thus disclosed may then be of assistance to consumers in evaluating the quality of the product or service offered and, in this way, the mechanism through which behaviour is influenced operates in a broadly similar fashion to schemes in which suppliers are compelled by law to disclose particular kinds of information.

(c) Public communications management as a regulatory instrument
[Disclosure-based techniques rely] upon the disclosure of information by *regulated entities*, while [public communications management techniques] rel[y] upon the communication of specific messages or information, by the *regulatory authority*. In other words, rather than compelling disclosure from those engaging in the regulated activity, public communications management techniques entail the state itself seeking to inform and educate the community, or specifically targeted sectors of the community, in an attempt to influence producer and/or consumer behaviour. Such approaches may be necessary or desirable in circumstances where it is considered impractical, inefficient or ineffective to compel those engaging in the social activity that the government seeks to regulate from disclosing the presence or magnitude of the hazard associated with that activity. For example, it would be highly impractical, if not impossible, to implement and enforce a mandatory disclosure regime requiring those suffering from sexually transmitted diseases to make full disclosure to potential sexual partners, or to require those prone to driving under the influence of alcohol to disclose to other road users the potentially dangerous nature of their driving. . . . there are various distinct but related ways in which public communications management may be used to implement government policy. . . .

Public information campaigns ("exhortation")
The most familiar way in which the state may engage in public communications management for the purposes of influencing social behaviour is through the use of public information campaigns, seeking to exhort the public to act in pro-social ways that are consistent with government policy objectives. The size and scale of such campaigns that have taken the form of direct advertising is far from trivial . . . [W]hile disclosure regimes regard consumer preferences as largely exogenous, education and advertising campaigns may regard consumer preferences as endogenous, and thus malleable and subject to external influences, allowing them to be moulded and shaped in ways that are considered to be aligned with, or at least more consistent with, the welfare of the community.

. . . [B]oth disclosure regimes and publicity management techniques rest on rather optimistic assumptions that individuals are receptive to, learn from and act upon, the information communicated. Yet there is a large and expanding literature broadly referred to as "risk communication", demonstrating that individuals behave in complex, contingent and sometimes unpredictable ways in response to risk information. In particular, a number of social psychological studies have documented the divergence between lay and expert perceptions of risk, often pointing to the significance of trust as an influence of risk perception and on responses to risk information, although the precise nature of the relationship between trust and risk perception remains contested and uncertain. Accordingly, the effectiveness of such education and awareness campaigns in securing changes to individual and collective social behaviour may be doubtful, contingent upon a range of variables, thereby precluding firm conclusions about the effectiveness of state-sponsored education campaigns in general.

Guidance ("explanation")

In seeking to identify why some state education campaigns may be regarded as largely successful, whilst others have been striking failures, Viscusi and Margat distinguish between state information campaigns which they term "browbeating", claiming that such campaigns have not been particularly successful, from programmes that provide "new" knowledge and are "genuinely informational" in nature. In other words, a distinction may be drawn between public communications activities that seek to exhort citizens to behave in desired ways, from communications that are less explicitly "evangelical" in orientation, pursuing the more modest goal of providing information and explanations to the public, thereby enabling them to make more informed choices concerning their behaviour. The matters upon which the government may wish to provide explanatory guidance to citizens need not be confined to conveying information warning about the nature and magnitude of particular hazards, but extends to general information concerning legal rights, obligations and tertiary rules outlining agency policy concerning the exercise of specific discretionary powers, information concerning specific agency decisions in particular cases, and public announcements inviting feedback or assistance from the community as part of a broader consultation process, or in soliciting information from members of the public who may be in a position to assist with agency investigations. Seen in this light, public communications management may be seen as a necessary and desirable adjunct to more conventional forms of regulation, rather than an independent technique of regulation, by informing and explaining to those affected by regulatory regimes their rights, obligations or range of options in settling upon a particular course of conduct, while raising general public awareness of the regulatory regime and the agency's activities.

Publicising compliance performance ("exclamation and excoriation")

Public communications activities taking the form of "exhortation" and "explanation" are underpinned by the notion that citizens will make "better" consumption, purchasing and production decisions if provided with fuller, more accurate and accessible information, thereby influencing individual behaviour. Another related but slightly different technique through which a regulatory agency might seek to utilise public communications to influence social behaviour might be referred to as "exclamation and excoriation", publicising details of the performance of particular members of the regulated community in adhering, or failing to adhere, to regulatory standards, following some form of agency investigation and appraisal of compliance performance. Publicity of this nature might take the form of published performance indicators or "league tables" ranking the performance of members of the regulated community highlighting "leaders and laggards", or may simply refer to the agency's findings following individual investigations and assessment. Perhaps the best-known British example of state-sponsored league tables entails the publication of official school performance tables and other performance indicators introduced in the early 1990s by the Major administration, despite strenuous opposition from teachers. The intention was to provide incentives to schools to improve their performance through anticipated reactions by schools before they faced inspection, and also to influence schools indirectly by better informing parents before they faced inspection. . . .

Rather than publicising the ranked performance of members of the regulated community in terms of their relative success or failure in complying with regulatory rules, public attention might simply be drawn to particular cases of exemplary ("naming and faming") or woeful ("naming and shaming") efforts to achieve compliance with regulatory rules and objectives. While publicity might take the form of drawing public attention to individual compliance performance, such as Ofsted's published inspection reports on the performance of individual schools, or publicising the winners of "award" programmes designed to recognise and reward demonstrable excellence, public condemnation of poor individual performance may range from publicising the names of those found to have contravened regulatory rules, such as the Health and Safety Executive's Public Register of Convictions, through to the issuing of press releases following successful conviction for regulatory violations and even alerting the public to the initiation of a prosecution against specific individuals or firms.

The mechanism through which publicity of this nature may be thought to influence social behaviour may be understood in several overlapping ways. First, publicity may be seen as a form of non-financial incentive: by "praising" superior performance, others may be motivated to strive for excellence, whilst the fear of being publicly singled out and censured as "laggards" for poor performance may deter others from allowing their compliance efforts to fall short of regulatory requirements. In other words, publicity may serve as both a "carrot" and "stick", depending upon which end of the performance table is being focused upon. At the same time, publicity of this nature may also serve an educative and informative purpose, facilitating more informed consumer choice in making their purchasing decisions, at least in so far as consumers seek to obtain the highest quality of service, or engage in so-called "ethical" consumption practices, consciously refraining from purchasing products manufactured by those known to act in unlawful ways. Finally, in circumstances where instances of non-compliance are singled out by the agency, the associated adverse publicity may operate as a form of "shaming", serving to punish the offender and deter others from engaging in similar behaviour while also claiming to protect the community by warning of the potential risks associated with dealing with those found to have committed past violations. Although there is no universally accepted definition of shaming, one leading commentator has defined it as "all social processes of expressing disapproval which have the effect of invoking remorse in the person being shamed and/or others who become aware of the shaming". One way in which shaming may improve compliance with regulatory rules is through its deterrence impact: would-be offenders may be deterred by the threat of being publicly shamed for their offences. Those who advocate the use of shaming sanctions claim, however, that the primary essential component of shaming lies in its attempt to "moralise with the offender". It is the expressive dimension of shaming, the communication of society's disapproval of the impugned behaviour and the reasons for that disapproval to the offender, that is claimed to undermine the offender's reputation and is regarded as crucial to its effectiveness.

Each communication-based mechanism discussed in the above extract draws upon the law in different ways. Mandatory disclosure regimes rely upon the law's coercive force in requiring members of the regulated community to disclose mandated information on pain of legal penalty for violation. Voluntary disclosure regimes that involve agreement between two or more producers rely upon the law's facilitative function to respect and uphold the terms of their agreement. Even in the absence of co-ordinated producer behaviour, in which individual producers voluntarily disclose information about the nature and characteristics of their product, the law's task is to provide a stable, open and fair market framework that permits producers to persuade buyers of the superiority of their product, and in which the security of market transactions is assured.

The collection of techniques referred to in the above extract as 'public communications management' also depend upon the law to facilitate behavioural change, but instead of providing for the security of transactions, here the law's role – at least in democratic states – is to facilitate the creation of a stable framework within which the 'marketplace of ideas' may flourish freely. The law underpins communication-based techniques insofar as it confers, at least in many of the liberal democratic contexts which the framework of this book assumes, a constitutional right on all persons to express ideas and opinions freely, subject only to legally recognised restrictions on expression (for example, laws of defamation, obscenity and contempt of court).

3.2.5 Code

While communication-based techniques appeal to rational human reasoning in seeking to bring about behavioural change, code-based (or architecture-based) techniques operate in direct contrast, seeking instead to eliminate undesirable behaviour by designing out the possibility for its occurrence. Although the use of architecture as a form of control has a long history, it is re-emerging in more recent debates in response to the rapid advances of technology. Lawrence Lessig's work on the regulation of cyberspace has been particularly influential: he argues that regulation in cyberspace may be perfectly achieved through modifications to software codes, foreshadowing the possibility that "Law as code is the start to the perfect technology of justice".

In the following extract, Brownsword seeks to identify the distinctive qualities of 'code as control', its identifying feature resting on its capacity to eliminate the possibility of violation and to by-pass practical reason in its entirety.

R. Brownsword, 'Code, control and choice: Why East is East and West is West' (2005)

In this article, I want to sketch ... an ideal-type that I will term 'techno-regulation'. This ideal-type does not merely recognise code as part of the regulatory repertoire;

it does not simply make use of CCTV, forensic data bases, tracking devices, and the like; instead, it relies entirely on design . . . .

. . . . What is it that is distinctive about techno-regulation . . . ? It is perhaps easier to start by identifying three features that are not the key to its distinctive (ideal-typical) nature.

First, there is no suggestion that code or design cannot be applied for virtuous regulator purposes . . . . Lessig suggests various examples of virtuous design – for instance, the architecture of Paris after the mid nineteenth-century introduction of the boulevards, the placement of the White House in relation to the Capitol, the removal of constitutional courts away from the seat of the legislative and executive branches, speed bumps, and so on. However, design is not always applied with such virtuous intent – Lessig gives examples of the bridges built on Long Island by Robert Moses so that buses carrying African Americans would not be able to get through to public beaches . . . .

Secondly, it is not the use of technology, or technical support, as such that characterises [techno] regulation. Where technology is deployed to monitor compliance and/or to enforce the regulatory standard, design is functioning in some regulatory dimensions but this falls short of ideal-typical techno-regulation. With techno-regulation, design operates alone in the three regulatory dimensions [i.e. cybernetic division of regulatory tasks into standard setting, information gathering and behaviour modification]. Moreover, it functions in such a way that regulatees have no choice at all but to act in accordance with the desired regulatory pattern – it is the difference, for example, between systems that make it physically impossible to exit the Underground (or Metro) without a valid ticket and low level barriers that make it more difficult (but not impossible) to do so . . . .

Thirdly, while techno-regulation might focus on designing the environment in which regulatees act, it is not so restricted; it is not co-extensive with situational crime prevention. In principle, techno-regulation might focus on designing people, products, or places. If Lessig sees emerging design responses in the field of information and communications technology, . . . then the revolution in biotechnology might one day offer a further suite of design options, ones that tackles people rather than products or environments . . . [C]onsider Garland's remarks to the effect that the emphasis of the new criminological approach is on 'social order as a problem of *system* integration'.

Thus:

'It isn't people who need to be integrated, but the social processes and arrangements that they inhabit. Instead of addressing human beings and moral attitudes or psychological dispositions, the new criminologies address the component parts of social systems and situations. They consider how different situations might be redesigned so as to give rise to fewer opportunities for crime, how interacting systems . . . might be made to converge in ways that create fewer security weaknesses or criminological hot spots. For these frameworks, social order is a matter of aligning and integrating the diverse social routines and institutions that compose modern society.

It is a problem of ensuring co-ordination — getting the trains to run on time — not of building normative consensus.

In the paragraph, immediately following this, Garland continues:

'The criminologies of everyday life thus offer an approach to social order that is, for the most part, amoral and technological. They bypass the realm of values and concentrate on the routine ways in which people are brought together in time and space. Their conception of social order is a matter not of shared values but of smart arrangements that minimise the opportunities for disruption and deviance. This is a very self-conscious, very sophisticated approach to social order in a complex, differentiated society. It flies in the face of traditionalist ideas that see order as emerging out of moral discipline and obedience to authority'.

This is now very close to the mark. Techno-regulation approaches the problem of social order in way that does not rely on building a normative consensus; it is amoral; it does by-pass the realm of values; and it does not rely on moral discipline or obedience to authority. However, this is not because techno-regulation favours non-moral reason over moral reason, but more dramatically because it by-passes practical reason altogether. Unlike the new criminological approach, though, this is no adaptation to crime as a normal feature of social existence; to the contrary, far from normalising crime, techno-regulation seeks to eliminate it as an option.

If we turn these negative features round, we can express the distinctive nature of techno-regulation in the following way. Where the ideal-type of techno-regulation is instantiated by regulators, having identified a desired pattern of behaviour (whether morally compliant or not), secure that pattern of behaviour by designing out any option of non-conforming behaviour. Such measures might involve designing regulatees themselves, their environments, or the products that they use in their environments, or a combination of these elements. Where techno-regulation is perfectly instantiated there is no need for either correction or enforcement.

The use of 'code' or architecture as a control device appears, at least at first sight, to avoid the reach of the law. But on closer inspection, the capacity to use architecture as means for shaping and constraining social behaviour relies upon the freedom to mould and manipulate the physical environment through which control is effected. In the physical world, this is achieved through rights of property ownership: local authorities may use speed humps to calm traffic in particular neighbourhoods because of their legal right to assert dominion over roads and other public rights of way. Although rights of exclusive possession and control may often be understood as arising 'naturally' by virtue of property ownership, at least in industrialised economies, those rights exist only *because* they are recognised by law as legal incidents of ownership. In other words, the law may be seen as operating in a facilitative and permissive fashion, although its force may appear almost invisible to those operating within an architecturally designed regulatory environment, particularly when architectural controls operate within 'virtual' rather than physical space.

In built-environments (including cyberspace), the capacity to assert control over that space or environment through code arises from the nature of that space as technologically designed, exemplified in cyberspace where access to and participation in that space is dependent upon software code. Academic commentators differ in their views on the capacity of law to penetrate such environments, as the continuing debate about the nature of cyberspace attests. Cyber-libertarians envisage cyberspace as beyond the effective reach of law owing to the possibility for anonymous participation and the high degree of mobility of participants in cyberspace enabling them to relocate freely to other areas of cyberspace where different regulatory constraints obtain. In contrast, cyber-paternalists (such as Lessig) claim that there is nothing inherent in the nature of cyberspace that renders it beyond the reach of law. For Lessig, there is nothing to prevent governments from seeking to deploy code as a means for regulating cyberspace, where law may not only continue to regulate behaviour in cyberspace through ordinary laws that apply to behaviour in the physical world (through the laws of copyright, defamation and so forth), although its effectiveness will vary depending upon the characteristics of cyberspace, but it may also regulate through the control of code itself, or the institutions (i.e. coders) who produce the code that shapes the contours of cyberspace. Although this is not the place to engage in debate about the regulability of code, it suffices to observe that the present capacity for shaping the design of cyberspace through code is at least partly a product of the underlying legal framework affecting the freedom of cyber-participants to alter the architecture of cyberspace. For example, when hackers succeeded in 'cracking' codes designed into media players to prevent unauthorised use of digital data, anti-circumvention legislation was introduced. Such legislation effectively characterised hacking as tantamount to illegal trespass to property, attempting to alter the architecture of cyberspace by legal means.

3.2.6   Classification and hybridisation

In the opening remarks of this discussion, we observed that tool classification systems (including the one adopted here) are not watertight, and many instruments rely upon more than one mechanism to regulate behaviour. Nor are the boundaries of each class of instrument clearly defined, and it may be possible to classify any given instrument in different ways, depending upon the characteristics under examination. So, for example, there is inescapable overlap between competition-based and consent-based tools, in so far as the former rely on the market forces of demand and supply to enable participants to find an agreed price for the commodity or service that is offered by competing 'sellers'. The law facilitates these mechanisms by providing a stable legal framework for a freely functioning market. In particular, it ensures the security of transactions concluded on the market by upholding agreements, with coercive force if necessary and, in some circumstances, providing a mechanism for dispute resolution.

Hybridity in tool mechanics is particularly prevalent in relation to various forms of self-regulation. Even within classical self-regulation, which ultimately relies upon agreement between members of the regulated community, the promulgation and enforcement of norms by the regulatory body established under that agreement resembles command-based regulation. While the sanction for violation might not satisfy strict legal definitions of punishment, it may nonetheless be regarded by the sanctioned member as punitive in its social effects. Yet because each member of the self-regulatory community is taken to have consented to the imposition of sanctions by the regulatory body for violations of the community's code of conduct, the consensual basis of the underpinning regulatory arrangements remains intact. In other words, classical self-regulation can be understood as a hybrid of consent and command-based mechanisms. The law's role is essentially to facilitate the security of the association's rules of conduct, which acquire legal force by virtue of the underpinning legally enforceable agreement between its members.

In the preceding discussion of consent-based instruments, we observed that the extent to which such instruments relied upon the law's coercive force may vary, enabling the creation of a range of hybrid command and consent-based techniques. While some self-regulatory arrangements are informal in nature, relying upon social norms rather than legal coercion as the means for exerting control over the regulated activity, it is possible to extend the reach of the law's intervention in the opposite direction. By bringing the law's coercive threat closer to the foreground of self-regulatory arrangements, scholars have sought to modify the classical model of self-regulation so as to reduce the risk that self-regulatory arrangements will be invoked by industries in pursuit of self-serving ends. One particularly prominent variant is propounded by Ian Ayres (an economist) and John Braithwaite (a criminologist), whose work we have already introduced in the previous chapter. They develop a notion of 'enforced self-regulation', which they describe as a form of 'subcontracting regulatory function[s] to private actors'. This constitutes only one plank of a broader set of policy prescriptions they term 'responsive regulation', which we will explore more fully in the next chapter. In the following extract, Ayres and Braithwaite develop and explain their notion of enforced self-regulation:

I. Ayres & J. Braithwaite, '*Responsive regulation*' (1992)
The model

The concept of enforced self-regulation is a response to the delay, red tape, costs, and stultification of innovation that can result from imposing detailed government regulations on business, and to the naiveté of trusting companies to regulate themselves. Under enforced self-regulation, the government would compel each company to write a set of rules tailored to the unique set of contingencies facing that firm. A regulatory agency would either approve these rules or send them back for revision if they were insufficiently stringent. At this stage in the process, [public interest groups] ('PIGs') would be encouraged to comment on the proposed rules. Rather than having governmental inspectors enforce the rules, most enforcement duties and costs would be internalized by the company, which would be required to establish its own independent inspectorial group. Where feasible, PIGs would be represented on this inspection group (e.g., the union on the workplace occupational health and safety group). The primary function of governmental inspectors would be to ensure the independence of this internal compliance group and to audit its efficiency and toughness. Naturally, old-style direct government monitoring would still be necessary for firms too small to afford their own compliance group.

State involvement would not stop at monitoring. Violations of the privately written and publicly ratified rules would be punishable by law. This aspect of the enforced self-regulation model, perhaps sounding radical, is actually not as extreme as it first might seem. Regulatory agencies would not ratify private rules unless the regulations were consonant with legislatively enacted minimum standards. To say that rules would be rejected if they failed to meet a minimum standard is not to say that the goal of the approval process ought to be standards as uniform as possible. It can be argued that striving for uniformity of standards under enforced self-regulation would not be desirable. Viscusi and Zeckhauser (1979) have developed the following rationale for nonuniformity. People normally assume that the higher the standards set by government for pollution, safety, and the like, the better will be industry's performance in meeting these criteria. Viscusi and Zeckhauser show formally that this is not the case. It is not so because whenever a standard is set, some firms will decide that the costs of compliance are greater than the costs of noncompliance (the probability of detection multiplied by the costs if detected). As standards are made more stringent, the costs of compliance increase steeply while the costs of noncompliance remain more or less constant. Hence, as standards become more stringent, the performance of firms that comply improves, but additional firms choose to risk penalties for non-compliance. Viscusi and Zeckhauser thus demonstrate that at some point further tightening of a standard may lower overall performance. But this point will be different for different types of firms. For firms with enormous sunk costs in old plants, the costs of compliance will be greater than for firms about to construct their factories. ...

Because of economies of scale in pollution control, the point at which further tightening of standards will increase the output of pollution may be higher for large firms than for small ones. In other words, the environment and the public may be better protected by nonuniform standards. Hence, nonuniformity under enforced self-regulation could be an advantage. More stringent rules could be demanded of firms with lower compliance costs. In some ways, environmental protection agencies already accept this principle by requiring more stringent emission controls on new automobiles than on those already on the road, and by requiring pollution control technology to be installed in new plants, controls not demanded of old ones.

Theoretically, enforced self-regulation makes possible nonuniform optimal standards that would give greater protection than any (stricter or more lenient) uniform standard. There are a number of ways that a legislature could frame broad statements of what is required of privately written regulations that were not at the same time platitudinous. Consider, for example, an act to set guidelines for the U.S. Mine Safety and Health Administration to follow in approving rules written by coal companies. The Act might recognize in its preamble that the minimum level of safety guaranteed by the Federal Coal Mine Safety and Health Act of 1977 was unsatisfactorily low and instruct the Administration not to approve any corporate safety rules that do not guarantee better safety performance than that ensured by the 1977 Act. Recognizing that American coal miners are three times more likely to be killed at work than British miners, the Act might further instruct the Administration not to accept the existing "state of the art" in safety standards. As a third option, the Administration could be directed to structure its approval process so as to halve coal mine fatality and injury rates by a certain year . . . .

Contracting around regulatory defaults

Instead of mandating that individual firms promulgate self-regulating standards, agencies could allow individual firms to promulgate such standards as an alternative to "backstop" or "default" regulations. Maintaining a regulatory default would still allow regulators to learn from the privately promulgated rules, but would allow some (especially smaller) firms to avoid the costs of rulemaking.

Borrowing from a more general theory of default rules, a self-regulatory system of defaults would need to establish not only "the defaults" – what regulations would apply in the absence of private mutation – but also the necessary and sufficient conditions for "contracting around" – what firms would need to do to supplant the default regulations.

In some instances, regulatory defaults would be set at what would be most appropriate for the majority of firms (i.e., what the firms and the state would have negotiated). Such majoritarian rules would allow individual firms to tailor rules to their needs without having to reinvent the wheel for standard provisions. At other times more stringent default regulations should be used even if they may be appropriate only for a minority of firms. For example, if consumers are relatively disenfranchised in the tripartite process, then setting regulatory defaults in their favor (or in favor of any affected, but powerless group) puts the burden on the relatively powerful to justify new regulations. Procedurally this could mean bipartite negotiation of defaults between state and PIG, with the process only becoming tripartite when the firm affirmatively moves to participate in enforced self-regulation. In the extreme case, such nonmajoritarian default rules will act as "penalties" to induce all firms to contract around the unpalatable backstop regulations.

The efficacy of such an approach would also crucially turn on the system of agency ratification – which in a sense would determine the necessary and sufficient conditions for contracting around the regulatory default. Especially when defaults are set to protect the disempowered, it will be appropriate for agencies to apply a higher level of scrutiny to the justifications for individual mutation.

In the United States, insurance regulation displays a default structure in which the status quo represents a default that can be contracted around only by filing before the state insurance commissions. More generally, the corporation statutes of the individual states represent a default form of corporate governance that the individual corporations are allowed to change by filing their corporate charters with the secretaries or state. We envision instances in which regulators should develop different sets of defaults that the regulated firms can choose between as an additional alternative to developing idiosyncratic self-regulation. Indeed, in the United States the diversity of corporate law among the states allows corporations to opt for a variety of forms of corporate governance simply by choosing a state of incorporation, a situation that has a variety of desirable and undesirable consequences . . . .

A distinguishing feature of enforced self-regulation is the use of individually negotiated agreements between the state and individual members of the regulated community. Unlike classical self-regulatory arrangements, the members of the regulated community enter into contractual arrangements with the state, but not with other members of the regulated community. It is therefore possible to locate enforced self-regulation within a distinct subset of consensual-based tools that differ from classical self-regulatory forms of control because they do not involve the consensual participation of all the members of the regulatory community. Instead, control is exerted through bilateral or multi-lateral partnerships between the state and one or more members of the regulated community. The state may try to extend its influence over the entire policy sector by establishing a series (or network) of such partnerships under separate and distinct partnership agreements, the terms of which are individually negotiated with the participants involved and may therefore be non-uniform across the sector.

For example, the essential framework for the regulation of British utilities immediately following privatisation entailed the grant of licences from the state to individual utility enterprises. The conditions of the licences were determined by individual private negotiations between the utility enterprise and the minister, rather than being in standard form and determined unilaterally by the relevant utility regulator. The approved code of conduct scheme, established by the Office of Fair Trading, may also be seen in this light: it allows trade associations to submit codes of conduct to the Office for approval, which will only be granted if the proposed code is considered to meet specified standards intended to protect consumer interests. Code approval entitles members of the association to display the OFT's logo. Industry providers who are not members of the relevant trade association are not so entitled. Accordingly, service standards may vary within a given sector, provided that all providers observe minimum legal requirements. In the following extract, Salamon suggests that programmes of this kind have become sufficiently pervasive to form the basis of a distinct paradigm of governance.

L. Salamon, '*The tools of government*' (2002)

... this book suggests a new approach to public problem solving for the era of 'third-party government' in which we find ourselves. I call this approach 'the new governance' to underline its two defining features. The *first* of these, signified by use of the term 'governance' instead of 'government', is an emphasis on what is perhaps the central reality of public problem solving for the foreseeable future – namely, its *collaborative nature*, its reliance on a wide array of third parties in addition to government to address public problems and pursue public purposes. Such an approach is necessary, we will argue, because problems have become too complex for government to handle on its own, because disagreements exist about the proper ends of its will on other crucial actors without giving them a meaningful seat at the table. The *second* feature, signified by the use of the term 'new', is a recognition that these collaborative approaches, while hardly novel, must now be approached in a new, more coherent way, one that more explicitly acknowledges the significant challenges that they pose as well as the important opportunities they create . . . .

The new governance paradigm

Like any new approach to a topic as old as public administration, the "new governance" is hardly entirely novel. Rather, it builds on a rich history of past thinking, changing emphases, and incorporating new elements, but hardly replacing all that has gone before. The result, however, is a new synthesis, a new paradigm, that brings prevailing realities into better focus and consequently makes more sense of some of the central dynamics at work. In particular, five key concepts form the core of this approach, as outlined in Table 1.4 below . . .

From agency and program to tool

At the heart of the new governance approach is a shift in the "unit of analysis" in policy analysis and public administration from the public agency or the individual public program to the distinctive *tools* or *instruments* through which public purposes are pursued. As we have seen, such instruments have mushroomed in both number

Classical public administration	New governance
Program/agency	Tool
Hierarchy	Network
Public vs private	Public + private
Command and control	Negotiation and persuasion
Management skills	Enablement skills

Figure 3.1 [Table 1.4] The new governance paradigm.

and scale in recent decades. A central argument of the "new governance" is that this has altered the nature of public management and the pattern of public problem solving in rather fundamental ways, but ways that are only partly acknowledged in existing theories and approaches . . . .

From hierarchy to network

In shifting the focus in public problem solving from agencies and programs to generic tools, the *new governance* also shifts the attention from hierarchic agencies to *organizational networks*. The defining characteristic of many of the most widely used, and most rapidly expanding, tools, as we have seen, is their indirect character, their establishment of *interdependencies* between public agencies and a host of third-party actors. As a result, government gains important allies but loses the ability to exert complete control over the operation of its own programs. A variety of complex exchanges thus come into existence between government agencies and a wide variety of public and private institutions that are written into the operation of public programs. Under these circumstances, the traditional concerns of public administration with the internal operations of public agencies – their personnel systems, budgetary procedures, organizational structures, and institutional dynamics – have become far less central to program success. At least as important have become the internal dynamics and external relationships to the host of third parties . . . that now also share with public authorities the responsibility for public programs operations.

Not only does this broadening of the focus from public agencies to "networks" of organizations differentiate the new governance from traditional public administration, it also differentiates it from the "privatization" and "reinventing government" perspectives that have surfaced in recent years . . . .

From public vs. private to public + private

In moving the focus of public management and policy analysis from the program and the agency to the tool and the network, the *new governance* also brings a new perspective to the relationship between government and the other sectors. Traditional public management posits a tension between government and the private sector, both for-profit and not-for-profit. The public sector is distinguished, in this view, by its monopoly on the legitimate use of force, which it acquires by virtue of its responsiveness to the democratic will of the people. Public agencies are thus imbued with sovereignty, the power to act on behalf of the public. Many of the central precepts of classical public administration flow from this central premise and are designed to ensure that the administrative officials so empowered do in fact respond to the public's will and not the partial will of some private group. Without this clear differentiation, accountability for the spending of public funds and the exercise of public authority becomes impossible and the public sphere polluted by the intrusion of private interests. Keeping private interests and private organisations at arm's length thus becomes a central motivation of the organizational design . . . .

Many of the new tools of public action defy these precepts rather fundamentally, however. Instead of a sharp division between the public and private spheres, they blend the two together. This is not to say that sectoral differences are blurred, as is often suggested. A central precept of network theory, after all, is that the participants in a network retain important elements of their individuality. However, *collaboration* replaces *competition* as the defining feature of sectoral relationships . . . .

From command and control to negotiation and persuasion

. . . Traditional public management, with its focus on the operation of public agencies, emphasises *command and control* as the modus operandi of public programs. This assumes that public action is carried out by hierarchically organised agencies whose central spinal chord is the chain of command. Such centralised control is, in fact, vital to the preservation of democratic accountability. Much of traditional public administration thus is preoccupied with clarifying lines of control and centralizing authority.

The privatisation school, by contrast, downplays the need for administrative management altogether. Instead, it posits the market as a superior mechanism for achieving coordination and advancing public goals. Market competition, in this view, replaces public decisionmaking and obviates the need for administrative control.

The "new governance" rejects . . . these approaches and suggests a third route for achieving public purposes in the world of third-party government that now exists. Unlike the privatisation school, it emphasizes the continued need for public management even when indirect tools are used. This is so because private markets cannot be relied on to give appropriate weight to public interests over private ones . . . . While stressing the continued need for an active public role, however, the new governance acknowledges that command and control are not the appropriate administrative approach in the world of network relationships that increasingly exist. Given the pervasive interdependence that characterizes such networks, no entity, including the state, is in a position to enforce its will on the others over the long run. Under these circumstances, *negotiation and persuasion* replace command and control as the preferred management approach, not only in the setting of policy but in carrying it out . . . .

From management skills to enablement skills

Finally, because of the shift in emphasis from command and control to negotiation and persuasion, the world of third-party government necessitates a significantly different skill set on the part of public managers and those with whom they interact. Both traditional public management and the "new public management" emphasise essentially *management* skills, the skills required to manipulate large numbers of people arrayed hierarchically in bureaucratic organizations . . . . the "new governance" shifts the emphasis . . . to *enablement* skills, the skills required to engage partners arrayed horizontally in networks, to bring multiple stakeholders together for a common end in a situation of interdependence.

3.2.7 Discussion questions

1. Imagine a situation in which domestic noise from neighbouring properties had risen to unacceptably high levels. How could each of the regulatory techniques identified above be utilised in order to respond to this problem?
2. Are there any circumstances or contexts in which one or more regulatory instruments cannot be deployed?
3. How robust are the justifications made in favour of self-regulation? Are weaknesses in those justifications adequately met by the model of 'enforced self-regulation' proposed by Ayres & Braithwaite?
4. Is self-regulation best explained by public or private interest theories of regulation?
5. Does 'code' as a regulatory technique completely eliminate moral agency?
6. Are command-based techniques best understood in opposition to regulatory instruments which are:

    (i) competition-based;
    (ii) consent-based;
    (iii) communication-based; or
    (iv) code-based?

7. How would you assess the relative 'intrusiveness' of regulatory instrument or technique? Which do you consider to be the least intrusive? The most intrusive?
8. In what ways, if any, does the law contribute to the mechanics of each regulatory instrument?
9. How, if at all, is each of the principal constitutional organs of state (i.e. the legislature, executive and judiciary) involved in the introduction and operation of each of the above regulatory techniques?
10. Consider the parallels between Salamon's 'new governance paradigm' and institutionalist theories of regulation discussed in Chapter 2.

3.3 Instrument choice

Having surveyed the various tools and techniques that may be deployed to regulate behaviour, we now turn our attention to questions of tool choice. How are policy-makers to choose between the broad array of instruments available to them in pursuing their chosen regulatory objectives? The following extract from Ogus compares the relative advantages and disadvantages of command-based techniques with competition-based techniques (which he labels 'economic instruments').

A. Ogus, 'Regulation' (1994)

As the [above extract] has revealed, environmental protection has been the primary area both for the limited existing experience of EIs and for proposals to adopt them on a more extended basis. In evaluating their merits, and in particular the advantages which they are alleged to possess over CAC regulation, we shall therefore concentrate on their application to that problem. To reduce the complexity of the comparison, we shall assume that CAC regulation seeks to emulate EIs by using differentiated, rather than uniform, standards. As we have seen elsewhere, uniform standards reduce administrative costs but generate significant allocative inefficiencies by failing to take account of differences in abatement costs.

(a) Information

Regulating pollution by traditional CAC techniques normally involves the agency setting standards which balance the pollution abatement costs to individual firms (PAC) against pollution damage costs (PDC), thus requiring adequate information on both sets of costs. An important advantage claimed for EIs is that, provided the agency can make a reasonable estimate of PDC, it need have no knowledge of PAC. Once a tax has been set so as to reflect the impact on PDC of particular concentrations of pollutant, it is left to individual firms to decide whether it is cheaper to pay the tax or else to abate. Further, the system provides better information for firms on the costs they will incur from pollution: the tax represents a certain sum, whereas what they will have to pay if they contravene a standard depends on such uncertain variables as the enforcement discretion of the agency and the sentencing discretion of the court.

These are powerful arguments, but some qualifications need to be made. First, there is the problem of estimating PDC and thus of setting an appropriate price on discharges. Evaluating environmental harm raises immense difficulties not only because of its geographical and temporal dimensions, but also because of the complex interaction of different polluting sources and such variables as weather and diverse patterns of consumer use. Secondly, without information on PAC, an agency will be unable to predict how much pollution will actually result from a given set of prices and thus how effective those prices will be in relation to the efficiency goal of optimal pollution. To overcome both difficulties, the agency will in practice have to adopt an iterative or 'trial and error' approach: an initial set of prices is established, but these are subsequently modified as their impact is observed and as account is also taken of other variables. The instability of this process will undermine the predictability of the costs imposed on firms, one of the principal benefits claimed for EIs.

Of course, agencies setting standards under a CAC regime face similar difficulties; but the flexibility inherent in negotiating and enforcing individualized standards enables them to adjust to changing conditions in a way that is not possible under a tax system.

(b) Incentives

Since under a tax or subsidy system the cost to a firm of polluting increases proportionately to the pollution, there is an incentive for the firm to abate as much as possible. It will do so up to the point where the marginal abatement cost is equal to the marginal tax (or subsidy) cost, and there is therefore also an incentive to develop cheaper methods of pollution abatement. A tradeable emission rights regime engenders the same incentives: firms which reduce their abatement costs can profitably sell their rights to firms with higher costs. In this respect, it would appear that EIs are superior to CAC regulation: although a firm will seek to find the cheapest way of meeting a CAC standard, once that standard has been achieved it has no incentive to reduce pollution further. It is true ... that the standards imposed under some CAC regimes are formulated by reference to the 'best available techniques' not entailing excessive cost', but the agency's perceptions of what is 'best' are unlikely to encourage firms to develop new technologies.

(c) Accidents

A point frequently overlooked in discussions of control instruments is that many cases of serious environmental damage are the result of accidents, rather than deliberate polluting activity. Under CAC regimes, the amount payable by way of penalties can be tailored to reflect the more serious external costs generated by accidents, because it is determined after the accident has occurred. A tax system normally involves an *ex ante* assessment of harm and thus can meet the problem only if the amounts levied reflect the risks of accidental discharges from the individual firm.

As regards industrial health and safety, the contributions levied from firms to finance the compensation payable to victims are in many countries (though not Britain) calculated by reference to the firms' accident record. It is generally acknowledged that the system is effective, at least when applied to firms large enough for the statistical evidence to be reliable. But that very qualification indicates why a tax system cannot create appropriate incentives for avoiding serious pollution accidents. The infrequency of such accidents would render the system arbitrary: the tax would either be too high, for firms with an accident record, or too low, for firms without one.

(d) Enforcement

The assertion that EIs are cheaper than CAC systems in terms of enforcement costs is not easily sustained. Both generally entail the monitoring of discharges. The costs in some individual CAC cases may be high, where protracted negotiation or prosecution follows a detected contravention, but that has to be balanced against the administrative burden of collecting taxes in a larger number of cases and dealing with the proceeds. In justifying its hesitation to adopt EIs more widely, the British government referred to the difficulty and expense of the administrative support which would be required. It has been reported that more than half of the revenue derived from the German system of water effluent charges is absorbed by administrative costs.

(e) Distributional considerations

One apparently clear advantage of taxes and auctioned tradeable emission rights (but obviously not subsidies) over CAC regulation is that they generate funds which can be used to compensate the victims of pollution. However, the distributional argument for preferring EIs is not so straightforward as may appear. One reason is that the estimation of the distributional consequences of various control instruments is a complex matter: the conditions prevailing in different product, labour, and capital markets as well as the nature of the instruments influence the way in which the ultimate financial burden is shared between shareholders, the labour force, and consumers. Secondly, even if EIs might in theory operate to redistribute resources from (say) the shareholders of polluting firms to householder pollution victims, in practice such transfers are limited. Tax revenues tend to be earmarked, if at all, for government clean-up programmes, and schemes which directly compensate pollution victims are rare.

(f) Empirical evidence

Although there have been a number of studies of environmental EIs, they provide a far from adequate basis for evaluating the impact of these instruments. One problem is that EIs are generally combined with traditional CAC regimes and it is not possible to isolate the effects of the different approaches. As regards taxes, there is the additional difficulty that the instruments are frequently designed primarily for revenue purposes and the amounts imposed are often significantly lower than would be required for incentive purposes.

Some generalizations have, nevertheless, emerged. The taxes imposed on leaded petrol appear to have had important incentive effects. Effluent charges seem to have made some improvement to water quality, though not to the extent predicted by economists. This is explained on the ground not only that the amounts levied have been too small, but also on the prevalent use of 'grandfather clauses': typically the charges are applied only to new emission sources or to levels of discharges exceeding those current at the time the system is introduced. An exception is the Dutch system, where the charges have been significantly higher and the impact on polluter behaviour significantly greater.

As the above extract demonstrates, evaluating the relative strengths and shortcomings of different kinds of instruments can be complex, so that the task of choosing between policy instruments may be difficult. In order to orient ourselves in exploring the academic and policy literature on questions of instrument choice, it is helpful to classify this literature into two groups: those concerned with questions of efficacy and those focusing on legitimacy.

3.3.1   Prescriptive approaches and tool-efficacy

There is a large and growing body of scholarship that is broadly concerned with identifying the conditions under which particular instruments are most likely to be effective in achieving the desired behavioural change. It is now generally accepted that sensitivity to the context in which regulation takes place is vital, and it cannot therefore be claimed that any particular tool or tool-class is necessarily more efficacious than any other. Yet scholars have adopted quite different intellectual and methodological assumptions in specifying the conditions under which particular instruments should be preferred. In the following extract, Cooter begins by observing that legal scholars typically view law as a set of obligations backed by sanctions, or commands backed by threats, while economists typically view the law as a set of official prices. For Cooter, both viewpoints are characteristically blind to each other's perspectives: lawyers are blind to the fact that officials cannot regulate the economy efficiently by giving orders, and economists are blind to the distinctively normative aspect of law, viewing a sanction as what is forbidden merely as the price for doing what is permitted. Hence he claims that the challenge is to combine both these approaches by developing a theory about the difference between the behavioural effects of prices and sanctions.

R.   Cooter, *'Prices and sanctions'* (1984)
I. Contrasting prices and sanctions

A. Definitions

The mere existence of an obligation or issuance of a legal command may provide insufficient motivation for obedience. In addition, a sanction or threat may be needed to induce conformity. A sanction is a detriment imposed for doing what is forbidden, such as failing to perform an obligation. For example, a defendant in a tort dispute may be ordered to pay compensatory damages for an injury caused by his negligence, or a convicted criminal may be sentenced to jail.

In contrast, a price is payment of money which is required in order to do what is permitted. For example, a company may buy goods in the market-place, but it must pay the seller's price. Similarly, individuals are permitted to earn income, but obliged to pay taxes on their earnings.

These definitions of sanction and price are not always consistent with ordinary speech. Tax evasion is forbidden, but in casual speech people often say a fine is the price of tax evasion, when by these definitions it is a sanction. Furthermore, these definitions are unlikely to satisfy philosophers in search of necessary and sufficient conditions for "sanction" and "price". To illustrate, paying an arsonist not to burn down a store is extortion, yet protection money fits the definition of a price—an exaction for doing what is permitted. Despite such shortcomings, these definitions lay the basis for the behavioural model developed in the next section.

B. Incentive effects of prices and sanctions

Assume that someone engages in an activity that imposes costs upon others – external costs. The external cost might be the harm caused by an accident, the nuisance created by a polluter, or the injury that arises from breach of contract. External costs can usually be reduced by the injurer at some expense to himself—accident costs can be reduced by precaution, pollution can be reduced by abatement, and the probability of breach can be reduced by care in performance. This Article uses "precaution" as a generic term to refer to any costly activity that reduces external costs.

The relationship between precaution and external costs is summarized in Figure 1[3.2]. Social costs, which refer to the sum of external costs and the cost of precaution, are shown on the vertical axis, and the actor's precaution is shown on the horizontal axis. This Article assumes that a small increase in precaution reduces external costs by a large amount when precaution is low, and a small increase in precaution reduces external costs by a small amount when precaution is high. Consequently, the graph of social costs is U-shaped and there is a level of precaution, denoted x', which minimizes social costs.

1. Incentives in the general case

Now consider two rules for allocating the costs represented in Figure 1[3.2]. Rule A partitions levels of precaution into a permitted zone and a forbidden zone. Specifically, Rule A creates a legal standard of precaution x^*, permitting the actor to take precaution as great or greater than the legal standard $(x \geq x^*)$, and forbidding the actor to take less precaution than the legal standard $(x < x^*)$. Furthermore, under certain conditions, Rule A exacts a sum of money as a sanction for being in the forbidden zone.

Figure 2[3.3] illustrates Rule A. It shows precaution on the horizontal axis and the actor's private costs on the vertical axis. There are two components of the actor's private costs: precaution and sanctions. When precaution is below x^*, the actor bears the cost of his precaution and he must also pay the sanction; when the actor's precaution is above x^*, he pays only for his own precaution.

To keep Figure 2[3.3] simple, this analysis assumes that the sanction equals the external cost of the act—the actor is liable for the full harm which he causes. Thus, the curve in Figure 2[3.3] is identical to the curve in Figure 1[3.2] at those values of x below x^*. As precaution increases, there is a jump or discontinuity in the cost curve at the legal standard x^*, because that is the cutoff point for imposing the sanction. Above x^*, the sanction is not exacted, so the actor's private costs equal the cost of his precaution.

A person who is rationally self-interested will choose his level of precaution to minimize his private costs. If he faces costs like those created by Rule A, he will search

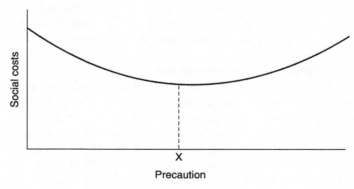

Figure 3.2 [Figure 1] Social costs.

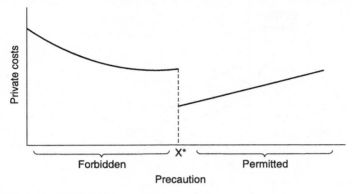

Figure 3.3 [Figure 2] Rule A.

for the lowest point on the cost curve. This point occurs when his precaution equals the legal standard x^*. Thus, a self-interested person subject to Rule A will take just enough precaution to satisfy the legal standard and escape liability.

It is not essential that the sanction equal the harm caused by the act to induce the self-interested actor to take precaution x^*. It is only essential that the sanction be large enough so that his private costs are minimized by conforming to the legal standard x^*. This point is illustrated in Figure 3[3.4], which shows the actor's private costs under four different assumptions about the sanction. The crucial feature of Figure 3[3.4] is that the lowest point in the graph is at x^*, regardless of whether the sanction corresponds to the high level A, the medium level B, or the low level C. Any one of these three sanctions will induce conformity with the legal standard x^*. However, if the sanction falls to the very low level indicated by D, then x∗ is not the lowest point on the cost curve, so the actor will minimize his private costs by taking less precaution than the legal standard.

Another kind of rule achieves similar ends by different means. Instead of dividing precaution into permitted and forbidden zones, Rule B requires the actor to pay the external costs that his activity imposes upon others. Under Rule B, the private costs of the actor are equal to the social costs of his activity; thus the social cost is internalized. To illustrate Rule B, relabel the vertical axis in Figure 1[3.2] to read "private costs = social costs." Because the actor's private costs are lowest at x′ when he is liable for the external cost of his acts, his private costs are minimized at the same level of precaution that minimizes social costs.

The incentives created by the two rules work in different ways. With Rule B, the actor balances the cost of additional precaution against the resulting reduction in the external costs for which he is responsible. His private costs are minimized when the benefits and costs of a small change in precaution offset each other. By contrast, with Rule A, the benefits and costs of a small change in precaution are not offset, because the actor's private costs are much lower when he just satisfies the legal standard than they would be if he just failed to satisfy it.

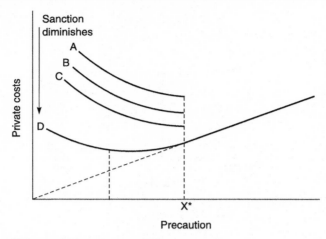

Figure 3.4 [Figure 3] Response to different sanctions.

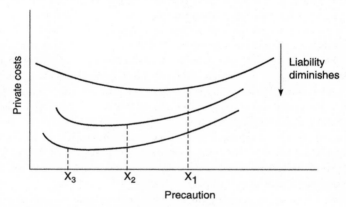

Figure 3.5 [Figure 4] Change to liability under Rule B.

The incentive effects of prices and sanctions are different because benefits and costs are usually equipoised with prices but not with sanctions. When benefits and costs are equipoised, a small change in them causes a change in behavior. Thus, under Rule B, the actor's precaution is responsive to changes in the price. If the price equals a fraction of the external harm, then reducing the fraction will cause the level of precaution which minimizes private costs to be reduced. This fact is illustrated in Figure 4[3.5], where lowering the price causes the lowest point on the cost curve to shift to the left. By contrast, when benefits and costs are not equipoised, moderate changes in them do not cause behavior to change. Thus, as was shown in Figure 3[3.4], the actor's precaution is unresponsive to modest changes in the sanction or the frequency of its application.

The difference in responsiveness can be summarized in a sentence: The amount of precaution an actor takes is more elastic with respect to changes in prices than to changes in levels of sanctions. On the other hand, an actor's precaution is responsive to a change in the obligation backed by a sanction, which corresponds to a change in the legal standard x^* under Rule A ....

... Thus, a small change in a sanction usually causes a small number of people to change their behavior a lot. In contrast, pricing the behavior causes most people to balance benefits and costs at the margin. Since many people would then be on the margin, a small change in a price will cause many people to change their behavior a little. In aggregate, then, behavior is more elastic with respect to prices than sanctions.

II. A normative theory of lawmaking

The difference in the incentive effects of prices and sanctions is important for lawmakers deciding whether to price or sanction behavior. If officials always possessed perfect information, socially desirable behavior could be induced by either prices or sanctions. Officials could either charge the price which exactly internalizes costs — which would induce individuals to choose the socially efficient level of behavior x' — or officials could create a legal standard — $x^* = x'$ — and back that standard with a sanction strong enough to induce conformity. Regardless of the approach, individuals would respond by choosing the efficient level of precaution.

In reality, however, lawmakers and officials who administer the law often make mistakes because they lack information or the incentives to use information. The behavioral consequences of mistakes are different depending upon whether the law creates a sanction or a price. A normative theory for choosing between sanctions and prices can be based upon the propensity of lawmakers to make mistakes, which depends in part upon the cost of information to them.

Most people conform to a reasonable obligation backed by a reasonable sanction, even if the legal standard is inefficient or otherwise undesirable. Consequently, lawmakers who create an obligation backed by a sanction must be certain that the partition between permitted and forbidden zones is in the right place. On the other hand, mistakes in computing the level of the sanction or the frequency of its application are not crucial, because most people will conform in spite of these mistakes.

In contrast, pricing behavior does not require dividing action into permitted and forbidden zones, so lawmakers need not compute the socially optimal behavior. Instead, the lawmakers must choose the price accurately. For efficiency, the price must fully reflect the external harm caused by the behavior. Since individuals are responsive to the magnitude of the price and the frequency of its collection, accuracy is crucial to induce behavior that is efficient or otherwise desirable ....

These observations lead to a simple decisional rule for lawmakers: If obtaining accurate information about external costs is cheaper for officials than obtaining accurate information about socially optimal behavior, then they should control the activity by pricing it; if the converse is true, then they should control the activity by sanctioning it ....

... In reality, such decisions are difficult for officials to make, especially when the affected individuals are heterogeneous. To illustrate, if pollution has many sources and many victims, it will be excessive in the absence of government intervention. If officials try to prescribe efficient pollution standards, they must know the abatement costs and the external harm for every source of pollution. It is impossible for officials to possess that much information, as the recent history of the Environmental Protection Agency has demonstrated. Obligations backed by sanctions will not succeed unless individual differences in compliance costs are comparatively small or receive no social weight.

When individual differences in compliance costs are important, the amount of information officials need can be reduced by relying upon prices instead of sanctions. Assigning the correct price to an activity only requires officials to compute the external cost, as opposed to balancing the costs and benefits. For example, if government creates pollution rights and encourages their exchange in a market, polluters will abate until the abatement cost at the margin equals the price of pollution rights. Thus, the market in pollution rights will reveal the marginal abatement cost of polluters without officials having to know anything about the technology of abatement.

Once the market reveals marginal abatement costs, officials can compare these costs to their computation of the external harm from pollution and adjust the amount of pollution until it is efficient. If the external harm caused by pollution exceeds the marginal abatement cost, then efficiency requires further abatement, so government should buy back some pollution rights to reduce their number. If the relative magnitudes are reversed, government should create and distribute additional pollution rights. These observations lead to the conventional conclusion that controlling pollution through prices requires less information than controlling it through obligations backed by sanctions ....

III. Distinguishing prices from sanctions

The prescription for lawmakers developed in Part II can be tested to see whether it is being followed in various bodies of law. First, however, it is necessary to be able to distinguish prices from sanctions. Sometimes a rule clearly resembles Rule A, in which case it is an obligation backed by a sanction, and sometimes it clearly resembles Rule B, in which case it imposes a price. However, some rules appear opaque upon first examination, so it is useful to have a criterion for preliminary classification.

A criterion can be developed by recalling that sanctions attach to forbidden acts and prices attach to permitted acts. Since the purpose of a sanction is to deter people from wrongdoing, the sanction will be adjusted to achieve this goal. Deterring actors whose fault is intentional, deliberate, or repeated requires a more severe sanction than deterring actors whose fault is unintentional, spontaneous, or committed for the first time. Therefore, sanctions increase with certain mental qualities of the act indicating more resistance to deterrence.

The efficient price depends upon the extent of external harm, not the actor's state of mind. If, contrary to fact, prices varied with the actor's state of mind — making the price higher if the act were done intentionally — then people would be deterred from doing the very acts that are permitted. Since a typical purpose of prices is to internalize costs, and since the external cost of an act is unrelated to the actor's state of mind, a price should not increase just because the activity is intentional, wilful, or repeated.

These observations point to a simple test for deciding whether a law creates a sanction or a price: Sanctions increase with the need for deterrence, as indicated by the actor's state of mind, whereas prices increase with the amount of external harm caused by the act, which is invariant with respect to the actor's state of mind.

IV. Relation to various areas of law
... This Part distinguishes prices from sanctions in several bodies of law — ... [including] regulation — to determine whether Part II's prescription is followed.

D. Regulation
Most regulations consist of obligations backed by sanctions. Economists have consistently advocated replacing many regulations with prices. This section examines this policy problem using the analytical framework developed in Parts I and II.

The normative issue
An example of the policy question is: Should pollution standards be replaced with pollution taxes? To compute the efficient tax, government officials must know the amount of external harm caused by the polluter and nothing more. By contrast, to discover the efficient standard, officials must balance the external harm against the cost of abatement, which requires complete information on each polluter's abatement technology. Since knowledge of the technology of each polluter is difficult or impossible for officials to obtain, some economists recommend replacing regulations with taxes.

There is, however, a problem with prices that does not arise with standards. It is in the interest of most people to conform to standards backed by sanctions, even though violations often go unpunished. Specifically, if reasonable pollution standards are backed by reasonable sanctions, most polluters will comply, even though pollution sometimes goes undetected. By contrast, if a price sometimes goes uncollected, then most self-interested people will change their behavior. Polluters will respond to a decrease in the frequency of collection of pollution fees by increasing the amount of pollution. In general, a sanction requires lower enforcement costs than a price, even if the two are equal in magnitude, because precaution is elastic with respect to imperfections in collecting prices and inelastic with respect to imperfections in enforcing sanctions.

Thus the choice between prices and sanctions in regulating pollution is a choice between the low enforcement costs of obligations backed by sanctions and the low information costs of prices.

Cooter's theory of prices and sanctions employs a methodological approach known as the economic analysis of law, an approach that has become particularly influential in North American legal scholarship. Another influential and expanding body of literature also focuses on the effectiveness and efficiency of regulatory instruments, although its underpinning methodological approach differs markedly, and which one leading political scientist has identified as distinctively Australian, referring to the large number of Australian regulatory scholars adopting this methodological approach. This self-titled 'regulatory' literature adopts a 'toolkit' approach, employing a methodological mix of empirical case-study observation, broad theoretical precepts and policy pragmatism in order to construct a series of normative prescriptions that purport to specify the conditions in which particular regulatory tools are likely to achieve behavioural change most effectively and efficiently. For example, Gunningham and Grabosky (whose work is emblematic of this approach) develop a set of normative principles and policies to inform the task of regulatory design, building upon the groundwork laid by Ayres and Braithwaite. They claim to adopt the standpoint of public policy in order to answer the question 'How can we achieve smarter and more effective regulation?' Their concern is to suggest ways in which policy makers, 'acting in good faith and intending to design successful environmental regulation, might best approach that task'. In so doing, their methodological approach draws upon the experience of several industry sectors which are claimed to operate as 'testing grounds' for developing policy prescriptions and design principles of general relevance. Although they identify the following criteria for a 'successful' regulatory strategy — effectiveness, efficiency, equity and 'political acceptability' — they claim that:

> Of these, we choose to make effectiveness and efficiency the pre-eminent criteria, because we believe that, in the majority of cases, the effectiveness of regulatory policy in reaching an environmental target, and its efficiency in doing so at least cost, will be the primary concern of policy makers . . . .We consider effectiveness and efficiency to be the two criteria most likely to yield substantial results in terms of improved environmental performance. These criteria are the essence of the term 'optimality', which is concerned with whether instruments will do the desired task at an acceptable performance level.

The design principles which they identify are discussed in the following extract:

N. Gunningham & P. Grabosky, '*Smart regulation*' (1998)

In pursuing our quest for 'smart' regulation we draw sustenance from two sources: one theoretical and academic; the other pragmatic and policy-oriented. While both illuminate our search, neither provides the answers we seek.

Turning to the former, there is some evidence that a new paradigm for the analysis of regulation may be evolving: one capable of transcending the regulation-deregulation dichotomy and of providing a much broader perspective of what regulation can involve. The most influential work within this paradigm, is that of Ayres and Braithwaite, who argue the case for 'responsive regulation' capable of providing 'creative options to bridge the abyss between deregulation and preregulatory rhetoric' and of achieving 'win-win' solutions through innovations in regulatory design. In particular, they emphasise the contributions of enforced self-regulation (whereby regulatees develop their own compliance programme, which is then subject to approval by regulatory authorities) and regulatory republicanism (where an enlightened private sector and an informed public, through deliberation and constructive participation, can contribute productively to the regulatory process). We build both on that work and, more generally, on the broader literature on legal pluralism to which it is related.

Scholars within the legal pluralism tradition focus upon the interrelationship between state law and private forms of social control and conflict resolution. They recognise that the law is just one element in a web of constraint on behaviour, some of whose strands are barely discernible, and many of which are non-governmental. For our purposes, the central insight of legal pluralism is that, contrary to conventional wisdom, most regulation is already 'in the hands not of government officials but of the myriad individuals employed in the private sector' and that, often, more can be achieved by harnessing the enlightened self-interest of the private sector than through command and control regulation. It is through the theoretical lens of pluralism, that we will elucidate the relationships which exist between the state industry, and third parties, and the way in which the law relates to each and operates in the shadow of the other. From this perspective, the limitations of a government-specific approach become readily apparent, as do the virtues of 'de-centering the state' and developing a broader and more inclusive conception of the regulatory process.

However, beyond these general perspectives, there has been little analysis of regulation which assists in addressing the central theme of this book: the design of efficient and effective 'optimal' policy mixes. For example, little work has been done to assess the relative advantages of different combinations of mechanisms in different institutional, economic, or social contexts. Neither is there any substantial body of literature which assists in addressing specifically environmental issues in the broader manner we envisage. For example, the environmental literature substantially overlooks means by which public agencies may harness commercial institutions and resources residing outside the public sector to further policy objectives, or how governments might foster conditions conducive to the operation of 'naturally occurring' private initiatives . . . .

Our second source of sustenance in designing smarter regulation is the rapid expansion of different types of environmental policy instruments over the last decade. These policy innovations include: self-regulation and co-regulation; environmental audits; environmental management systems (EMSs); eco-labelling schemes; liability rules for banks and insurers; environmental reporting; community right-to-know legislation (CRTK); and good neighbour agreements.

While these instruments open up a range of policy options far broader than traditional regulation, they have rarely been used to their full potential. This is

because most of these developments have been driven by pragmatic policy considerations and the desire to rectify specific problems, rather than by broader theoretical
concerns. As a result, they have also tended to develop in an ad hoc manner, often
without any serious attempt to design them as part of an integrated system. Nor has
there been much systematic enquiry into how such instruments might interact with
each other and other forms of regulation. Rather, policymakers have commonly
fallen into the trap of simply adding a new instrument to their arsenal of weapons
without giving sufficient thought to how this will impact on their overall regulatory
strategy.

Also introduced, but with a much more coherent and sophisticated theoretical
underpinning, has been a range of economic instruments including taxes, charges,
and tradeable property and pollution rights. However, even most of the economic
literature shows only a limited appreciation of the extent to which some economic
instruments at least might be viewed not just as a complement to direct regulation
(or a more flexible form of it), but integrated with a range of other policy
instruments.

Overall, there remains a tendency to treat the various policy instruments as
alternatives to one another rather than as potentially complementary mechanisms
capable of being best used in combination. As a result, policy analysts have tended to
embrace one or other of these regulatory approaches without regard to the virtue of
others. Perhaps predictably, economists have focused on economic instruments,
lawyers and government regulators on direct regulation, industry on self-regulation,
and scientists on research.

We will argue that such 'single instrument' or 'single strategy' approaches are
misguided, because all instruments have strengths and weaknesses; and because none
are sufficiently flexible and resilient to be able to successfully address all environmental problems in all contexts. Accordingly, we maintain that a better strategy will
seek to harness the strengths of individual mechanisms while compensating for their
weaknesses by the use of additional and complementary instruments. That is, we will
argue that in the large majority of circumstances (though certainly not all), a mix of
instruments is required, tailored to specific policy goals. Moreover, such a mix of
instruments will work more effectively if a broader range of participants are capable
of implementing them. This means the direct involvement not only of governments
(first parties) but also of business and other 'targets' of regulation (second parties)
and a range of other interested actors (third parties), both commercial and non-
commercial. To date, the use of third parties has been restricted to public interest and
community groups. Commercial third parties, in particular, remain a largely
untapped resource in the environmental arena, despite their considerable potential
to act both as quasi-regulators and to influence the behaviour of regulatees more
generally.

Towards a successful policy mix

[Our] central thesis ... is that recruiting a range of regulatory actors to implement complementary combinations of policy instruments, tailored to specific

environmental goals and circumstances, will produce more effective and efficient policy outcomes. Further, that this approach will reduce the regulatory burden on government, thus freeing up scarce public resources to be allocated to situations where government intervention or assistance is most required . . . .

We do not, however, advocate a 'smorgasboard' approach, where the greater the number of different instruments and actors the better. There are limits to government and private actor resources which necessitate a careful selection of the most cost-effective regulatory combinations. There are also limits to the administrative burden that can reasonably be placed on regulatees in satisfying the multiplicity of regulations. Excessive administrative burdens may well divert internal firm resources away from more productive pollution prevention activities. Finally, appropriate mixes of instruments and actors will vary depending on the nature of the environmental problem and industry sector or sectors being addressed, making it difficult if not impossible to generalize concerning optimal combinations.

Nor do we assume that any combination of instruments will be better than a single instrument approach. On the contrary, different combinations of instruments, or the introduction of a new instrument to an existing policy mix, could have a variety of effects, not all of which are positive. These range from synergy (where two instruments enhance each other's effects) to neutralisation (where one instrument negates or dilutes the effect of another). For example, uniform pollution standards for individual firms may well undermine the efficiency of a broad based pollution tax. What is needed then, is not simply the introduction of a broad range of policy instruments, but the matching of instruments with the imperatives of the environmental issue being addressed, with the availability of different regulatory actors, and with the intrinsic qualities of each other . . . .

Designing environmental policy

. . .[W]e believe . . . that notwithstanding the context-specific nature of most environmental problems, it is possible to build a process and principle based framework for designing environmental regulation in any given circumstances. By this, we mean an approach which, while falling short of providing determinative regulatory solutions, leads policymakers to ask the crucially important questions (processes) and assess their decisions against a set of design criteria (principles) which form the basis for reaching preferred policy outcomes.

Specifically, we seek to demonstrate that there is a middle path. This path involves drawing lessons from both the theoretical literature on regulation and from empirical study of what works and what doesn't work in specific contexts (drawing, in particular, on our case studies of the chemical industry and agriculture) to provide a series of policy prescriptions of broad application. These are intended to guide policy makers in seeking to design regulatory or policy solutions to any given environmental problem, on how best to approach that task.

. . . [W]e address the three major components we believe are crucial to successful regulatory design. First, and briefly, we examine regulatory design processes: the preliminary steps which policy makers must go through in identifying their objectives, the characteristics of the environmental problem they confront, the available policy options, and issues of consultation and participation. These processes can be mechanistic, except if they are used in an open-ended way to challenge assumptions and fully explore possibilities. While the questions making up the processes are not new they are essential, and a failure to understand them causes policy failure.

Secondly, we identify a series of regulatory design principles. We argue that adherence to these principles is at the very heart of successful policy design. Not least, we argue that policy makers should take advantage of a number of largely unrecognised opportunities, strategies and techniques for achieving efficient and effective environmental policy. These include:

- the desirability of preferring complementary instrument mixes over single instrument approaches while avoiding the dangers of 'smorgasboardism' (i.e. wrongly assuming that all complementary instruments should be used rather than the minimum number necessary to achieve the desired result) [i.e. Principle 1: prefer policy mixes incorporating a broader range of instruments and institutions];
- the virtues of parsimony; why less interventionist measures should be preferred and how to achieve such outcomes; [Principle 2: prefer less interventionist measures];
- the benefits of an escalating response up an instrument pyramid (utilising not only government but also business and third parties) so as to build in regulatory responsiveness, to increase dependability of outcomes through instrument sequencing, and to provide early warning of instrument failure through the use of 'triggers' [Principle 3: Ascend a dynamic instrument pyramid to the extent necessary to achieve policy goals];
- empowering third parties (both commercial and non-commercial) to act as surrogate regulators, thereby achieving not only better environmental outcomes at less cost, but also freeing up scarce regulatory resources which can be redeployed in circumstances where no alternatives to direct government intervention are available; [Principle 4: empower participants which are in the best position to act as surrogate regulators] and
- maximising opportunities for win-win outcomes, by expanding the boundaries within which such opportunities are available, and encouraging business to go 'beyond compliance' with existing legal requirements [Principle 5: Maximise opportunities for win-win outcomes];

Thirdly, we stress the crucial importance of designing instrument combinations and discuss how such permutations might be inherently complementary, inherently counter-productive, or essentially context-specific in nature. We also explain how instrument combinations can be sequenced in order to avoid dysfunctional results and so as to expand the range of circumstances in which particular combinations will be complementary rather than counterproductive.

The policy prescriptions developed in the two preceding extracts proceed from the assumption that both policy-makers, and the instruments which they seek to deploy, can be faithfully relied upon to adopt and implement policies that will most effectively achieve regulatory goals. In so doing, they develop policy prescriptions which seek to employ the law's instrumental force directly. However, we saw in the previous chapter that one of the principal observations of systems theoretical approaches is the limited effectiveness of one social system (including the legal system) in exerting direct influence over other social systems, due to the normative closure of social sub-systems. For systems theorists, effective regulatory control is best pursued through indirect influence, drawing upon the 'cognitive openness' of social sub-systems in order to overcome the limits of their normative closure, advocating an approach referred to as 'proceduralisation', explained in the following extract.

C. Scott, *'Regulation in the age of governance: The rise of the post-regulatory state'* (2004)

For the legal theory of autopoiesis (LTA) the problem of control is a problem of communication. Autopoiesis is a term developed initially in biological sciences, derived from Greek words meaning self-producing, and refers to the idea that law reproduces itself according to its own norms. The problem which the theory addresses is centrally concerned with the difficulties that politics, economy, society and law have in communicating with each other and thus exercising control. Can legislatures create new legal rules and simply expect that they will be translated into laws which are effective in the legal system and which produce the desired changes in behaviour by economic and social actors? The central hypothesis of LTA is that such an expectation would, generally, be far-fetched. LTA provides an explanatory theory for the problems of regulatory control with some ideas as to how such problems might be addressed.

Developing a systems theory perspective associated with the work of Niklas Luhmann LTA perceives the world as consisting of differentiated and autonomous social subsystems. These subsystems — the political, the legal, the social and the economic are the subsystems central to regulation — are said to be cognitively open but normatively and operatively closed. Thus a subsystem is open to 'facts, situations and events of its environment'. This means that no subsystem is immune from the stimulation of its external environment, but such stimulation occurs as disturbance or perturbation. Stimuli are processed according to the normative structure of the subsystem and not the normative structure of the external environment. In the case of the legal system the distinctive character of its differentiation is its adoption of a binary code — in which actions are classified as legal or illegal, lawful or unlawful — to which its operations are oriented.

To take a simple regulatory example, within the political subsystem there may be legislation created which assigns criminal penalties to breaches of rules set down in a regulatory statute. The legislation is the instrument of communication between political and legal subsystems. The legal subsystem, operationalized through a court, receives the legislation on its own terms, processing it according to the wider normative principles of criminal law. The instrumental objectives of the political subsystem in prohibiting the targeted conduct are of no interest within the legal subsystem. The legal norms emphasize principles protective of defendants such as a requirement that intent is proven, that guilt is proved beyond reasonable doubt, and so on. The stringent application of these principles often cuts across the instrumental objectives of a regulatory regime.

It may be the case that differentiated subsystems are well aligned with each other in particular domains. It is said, for example, that in many legal systems contract law and market principles of exchange within the economy have a reasonable fit with each other. Similarly the organizational forms used for business organizations' and corporations' law statutes are often quite well aligned. For LTA these alignments represent 'structural coupling' between systems. Such linkages are perceived as being a product of 'co-evolution'.

The leading exponent of LTA, Gunther Teubner, describes his hypothesis as to the effects of the inherent problems of communications between subsystems in terms of a 'regulatory trilemma'. At its simplest the trilemma describes the three types of problem that can arise in the relationship between law and other subsystems: law may be irrelevant to the other subsystem and of no effect ('mutual indifference'); through creeping legalism law may damage the other system which is to be regulated by inhibiting its capacity for self-reproduction; the self-reproductive capacity of the legal subsystem may be damaged through an 'oversocialisation of law'.

The aspect of the analysis which has received most attention is creeping legalism or juridification damaging other subsystems. This is as much a problem for the welfare state as for the regulatory state. If we take the example of a regulatory regime over a utilities sector, decisions might largely be taken through negotiation over the needs of the sector consistent with a view as to what the regulatory policy requires. Law is present, but on the boundaries of regulatory interaction. Changes within the regulated sector, for example liberalization and an influx of new firms, might shatter the regulatory consensus and cause law to be drawn into the resolution of disputes more frequently. This is not simply about litigation, but also an increasing presence for lawyers in drafting documents and negotiating over regulatory decision-making. To the extent that lawyers operate within the meaning structures of the legal system they will seek to import legal norms about how things are done. This is perhaps most true in court settings, where judges are likely to resolve questions through appeal to the general norms of administrative or contract law rather than values more directly related to the instrumental objectives of the regulatory regime. For Teubner this poses the risk that private law will be further fragmented as it is asked to provide solutions to problems outside its normative experience or it will be hybridized and combined with other normative structures as it seeks to respond.

Applying LTA to empirical questions provides a distinctive insight into problems of regulatory control. It displaces a linear governance pattern in which policy is translated into legislation, then regulatory action and regulatory effects with an image of 'a multitude of autonomous but interfering fields of action in each of which, in an acausal and simultaneous manner, recursive processes of differences take place'. The challenge, in these terms, is to find ways to reduce or minimize the differences between the different fields of action through securing 'structural coupling'. Such effects arise in quite unpredictable ways. This may be investigated empirically by drawing complex cognitive maps to demonstrate the self-regulatory processes of the various fields of action and to show their points of communication or non-communication.

LTA envisions a post-regulatory state in which the legal subsystem relates to other subsystems not through highly specified, or materialized, regulatory law, but rather through working with the grain of the understanding of ordering within other subsystems. Put another way, the successful implementation of regulatory law is dependent on achieving some measure of 'structural coupling'. For Teubner the interesting ways to address the problem do not follow the economic theorists down a deregulatory route emphasizing the control functions of markets, but rather towards more sophisticated, abstract and indirect forms of regulatory inter-vention, which he describes as 'control of self-regulation', but which is also captured in the concepts 'collibration', 'reflexive law', 'meta-governance', and 'meta-regulation'. This approach recognizes the 'inner logic' of social systems and sets law the challenge of seeking to steer those social systems. A key aspect of this approach is re-casting the function of law from direct control to proceduralization. Such a shift in regulatory law would not end processes of juridification, but 'would help steer the process into more socially compatible channels'. This modest concep-tion of law's capabilities has led to a concern with targeting the internal management systems of regulated entities in order to secure compliance with regulatory goals.

Thinking about the problem of the relationship between mechanisms of global governance and regulatory law, Teubner himself has invoked ideas of legal pluralism as a complement to LTA. It is, claims Teubner, civil society rather than international governance organizations which is generating effective global regulatory rules, effec-tive in the sense that they are structurally coupled to the economic subsystem to which they apply. The key example he cites is the *lex mercatoria*, the ancient system of legal rules governing economic transactions, but he refers also to the regimes estab-lished within multinational enterprises to govern their global affairs. We could think also of international rules governing such matters as sustainability of forests and the protection of the environment from chemical pollution.

The legal theory of autopoiesis highlights important limitations to the use of law as a regulatory instrument, encouraging us to think about the normative structures within other subsystems which might provide the key to control in respect of par-ticular sets of values. The theory suggests a modest role of law in steering or proce-duralizing those activities over which control is sought, thus seeking control indirectly. It is implausible to think of direct hierarchical control, and thus we must think of ways of intervening which work with the recursive practices of subsys-tems, seeking, for example, the alignment of regulatory norms set by legislators, legal norms generated as a response by the legal subsystem, and the activities over which control is sought. The capacity of the analysis to offer causal explanations and to predict the outcomes of particular interventions makes it extremely difficult to sell as a policy tool.

3.3.2 Politics, legal culture and institutional variety

The literature referred to in the preceding section (apart from the previous extract's discussion of an autopoietic approach to social sub-systems), views the question of 'how to regulate' as a technocratic one, driven by the quest for effective and efficient solutions. Another body of academic scholarship is also concerned with questions of instrument choice, but instead of focusing on efficacy, it seeks to explore broader questions of legitimacy. These analyses emphasise the relevance and importance of non-instrumental influences on the choice of instrument, not only as a matter of political pragmatism, but also arising from a commitment to non-instrumental values and principles. These values and principles are based on assumptions about the role of law, the rule of law and the need to ensure the legitimacy of control regimes within democratic states. In other words, scholars working from this intellectual perspective tend to reject the notion that the tools within a policy-maker's toolkit are directly substitutable in a context of choice driven by efficacy criteria. Rather, they highlight the importance of institutional, political and ideological constraints that may or should influence instrument choice. There are a wide variety of such non-instrumental concerns, and the following extracts have been chosen in order to illustrate their richness and diversity.

Throughout this chapter, we have drawn attention to the law's instrumental role in providing foundational support for regulatory tools. But the law may also serve an important *expressive* function, the potency of which is likely to vary, depending upon the law's visibility in particular contexts. In the following extract, Neiman expresses concern at the growing popularity of market-based tools within policy literature across a range of social domains, including metropolitan reform, pollution control and urban development.

M. Neiman, '*The virtues of heavy-handedness in government*' (1980)

With the advance of history, especially in the democracies, there has been an increased reliance by government on non-coercive methods of influencing human behavior. As one scholar has claimed:

Our generation, more than any other, shrinks from inflicting pain. We are less confident than any of our predecessors in imputing guilt. The Christian ideal of forgiveness, the democrat's hatred of seeing one man held down by another, the psychologist's exposure of the element of sickness in sin and crime — all join together in our period. They cause us to look askance at the whole idea of punishment.

I believe, however, that the omnibus disdain for coercion as a mode of government action is an attitude too easily accepted. I believe that insufficient scrutiny has accompanied the proliferation of such "noncoercive" approaches as market incentive tax breaks, or other forms of reward and alternatives to coercion and punishment. I am especially concerned about those formulations that propose to structure incentives in order to pose more subtle and presumably more efficient methods of manipulating human conduct. At the risk of attracting ridicule and scorn I believe it is useful to adopt, as at least a working, devil's advocate-like assumption, the proposition that the heavy, visible and coercive, hand of government is in some respects desirable; that coercion from our public institutions has its virtues . . . .

The benefits of coercive approaches

[O]ne of the major sources of contemporary criticism of the more intrusive and coercive methods of government intervention is the resurgence of classical liberalism among economists, with its distrust of political decisions and the primacy it accords to the private domain. Even among those who accept the need for substantial interventions by government in the affairs of citizens, there is a preference for relying on the methods of incentives, prices, and the like. No one better summarizes this view than Schultze, who in his book *The Public Use of Private Interest* makes the following statement:

The desirable mode of carrying out economic and social activities is through a network of private and voluntary arrangements — called, for short, "the private market." A theory of social intervention is thus concerned with defining the conditions under which that presumption is indeed rebuttable. We think of the public sector as intervening in the private sector, and not vice versa. In short, it is privatism and the calculus of exchange that is paramount, while politics is residual and complementary.

To a political scientist, this is a dismal characterization of the role and essence of the political; this diminution of politics implies a kind of supremacy for consumership over the functions of citizenship.

. . . My concern extends beyond simply being insulted by economists or so-called public choice theorists; many who call for more emphasis on noncoercive approaches to public intervention in individual decisions also ignore society's political component, the most important elements of which are, in this context, the formulation and enforcement of rules governing "publicly significant behavior". There seems to be an implicit notion among critics of government coercion that the purpose of law, regulation, and rule making is merely to influence physical behavior. It would appear that this view of public directives of one kind or another as mere technique overlooks the act of rule making as embodying what is viewed as proper, virtuous, just, good, and sacred. While much public policy, regardless of how it is expressed, is often a matter of convenience or a response to pressures by special interests, public policy is also one of the only ways in which secular virtue can be expressed. Focusing entirely on whether administrative regulations, ordinances, and laws are more or less efficient in influencing behavior than are markets, prices, and profit motive tends to underscore the mere directing of behavior as the paramount function of public intervention.

Consequently, tinkering with the calculus of private transactions in order to direct egoistic behavior to public ends ignores the important need to wreak retribution and punishment on those who refuse to satisfy public goals. After all, how can one "punish" someone who merely refuses publicly offered rewards and payments and continues to behave in ways that contravene publicly expressed goals. To diminish the practice of enforcing rules by punishment and other heavy-handed, even violent, means is to diminish the role of the sacred in human affairs. And to diminish the sacred is to invite increased difficulty in encouraging individuals to act individually in ways to achieve collective goals and satisfactions. As Hirsch has asserted in his complex analysis of the moral components of economic growth:

Appeal to ... private self-interest remains in many situations the most effective instrument available for attaining the immediate objective. But by weakening the norms of deliberate co-operation, and social restraint, reliance on this appeal as the dominant value of society produces an unstable system over time. The effectiveness of the miracle drug is eventually weakened by its side effects.

These observations contain considerable merit ....

Once the issue of influencing human beings to behave in particular ways is narrowed so that it becomes one of technique there is then a tendency to obscure the distinction between the application of coercion to discourage undesired behavior and the bestowing of rewards for desired behavior. In a broad sense the two approaches are different in profound ways. When punishing a person, for example, it is claimed that the person had no right to behave as he did and that society, through its designated institutions, considers the punished behavior as improper, immoral, or contemptuous of the popular will, expressed through democratically designed public policies. To pay people so that they behave in desired ways seems, on the other hand, to suggest that it is the right of a person to behave in ways that society may find undesirable, and that the wish of society to elicit other behavior must not be imposed; indeed individuals must be compensated in order for them to change their behavior in a manner consistent with popular will.

While it must be acknowledged that not everything desired by the public can be imposed upon individuals without compensation, particularly where individuals are obliged to suffer disproportionate burdens, one chafes at the idea that a safe and clean supply of air, for example, must be guaranteed by paying potential air polluters a bribe not to pollute. Similarly, it is bothersome to compensate land speculators for the loss in property values that were generated by the public in the first place. But all this aside, viewing coercion versus noncoercion as only alternative *techniques* obscures the moral and ethical dimension of human affairs and the role of rule making and punishment as important sources of a moral consciousness, something that the "ethics" of economic transactions cannot provide.

Thus the threat of coercion for violating rules of conduct or important social goals is important not simply because it is one way of trying to influence people's behavior, but also because it provides the basis for inflicting retribution on noncomplying individuals. Without allowing for the initial threat, it is far more difficult to impose coercion. But without punishment there is little sense of retribution and "without retribution we may lose our sense of wrong". Any system that tries to influence human conduct and does not have a substantial moral and coercive component tends to ignore the evident desire and need of citizens not merely to want to change conduct, but also to punish the wrongdoers.

This is not to assume that the angels amongst us want to punish the devils in our midst. Rather, there are enough of us who are self-righteous or hypocritical on an ongoing basis to provide a strong demand for punishing those of us caught doing wrong. As Pakenham declares, "the conviction on which the retributive theory is based is strong and genuine and almost universal, so that it would be very rash to ignore it as mere fallacy." Any evaluation of the relative merits of coercive and noncoercive approaches should consider what role, if any, a particular approach or method has in the system of punishment and in the satisfaction of at least minimum demands for retribution . . . .

The 'symbolic' or expressive dimension of some instruments may vary, just as the social meaning attached to various activities and behaviour may vary across communities. The meaning or symbolism attached to particular tools will inevitably be a product of the legal, constitutional and social culture of the community in which it is adopted. Yet the relationship between policy instruments and legal, constitutional and social culture is a reflexive and dynamic one, so that the latter is likely to influence the range and choice of instruments and institutions used within any given legal system in various ways, outlined by Ogus in the following extract.

A. Ogus, 'Comparing regulatory systems: Institutions, processes and legal forms in industrialised countries' (2002)

Comparisons between national systems risk superficiality if no account is taken of the cultural and constitutional context in which the regime is to be found. We may find a strong resemblance between the regimes in two different jurisdictions: for example, similar conditions may be stipulated for the grant of a licence; and similar processes may be laid down. But the functioning of the regulatory system may be strikingly different if, for example, State A has a panoply of process values incorporated into its general administrative law and enforced by an independent judiciary, whereas in State B the matter is simply one of bureaucratic diktat. So also the concrete decisions made may depend not only on the merits of applicants and the use of highly detailed legislative or administrative criteria, but also on the constitutional basis of the system. State A may enshrine a general principle of freedom of economic activity in relation to which the requirement for licensing constitutes a necessarily limited exception; State B may, in contrast, regard the system as simply an instrument facilitating government control of the economy.

Indeed, above and beyond substantive constitutional norms may be other significant aspects to be considered under what may be loosely called 'cultural' variables. Historically, different bureaucratic and regulatory traditions have emerged in different countries relating to the style of rule-making and enforcement. Such traditions may stem from the cultures associated with different legal families (for example, common law; civil law; Scandinavian; Latin American...) or operate quite independently of the latter. The report begins, therefore, with an attempt to identify how regulation fits into the constitutional and cultural environment.

Constitutional and cultural environment
Constitutional framework

Regulation, in our conception, involves individuals and firms being induced to outcomes which, in the absence of the instrument, they would not have attained. It therefore necessarily involves the exercise of power by the state or an agency of the state. Constitutions control power and allocate it between different organs of the state, more specifically between legislature, executive and judiciary. Under most modern Western constitutions, the power to regulate is acquired, if only implicitly, by the legislature.

If our interpretation of regulation as importing collectivist goals is accepted, conferring sovereign power on the legislature to regulate might seem, in the light of democratic principles, to be obvious. However democratic ideals must, to some extent, cede before other values and in consequence constitutional arrangements governing regulation are more complex.

First, and most obviously, in practice much regulatory power is delegated by legislatures to the executive; while primary legislation may lay down objectives and general principles, subordinate legislation or other administrative instruments provide the detailed rules. The costs of legislators being sufficiently informed to make good decisions and of the necessarily frequent technical amendments make this inevitable.

Secondly, in some countries, notably France, the power of the executive to regulate at least in some sectors is derived directly from the Constitution. This may reflect a political or ideological choice in favour of limiting democratic influences on decisions in such areas, a tradition persisting from monarchist concepts of the state.

A third exception, sometimes overlooked by political scientists and economists, is the residual power of the judiciary to regulate. In many jurisdictions, the courts refuse to enforce contractual obligations which are contrary to the *ordre public*, a concept sufficiently broad to encompass a large number of social and economic values. In the common law world, judges have developed principles not only to constrain monopolistic behaviour, but also, under the doctrine of 'common callings', where such conditions are justified or inevitable − as in natural monopolies − to guarantee services and to regulate prices. And, in New Zealand, attempts have been made to invoke the principles to post-privatisation utility arrangements. In the absence of a bureaucracy, the approach may be justified but it is problematic insofar as it requires a legal claim for it to be activated and (in modern times) makes great demands on the technical expertise of judges.

A fourth qualification arises from the possibility of an allocation of legislative competence between national and provincial legislatures under a federal system of government. Inspired by notions of political decentralisation, these constitutional arrangements raise difficult questions whether they inhibit trade across the federation and/or encourage 'regulatory competition' between regions, with beneficial or adverse economic consequences. And the same issues arise in a transnational context, such as the European Union.

Note too that in some countries the constitution itself may exert constraints on the power of the legislature to regulate; and this in turn will depend on the set of politico-economic values to which that document gives expression. Thus we may have, as in the United States, a constitution which is interpreted as being based on a premise of freedom of economic activity. Then regulation has to find its constitutional legitimacy in the (admittedly broad) range of 'police powers' (e.g. protection of the health, safety and welfare of the community) the exercise of which can interfere with that freedom. This approach may be contrasted with another tradition which defines the role of the state as in some way directed towards social welfare ends which may diverge from unregulated market outcomes. Thus the German Basic Law of 1949 has, at its base, the concept of *soziale Marktwirstchaft* (social market economy) impliedly legitimising more active regulatory interventions. But the language used to define such powers tends to be very vague, making constitutional challenges easy to resist. For example, Article 41 of the Italian Constitution provides that 'the law will set up appropriate schemes and controls in order that public and private economic activities may be directed and coordinated for the benefit of society'. This in turn should be distinguished from a third type of constitutional framework which assumes a planned economy and gives the legislature or government all the powers necessary to control it.

Administrative law

Administrative law deals with the decisions and activities of public institutions and, in particular, specifies the means of challenging their validity and providing remedies for grievances. It plays a number of vital roles in relation to regulatory systems, ensuring that regulatory institutions use proper procedures and act not only within their legislative mandate, but also fairly and reasonably within the light of those objectives.

There are major differences between countries regarding the character and effectiveness of administrative law and an obvious variable is the strength and independence of the judiciary who are primarily responsible for making and enforcing decisions against public institutions. In this connection, it would be wrong to assume that the power of judges to control administrative activity is a reflection of the state of the jurisdiction's economic development and therefore to be found predominantly in Western industrialised countries. It has been persuasively argued that the world's most active judiciary (in this sense) are to be found in India.

In any event, there are important differences between administrative law systems in countries which show equal respect for the separation of powers and ensure the independence of judges. There is, on the one hand, the continental European, civil law jurisdictions, which have a system of public law tribunals, separate from the main judicial system; and, on the other, the common law jurisdictions where administrative action is largely controlled by the ordinary courts, the state being regarded as simply *primus inter pares*.

And even within these two systems there are important variations. So, for example, the question whether a court has the power to annul legislation on the ground that it is inconsistent with the constitution is not one which receives the same answer within each tradition. The German *Verfassungsgericht* has the power; but that of the French *Conseil Constitutionnel*, which in any event is not a court, is more limited. The United States Supreme Court has the power; the British House of Lords has not.

Other differences may be questions of emphasis and therefore more difficult to categorise. German administrative law centres on the notion of the *Rechtsstaat*, the main principle being that all instances of public administrative activity must be legitimised by formal legal norms. While this idea would not be treated as wholly alien to the French *droit administratif*, that system takes as its focal point the 'public interest'. This not only enables constitutional texts to be interpreted in such a way as to justify appropriate administrative action; it also protects private citizens, in the sense of requiring public authorities imposing losses on individuals in the furtherance of the public interest, to provide compensation.

Then as between two of the leading common law jurisdictions, the USA and the UK, administrative law has clearly diverged. American judges take a harder look at the reasonableness of administrative actions (so-called 'substantive judicial review') whereas their English counterparts have rather concentrated on whether appropriate procedures have been observed. American administrative law has also gone further in terms of process values, requiring a greater degree of transparency of decision-making and encouraging participation by interested third parties.

Regulatory traditions and styles

Characterising and placing what we have come to call 'regulation' within legal systems are highly problematic tasks, as an impressionistic comparison of how law librarians classify books bearing that title would at once reveal. The question is not unconnected with the politico-economic basis of the law. Thus we find that civil law systems which have rationalised the concept of the state, and particularly its role in the economy, have developed formal legal categories for this purpose, for example, the French *droit public economique* and the German *Wirtschaftsverwaltungsrecht*. These terms have been used to bring under a single umbrella the law relating to public enterprise, public finance, state controls of private enterprise and competition law – and therefore without difficulty have incorporated the regulation of privatised entities. In contrast, in Anglophone jurisdictions with their common law emphasis on the control of government power, equivalent classifications do not exist. Of course, the same areas of law can be identified, but there has been nothing in legal doctrine to link them. Rather they have been seen as disparate aspects of administrative law, the main concern of which was to control executive discretion, rather than facilitate outcomes considered as economically desirable. Interesting, but not entirely successful attempts were made by German emigrants to impose continental patterns on the American and British systems.

Paradoxically, the concepts of 'regulation' and 'regulatory law' which became so dominant in the 1980s and afterwards were predominantly Anglo-American in origin. They had as their base the economic notion of public law responses to instances of market failure and, as such, were rationalised by legal scholars from a law-and-economics background. Undoubtedly this literature had an impact on administrative lawyers who began to forsake their traditional preoccupation with discretion and judicial review to join 'the economists' pilgrimage to the new Jerusalem, which beckons with responsive regulation, regulatory negotiation and regulation by performance outcome and through economic incentives'. While public lawyers from the common law world were thus acquiring a vision which was closer to that of continental exponents of 'economic law', the latter were adjusting to the somewhat narrower notion of 'regulation' which became in French *reglementation* and in German *Regulierung*.

Notwithstanding this convergence of the conception and rationalisation of regulation between the two principal legal cultures, the practical application retained important differences. ... [H]ere we can mention some examples which result from the historical traditions.

- The focus on the 'state' and the greater degree of state intervention in the continental tradition, leads to a culture of 'public interest' regulation which is somewhat broader than the Anglo-Saxon emphasis on 'market-failure' regulation.
- The style of the legislation used for regulatory purposes in common law systems tends to aim at a high level of precision, thus generating lengthy and very complex provisions; the continental approach adopts more general and abstract language, leaving more room for discretionary interpretation. Historically this can be explained as a consequence of the ideology that regulation was an incursion on the general principles of the common law and, thus, to be protected against judicial conservatism, required to be formulated in very specific terms. Given their long tradition of state intervention and centralised bureaucracy, continental European systems have been less comfortable than common law jurisdictions with regulatory agencies which are, at least to some degree, independent of government.
- While continental regulatory authorities are given powers themselves to impose sanctions for non-compliance, the British regulatory systems predominantly use the criminal justice process to enforce regulation. The latter appears to be a consequence of the fact that, before modern bureaucracies, regulation was enforced by justices of the peace, the local arm of the criminal law.
- In common law systems, again because historically intervention was regarded as exceptional rather than routine, regulatory techniques and principles have tended to emerge piecemeal, with little attempt at coherence across different sectors. In some European continental jurisdictions, particularly Germany, attempts have been made to develop general principles of regulatory administrative justice.

In the preceding extract, Ogus identifies how several features of a community's legal, constitutional and institutional traditions can shape that community's policy choices in seeking to regulate social behaviour. But such choices are also particularly susceptible to the influence of political ideologies that may transcend particular legal or constitutional cultures, such as the deregulatory movement that swept across industrialised democratic economies throughout the late 1970s and gained accelerating pace in the decade which followed. While the notion of deregulation is rather imprecise, it essentially refers to the process by which the governments of industrialised economies sought to reduce state control over an industry or activity so as to make it structurally more responsive to market forces. Given that empirical evidence concerning the superior efficiency of competition-based policy instruments over command-based techniques is inconclusive, the popularity of the former within political rhetoric can be at least partly explained by their ideological attraction. In other words, competition-based techniques resonated with the rise of a political ideology associated with liberal capitalism that sought to 'roll back the frontiers of the state' and remove (or at least reduce) the apparent burdens of regulation from the shoulders of industry. In the context of this macro-political and ideological rhetoric, competition-based tools represented a move away from a paternalistic, interventionist state, enabling greater scope for free enterprise, participation and individual autonomy. But despite this powerful deregulatory rhetoric and the theoretical appeal of competition-based techniques, they have been used relatively infrequently in practice. Ogus offers possible [micro] political explanations.

A. Ogus, 'Regulation' (1994)

Whatever the merits of EIs, it is not difficult to understand the reluctance of legislatures to use them. In general, as we have seen, in formulating regulatory policy politicians are expected to respond to pressures from both sectional interest groups - notably those representing industry — and ideological interest groups, e.g. environmentalists. Although the influence of the former tends to be stronger than that of the latter, some compromise between the respective demands of the two groups normally emerges. In the present context, however, the environmentalist lobby has combined with the industrial lobby in opposing EIs.

The opposition of environmentalists to EIs can be explained on several grounds. First, they expect governments to respond to the pollution crisis by the adoption of immediate and tough measures. Mandatory CAC standards, cast in a suitably rigorous form, are seen to meet this demand; EIs, which rely on voluntary behaviour and are characterized as 'licences to pollute', are not. Secondly, the use of the criminal law and its institutions stigmatizes pollution; EIs, which involve merely administrative intervention, are morally neutral. Thirdly, the assumption of rational economic behaviour which underpins the arguments for EIs is treated with scepticism. How does economism deal with the crusty general-manager who believes that the old ways of disposing of toxic wastes are the best and that no new-fangled effluent tax is going to change his tried and true practices? Legalism does have a way of dealing with this not-so-uncommon menace to the public health; it takes him to court and threatens to shut his plant down.

Fourthly, as regards taxes, governments cannot be trusted to use the proceeds for environmental purposes; and, as regards subsidies, why should taxpayers support polluters?

The political appeal of this last point is overwhelming and certainly sufficient to dampen the demand by polluting industries for subsidies. Industrial opposition to tax systems is no less difficult to comprehend. Such systems would seem to require polluting firms to pay twice: they pay not only for the technical equipment necessary to abate pollution, but also for emissions which they are unable to abate. Moreover, the collection of taxes is a matter of administrative routine and difficult to obstruct. The very effectiveness of tax systems in imposing costs therefore makes them much less attractive to polluters than CAC regimes, the enforcement agencies of which can be persuaded not to prosecute.

Finally, the influence of the agencies themselves in resisting EIs should not be underestimated. The discretion conferred on them by CAC regimes enables them to enjoy power, prestige, and job satisfaction; administration of a tax system provides little by way of equivalent benefit.

While the above extract from Ogus demonstrates how political considerations may favour *command*-based tools, the rise of 'third way' politics associated with the Blair administration's first term of office in the UK, or the Clinton administration's second term of office in the US, provides ideological underpinnings in favour of *consensual*-based techniques involving 'public-private partnerships' (see Section 3.2.6) and *communication*-based techniques of control that seek to preserve individual choice. The ideological appeal of these techniques is discussed in the following two extracts.

K. Yeung, '*Securing compliance*' (2004)

... Ayres and Braithwaite's responsive regulation may be viewed in the context of increasing calls to develop regulatory processes and institutional structures that will enhance deliberation and enable participation, which Black identifies as proceeding under the banners of reflexive law, responsive regulation, or most broadly, 'proceduralisation', all of which ascribe a critical role to deliberative, participatory procedures as a means for securing regulatory objectives ....

In seeking to understand the disagreement concerning the desirability of [collaborative] ... approaches, we may draw from the voluminous literature that has developed in response to the 'alternative dispute resolution' ('ADR') movement ...

... As a means of dispute-resolution and form of social ordering, negotiation and bargaining in general are often claimed by ADR advocates to generate a number of other practical benefits when contrasted with formal adjudication. ADR advocates seek to emphasise its informality (implying that it is less alienating and intimidating to ordinary citizens), low cost, width and ease of access, and speed of operation. But in addition to these practical claims, all of which can be regarded as various aspects of the negotiation process that may promote effectiveness in decision-making, lies a further ideological dimension. In particular, it is claimed that because the resolution of disputes through negotiation and bargaining relies primarily on the consent of its participants, who together arrive at a mutually satisfactory outcome, it is more consistent with individual autonomy and freedom than is formal adjudication. Because the latter operates predominantly on the basis of coercion rather than consent, it thus reflects a paternalistic and interventionist state. Modes of resolution that are primarily consent-based are thus claimed to be associated with images of accommodation, conciliation, inclusiveness and participation. Court adjudication, on the other hand, is alleged to be associated with notions of combat, hostility, formality, resistance and exclusion.

Bargaining and the rule of law

Enthusiasm for dispute processing by means that do not involve the formal process of law is, however, far from universal. Richard Abel, one of the staunchest critics of the movement to introduce large scale ADR mechanisms in North America, argues that processes of 'informal justice' involve techniques of subtle manipulation in which the state is able to expand its apparatus of control over citizens. Informal processes simply disguise rather than eliminate coercion, providing the forum in which the 'velvet glove has largely hidden the iron fist.' In a similar vein, Auerbach claims that ADR techniques have operated in practice to disempower and exclude the socially disadvantaged. It is the weak and the poor who are denied the opportunity to avail themselves of their formal legal rights which remain the domain of the bourgeois elite who can afford to invoke the formal process and protections of the law. These largely political objections are essentially grounded in deep-seated scepticism of the ability of methods of alternative dispute resolution to live up to their promises when translated into a world fraught with distributional inequalities.

Both Abel and Auderbach acknowledge, however, that the values to which ADR aspires are nevertheless worthy of allegiance. In this respect, Fiss's arguments 'against settlement' reach further still. To him, '[t]o settle for something means to accept less than some ideal.' Fiss's objections to settlement rest on a particular view of the proper function of adjudication. In his view, the purpose of adjudication is not merely to resolve disputes, but to explicate and give force to the authority of legal rules, to interpret the values upon which they are grounded and to bring reality into accord with them. Thus, when legal disputes are resolved outside the court, this purpose is left wanting. For Fiss, informal non-adjudicative justice is justice denied ....

... Fiss's objections point to an inherent tension between the use of negotiation and bargaining as a mechanism of decision-making and dispute-resolution and the rule of law, objections which resonate strongly in the critiques of the North American collaborative compliance approaches to regulatory policy implementation alluded to in the preceding section.

... Because the resolution of disputes through negotiation is shaped by the reciprocal needs and interests of the parties worked out through their bargain, rather than dictated by legal rules, it can be seen as contrary to the rule of law ideal. This is not to say, however, that legal rules have no part to play in the resolution of disputes by negotiation. Rather, participants are claimed to bargain 'in the shadow of the law' so that the outcome ultimately agreed to will be shaped and constrained by the strict legal rights and duties of the parties. But when legal disputes are settled by agreement rather than by adjudication, the resulting agreement need not reflect that which would have resulted from court adjudication through the application of legal rules.

While the preceding extract draws attention to the ideological attractions of negotiation and bargaining, on the one hand, contrasting them with rule of law values typically associated with adjudicatory processes on the other, the following extract explores the ideology associated with communication-based tools.

K. Yeung, '*Government by publicity management: Sunlight or spin?*' (2005)

... despite [its] limitations, communications management techniques (both in the form of public communications management and mandatory disclosure regimes) may offer considerable ideological appeal. Although many of the tools and techniques available to the government in seeking to implement its policy objectives are often viewed in dichotomous pairs, information-based techniques of control tend not to be discussed in contrast to, or in opposition from, a particular "partner" tool or technique. But, rather than being viewed as the unhappy singleton within a broader community of regulatory tools and techniques, information-based approaches may be seen as offering an attractive "third way" form of government intervention. Such approaches may be seen as offering an appealing compromise between heavy-handed paternalistic intervention (such as banning or restricting production), on the one hand, and a laissez-faire approach on the other. Central to such approaches is the preservation of individual choice. By providing knowledge and information, the state may be seen as acting deliberately and positively to empower and enable citizens to take decisions that best reflect their personal preferences, rather than constraining or restricting their available choices, whilst avoiding the charge of sitting idly by and providing no assistance to citizens confronted by a barrage of social and industrial hazards on a daily basis. It is the rhetoric of choice that may be seen as underpinning many of the techniques employed from the early 1990s onwards in the regulation of state schools in England which included the publication of official school league tables and the naming and shaming of so-called "failing schools" by Ofsted with the aim of promoting the education market-place. The publication of official school league tables was intended to operate in the context of giving parents (theoretically at least) the right to express a preference over choice of school, in which funding follows the pupil so that school budgets were determined largely by pupil numbers, providing schools with incentives to attract as many pupils as possible. As a result, popular schools would be expected to grow whilst unpopular ones would shrink. While this is not the place to provide a critique of regulatory reforms in the delivery of secondary education, it provides a useful illustration of the political and ideological appeal of communication-based policy techniques and may serve to provide at least a partial explanation of their increasing popularity within the current political climate.

The rhetoric of choice that is often associated with the use of public communications management techniques points to another claim that magnifies their attractiveness to policymakers. By providing a potential means for enhancing transparency in government, such techniques may be seen as promoting an informed citizenry and giving concrete expression to the so-called "right to know" that is considered fundamental to a flourishing democratic society. Attempts by regulatory authorities to draw public attention to their activities may thus be seen as laudable attempts to open up the "black box" of government activity and decision-making to public scrutiny. Just as the "open justice" principle requires transparency in the making of judicial decisions, so too is transparency required in the making of governmental decisions. Seen in this light, agency-generated publicity drawing attention to their activities may be regarded as a welcome means by which transparency and accountability in governmental decision-making is promoted.

While the arguments from transparency and accountability in government appear to provide powerful support for public communications management techniques, they might not withstand critical scrutiny. In reflecting upon these claims, the argument from choice may be seen as directly linked to the argument from transparency. By increasing the level of publicly available information about a particular service or activity, the level of transparency associated with the conduct of that activity is enhanced, and the citizen is correspondingly empowered to make more informed choices about the activity in question. But ... although public communications management techniques may involve the dissemination of factual information, they may also include strategies of selective disclosure and the communication of particular ideas or messages with relatively little or no factual content. In other words, public communications management may be seen as a strategic, purposive communicative activity, undertaken by government to achieve particular objectives, seeking to shape public attitudes towards particular activities or issues rather than being necessarily concerned with disseminating factual information. Although some might regard such techniques as enhancing transparency and openness in government, others might regard them more cynically as attempts by the administration to influence and shape public opinion so as to portray itself in a positive light. ...

When viewed in this light, the public communications management activities of government agencies may be indistinguishable from the various communications-based strategies adopted by other social institutions in the political arena striving to win the support of public opinion as part of the on-going, dynamic struggle for wealth, prestige, power and influence. So conceived, public communications management techniques adopted by government authorities may be no different from the strategies and techniques adopted by private firms in seeking to harness media publicity to market their products, or in seeking to sway the tide of public opinion in their favour as an indirect means of lobbying politicians to adopt pro-business policies. To this end, public relations professionals are engaged in ever increasing numbers with Davies observing that, over the last two decades, British organisations from a wide range of sectors, including unions, pressure groups, religious organisations, charities, local councils and other state institutions have engaged public relations professionals to help achieve their objectives. Davies also claims that public relations professionals are not simply being utilised to improve organisational image (or "brand") with the public, but to achieve a number of specific objectives, including influencing policy makers, raising share prices, winning industrial disputes, increasing income, and generating interest in particular issues and new cultural products. Similarly, while Jackall observes that public relations serves a number of functions, its basic goal is to "get one's story out to important publics" enabling managers to "try to shape and control the main dimensions of public opinion in an unsettled social order".

If the use of public relations professionals and public communications management techniques are understood in this way, such techniques appear broadly consistent with the activities referred to by political scientists as "presentational strategies" (techniques adopted by politicians and bureaucrats, selecting arguments to minimise or avoid blame as part of the so-called "blame game") or as "impression management" strategies by scholars of organisational communications (a sub-field of organisational theory within management studies) drawing from studies and observations by social psychologists. Impression management has been defined as "any behaviour that has the purpose of controlling or manipulating the attributions and impressions formed of that person by others by controlling the information that is presented about the actor." From these perspectives, "public communications management" may provide a more respectable label for what may otherwise be understood as propaganda. Although the term "propaganda" is typically reserved for the spreading of subversive, debatable or slanted information, Lasswell (a leading communications sociologist) has defined it "in the broadest sense" as "the technique of influencing human action by the manipulation of representations", in which the propagandist's aim is "to intensify attitudes favourable to his purposes, to reverse obstructive attitudes, to win the indifferent or at least prevent them from becoming antagonistic". Lasswell's understanding of the task of a propagandist appears largely to mirror the tasks of the public relations professional, which may suggest that the government communications professional is simply a species of propagandist, employed to facilitate the government's public communications aims and objectives.

Although government communications professionals may object to being described as propagandists, the term is useful for it both calls into question the claim that public communications management techniques enhance transparency and accountability and highlights the importance of articulating the underlying assumptions upon which any normative critique of policy instruments is based. As Weiss has observed, the intrusiveness of government information policies is a vigorously contested matter. Optimistic critiques accept that public communications activities bolster transparency in government and enhance citizen choice, regarding such techniques as the "softest and most lenient instrument in the government toolkit". In contrast, more pessimistic critiques may regard such activities as a potentially dangerous form of propaganda, distorting the information and ideas available to citizens, utilising the power and resources of government to spread some ideas and perspectives (but not others), thereby disempowering, manipulating and inducing passivity in citizens, yet enhancing the power and status of government officials. Accordingly, reliable generalisations about the contribution of such techniques towards enhancing or undermining transparency and accountability in government, or in enriching citizen choice, are likely to remain elusive. Any such evaluation will inevitably be a function both of the quality of information and messages communicated and the ways in which the policy implementation and democratic processes are conceived and understood.

3.3.3   Discussion questions

1. How can Cooter's suggested distinction between prices and sanctions assist in choosing between alternative regulatory instruments?
2. What do Gunningham and Grabosky mean by 'smart' regulation?
3. How do you think Neiman would view 'smart' regulation?
4. Do notions of 'punishment' and 'retribution' have a legitimate role to play in regulatory design?
5. Is there any relationship between the role that law plays in the operation of particular regulatory tools and the legitimacy of those tools?
6. How, if at all, are ideological concerns relevant to instrument choice?
7. What are the implications for regulatory design of an autopoietic approach to regulation?
8. What is the relationship between tool-efficacy and tool-legitimacy?
9. How, if at all, would the various theories of regulation affect the choice of regulatory instrument?

3.4   Conclusion

This chapter's selective survey of literature on how to regulate reveals a broad and diverse terrain, encompassing disciplinary concerns and methodological approaches that vary widely in the scope of their analysis, the kinds of questions asked and the assumptions they make. In order to acquire a better understanding of the mechanics by which regulatory instruments affect behaviour, scholars have developed many different classification schemes. The system adopted in this chapter groups instruments into five broad classes: command, competition, consensus, communication and code, with each class based on the modality of control primarily in operation. This classification system bears no claim to superiority, let alone infallibility, but it provides a heuristic device for examining the mechanics of control and – in particular – it helps to illuminate the law's role in supporting regulatory instruments. Drawing together the strands of that discussion, the law's facilitative role operates in two different but related ways, represented by two images: *law as threat* and *law as umpire*. In the former case, it is the law's coercive force — its capacity to intervene directly in the affairs of its citizens — that is highlighted. In the latter, as we discussed in the previous chapter, it is the law's capacity to create stable frameworks in which citizens are free to interact and transact with each other.

The exploration of regulatory tools is especially helpful for illustrating how the visibility of the law's threatening face may vary, depending upon the class and particular type of tool under consideration. As we emphasised in Chapter 1, our use of 'images' such as law as threat is meant as a broad indicia that helps summarise empirical variation, and not as an abstract philosophical claim about the nature of law. Law's threatening face is most apparent in the use of command-based instruments, operating in the foreground of regulatory regimes with the aim of deterring undesirable behaviour through fear of the sanctions that may be imposed if the law's command is violated. At its most hidden, the law's threat recedes from view — particularly where consent-based systems rest on social norms and consensus, rather than legal coercion, as the means through which behaviour is influenced. In these instances, the law provides a background threat, reflected in the regulated community's fear that interventionist mechanisms may be introduced if regulation through social consensus is considered inadequate. But the law's threat may also operate at an intermediate level, lurking in the shadows but not entirely hidden, as a means for buttressing the law's umpiring function: providing fall-back coercive mechanisms to establish structural frameworks that enable and facilitate freedom of action and expression. At this intermediate level, the law's facilitative dimension is brought to the fore, in seeking to create and maintain a stable, open and fair space in which people may transact freely in response to the competitive forces of the market: be it in the product market (underpinning competition-based tools), quasi-markets within bureaucracies, or the marketplace of ideas (underpinning communication-based tools) by guaranteeing the security of transactions and expression, respectively.

The law's influence upon the mechanics and choice of regulatory tool is not, however, limited to its facilitative functions. In reflecting upon questions of tool choice, scholars have also drawn attention to the law's expressive dimension. In this guise, the law operates not as deterrent, or in ensuring adherence to regulatory requirements, but as a means of institutionalising values, be they moral principles expressed in legal prohibitions, community desires demanded through democratic processes or constitutional values. The law's expressive dimension is most apparent within command-based mechanisms, where punitive sanctions may be imposed for violating the law's command. Expressive dimensions of law are also present in the influence of political, ideological, constitutional, cultural and social traditions on questions of tool choice and implementation. But the contours and application of law's expressive dimension are sites of scholarly disagreement and debate. Variations in the law's expressive role will be one of the important themes which we will explore in the next chapter, especially where socio-legal scholars have examined how regulatory officials behave when enforcing regulatory norms.

References

Abel, R. 1982. *The Politics of Informal Justice*, Los Angeles: Academic Press.

Auerbach, J. 1983. *Justice Without Law?*, New York: Oxford University Press.

Ayres, I. and Braithwaite, J. 1992. *Responsive Regulation*, New York: Oxford University Press, 101–132.

Black, J. 1998. 'Talking about regulation', *Public Law* 77–105.

    2000. 'Proceduralising regulation', *Oxford Journal of Legal Studies* 20: 597–614.

Breyer, S. 1982. *Regulation and its Reform*, Cambridge: Harvard University Press, 156–181.

Brownsword, R. 2005. 'Code, control and choice: Why East is East and West is West', *Legal Studies* 25: 1–21.

Calabresi, G. and Melamud, A.D. 1972. 'Property rules, liability rules, and inalienability: One view of the cathedral', *Harvard Law Review* 85: 1089–1128.

Cooter, R. 1984. 'Prices and sanctions', *Columbia Law Review* 84: 1523–1552.

Daintith, T. 1994. 'The techniques of government' in Jowell and Oliver (eds.), *The Changing Constitution*, Oxford: Clarendon Press , 209–236.

Davies, A. 2002. *Public Relations Democracy*, Manchester: Manchester University Press.

Fiss, O. 1984. 'Against settlement', *Yale Law Journal* 93: 1073–1090.

Garland, D. 2001. *The Culture of Control*, Oxford: Oxford University Press.

Gunningham, N. and Grabosky, P. 1998. *Smart Regulation*, Oxford: Clarendon Press.

Hirsch, F.L. 1978. *The Social Limits to Growth*, Cambirdge, MA: Harvard University Press.

Jackall, R. 1995. 'The magic lantern: The world of public relations', in Jackall (ed.), *Propaganda*, London: Macmillan.

Lasswell, H. 1995. 'Propaganda', in Jackall (ed.), *Propaganda*, London: Macmillan.

Luhmann, N. 1991–92. 'The coding of the legal system', in *European Yearbook in the Sociology of Law*, 145–185.

Magat, W.A. and Viscusi, W.K. 1992. *Informational Approaches to Regulation*, Cambridge, MA: MIT Press.

Neiman, M. 1980. 'The virtues of heavy-handedness in government', *Law & Policy Quarterly*, 2: 11–34.

Ogus, A. 1994. *Regulation*, Oxford: Clarendon Press, 245–256.

    1995. 'Rethinking self-regulation', *Oxford Journal of Legal Studies*, 15: 97–108.

2002. 'Comparing regulatory systems: Institutions, processes and legal forms in industrialised countries', *Centre on Regulation and Competition*, University of Manchester, Working Paper No. 35.

Pakenham, F. 1961. *The Idea of Punishment*, London: Geoffrey Chapman.

Salamon, L. (ed.) 2002. *The Tools of Government*, Oxford: Oxford University Press.

Schultze, C. L. 1977. *The Public Use of Private Interest*, Washington: Brookings Institution.

Scott, C. 2004. 'Regulation in the age of governance: The rise of the post-regulatory state', in Jordana and Levi-Faur (eds.), *The Politics of Regulation*, Cheltenham: Edward Elgar, 145–174.

Teubner, G. (ed.) 1987. *Juridification of Social Spheres: A Comparative Analysis of Labor, Corporate, Antitrust and Social Welfare Law*, Berlin: Mouton de Gruyter.

1997. 'Global Bukowina: Legal pluralism in the world society' in Teubner (ed.), *Global Law without a State*, Dartmouth: Aldershot, 3–30.

1998. 'After privatization: The many autonomies of private law', *Current Legal Problems* 51: 393–424.

Viscusi, W. and Zeckhauser, R. J. 1979. 'Optimal standards with incomplete enforcement', *Public Policy* 27: 437–456.

Weiss, J. 2002. 'Public information', in Salamon (ed.) *The Tools of Government: A Guide to the New Governance*, New York: Oxford University Press.

Yeung, K. 2004. *Securing Compliance: A Principled Approach*, Oxford: Hart Publishing, Oxford.

2005. 'Government by publicity management: Sunlight or spin?', *Public Law*, 360–383.

Suggested further reading

Braithwaite, J. 2002. *Restorative Justice and Responsive Regulation*, New York: Oxford University Press.

Brigham, J. and Brown, D. 1980. 'Distinguishing penalties and incentives', *Law & Policy Quarterly* 2: 5–10.

Collins, H. 1999. *Regulating Contracts*, Oxford: Oxford University Press, Chapter 4.

Daintith, T. 1998. 'Legal measures and their analysis' in Baldwin, Hood and Scott (eds.), *A Reader on Regulation*, Oxford: Oxford University Press, 349–372.

Dana, D. 2000. 'The emerging regulatory contract paradigm in environmental regulation', *University of Illinois Law Review* 9: 35–60.

Hood, C. 1983. *The Tools of Government*, London: Macmillan

Majone, G. 1997. 'The new european agencies: Regulation by information', *Journal of European Public Policy* 4: 262–275.

Scott, C. and Murray, A. 2002. 'Controlling the new media: Hybrid responses to new forms of power', *Modern Law Review* 65: 491–516.

Sinclair, D. 1997. 'Self-regulation and command and control: Beyond false dichotomies', *Law and Policy* 19: 529–560.

Tietenberg, T. H. 1990. 'Economic instruments for environmental regulation', *Oxford Review of Economic Policy* 6: 17–33.

Twining, W. and Miers, D. 1991. *How to Do Things with Rules*, London: Weidenfeld, 3rd ed.

Vickers, J. and Kay, J. 1994. 'Regulatory reform – an appraisal' in Wheeler (ed.), *A Reader on the Law of the Business Enterprise*, Oxford: Oxford University Press.

4

Regulatory enforcement and compliance

4.1   Introduction

In the previous chapter, we considered various techniques of regulation. In so doing, our aim was to answer the question of how to regulate; this chapter deepens and extends that inquiry by considering questions of regulatory enforcement and compliance. The previous chapter's analysis of regulatory techniques sought to understand the range of instruments used in pursuit of regulatory goals. But all regulatory techniques must be given flesh through the enforcement process if they are to achieve their intended purpose. By focusing on enforcement and compliance, we begin to draw into focus the dynamic, messy and socially contextual nature of the regulatory process.

Before proceeding, it is helpful to clarify our terminology. Within regulatory regimes that rest upon a command and control framework, there is a tendency in common parlance to equate enforcement with the prosecution of offences: the formal invocation of the legal process in order to impose sanctions for violating the law. One important contribution of the regulatory compliance and enforcement literature, however, is to highlight the pervasiveness of informal practices throughout the enforcement process. As Hutter points out:

> Compliance is a concept relevant to all forms of enforcement, but the concept is used in a variety of ways in the regulation literature . . . A theme running through much regulation literature is that compliance with regulatory legislation should be regarded as much as a process as an event. Regulatory officials may regard compliance both as a matter of instant conformity and an open-ended and long-term process which may take several years to attain. Edelman seeks to shift the emphasis to the process of compliance, especially in view of the belief that compliance is a social and political process that evolves over time. . . . Many early studies of regulatory enforcement began with the question of how regulators use the law and what they aim to achieve. . . . It was argued that enforcement of the law did not refer simply to legal action but to a wide array of informal enforcement techniques including education, advice, persuasion and negotiation. These were used by all law enforcement officials, but came into particular prominence in the regulatory arena. (Hutter 1997: 12–14)

The widespread and extensive use of informal techniques for securing compliance may indicate uncertainty over the objectives or purposes of compliance and enforcement activity. As Yeung has observed:

> Throughout the literature concerned with regulatory enforcement, it is typically claimed, rather ambiguously, that the purpose of regulatory enforcement is to 'secure compliance'. But with what must compliance be secured? Regulatory theorists appear to use the phrase not only by reference to compliance with the collective goals underpinning a regulatory scheme, but also by reference to compliance with regulatory standards. The lack of clarity is exacerbated by the tendency of some theorists to use the term interchangeably and inconsistently, sometimes referring to compliance with regulatory standards, but on other occasions referring to compliance with collective goals. The issue is not merely a linguistic, terminological difficulty, for the two reference points, collective goals and regulatory standards, may not necessarily be consistent. So for example, the phenomenon of 'creative compliance', whereby technical compliance with rules may be achieved yet the underlying spirit and purpose of those rules might be simultaneously undermined, is well known. If regulatory standards have been poorly designed, they may fail to influence behaviour in the manner intended, with the result that compliance with regulatory standards may not promote compliance with the scheme's collective goals. And even if standards are well-designed, it is possible to envisage circumstances in which insistence on compliance with standards in situations involving technical or trivial violations could be counterproductive, undermining a general culture of commitment on the part of the regulated community towards the scheme's collective goals. In short, it is possible to distinguish between "rule compliance" on the one hand and "substantive compliance" with collective goals on the other, and the two may not always be coextensive. (Yeung 2004: 11)

In the previous chapter, we observed a tendency for lawyers and policy-makers to think of regulation primarily in terms of classical regulation in command and control form. Although enforcement action is necessary within all regulatory regimes, the literature on enforcement and compliance has predominantly focused on enforcement taking place within a command and control regime. Accordingly, the chapter begins with an examination of the problems associated with the design, interpretation and application of the law's command, where that command takes the form of legally enforceable rules. While the problems of rules are rooted in the uncertain and imprecise character of human communication, communication is also the avenue through which some of the limitations of rules can be overcome. It is the human dimension of regulatory enforcement that forms the focus of a well-developed socio-legal literature concerned with observing, understanding and documenting the behaviour of regulatory enforcement officials in agency-specific contexts.

The second part of our examination considers prescriptive models constructed by regulatory scholars, often with the aim of guiding public enforcement officials in making enforcement decisions. While much of the literature in this field has concerned variety in regulatory enforcement styles, there is also a related but distinct literature concerned with regulatory sanctions and the liability rules attaching to those sanctions; this is examined in the third part of the chapter when considering the role of public and private actors in the enforcement process. The chapter concludes by reflecting on the role of law in regulatory enforcement and compliance. As the chapter unfolds, we shall see that central to the study and analysis of regulatory enforcement is the width of discretion within regulatory systems (in the hands of both public and private actors), providing ample scope for human action, error, manipulation and creativity.

4.2   The limits of rules

All regulatory regimes requiring some form of enforcement mechanism to achieve their goals rely upon the use of rules to guide the conduct of members of the regulated community. But rules are not self-executing, and scholars have devoted considerable energy to understanding the challenges associated with the use of rules as a mechanism for guiding behaviour. Many (although by no means all) of these problems are attributable to the indeterminate nature of rules, which is itself a product of the inherent indeterminacy of language and the subjective and contingent nature of how the surrounding factual context in which rules are applied is understood. The nature and source of these difficulties are highlighted in the following extract.

J. Black, '*Rules and regulators*' (1997)
The nature of rules
> The three main problems associated with the use of rules in any context, and on which all who write about rules agree, are their tendency to over- or under-inclusiveness, their indeterminacy, and their interpretation. These problems stem from two roots: the nature of rules and the nature of language. Prescriptive rules are anticipatory, generalized abstractions, and when endowed with legal status are distinctive, authoritative forms of communication. They are also linguistic structures: how we understand, interpret, and apply rules depends in part on how we understand and interpret language. In considering the nature and limitations of rules, a legal analysis of the roles which rules are asked to play in a regulatory system needs thus to be coupled to an examination of these linguistic properties.

> **Inclusiveness**
> Rules are generalizations: they group together particular instances or attributes of an object or occurrence and abstract or generalize from them to build up a category or definition which then forms the operative basis of the rule. Say, for example, that following a lunch in a restaurant in which my black labrador dog, Rufus, has been particularly disruptive the proprietor wants to make a rule to

ensure such disruption does not happen again. She will consider which aspects of the event should form the operative basis of the rule, what the rule should 'bite' on. In doing that, she would need to assess which of the various aspects of Rufus (Rufus, black, dog, mine, in restaurant) were relevant to the fact of the disruption. She could consider banning all black things or all things called Rufus, but, as far as we know, not all black things or indeed Rufuses are necessarily disruptive, and the fact that Rufus was black or his name was Rufus were not causes of the disruption. Rather she should focus on the fact that Rufus was a dog, and so form a rule, 'no dogs allowed'.

The rule in this example is straightforward, but the process of rule formation is not. In making the generalization, the rule maker is choosing from a range of individual properties which an event or object possesses; in making that choice she searches for the aspect of the particular which is causally relevant to the aim of the rule: the goal which is sought to be achieved or the harm which is sought to be avoided. It is thus the overall aim or purpose of the rule which determines which among a range of generalizations should be chosen as the operative fact or facts for the ensuing rule. However in forming the generalization, which is the operative basis of the rule, only some features of the particular event or object are focused on and are then projected onto future events, beyond the particulars which served as the paradigm or archetype for the formation of the generalization. The generalizations in rules are thus simplifications of complex events, objects or courses of behaviour. Aspects of those events will thus be left out, or 'suppressed' by the generalization. Further, the generalization, being necessarily selective, will also include some properties which will in some circumstances be irrelevant.

Purpose thus interacts with the generalization. The inclusiveness of a rule (or more accurately, its generalization) is a function of the rule's purpose or justification. It is the imperfect match between the rule and its purpose which is represented in the description of rules as over- or under-inclusive. This mismatch can occur for three reasons. First, as noted, the generalization which is the operative basis of the rule inevitably suppresses properties that may subsequently be relevant or includes properties that may in some cases be irrelevant. Secondly, the causal relationship between the event and the harm/goal is likely to be only an approximate one: the generalization bears simply a probable relationship to the harm sought to be avoided or goal sought to be achieved. Thirdly, even if a perfect causal match between the generalization and the aim of the rule could be achieved, future events may develop in such a way that it ceases to be so. ...

It follows from this that over or under-inclusiveness, although inherent, is likely to be exacerbated in certain circumstances, viz., where the context in which the rule operates is one which is subject to frequent change, where the course of change is unforeseeable, where the range of situations in which the rule will apply is great, and where there is an uncertain causal relationship between the events, objects or behaviour focused on and the harm to be avoided or goal to be achieved....

Inclusiveness can be taken as a sign of the 'success' or 'failure' of a rule. Legal rules, and particularly regulatory rules, perform social management and instrumental functions. Rules are embodiments of policy decisions, and their success is measured in terms of the extent to which they ensure that the substance of policy is achieved. The fundamental demand for congruence between the rule and its purpose derives from this instrumental view. Under-inclusion can represent 'missed targets'; over-inclusion, excessive intrusion. . . . Where over inclusiveness at 'rule-level' is not mitigated by flexible application at the 'site-level', Bardach and Kagan argue, this leads to both economic inefficiencies and in particular to damaging social implications, as regulatees suffer the experience of being subjected to unreasonable regulatory requirements. This in turn affects their attitude to the regulation, undermining commitment to it, destroying co-operation, generating perceptions of injustice, and stimulating political and legal resistance . . . .

Indeterminacy

Rules are also inherently indeterminate. Their indeterminacy arises in part from the nature of language, in part from their anticipatory nature, and in part because they rely on others for their application. Their indeterminacy matters because rules, particularly legal rules, are entrenched, authoritative statements which are meant to guide behaviour, be applied on an indefinite number of occasions, and which have sanctions attached for their breach. It is thus important to know whether this particular occasion is one of those in which the rule should be applied. The most familiar exponent of the indeterminacy of legal rules is Hart, who described rules as having a 'core' of meaning and a 'penumbra of uncertainty' or 'fringe of vagueness'. The indeterminacy arises not because the meaning of the word is unclear in itself, but because in applying the rule the question would always arise as to whether the general term used in the rule applied to this particular fact situation. 'Particular fact situations do not await us already marked off from each other, and labelled as instances of the general rule, the application of which is in question; nor can the rule itself step forward to claim its own instances.' There will be cases in which the general expression will be clearly applicable; in others it will not. There may be fact situations which possess only some features of the plain case, but others which they lack. This indeterminacy in application Hart described as the 'open texture' of rules. The concept of open texture was drawn from a theory of language developed by Waismann, although Hart recast it in his theory of rules, and it has been used by others, notably Schauer, to show why rules can be inherently indeterminate. In Hart's analysis, as in Schauer's, open texture stems from the inability of rule makers to anticipate all future events and possibilities: 'the necessity for such choice is thrust upon us because we are men, not gods'. So even if consensus could gradually be built up as to the 'core meaning' of a particular term, the vagaries of future events would mean that there would still be instances 'thrown up by nature or human invention' which would possess only some of the features of the paradigm case or cases but not others . . . Rules thus have an inherent vagueness which stems not from language but from the prospective generalizations which characterize rules - even if determinant, the limits of human foresight mean that the least vague term may turn out to be vague when applied to a situation unforeseen when the term was defined.

Interpretation

... Rules need a sympathetic audience if they are to be interpreted and applied in a way which will further the purpose for which they were formed; rule maker and rule applier are to this extent in a reciprocal relationship. Such a sympathetic interpretation is essentially what those who advocate a purposive approach to interpretation demand. Problems of inclusiveness and determinacy or certainty can be addressed by interpreting the rule in accordance with its underlying aim. By contrast, the purpose of the rule could be defeated if the rule is interpreted literally, if things suppressed by the generalization remain suppressed.

Rules also need an informed audience, one which understands the context of assumptions and practices in which the rule is based, which gave rise to it, and which it is trying to address. As practices change, the application of rules needs to change with them. As we have seen, rules can never be sufficiently explicit to cover every circumstance. Nor can they ever express all the tacit understandings on which the rule is based as to those practices or to the state of the world. A rule 'no dogs allowed' relies on the shared understanding of what a 'dog' is; it does not need to then go on to define 'dog' into its semantic components. To the extent that the rule does have to define the terms which it contains, it becomes increasingly precise, with consequent implications for inclusiveness and formalism, complexity and certainty, discussed below.

A rule, then, is only as good as its interpretation. To follow Hart again, rules cannot apply themselves, they rely on others for their application. To be applied, rules have to be interpreted. ... Although a purposive interpretation could ameliorate some of the limitations of rules, such an interpretation may not in practice be that which the rule receives. The problems of interpretation ... also cover the honest perplexity of those subject to the rule of its application in a particular circumstance, which in turn can affect the certainty of the rule's operation. Given then the centrality of interpretation for the operation of rules, how can the rule maker know how the rule will be interpreted and applied? What is the relationship between rules and their interpretation? The theoretical literature exploring the relationship between rules and interpretation is considerable ... and [it] could provide a basis for addressing one of the central problems with rules: their interpretation and application (even by well-intentioned addressees concerned to 'do the best' by the rule) ....

[W]e are not concerned with meaning per se, and whether there is an objectively 'correct' or 'real' meaning, for example. Rather what we are concerned with is how that rule will be interpreted and applied by those it is regulating; not how it should be. In this vein, the most suggestive line of work is that of the conventionalist school, which is concerned with how the meaning of rules is constructed and hence how rules are interpreted and applied.

The writing in this area is extensive; however within it the writings of Wittgenstein have been some of the most influential. Wittgenstein was concerned with unreflective rule following, in mathematics or language, and not with legal rules. His theory has nevertheless spawned a considerable debate on legal rule following and application.

He argued that automatic, unreflective rule following arose from shared judgements in the meaning and application of that rule. If language is to be a means of communication there must be agreement not only in definitions but also (queer as this may sound) in judgements.

Judgements include all the connections we make in our actions between language and the world: between a rule and its application, for example, or between how we have used a term in the past and whether we apply it to a particular new instance. Agreement in judgements arises in turn from shared understandings arising from shared 'forms of life'. The concept of forms of life is cultural; different educations, interests, concerns, human relations or relations to nature constitute distinct forms of life. It includes social contexts, cultures, practices, and training and forms the framework in which our use of language occurs (or our language-game is played, to adopt Wittgenstein's terminology). There are no shared rules without shared patterns of normative actions, and so shared judgements about justifications, criticisms, explanations, descriptions. The interpretation and application of a rule will thus be clear where there is agreement as to the meaning of the rule; agreement in turn comes from shared forms of life.

. . . What relevance has this for the formation and use of rules? . . . What can be drawn from Wittgenstein's analysis for the purposes of understanding the nature of legal rules and their interpretation . . . are three things.

First, that saying a word or rule has a 'literal' or 'plain' meaning means simply that meaning which participants from a community would unreflectively assign to it. A word may have a different 'literal' meaning in different languages, dialects, communities or contexts. It may be that in a community certain terms have very specific meaning; that meaning may not be shared by others outside. So 'jellies' may mean a particular drug to one community, or a type of dessert to another. Words may have particular technical meanings which may be alien to other language users: legal terms provide obvious examples ('consideration' in forming a contract does not mean a display of kindness), others could be terms commonly used in a particular industrial or commercial sector. However, it may nevertheless be the case that some words or phrases commonly have clearer meanings than others. In particular, evaluative terms will normally have a greater range of potentially acceptable interpretations than descriptive terms, particularly quantifiable ones ('reasonable speed' as opposed to '30 miles per hour'). Nevertheless, it may be that words which appear to be open to a wide range of interpretations, 'reasonable' or 'fair' for example, may in fact have very specific meanings in a particular community: what is considered to be a reasonable speed may be interpreted quite specifically (as 20 miles per hour, for example) in a particular community.

Secondly, because meaning and hence the application of a rule is not an objective fact but is contingent on the interpretive community reading the rule, there is no objectively clear rule or plain case. The clarity of a rule is not an objective assessment; rather as Fish notes it is a function of agreement within an interpretive community: 'agreement is not a function of clear and perspicuous rules; it is a function of the fact that interpretive assumptions and procedures are so widely shared in a community that the rule applies to all in the same (interpreted) shape'. This analysis bears directly on the question of certainty of the rule: certainty in relation to a rule means that all who are to apply the rule: regulated, enforcement official, adjudicator, will adopt the same interpretation of the rule. What the conventionalist theory indicates is that certainty is not solely a function of the rule itself, it is a function of the community interpreting the rule. This, it is suggested, has significant implications for forming and using rules. . . .

Finally, the idea of community constructed interpretations offers a theoretical basis for understanding many of the empirical observations as to the responses to rules of those subject to them in bureaucracies and regulatory systems. Studies of bureaucratic behaviour indicate that rules which contain wide, evaluative terms may be interpreted in a quite particular way by officials who are applying them. The regulated may adopt a deliberate interpretive strategy, one of literalism, to defeat the purpose of the rule. This is not simply a failure to adopt a purposive approach, however, although it is that; it is a refusal to 'read in' to the rule things which are suppressed by the generalizations or abstractions which the rule uses, and most significantly a refusal to recognize the tacit understandings on which the rule is based and on which it relies. These understandings may be as to the purpose of the rule, they may also be as to the state of the world or other unformulated rules of conduct. A rule maker can never make sufficiently explicit the tacit assumptions on which the successful application of the rule depends; she will always be prey to those who adopt a 'literal' interpretation of a rule.

The above extract emphasises the subjectivity involved in the interpretation of rules. Although not extracted here, Black goes on to suggest that the interpretative approach taken to any given rule is partly a product of the structure of the rule itself. In particular, she identifies four dimensions along which rules may differ: the substance or scope of a rule, the character or legal status, the sanction attached to a rule and its linguistic structure. The structural form of rules shapes the distribution of discretion or decisional jurisdiction within a regulatory system. So, for example, Black suggests that the use of vague, permissive language can alleviate the likelihood of formalistic interpretations. Like Black, the following extract by Colin Diver is also concerned with the problems arising from rule imprecision, but he adopts an economic rather than a sociological approach. Thus, his concern is not primarily to find ways of reducing interpretive disparity, but to minimise the social costs associated with rule imprecision (although the reduction of interpretive disparity may well reduce these costs). From an economic perspective, the uncertainty associated with the use of rules imposes social costs. The challenge, then, is to reduce the social costs associated with rule imprecision when designing rules to regulate behaviour, and Diver identifies a set of normative prescriptions for achieving the 'optimal' or socially efficient level of rule precision.

C. Diver, '*The optimal precision of administrative rules*' (1983)

I. I. The concept of rule precision

One would naturally expect the concept of rule precision to occupy a central place in any coherent philosophy of law. Yet legal philosophers differ considerably in both the relative significance they attach to formal rules and the attributes of rules with which they are most concerned. Commentators have identified a wide variety of parameters to describe legal rules: generality and clarity, comprehensibility, accuracy of prediction, determinacy, weight, value, and consistency with social purpose. Before we can begin to make useful prescriptions about the precision of administrative rules, we must give the concept some added precision of its own.

A. Three dimensions of rules

The success of a rule in effecting its purpose largely depends on the words a draftsman uses to express his intentions. A rational rulemaker will therefore be attentive to the probable effect of his choice of words upon the rule's intended audience. First, he will want to use words with well-defined and universally accepted meanings within the relevant community. I refer to this quality as "transparency." Second, the rulemaker will want his rule to be "accessible" to its intended audience-that is, applicable to concrete situations without excessive difficulty or effort. Finally, of course, a policymaker will care about whether the substantive content of the message communicated in his words produces the desired behavior. The rule should, in other words, be "congruent" with the underlying policy objective. . . .

. . . Since any criterion for evaluating the "precision" of administrative rules should include these three values, it would be tempting simply to define as "precise" a rule that combined the virtues of transparency, accessibility, and congruence. But two formidable obstacles lie in the path of such a venture — measurement and tradeoffs.

B. The problem of measurement

We must ask initially how to translate the goals of transparency, accessibility, and congruence into usable criteria for evaluating specific rules. To sketch the dimensions of that task, I offer a simple illustration. Imagine a policymaker who must establish certification criteria for commercial aircraft pilots. One aspect of that task is to define the circumstances under which a pilot, once certified, should no longer be eligible to serve in that capacity. Let us suppose our lawmaker has a rough idea of a policy objective: pilots should retire when the social cost of allowing them to continue, measured as the risk of accidents that they might cause multiplied by their consequences, exceeds the social benefit, measured as the costs avoided by not having to find and train a replacement. But how can the lawmaker capture this idea in a legal standard?

Let us initially offer three alternative verbal formulations for such a rule:

Model I: No person may pilot a commercial airplane after his sixtieth birthday.
Model II: No person may pilot a commercial airplane if he poses an unreasonable risk of an accident.

Model III: No person may pilot a commercial airplane if he falls within one of the following categories. (There follow tables displaying all combinations of values for numerous variables, including years and level of experience, hours of air time logged, age, height, weight, blood pressure, heart rate, eyesight, and other vital signs, that would disqualify a pilot from further eligibility to pilot aircraft.)

Which formulation is most transparent? The answer is easy: Model I. Everyone knows exactly what the words "sixtieth" and "birthday" mean. The crucial concept of Model II — "unreasonable" risk — seems, by contrast, susceptible to widely varying interpretations. Suppose, however, that among the rule's intended audience, the term "unreasonable risk of accident" had acquired a very special meaning: namely, "older than 60." In that case, the two rules would be equally transparent. That contingency, however implausible here, nonetheless reminds us of the danger of judging a rule's transparency without looking beyond its words to its actual impact.

The danger inherent in facial evaluation is even more evident in applying the other two criteria. Is the rule of Model II or Model III more accessible? The former is shorter and more memorable. It also apparently requires only a single judgment — the "reasonableness" of the risk. That judgment, however, may well rest on a set of subsidiary inquiries as numerous and complex as those encompassed within Model III's more explicit set of tables.

Similarly, our intuition that Model II is more congruent than, say, Model I, may be unreliable. The facial resemblance between Model II and the rulemaker's ultimate objective depends on the unverifiable assumption that "unreasonable" connotes "economically inefficient."

It might be possible to assess these alternatives by reducing our three values to some empirically measurable form. We could, for example, conduct an experiment in which we present a series of hypothetical questions to a random sample of a rule's intended audience and require them to apply it to specific situations. We might measure the rule's congruence by the ratio of agreement between the respondents' answers and the rulemaker's desired answers. We could use the ratio of internal agreement among respondents to measure the rule's transparency. Finally, we could construct an index of the rule's accessibility by assessing the average time (or money, in a more realistic experiment) that respondents invest in arriving at their answers. These measures, however, are at best only expensive proxies for the values that underlie them.

C. The problem of tradeoffs

Assuming that we could make reliable measurements along each of the three dimensions, we would still have to find a way to aggregate them in an overall evaluation. If transparency always correlated closely with accessibility and congruence, this would present no difficulty. Our three models of a pilot retirement rule, however, suggest that it does not. Each formulation has something to recommend it, but each also presents obvious difficulties. Model I may indeed be amenable to mechanical application, but it will undoubtedly ground many pilots who should continue flying and may allow some to continue who should be grounded. Even if we concede that Model II is simple and faithful to our policy-maker's intentions, it generates widely varying interpretations in individual cases. Model III is commendably objective and may even discriminate accurately between low and high risks. But it achieves this latter objective only at the cost of difficulty in application.

Attempting to escape from these tradeoffs with a fourth option seems hopeless. Suppose we begin with Model I's "age 60" version. Since this rule's greatest flaw is its apparent incongruity, we might try to soften its hard edges by allowing exceptions in particularly deserving cases. We could, for example, permit especially robust sexagenarians to continue flying. But this strategem merely poses a new riddle: how should we define the category of exempt pilots? There are, of course, many choices, but all of them seem to suffer in one degree or another from problems of opacity (e.g., "reasonably healthy"), incongruence (e.g., "able to press 150 pounds and run five miles in 40 minutes"), or inaccessibility (Model III's tables).

Similarly, starting from Model II's "unreasonable risk" standard, we could increase its transparency by appending a list of the components of "unreasonable risk" — for example, "taking into consideration the person's age, physical condition, mental alertness, skill and experience." Yet such laundry lists add relatively little transparency when both the meaning and relative weights of the enumerated terms remain unspecified. Providing the necessary specification, however, makes the standard less congruent or accessible.

II. The optimal degree of regulatory precision

The observation that various verbal formulations are likely to involve differing mixes of transparency, accessibility, and congruence offers little solace to a regulatory draftsman. Tradeoffs may be inevitable, but not all tradeoffs are equally acceptable. What our rulemaker needs is a normative principle for comparing formulations.

Invocation of moral values like fairness, equity, or community offers little promise. Each dimension of regulatory precision implicates important moral principles. Transparent rules help to assure equality by defining when people are "similarly situated" and divorcing the outcome of an official determination from the decision-makers. An accessible rule, by contrast, promotes communal and "dignitary" values by enabling members of its audience to participate in its application to their individual circumstances. Congruence directly fosters the law's substantive moral aims by promoting outcomes in individual cases consistent with those aims.

These principles frequently work at cross-purposes, however, precisely because tradeoffs occur along the three dimensions of precision. A perfectly transparent rule ("no person with a surname ending in a vowel may be a pilot") may assure similar treatment of categorically similar cases, but it may also fail to provide defensible applications. A morally congruent rule ("immorality is prohibited") can be too vague to satisfy the moral imperatives of fair warning and meaningful participation. A perfectly transparent and congruent rule may be so cumbersome as to deprive its audience of fair warning.

A. An efficiency criterion for rule precision

Since tradeoffs among values are unavoidable, the morally sensitive rulemaker must reduce those conflicting values to some common denominator. One candidate is the currency of welfare economics — "social utility." A social utility-maximizing rulemaker would, for any conceivable set of rule formulations, identify and estimate the social costs and benefits flowing from each, and select the one with the greatest net social benefit. Subject to a constraint on his rulemaking budget or authority, the rulemaker would continue adding to his stock of rules so long as the marginal social benefit of the last increment exceeded its marginal cost.

We can use our pilot retirement rule to sketch the dimensions of this task. Suppose our hypothetical policymaker wants to decide whether Model I or Model II is socially preferable. Several considerations argue in favor of Model I. It may, for example, produce a higher level of voluntary compliance, since the rulemaker can more readily charge pilots with its enforcement. For this reason, pilots are less likely to evade or sabotage the rule.

Model I also seems cheaper to enforce. Since it increases accuracy of prediction, there will be fewer requests for interpretation. Since it increases the level of compliance, there will be fewer violations to process. And since it is highly objective, the enforcement agency can quickly and accurately resolve the disputes that do arise. Model II, by contrast, will generate numerous and expensive conflicts. In the absence of clear standards, factfinding and offers of proof will range far and wide. The rule's audience will expend effort in interpreting the meaning of the standard and in making successive elaborations of its meaning in individual cases.

The increased compliance and reduced litigation are counterproductive, however, if a rule induces the wrong result. The age-60 rule will deprive society of the services of safe, experienced sexagenarians. Even the claim that Model I has lower transaction costs must be tempered with skepticism. Arbitrary rules invite demands for modification. Proponents of Model I will spend their days defending the rule and may in the end accede to some exceptions. Processing petitions for waiver will consume many of the same social resources required for the administration of Model II.

Varying the degree of precision with which a rule is expressed can have an impact on both the primary behavior of the rule's audience and the transaction costs associated with administering the rule. Refining these concepts further, one can identify four principal subcategories of potential costs and benefits:

1. *Rate of Compliance* — Increased precision may increase compliance and decrease evasion or concealment costs. First, it will reduce the cost of determining the rule's application to an actor's intended conduct. Second, the ease of enforcing transparent rules discourages would-be violators from making costly (and, from society's viewpoint, wasteful) efforts to avoid compliance. Increasing a rule's transparency may, however, eventually reduce compliance by increasing the cost of locating and applying the applicable provision, i.e., increasing the rule's inaccessibility and incongruence.

2. *Over- and Under-Inclusiveness* — Increasing the transparency of a rule may increase the variance between intended and actual outcomes. The rulemaker may be unable to predict every consequence of applying the rule or to foresee all of the circumstances to which it may apply. While the rulemaker presumably can change the rule after learning of its incongruence, the process of amendment is costly and gives rise to social losses in the interim. On the other hand, a more opaque rule, though facially congruent, may be under- or over-inclusive in application, because its vagueness invites misinterpretation. Increasing a rule's transparency may therefore substitute errors of misspecification for errors of misapplication.

3. *Costs of Rulemaking* — Rulemaking involves two sorts of social costs: the cost of obtaining and analyzing information about the rule's probable impact, and the cost of securing agreement among participants in the rulemaking process. These costs usually rise with increases in a rule's transparency since objective regulatory line-drawing increases the risk of misspecification and sharpens the focus of value conflicts. Yet, greater initial precision can also reduce the need for future rulemaking by leaving fewer policy questions open for later resolution by amendment or case-by-case elaboration.

4. *Cost of Applying a Rule* — The cost to both the regulated population and enforcement officials of applying a rule tends to increase as the rule's opacity or inaccessibility increases. Transparent and accessible rules can reduce the number of disputes that arise and simplify their resolution by causing the parties' predictions of the outcome to converge.

Having identified the costs and benefits associated with alternative rule formulations, the optimizing rulemaker computes the net social cost or benefit of each and selects the version generating the greatest net benefit.

B. Balancing the factors

Classifying the consequences of alternative rules in this way helps identify situations in which one factor may exert especially strong pressures for transparency, accessibility, or congruence. The rate of compliance, for example, is an especially important consideration in the analysis of rules regulating socially harmful conduct. This factor supports use of highly transparent and accessible standards. By "strictly" construing the language used in criminal statutes according to its most widely accepted meaning, for example, courts enhance the transparency of the criminal law. One would similarly expect a high degree of transparency in the rules used to define easily concealable regulatory offenses such as unsafe transportation of hazardous chemicals, unauthorized entry into the country, or overharvesting fisheries.

Concerns about over- or under-inclusiveness dominate when errors of misclassification are particularly costly. [Constitutional laws protecting freedom of expression], for example, reflect a belief that speech often has a higher value to society than to the individual speaker. . . . Less dramatic examples also abound in administrative regulation. For example, the social impact of discharging a given quantity of a

pollutant into a stream can vary widely from industry to industry (because of variations in costs of prevention) or from stream to stream (because of variations in harm
caused). Where the costs of over- or under-inclusiveness are high, rational policy-
makers will favor highly flexible or intricate regulatory formulas.

The costs of applying rules often loom especially large in the formulation of
standards designed to govern a large volume of disputes. In these situations a
desire to minimize litigation costs by using bright-line rules may outweigh countervailing considerations. Thus, agencies with particularly crowded enforcement dockets
tend to adopt the most transparent rules. A related transaction cost is incurred in
controlling the behavior of persons charged with a policy's enforcement. Numerous
scholars have documented the difficulties of controlling the behavior of police officers and other officials applying law at the "street level." In occupational safety and
health regulation or administration of the tax laws, which depend on large decen-
tralized enforcement staffs, the costs of applying rules often push rules to a highly
transparent extreme.

The cost of rulemaking may assume particular saliency in a collegial rulemaking
body such as a legislature or multi-member independent agency. The larger the
number of participants and the more divergent their values, the greater will be the
cost of reaching agreement. One would therefore expect collegial rulemakers to favor
formulas like Model II, which minimize the range of agreement required. This effect
is especially pronounced if the subsequent process of elaborating such open-ended
rules has fewer participants.

The implication of this analysis is that optimal precision varies from rule to rule.
The degree of precision appropriate to any particular rule depends on a series of
variables peculiar to the rule's author, enforcer, and addressee. As a consequence,
generalizations about optimal rule precision are inherently suspect.

Diver's economic approach is concerned with identifying a series of normative
prescriptions that seek to minimise the social costs associated with rule imprecision. One criticism of rule-based command and control approaches to regulation
is the possibility of formalistic interpretations that fail to reflect the underlying
purpose of the rule and which may also have counter-productive effects. In the
following extract, McBarnet and Whelan describe the essence of strategies
of avoidance that rely upon literalism in rule interpretation, which they label
'creative compliance'.

D. McBarnet and C. Whelan, '*The elusive spirit of the law: Formalism and the struggle for legal control*' (1991)

Formalism and the failure of legal control

Different approaches to law and control co-exist in legal policy and legal thinking,
but formalism is often presented as dominant. Formalism implies a narrow approach
to legal control − the use of clearly defined, highly administrable rules, an emphasis
on uniformity, consistency and predictability, on the legal form of transactions and
relationships and on literal interpretation.

Although the term formalism has been used in divergent ways, at its heart 'lies the concept of decision making according to rule,' rule implying here that the language of a rule's formulation – its literal mandate – be followed, even when this ill serves its purpose. Thus, 'to be formalistic... is to be governed by the rigidity of a rule's formulation.'

... Creative compliance uses formalism to avoid legal control, whether a tax liability or some regulatory obstacle to raising finance, effecting a controversial takeover or securing other corporate, or management, objectives. The combination of specific rules and an emphasis on legal form and literalism can be used artificially, in a manipulative way to circumvent or undermine the purpose of regulation. Using this approach, transactions, relationships or legal forms are constructed in order to avoid the apparent bounds of specific legal rules. In this sense, the detailed rules contribute to the defeat of legal policy. Though creative compliance is not limited to law and accounting, accountants are particularly conscious of its potential to reduce the effectiveness of regulations and to avoid tax. Much of the current impetus for a broad, open approach to professional standard setting stems from concern that a 'mechanistic "cookbook" approach... [which] is very precisely drafted... will be relatively easy to avoid.'

Creative compliance is often a prerequisite to a successful 'off balance sheet financing' transactions (OBSF). OBSF is currently perceived as a major problem in the regulation of financial reporting. It is the 'funding or refinancing of a company's operations in such a way that, under legal requirements and existing accounting conventions, some or all of the finance may not be shown on its balance sheet.' Assets or, more likely, liabilities are hidden from the reader of accounts, effectively destroying the purpose of financial reporting. There are many motivations for OBSF, for example to enhance market image, secure competitive advantage, increase credit, circumvent rules of corporate governance, increase management remuneration and avoid employee demands. This is not just a matter of cutting through formalities. In circumventing control, OBSF can also hide large scale financial risk, resulting in sudden insolvency, major creditor losses and redundancies....

... Creative compliance highlights the limits of formalism as a strategy of legal control. A formalistic approach, which relies upon a 'cookbook' or code of specific and rigid rules and emphasises the legal form of transactions, can 'fail' to control for a variety of reasons. Unless the rules promote the overall purpose of the law, compliance with them and insisting on their literal interpretation or enforcement will not achieve the declared objectives. The letter of the rule may not accord with the spirit in which the law was framed; a literal application of the rules may not produce the desired end, it may be counter-productive; there may be gaps, omissions or loopholes in the rules which undermine their effectiveness. The rules may be out of date and no longer relevant. There may be other problems too. The legal form of a transaction or a relationship may not reflect its legal or its economic or commercial substance. The totality of a transaction or relationship may not be reflected in any individual part. There may be a dynamic adaptation to escape rules. Formalistic regulation may increasingly drift from any relationship with the real world and any chance of effectively controlling it.

The subject matter of McBarnet and Whelan's extract shares with the preceding extracts a focus on rules which are legally enforceable. But regulatory rules need not be legally enforceable. Nor are rules (whether legally enforceable or otherwise) necessarily constructed in the form of a command. Although rules in the form of legal proscriptions against specified conduct are at their most visible within command-based regulatory regimes, they may also arise in various guises within other forms of regulatory control. So, for example, attempts to regulate behaviour through competition by providing financial incentives to act in pro-social ways through taxation or subsidy rely upon the formulation of rules or standards specifying the conduct or activity to which the tax or subsidy may attach. Even within a communication-based regime that relies upon published league-table rankings of members of the regulated community, the performance criteria against which members are evaluated and ranked must be specified. Yet even when rules take the form of non-legal performance criteria, rather than legal prohibitions backed by sanctions, scholars have observed that those targeted by such regimes may engage in avoidance or 'gaming' behaviour akin to the kind of conduct which McBarnet and Whelan label 'creative compliance' by those subject to legally enforceable rules. In other words, even outside formal legal contexts, members of a regulated community have been shown to respond to rules opportunistically, in ways that may be contrary to the underlying purpose of the regulatory regime, exemplified in the findings from the following study.

G. Bevan and C. Hood, '*What's measured is what matters: Targets and gaming in the English public health care system*' (2006)

Managing public services by targets: and terror?

In the mid-eighteenth century, Voltaire (in Candide) famously satirised the British style of naval administration with his quip 'ici on tue de temps en temps un amiral pour encourager les autres'. In the early twentieth century, the USSR's communist czars combined that hanging-the-admirals approach with a system of production targets for all state enterprises. The basic system survived for some sixty years, albeit with various detailed changes over time, before the Soviet system finally collapsed in 1991 — a decline that has been attributed by some to not hanging enough admirals to counter gaming produced by the target system.

In the 2000s, Tony Blair's New Labour government in Britain adopted a watered down version of that system for performance management of public services, especially in England. Having tagged a new set of government-wide performance targets onto the spending control system in 1998, in 2001 it added a key central monitoring unit working directly to the Prime Minister. From 2001, in England the Department of Health introduced an annual system of publishing 'star ratings' for public health care organizations. This gave each unit a single summary score from about 50 kinds of targets: a small set of 'key targets' and a wider set of indicators in a 'balanced scorecard'. While the Blair government did not hang the admirals in a literal sense, English health care managers (whose life was perceived to be 'nasty, brutish and short', even before the advent of targets) were exposed to increased risk of being sacked as a result of poor performance on measured indices and, through publication of star ratings, also to 'naming and shaming' as had been applied to schools and local government in the previous decade....

This paper seeks to explore some of the assumptions underlying the system of governance by targets and to expose those assumptions to a limited test based on such evidence as is available about responses to targets in the English public health care system up to 2004. How far did the system achieve the dramatic results associated with the Soviet target system in the 1930s and 1940s? Did it for instance produce a real breakthrough in cutting long waiting times, − chronic feature of the pre-targets system for 40 years − and how far did it produce the sort of chronic managerial gaming and problems with production quality that were later said to be endemic in the Soviet system?...

The theory of governance by targets and performance indicators

Governance by targets and measured performance indicators is a form of indirect control, necessary for the governance of any complex system....

Targets are sometimes kept secret. The type of regime considered here, however, is one in which targets and measures are published and so is performance against those measures. The rewards and sanctions include: reputational effects (shame or glory accruing to managers on the basis of their reported performance); bonuses and renewed tenure for managers that depend on performance against target; 'best to best' budgetary allocations that reflect measured performance; and the granting of 'earned autonomy' (from detailed inspection and oversight) to high performers. The last, a principle associated with Ayres and Braithwaite's idea of 'responsive regulation,' was enshrined as a central plank in the New Labour vision of public management in its 1999 *Modernizing Government* White Paper, as well as a major review of public and private regulation at the end of its second term.

Such rewards and sanctions are easy to state baldly, but are often deeply problematic in practice. Summary dismissal of public managers can be difficult and was so even in the USSR in its later years. The 'best to best' principle of budgetary allocation will always be confronted with rival principles, such as equal shares or even 'best to worst'. In addition, the earned autonomy principle of proportionate response implies a high degree of discretion accorded to regulators or central agencies that rubs up against rule-of-law ideas of rule-governed administration.

There are also major problems of credibility and commitment in any such system, given the incentives to 'cheat' both by target-setters and by target managers. One possible way of limiting cheating and establishing commitment is by establishment of independent third parties as regulators or evaluators. In the English variant of governance by targets and performance indicators in the 2000s − in contrast to the Soviet model − semi-independent bodies of various types, often sector-specific, figured large in the institutional architecture alongside central agencies and government departments. But the commitment and credibility such bodies could add was precarious, given that most of them had only limited independence.

We now consider two linked assumptions that underlie the theory of governance by targets. One is that measurement problems are unimportant, that the part on which performance is measured can adequately represent performance on the whole, and that distribution of performance does not matter. The other is that this method of governance is not vulnerable to gaming by agents.

Assumptions about measurement: Synecdoche

...[G]overnance by targets implies the ability to set targets relating to some domain (small or large) of total performance which is to be given priority.... So the task is to develop targets measured by indicators... to assess performance... The problem... is that most indicators... do not give answers but prompt investigation and inquiry, and by themselves provide an incomplete and inaccurate picture. Hence typically there will be a small set of indicators that are... good [performance] measures ($M[\alpha_g]$) for a subset of [performance within the domain of interest to controllers] (α)... a larger set of [imperfect performance measures] $M[\alpha_i]$ for another set of α for which there are data available, here denoted α_i; and [unmeasured performance] another subset of α, here denoted α_n... ...for which there are no usable data available....

Accordingly, governance by targets rests on the assumptions

(i) that any omission of ß [performance outside the domain of interest to controllers] and α_n [unmeasured performance] does not matter; and

(ii) *either* that [good performance measures] $M[\alpha_g]$ can be relied on as a basis for the performance regime, *or* that [good performance measures] combined with [imperfect performance measures] ($M[\alpha_g] + M[\alpha_i]$) will be an adequate basis for that regime.

What underlies these assumptions is the idea of synecdoche (taking a part to stand for a whole). Such assumptions would not be trivial even in a world where no gaming took place, but they become more problematic when gaming enters the picture.

Assumptions about gaming

Governance by targets rests on the assumption that targets change the behaviour of individuals and organizations, but that 'gaming' can be kept to some acceptably low level. 'Gaming' is here defined as reactive subversion such as 'hitting the target and missing the point' or reducing performance where targets do not apply [i.e. performance outside the domain and unmeasured performance] (ß and α_n). For instance, analysis of the failure of the UK government's reliance on money supply targets in the 1980s to control inflation led the economist Charles Goodhart to state his eponymous law: 'Any observed statistical regularity will tend to collapse once pressure is placed on it for control purposes' because actors will change their conduct when they know that the data they produce will be used to control them. And the 60-year history of Soviet targets shows that major gaming problems were endemic in that system. Three well-documented [ones] were ratchet effects, threshold effects and output distortions.

Ratchet effects refer to the tendency for central controllers to base next year's targets on last year's performance, meaning that managers who expect still to be in place in the next target period have a perverse incentive not to exceed targets even if they could easily do so... Such effects may also be linked to gaming around target-setting, to produce relatively undemanding targets... Threshold effects refer to the effects of targets on the distribution of performance among a range of, and within, production units, putting pressure on those performing below the target level to do better, but also providing a perverse incentive for those doing better than the target to allow their performance to deteriorate to the standard, and more generally to crowd performance towards the target. Such effects can unintentionally penalize agents with exceptionally good performance but a few failures, while rewarding those with mediocre performance crowded near the target range. Attempts to limit the threshold effect by basing future targets on past performance will tend to accentuate ratchet effects, and attempts to limit ratchet effects by system-wide targets will tend to accentuate threshold effects. Output distortions means attempts to achieve targets at the cost of significant but unmeasured aspects of performance ($ß$ and α_n). Various such distortions were well documented for the Soviet regime including neglect of quality, widely claimed to be an endemic problem from Stalin to Gorbachev.

The extent of gaming can be expected to depend on a mixture of motive and opportunity. Variations in the motives of producers or service providers can be described in various ways, of which a well-known current one is LeGrand's dichotomy of 'knights' and 'knaves'. Stretching that dichotomy slightly, we can distinguish the following four types of motivation among producers or service providers:

1. '*Saints*' who may not share all of the goals of central controllers, but whose public service ethos is so high that they voluntarily disclose shortcomings to central authorities. ...
2. '*Honest triers*' who broadly share the goals of central controllers, do not voluntarily draw attention to their failures, but do not attempt to spin or fiddle data in their favour. ...
3. '*Reactive gamers*': who broadly share the goals of central controllers, but aim to game the target system if they have reasons and opportunities to do so. ...
4. '*Rational maniacs*': who do not share the goals of central controllers and aim to manipulate data to conceal their operations. ...

Gaming as defined above will not come from service providers in categories (1) and (2) above (though there may be problems about measurement capacity as discussed in the previous sub-section at least for (2)), but will come from those in categories (3) and (4). Accordingly, governance by targets rests on the assumption that (i) a substantial part of the service provider population comprises types (1) and (2) above, with types (3) and (4) forming a minority; and (ii) that the introduction of targets will not produce a significant shift in that population from types (1) and (2) to types (3) and (4) or (iii) that [good performance measures] $M[\alpha_g]$... comprises a sufficiently large proportion of [performance within the domain of interest to controllers] α that the absence of conditions (i) and (ii) above will not produce significant gaming effects.

These assumptions are demanding. . . .

If central controllers do not know how the population of producer units or service providers is distributed among types (a) to (d) above, they cannot distinguish between the following four outcomes if reported performance indicates targets have been met:

1. All is well; performance is exactly what central controllers would wish in all performance domains (α_g, α_i, α_n, ß).
2. The organization is performing as central controllers would wish in domains [with good or imperfect performance measures] α_g and/or α_i, but this outcome has been at the expense of unacceptably poor performance in the domains where performance is not measured (α_n and ß).
3. Although performance as measured appears to be fine [indicated by good and imperfect performance measures] (M[α_g] and M[α_i]), actions are quite at variance with the substantive goals behind those targets (that is, 'hitting the target and missing the point').
4. There has been a failure to meet measured-performance targets [indicated by either or both good or imperfect performance measures] (M[α_g] and M[α_i]), but this outcome has been concealed by strategic manipulation of data (exploiting definitional ambiguity in reporting of data or outright data fabrication).

In the section that follows, we consider how far the demanding assumptions identified here as underlying the theory of governance by targets were met in the English National Health Service under its 'targets and terror' regime of the early 2000s.

Targets and terror as applied to the English NHS
The context and the institutional setting

The National Health Service (NHS) was created in 1948 as a UK-wide system for providing publicly-organized and tax-financed health care for the population at large, replacing a previous patchwork system of regulated private, charitable and local authority organization. . . .

From the 1980s, there were various attempts to generate incentives for improved performance before the Blair government introduced its targets-and-terror system for England in the early 2000s. In the 1980s there were attempts to make hospital managers more powerful relative to medical professionals. In the 1990s a Conservative government introduced an 'internal market' into the public health care system in which providers were intended to compete with one another. But . . . ministers continued to intervene to avoid hospitals being destabilized in the market. In adapting this system after it won government in 1997, Labour tried to devise a control system that did not rely on funds moving between competing providers. Central to that new approach was the targets-and-terror system of governance of annual performance (star) ratings of NHS organisations that was referred to earlier.

By the mid-2000s this system applied to over 700 NHS organizations in England . . . and was part of a broader control system for public service performance. There were two central agencies: the Prime Minister's Delivery Unit which from 2001 monitored a set of key public-service targets for the PM by a 'war room' approach, of which two or three applied to health; and the Treasury, which from 1998 attached performance targets (Public Service Agreements or PSAs) to financial allocations to spending departments (of which 10 or so applied to health care). In addition, there was the Department of Health, which continued to act as the overall overseer of the healthcare system, though operating increasingly at arms-length from health care providers; and freestanding regulators of health-care standards, of which the main one, called the Healthcare Commission at the time of writing, was responsible for inspections and performance assessment, including the published star ratings. Finally, there were two national audit organisations, the National Audit Office (NAO) that audited central government expenditure across the UK, including the Department of Health's spending, the Audit Commission, responsible for auditing the probity of NHS spending in England, and numerous other regulators and assessors of parts or all of the health care system. Taken together, it amounted to an institutionally complex and frequently changing set of overseers, inspectors and assessors of health care that lay behind the system of governance by targets in the early 2000s.

Reported performance data: Impressive improvements

On the face of it, the targets and terror system overseen by this army of monitors and assessors produced some notable improvements in reported performance by the English NHS. Three 'before' and 'after' comparisons in England and a fourth cross-country comparison relative to trusts elsewhere in the other UK countries without star ratings target systems may serve to demonstrate the point.

[[H]ospital accident and emergency (A&E) targets] The National Audit Office found that: 'Since 2002, all trusts have reduced the time patients spend in A&E, reversing a previously reported decline in performance. In 2002, 23 per cent of patients spent over four hours in A&E departments, but in the three months from April to June 2004 only 5.3 per cent stayed that long'. This reduction was achieved despite increasing use of A&E services, and the NAO also found evidence that reducing the time spent in A&E had increased patient satisfaction.

[[A]mbulance trust targets of reaching 75% of immediately life-threatening emergencies (category A calls) within 8 minutes.] [This] target had existed since 1996. After [it] became a key target for ambulance trust star ratings in 2002/3, [reported] performance . . . jumped dramatically and, at the end of that year, the worst achieved nearly 70 per cent.

[[H]ospital waiting times targets for first elective admission (in England).] Maximum waiting times were dramatically reduced in England after the introduction of the star rating system from 2000−01. This set targets for maximum waiting times for the end of March each year; and for 2003 and 2004 these were 12 and 9 months.

[[H]ospital waiting times for first elective admission in England as compared with other UK countries.] There was a notable difference between the dramatic improvement in reported waiting times for England, as against the other countries in the UK, which did not apply the targets-and-terror system of star ratings described earlier. Reported performance in the other countries did not in general improve, and at the end of March of 2003, when virtually no patient in England was reported as waiting more than 12 months for an elective admission, the equivalent figures for Scotland, Wales and Northern Ireland were 10, 16 and 22 per cent of patients respectively....

These improvements in reported performance are dramatic and on the face of it indicate the sort of results that the USSR achieved with its targets system from the 1930s to the 1960s, when it successfully industrialized a backward economy against a background of slump and unemployment in the capitalist West, emerged the victor in World War II and rebuilt its economy afterwards, to the point where, in 1961, publicly challenged the USA to an economic race over per capita production. We now examine how far the control system met the assumptions we set out in the previous section.

The assumptions revisited: Measurement and gaming
Measurement
... In the case of health care [the] distinctions we drew [above] turn out to be central to the design of any performance management regime.

At first sight waiting times for access to care at first sight may appear to be a clear case of [good performance measures] $M[\alpha_g]$, but even for this indicator several inquiries have revealed data limitations that are far from trivial. For A&E targets, the National Audit Office found weaknesses in arrangements for recording time spent and observed that the relevant management information systems mostly pre-dated the targets regime and some were over ten years old. There were apparent discrepancies between reported levels of performance officially and from independent surveys of patients in achieving the target for patients spending less than four hours in A&E: in 2002/03, officially in 139 out of 158 acute trusts 90 per cent of patients were seen in less than four hours, but only 69 per cent of patients reported that experience in the survey; in 2004/05, the official level had increased to 96 per cent, but the survey-reported level was only 77 per cent. For ambulance targets, there were problems in the definition of what constituted a 'life-threatening emergency' (the proportion of emergency calls logged as Category A ranged from fewer than 10 per cent to over 50 per cent across ambulance trusts) and ambiguity in the time when the clock started. For hospital waiting time targets, the Audit Commission, on the basis of 'spot checks' at 41 trusts between June and November 2002, found reporting errors in at least one indicator in 19 of those trusts. As we shall stress later, there was no systematic audit of measures on which performance data are based, so such inquiries were partial and episodic. But they raise serious questions as to how robust even the [good performance] measure $M[\alpha_g]$ was for this performance regime. . . .

As noted earlier, the quality problem bedevilled the Soviet targets regime and quality remained in the subset of [unmeasured performance] α_n. Likewise, the 1980s generation of health-care performance indicators in the UK [had earlier been criticised] for their failure to capture quality in the sense of impact or outcome. And that problem had by no means disappeared in the 2000s targets-and-terror regime for health care governance in England. Methodologically, measures of effectiveness remained difficult methodologically, required new kinds of data that were costly and problematic to collect and tended to rely on indicators of failure. The star ratings of the 2000s, like the predecessor performance indicators of the 1980s failed to capture key dimensions of effectiveness. There was a large domain of unmeasured performance (α_n) and measures of 'sentinel events' indicating quality failures (notably crude mortality rates and readmission rates for hospitals) were at best indicators of the [imperfect performance measure] type $M[\alpha_i]$. Risk-adjusted mortality rates could be calculated for a few procedures such as adult cardiac surgery. But even there, problems in collecting the detailed data required led to a failure to achieve a high-profile ministerial commitment − announced after the Bristol paediatric cardiac surgery scandal referred to earlier − to publish, from 2004, 'robust, rigorous and risk-adjusted data' of mortality rates.

Gaming
. . . As mentioned above, there was no systematic audit of the extent to which the reported successes in English health care performance noted [above] were undermined by gaming and measurement problems, even though much of the data came from the institutions who were rated on the basis of the information they provided. That 'audit hole' can itself be interpreted by those with a suspicious mind (or a long memory) as a product of a 'Nelson's eye' game in which those at the centre of government do not look for evidence of gaming or measurement problems which might call reported performance successes into question. In the Soviet system, as all bodies responsible for supervising enterprises were interested in the same success indicators, those supervisors connived at, or even encouraged, gaming rather than checking it. In the English NHS 'hard looks' to detect gaming in reported performance data were at best limited. Central monitoring units did mount some statistical checks on completeness and consistency of reported data, but evidence of gaming was largely serendipitous and haphazard, emerging from particular inquiry reports or anecdotal sources. We therefore cannot provide any accurate estimate of the distribution of the health-care-provider population among the four categories identified above (though examples of the existence of each of those types can be readily given, as we showed earlier). But . . . there is enough evidence of significant gaming to indicate that the problem was far from trivial.

We now present evidence of gaming through distortion of reported output for ambulance response-time targets, hospital A&E waiting-time targets and hospital waiting time targets for first outpatient appointment and elective admission.

[Evidence was found] that in a third of ambulance trusts, response times had been 'corrected' to be reported to be less than eight minutes. The kinds of different patterns discovered are illustrated by Figure 7[4.1]: an expected pattern of 'noisy decline' (where there has been no 'correction'), and of a 'corrected' pattern with a curious 'spike' at 8 minutes — with the strong implication that times between 8 and 9 minutes have been reclassified to be less than 8 minutes. There was also evidence that the idiosyncracies of the rules about Category A classification led in some instances to patients in urgent need being given a lower priority for ambulance response than less serious cases that happened to be graded Category A.

For hospital A&E waiting-time targets, five types of output-distorting gaming response were documented. First, a study of the distribution of waiting times in A&E found frequency peaked at the four-hour target — although this pattern was much less dramatic than that for ambulance response times. Surveys ... reported widespread practice of a second and third type of gaming responses: drafting in of extra staff and cancelling operations scheduled for the period over which performance was measured. A fourth practice was to require patients to wait in queues of ambulances outside A&E Departments until the hospital in question was confident that that patient could be seen within four hours. Such tactics may have unintendedly caused delays in responding to seriously ill individuals when available ambulances were waiting outside A&E to offload patients ... A fifth gaming response was observed in response to the so-called 'trolley-wait' target that a patient must be admitted to a hospital bed within 12 hours of emergency admission. The response took the form of turning 'trolleys' into 'beds' by putting them into hallways.

For hospital waiting time targets for first outpatient appointment and elective admission, the National Audit Office reported evidence that nine NHS trusts had

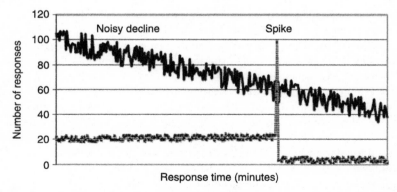

Figure 4.1 [Figure 7] Frequency distributions of ambulance response times.

'inappropriately' adjusted their waiting lists, three of them for some three years or more, affecting nearly 6,000 patient records. In five cases the adjustments only came to light following pressure from outsiders, though in four cases they were identified by the trusts concerned. The adjustments varied significantly in their seriousness, ranging from those made by junior staff following established, but incorrect, procedures through to what appears to be deliberate manipulation or misstatement of the figures. The NAO study was followed up by the Audit Commission, which found evidence of deliberate misreporting of waiting list information at three trusts. In addition, a parliamentary select committee report on targets in 2003 reported that the waiting time target for new ophthalmology outpatient appointments at a major acute hospital had been achieved by cancellation and delay of follow-up appointments, which did not figure in the target regime. Recording of clinical incident forms for all patients showed that, as a consequence, 25 patients lost their vision over two years, and this figure is likely to be an underestimate.

Further, the publication of mortality data as an indicator of quality of clinical care may itself have produced reactive gaming responses. There is anecdotal evidence that such publication results in a reluctance by surgeons to operate on high risk cases, who stand to gain most from surgery. Because mortality rates are very low (about 2%), one extra death has a dramatic impact on a surgeon's performance in a year, and risk-adjustment methods cannot resolve such problems.

. . .

Discussion and conclusion

We have argued that the implicit theory of governance by targets requires two sets of heroic assumptions to be satisfied: of robust synecdoche, and game-proof design. And we have shown that there is enough evidence from the relatively short period of its functioning to date to suggest that these assumptions are not justified. The transparency of the system in real time seems to have exacerbated what we earlier described as Gresham's law of reactive gaming,

We see the system of star rating as a process of 'learning by doing' in which government chose to ignore the problems we have identified. A consequence was that although there were indeed dramatic improvements in reported performance, we do not know the extent to which the improvements were genuine or offset by gaming that resulted in reductions in performance that was not captured by targets. Evidence of gaming naturally led many critics of New Labour's targets-and-terror regime to advocate the wholesale abandonment of that system. But the practical alternatives to such a regime . . . are well-tried and far from problem-free. Nor is health care truly governed by anything approximating to a free market in any developed state: regulation and public funding (even in the form of tax expenditures) take centre stage in every case . . . .

4.2.1   Discussion questions

1. Can Black's analytical framework for rule interpretation and application accommodate Diver's prescriptions for rule-making?

2. How, if at all, could Diver's rule-making prescriptions be employed to address the phenomenon of 'creative compliance' described by McBarnet and Whelan?
3. Can the findings of Hood and Bevans' study of the use of targets to regulate the English NHS be explained in terms of the problems associated with rules?

4.3   The enforcement of rules and agency behaviour

The 'gaming' behaviour of NHS institutions falling within the scope of the British government's target regime documented by Hood and Bevan serves as a stark reminder that regulatory rules do not automatically and unproblematically bring about the rule-maker's intended behavioural change. Rules are interpreted and applied by human actors. Many of the difficulties associated with the use of rules can ultimately be traced to the vagaries and complexity of human interaction and ingenuity. But just as variability in the use of rules may be attributed to different human responses to linguistic uncertainty inherent in rules, the flexibility and adaptability of human responses and interaction provide scope for overcoming their limitations. One example of how this has been achieved is through the use of what Julia Black refers to as 'regulatory conversations' between the regulator and members of the regulated community. She identifies a number of problems with such conversations, including the potential for exposing the regulator to charges of 'capture, inconsistency and inequity, emptying the law of any meaningful content, and undermining the regulation and, more particularly, its public interest or social objectives'. Despite these problems, the following extract focuses on the nature, utility and inevitability of such conversations:

J. Black, *'Talking about regulation'* (1998)
Forms of conversation
The conversations being referred to are communications and discussions between a regulatory official or officials and a regulated individual or firm as to the application of a generally applicable rule in their particular case. Rules in this sense include primary, secondary and tertiary rules, and so may be embodied in, inter alia, statute, regulatory rules, circulars, guidance, licenses or franchise agreements. Conversations are not synonymous with regulation, rather they are a feature of the day to day operation of a regulatory system and the interaction between regulator and regulatee concerning the meaning and application of rules. Conversations may involve guidance or rulings on the rule's application, its elaboration, either by the firm or the regulator, or its effective modification or waiver. No clear cut distinction is thus being envisaged between rule formation and rule application: conversations may involve the development of previously written rules in such a way that a rule is effectively revised; rule application may thus lead to rule re-formulation. What is not included in the idea of a "conversation" however is the broader policy formation

process and the initial construction of the regulatory framework. Rather, attention is placed on those conversations which occur within the regulatory framework once it has been set.

Conversations may occur at a number of different points within the regulatory process and with officials in different parts of the regulatory organisation. They may be centralised or decentralised. Conversations may be part of the inevitable course of the regulatory process, and may or may not have explicit sanction within the regulatory system. Alternatively (or in addition), they may be a consciously adopted regulatory strategy; the regulator may issue only very broad rules, anticipating that it will then engage in a process of negotiation, a conversation, with individual regulatees as to how those broad rules will apply to those circumstances, including perhaps the approval of rules written by the firm or individual to guide its own behaviour in compliance with the generally applicable norm.

Generalisations as to their nature can only take us so far. To illustrate the phenomenon, it is worth exploring some examples of different types or occasions of conversations. Three broad occasions for conversations are considered here: the process of rule application, that of supervised rule-formation, and that of monitoring and enforcement.

Rule application: guidance and waivers
Guidance given to individual regulatees as to the meaning or application of the rule may be given informally or as a result of a formal process. It may or may not have legal status, and it may or may not lead to further action, such as the granting of a waiver or no-action letter. . . . different systems of regulation, which are not of the archetypal "command and control" model, in which guidance and/or waivers play a central role [include] takeovers [and] tax collection . . . .

[For example,] the regulation of takeovers and mergers relies heavily on guidance, and indeed the conversational approach is one of its principal modes of operation. The Takeover Panel is a non-statutory body which regulates the conduct of takeovers and mergers of all public companies in the British Isles. Its code consists of 10 general principles and 38 rules, elaborated by sub-rules and notes, rules on substantial acquisition of shares and various disclosure forms. These are supplemented from time to time by statements of practice or policy issued by the Panel. The operation of the Panel is notable in that its authority is almost universally accepted, and its conduct largely praised.

. . . It is . . . common practice for the Panel, in the form of the executive, to be closely involved in takeover proceedings. The advice and rulings of the executive are frequently sought, and significantly, the executive will give rulings on hypothetical situations. The key to the Panel's operation is its flexibility and the speed of its responses: advice or rulings are sought or given mainly over the telephone, the executive requiring only two hours at most, and rulings are given within 24 hours. Guidance and rulings of the executive are authoritative; if the parties want to appeal against them they can do so to the Panel within one month, or sooner if the executive so stipulates. Alternatively, the executive can itself refer a matter to the Panel if it is a particularly difficult, unusual or important point. Both referrals and appeals are in fact rare, with the Panel seldom overruling the executive. Appeals are private and are conducted on an informal basis with no formal rules of evidence . . . [and] no party can be represented by counsel. The Panel operates in complete confidence: rulings are not published, and even Panel decisions on appeal remain confidential unless the issue is particularly important or controversial. In all events, the transcript of the appeal hearing is not disclosed unless all parties agree.

The operation of the Panel provides an example of a system of regulation which relies on quite a sophisticated form of conversation. The Panel is the final interpreter of its own rules, giving it the authority to provide a flexible system of regulation; its rulings are binding; the procedure is speedy, and third parties have some limited rights of participation. This form of conversation provides an interesting comparison to that of the Inland Revenue's practice of giving advice with respect to the application of tax legislation . . . . [which] . . . is of a quite different nature from that which occurs between the parties to a takeover and the Panel. The Revenue is not presumed to be the final authority in interpreting the tax legislation, and it is open to the taxpayer to adopt a different interpretation from that of the Revenue, and indeed not to tell the Revenue which has been adopted. The Revenue will not give rulings which are formally binding on the tax effect of transactions prior to their occurring (although the Revenue may treat such rulings as binding in practice), and unlike the Panel, will not give advice on hypothetical situations. Notably, the Revenue has a strong concern that in giving advice or rulings it should not assist individuals to reduce their tax burden, so depriving the Revenue of income. . . . Whilst informal advice is therefore available, and often freely so, conversations are significantly restricted in nature, and those which formally bind the parties only occur in very limited circumstances . . . .

Supervised rule formation
In the examples given above, the conversation which is occurring is as to the application of rules which have been formulated by the regulator or are embodied in some form of primary legislation. Other forms of conversation are possible. Firms could, for example, formulate their own rules under the supervision of, and in negotiation with, a regulatory body. The conversation here would be not just about the application of a general rule in a particular instance, but the application of a general set of rules to a particular firm, and ways in which the firm could formulate a rule system of a greater degree of specificity which would be tailored to its own operations, whilst achieving the general social objectives enshrined in the more general rules. This system of firm-written rules may take a range of forms: the regulatory body could formulate very simple, general rules, and the firm write their own more detailed rules under those; or the regulatory body could formulate a set of "default" rules which will apply to firms unless they choose to adopt their own, again, in negotiation with, and subject to, the approval of the agency.

Examples of regulatory systems which involve the use of self-written rules include aspects of U.S. environmental regulation, of health and safety regulation in mines in the U.S. and Australia, and nursing homes in Australia. The technique is also mandated by regulators in certain areas of banking and securities business. The international regulator of banking, the Basle Committee, has recently stated that firms will be able to use their own internally formed models to calculate the extent of their market risk, which will then be used to set capital requirements. The models have to conform to broad regulator-set parameters, but can otherwise take the form that the firm chooses. . . .

Monitoring and enforcement
In the examples given above, conversations have concerned the elaboration of and guidance on the application of rules in particular cases, the waiver of those rules, and approval of and reliance on firm-written rules. They have been both centralised and decentralised, and occurred at different levels within the regulatory organisation. The final example of conversations to be considered are those which occur during the process of routine monitoring and enforcement. These tend by their nature to be decentralised and relatively low level. They may involve the same elaboration, adjustment or waiver of the rule, or the same guidance as to its meaning, as that which is involved in the process of guidance or waivers discussed above. The principal differences are that the conversation is not necessarily initiated by the regulatee, but occurs in respect of application of the rule, and in situations where it has been breached. The issue may thus not be so much whether the rule applies, but what should happen in the case of its breach.

That such conversations occur as part of the enforcement process has been well observed by a number of empirical studies of the enforcement of social, particularly environmental and health and safety, regulation. These studies show the enforcement process to be one of negotiation, often involving bargaining (waiver of one rule breach in return for compliance with another), bluff (as to the legal requirements, the range of penalties at the agency's disposal), and the assertion and presentation of the legal authority of the agency . . . .

The reasons for conversations
The granting of rulings, waivers or comfort letters . . . provide advantages both for the regulator and the regulated. The regulated can address uncertainty in the rule's application by seeking an assurance that if it takes a particular course of action, the regulator will not proceed against it, or can seek an exception from the rule or its waiver in particular instances. From the regulator's point of view, this strategy enables tailoring of the regulation to fit particular circumstances, which the agency may want to ensure for a range of reasons. These may be concerns of regulatory equity (for example, if the application of the rule in particular circumstances would not further its purpose and nor would the waiver undermine the policy goal of the rule). Alternatively, waivers or exemptions may prevent or reduce hostility to the regulation and alienation of regulatees, and may simply be an attempt to provide regulation which suits the circumstances of the regulatee in the hope of saving time and resources later in attempting to ensure enforcement.

A slightly different set of advantages may accompany conversations which occur during a process of supervised rule formation. Such a process has the potential to avoid the problems of regulator written rules and, depending on its design, of "command and control" regulation. Rules could adjust more quickly to changing business environments, as the regulator could simply require firms to write rules to meet new situations rather than having to engage in a lengthy rule making process itself. The regulator could tap the knowledge and expertise of firms in designing regulation. Regulation would thus permit innovation and cover a greater range of corporate activity than regulator formed rules. Companies would be more committed to the rules they have written. Overall costs of regulation would be reduced: the regulator would not have to bear the costs of rule formation and the firm does not have to undergo the costs and confusion of having two rule books—the regulator's and its own in-house rules. Further, by giving to the firm the opportunity to design regulation, it could avoid what may be termed the "rationality clash" which is seen by some as the underlying cause of regulatory failure. Regulators may use the technique in such a way as to ensure that the tailored rules structure the regulated's incentives to improve compliance, fine tuning requirements as becomes necessary (as in the examples of prudential regulation given above).

Conversations which occur during the enforcement process are also frequently accompanied by their own set of rationales and advantages. The enforcement process is often as much about promoting a willingness to comply as it is about ensuring exact compliance with a particular rule. The reasons for the adoption of a compliance approach may relate to the resource constraints, both temporal and financial, of the agency, but they are likely to be more complex. A compliance approach tends to be adopted where there is an on-going relationship between regulator and regulated, and particularly where the individuals involved know one another or share a common background or outlook. It is usually adopted to prevent the alienation of the regulated since the more "bullying" approach of sanctioning every breach can stimulate opposition to the regulation by the regulated, prompting non-co-operation in investigations and the compliance process. More significantly, the greater the feeling of alienation, the less are firms likely to implement the necessary measures to ensure on-going compliance with the regulation in the periods between inspections, and perhaps the more likely they are to engage in minimal or creative compliance strategies. A compliance approach can thus be used in an attempt to stimulate compliance. The adoption of a compliance approach may thus have significant strategic advantages. It may also be adopted as a matter of necessity, and . . . because of the moral ambivalence surrounding the issue of regulatory rule breaches.

There are more fundamental reasons for conversations in regulation, however, which suggest that conversations are an inevitable feature of regulation, even if they are not formally mandated or do not form part of the central strategy of regulation. Conversations provide a means of addressing one of the central problems which pervade any system of regulation, whatever its design: the limitations of rules . . .

. . . Focus has been placed on the interpretive aspect of rule use, on the need to foster an understanding between the rule maker and the rule's addressees as to the rule's meaning and intended application through the development of interpretive communities.

A conversational use of rules is a further way in which some of the problems of rules, notably those of interpretation, inclusiveness and entrenchment, can be overcome. . . .[P]art of the problem of rules is that they are legally binding statements or reasons for action. As they are anticipatory and generalised, they may over- or under-include; but their entrenchment means that they cannot easily be adjusted, hence the charge of the "inflexibility" of rules. The contrast is sometimes drawn with conversations. Conversations allow for adaptability. In conversation, the problems of generalisations and to an extent of open texture can be, and are, resolved by latitude in interpretation and understanding on the part of those participating in the conversation, and by the possibility of further elaboration or definition of generalisations made and statements uttered. For example, I may state that the weather is always miserable in February, but it is open to me then immediately to qualify that by saying there may be days in February in which the sun shines; or accept that in Australia the weather in February is in fact very pleasant. Conversation uses generalisations, and can tolerate them simply because it has the capacity for retraction, modification, qualification, clarification and embellishment. It is when this process cannot or does not occur that the over- or underinclusiveness of generalisations poses a problem.

Conversations not only allow for adjustment, they also aid interpretation. As has been well observed, rules do not apply themselves; they need to be interpreted. Interpretation is however a contested exercise. There is no inherent, fixed meaning to rules or to language; the meaning, and hence the application, of a rule is not an objective fact but is contingent on the interpretive community reading the rule. The contingency of the application of the rule on the interpretation it receives suggests a particular vulnerability of rules. Rules may receive a number of interpretations and thus be applied in a number of ways. Conversations which involve elaboration of the rule's meaning allow the problem of interpretation to be addressed. They can thus meet the need for certainty in the rule's operation, a need which itself stems from the legal status of rules, and the concomitant rule of law concerns that rules should be able to guide behaviour and allow individuals to plan their lives.

4.3.1 Observational studies of agency behaviour

Conversation between regulatory officials and those they regulate highlights the necessity of human agency in breathing life into regulatory regimes. In the preceding extract, Black refers to conversations taking place during various stages of regulatory implementation, including the enforcement process. It is the study of the behaviour of regulatory enforcement officials in applying regulatory rules that forms the focus of a varied range of ethnographic studies. Indeed, for many regulatory scholars, the study of regulation is regarded as synonymous with the study of human behaviour in the context of regulatory enforcement by a public agency or official. Through agency-specific ethnographic analysis, a rich body of socio-legal scholarship has developed, documenting this behaviour. An early, and perhaps the best-known, ethnographic study of agency behaviour is Hawkins's study of British officials responsible for enforcing environmental regulations. In the first part of the following extract, Hawkins gives an account of two distinctive enforcement 'styles', one which he terms a 'compliance' approach, contrasting it with an alternative 'sanctioning' approach. In the second part of the extract, he offers an explanation as to why a compliance approach is not merely important, but 'morally compelled'.

K. Hawkins, *'Environment and enforcement'* (1984)

... In this book the enforcement of regulation is analysed in terms of two major systems or strategies of enforcement which I shall call compliance and sanctioning. I shall also talk of a conciliatory style of enforcement as characteristic of compliance strategy, and a penal style as distinctive of sanctioning strategy. The terms 'conciliatory' and 'penal' are adopted from Black who discusses dominant styles of law which have counterparts in wider and more pervasive forms of social control. A conciliatory style is remedial, a method of 'social repair and maintenance, assistance for people in trouble', concerned with 'what is necessary to ameliorate a bad situation'. Penal control, on the other hand, 'prohibits certain conduct, and it enforces its prohibitions with punishment'. Its nature is accusatory, its outcomes binary: 'all or nothing — punishment or nothing'.

Since the characteristics of sanctioning and compliance strategies are pervasive themes throughout the book, it would be as well to preface the analysis with a brief exploration of some of their general features. ... Central to a sanctioning strategy is a concern for the application of punishment for breaking a rule and doing harm. Conformity with the law may be the consequence of this, but that is not the main issue. The formal machinery of law is crucial to this concern, and exacting a legal sanction by means of the legal process is a relatively routine matter. Enforcement agents who adopt a compliance strategy, however, are preoccupied with securing conformity to a rule or standard when confronted with a problem. Compliance strategy seeks to prevent a harm rather than punish an evil. Its conception of enforcement centres upon the attainment of the broad aims of legislation, rather than sanctioning its breach. Recourse to the legal process here is rare, a matter of last resort, since compliance strategy is concerned with repair and results, not retribution. And for compliance to be effected, some positive accomplishment is often required, rather than simply refraining from an act.

These differences are reflected in enforcement style. A penal style is accusatory and adversarial. Here enforcement is reflective: a matter of determining what harm was done, of detecting the law-breaker and fixing the appropriate sanction. The primary questions are whether a law has been broken, and whether an offender can be detected. If so, then the breach deserves punishment. In a compliance strategy, on the other hand, the style is conciliatory and relies upon bargaining to attain conformity. Enforcement here is prospective: a matter of responding to a problem and negotiating future conformity to standards which are often administratively determined. Since such standards are generally designed to prevent harm by accumulation, violations consist of rule-breaking which could lead to harm, as well as rule-breaking where actual harm is demonstrated. This makes retribution inappropriate. If prevention of future misconduct occurs, it does so as a result of negotiation rather than the deterrence which (presumably) inhibits future rule-breaking in a sanctioning system.

A standard which has not been attained in a compliance system needs remedy. The emphasis given to detection and punishment in a sanctioning system is linked with a special concern for proof of violation. Decision outcomes tend to be binary and matters are ultimately settled by means of adjudication. As such, the process is visible, and a central role in adjudication is given to a stranger. In a compliance system, in contrast, there is much less concern for proving a violation took place; indeed widespread reliance on strict liability would make the question of proof relatively straightforward if matters ended up in court. Detection is important, however, but rather as a means of monitoring compliance and of enhancing prevention; indeed the commitment to repair of a potential source of harm produces a concern for the effectiveness of enforcement procedures in securing conformity. On the evidence of this study, the dominant conception of enforcement agents in a compliance system is a notion of efficiency: the attainment of a social goal at least cost to them and their work. Punishment is an unsatisfactory operational philosophy because it risks damage to the ultimate end of enforcement, and control of the case does not remain in their hands.

Decisions in a compliance system are graduated in character, and though in rare cases matters are ultimately settled by adjudication, they are normally controlled by the parties themselves in private, intimate negotiations which rely on bargaining, not adjudication. Where enforcement relationships in sanctioning systems tend to be compressed and abrupt, compliance enforcement is marked by an extended, incremental approach. There are implications in all of this for what are regarded as indices of success for enforcement officials and agencies. Statistics of process, such as arrests and clearance rates are accustomed indices of organizational success in a sanctioning system. In a compliance system, however, statistics of impact are more likely to be employed to display the organization's effectiveness in repairing harm.

. . .

Compliance

Enforcement behaviour in pollution control is determined by the play of two interconnected features: the nature of the deviance confronted and a judgment of its wilfulness or avoidability . . .

Compliance, then, is much more than conformity, immediate or protracted, to the demands of an enforcement agent. The continuing relationship between officer and polluter, the open-endedness of problems encountered, and the pragmatism of field staff encourage a focus upon the deviant's efforts at compliance, an opportunity denied the deviant in breach of a rule in the traditional criminal code where an act committed is over and done with and beyond repair. A polluter who displays an immediate willingness to take whatever action is necessary may well discover that the gravity of the pollution itself is accorded less importance by the officer: 'it can become a secondary feature,' said one field man, 'if co-operation from the firm is complete.'

Compliance, in short, has a symbolic significance. Enforcement agents need, as much as a concrete accomplishment, some sign of compliance. Planning is as important as building; intention as important as action. Assessments of conformity thus tend to be fluid and abstract, rather than concrete and unproblematic. 'Attitudes' are judged as much as activities:

KH: How important is the attitude of the other person?

FO: Oh, I think that's the most important thing, is his attitude. Because the pollutions themselves can be so variable.... If he's trying to solve it, I go along with him. If he's not interested in it and thinks 'Well, it will go away in time anyway,' then obviously I'm going to press him harder then. Yeah, it is the most single important parameter I think, his attitude. [His emphasis]

The discharger who does what the field man asks — even though he may still be polluting — will be thought of as compliant. Compliance in practice is a continuing effort towards attainment of a goal as much as attaining the goal itself. The extent to which pollution is controlled is no more significant in a compliance strategy than the extent of the polluter's good faith. How 'good' the faith is, however, depends on the kind of polluter encountered....

A more important categorization,... one continually open to redefinition, is a judgment of polluter's co-operativeness. To regard a discharger as 'co-operative' or having a 'good attitude', or, in contrast, as 'unhelpful' or 'bolshie' informs an officer's expectations about the nature of his relationship with that polluter. Co-operativeness is welcomed for facilitating the job of enforcement and for encouraging principled compliance: 'If you get on well with them, they're more likely to look at the moral issue [of complying] than the economics.' The suggestion of willing compliance from the 'co-operative' polluter announces a respect for the officer's authority and reassures him that his demands are not only reasonably put, but legitimate. Besides, a show of compliance is a means of coping with uncertainty, as 'something is being done'....

The officer's understanding of the reasons why particular kinds of polluters comply helps shape his choice of enforcement tactics, especially in those cases where the field man expects or is already experiencing 'trouble'. One assumption, with profound implications for enforcement behaviour, is that dischargers are sensitive creatures whose feelings may be easily bruised if urged to do too much, too soon. To 'use the big stick' or 'crack the whip' too zealously may be counterproductive. To be too eager or abrasive in enforcement work is to risk encouraging in polluters an unco-operative attitude or even downright hostility. This is a major foundation of the commitment to a conciliatory style of enforcement relying on negotiation as a means of securing compliance, 'co-operation cannot be established in the atmosphere of suspicion and distrust that rigid application of the law generates.' In practical terms this assumption supports two related imperatives for field staff aimed at preserving relationships: 'be reasonable' and 'be patient'. Rather than explicitly seeking to secure compliance at the outset by coercion, officers must demonstrate an understanding of the polluter's problems by discussion and negotiation. Enforcement takes time . . . .

Bargaining
The voluntary compliance of the regulated is regarded by the agencies as the most desirable means of meeting water quality standards. For the agencies it is not only viewed as the most effective strategy, it is a relatively cheap method of achieving conformity. For agency staff it is a means of promoting goodwill, a matter of profound importance in open-ended enforcement relationships which must be maintained in the future. Compliance takes on the appearance of voluntariness by the use of bargaining. Bargaining processes have 'a graduated and accommodative character' which draw their efficacy from the ostensibly voluntary commitment of the parties. The more legalistic style of penal enforcement with decision-making by adjudication and the imposition of a sanction risks, according to agency staff, continued intransigence from the guilty polluter. Bargaining is central to enforcement in compliance systems; control is buttressed for it is derived from some sort of consensus. Bargaining implies the acquiescence of the regulated, however grudging. And it inevitably suggests some compromise from the rigours of penal enforcement.

The essence of a compliance strategy is the exchange relationship, a subtle reminder of the mutual dependence which Edelman regards as central to the conception of the game. The polluter has goodwill, co-operation and, most important, conformity to the law to offer. The enforcement agent may offer in return two important commodities: forbearance and advice.

The offer of forbearance is the opportunity for another display of the officer's craft. He will not ask for costly remedies unless the problem is a major one or the polluter is undoubtedly wealthy. He will recognize inherent constraints facing the polluter, such as lack of space. He will respect a previously co-operative relationship. Most important, he will offer a less authoritarian response than that legally mandated. He offers the polluter time to attain compliance, for bargaining strategies 'are based on the principle that success in pollution control is "bought" by giving up some of the demands that are fixed in the legal norms to be implemented'.

Bargaining is possible, then, only because the law need not be formally enforced. Rules are a valuable resource for enforcement agents since, as Gouldner has observed, they represent something which may be given up, as well as given use. The display of forbearance is valuable in obliging the polluter to take action in response to the show of leniency:

'. . . instead of leaving the impression that you're some jumped-up little upstart from an office using the law to tell him what he must do, if you talk to him right, you finish up leaving him with the view that "Well, he's a damn good chap. . . . I could've been prosecuted for this. I'm breaking the law, but he's obviously going to shoot it under the carpet and let me get away with it." So . . . he does what he has to do, with goodwill, and everybody's happy.'

... A sense of mutual trust is important in sustaining the bargaining relationship: trust that the polluter will not 'pull a fast one', trust that the officer will not penalize theoretically illegal conduct. Field staff generate a sense of trust by showing how 'reasonable' — that is forbearing — they are, polluters by displaying a willingness to conform and a readiness to report 'problems'. Forbearance aids the detection of pollution by encouraging self-reporting whenever there is an escape of effluent. The polluter himself is, after all, in the best position to discover and control the pollution and prevent it from becoming a public matter. 'You do tend to learn an awful lot more,' said a supervisor based in a major conurbation, 'particularly if they know what your actions are going to be. And also if they realize that when things do go wrong, if they tell you ... you're going to react in a sensible sort of way. And when something goes wrong that they could be prosecuted on, they would still tell you because they know that ... you're going to be more reasonable with them, because you know that they haven't hidden things in the past.'...

Postscript

Compliance is often treated as if it were an objectively-defined unproblematic state, rather than a fluid, negotiable matter. Compliance, however, is an elaborate concept, one better seen as a process, rather than a condition. What will be understood as compliance depends upon the nature of the rule-breaking encountered, and upon the resources and responses of the regulated. The capacity to comply is ultimately evaluated in moral terms, and is of utmost importance in shaping enforcement behaviour. A greater degree of control is likely where a discharger is regarded as able to bear the expenditure for compliance; this issue is still a moral one, fundamentally, not one of economics.

Compliance is negotiable and embraces action, time, and symbol. It addresses both standard and process. It may in some cases consist of present conformity. In others, present rule-breaking will be tolerated on an understanding that there will be conformity in future: compliance represents, in other words, some ideal state towards which an enforcement agent works. Since the enforcement of regulation is a continuing process, compliance is often attained by increments. Conformity to this process itself is another facet of compliance. And when a standard is attained, it must be maintained: compliance here is an unbounded, continuing state. It is not simply a matter of the installation of treatment plant, but how well that plant is made to work, and kept working. And an ideal, once reached, may be replaced or transformed by other changes.... Central to all of this is the symbolic aspect of compliance. A recognition of the legitimacy of the demands of an enforcement agent expressed in a willingness to conform in future will be taken as a display of compliance in itself. Here it is possible for a polluter to be thought of as 'compliant' even though he may continue to break the rules about the discharge of polluting effluent.

A strategy of compliance is a means of sustaining the consent of the regulated where there is ambivalence about the enforcement agency's mandate. Enforcement in a compliance system is founded on reciprocity, for conformity is not simply a matter of the threat or the rare application of legal punishment, but rather a matter of bargaining. The familiar discrepancy between full enforcement and actual practice is 'more of a resource than an embarrassment'. Compliance strategy is a means of sustaining the consent of the regulated when there is ambivalence about an enforcement agency's legal mandate. The gap between legal word and legal deed is ironically employed as a way to attaining legislative objectives. Put another way, bargaining is not only adjudged a more efficient means to attain the ends of regulation than the formal enforcement of the rules, bargaining is, ultimately, morally compelled.

A number of observational studies of the enforcement behaviour of various agencies have subsequently identified a spectrum of enforcement styles that range between the two ideal types identified by Hawkins, and refining or adding to these ideal types based on their observations. So, for example, Hutter contrasts a 'persuasive strategy', which broadly approximates the 'compliance' strategy outlined by Hawkins, with an 'insistent' strategy, which is less benevolent and flexible yet directed towards gaining compliance, rather than seeking retribution. It is this purposive dimension which she claims distinguishes it from the 'sanctioning' strategy described by Hawkins.

It is evident from the literature described in this section that scholars have identified a broad spectrum of factors that influence the enforcement style adopted by regulatory officials. Yet definitive explanations capable of providing a comprehensive account for observed variance in agency behaviour have proved elusive. In the following extract, Kagan provides a useful framework for collecting together a range of explanations that scholars have offered in seeking to explain such variation.

R. Kagan, 'Regulatory enforcement' (1994)

Why do regulatory agencies lean toward one enforcement style rather than toward another? The answer, as our review of the case study literature will make clear, is complicated. One wonders if it can ever be formulated with economy and precision. Perhaps the best that can be done at this stage is to organise the search for explanations as clearly as possible, differentiating carefully among different kinds of regulatory programs and types of explanatory factors.

Social scientists tend to offer two basic kinds of explanations. In one perspective, official action is shaped by the technical, economic and legal problems the agency encounters. Regulatory officials, it is assumed, are like public-spirited carpenters. The laws they enforce provide the blueprint that sets forth their mission and define the tools they cause. Working with those constraints, the regulatory carpenters adapt the plans to the raw material with which they work: the hazards to be abated; the attitudes, capabilities and economic resilience of regulated entities; the problems of detecting and preventing non-compliance; the unexpected disjunctions between the plans of what seems feasible in the particular situations. To understand enforcement style, therefore, one must look first of all to the 'legal design' of the regulatory program: its substantive goals and standards, the powers it gives the agency, and the constraints it imposes on agency discretion. In addition, one must consider the features of the 'task environment' to which the regulatory administrator must adapt: the nature and seriousness of non-compliance, the character of regulated enterprises, and the detectability of violations.

The second explanatory approach emphasises the regulatory agency's 'political environment'. Regardless of the law and the regulators' notions of what would be best, it is assumed, regulators work within a charged political atmosphere. Interest groups attempt to control agency leadership. Officials who offend politically significant government officials or private organisations face public criticism, budgetary cutbacks, and replacement. Understanding variation in enforcement style, therefore, requires us to focus on the intensity and predominant direction of political pressures brought to bear on regulatory officials by political leaders, industry, proregulatory advocacy groups, and the news media.

```
Legal design factors
        Stringency of regulatory mission
        Legal powers
        – Ex ante/ex post controls
        – Potency and immediacy of sanctions
        – Legal rights of regulated
        – Legal rights of complainants
        Specificity of legal standards and penalties

Task environment factors
        Visibility of violations
        – Frequency of interaction with regulated entities
        – Visibility of violations to complainants
        Regulated entities' willingness to comply
        – Size and/or sophistication of regulated entities
        – Cost of compliance/economic resilience
        Seriousness of risks to be prevented

Political environment factors
        Strength and aggressiveness of proregulation interests
        Preferences of political authorities, as influenced by:
        – Recent catastrophes or scandals
        – Economically urgent projects subject to regulation
        – Political controversy over enforcement style
        – Electoral shifts/changes in regulatory leadership
        – Budget cutbacks
        – Resistance by regulated governmental entities

Leadership factors
        Reactive vs strong-minded regulatory leaders. If strong
        – Leaders' policy Benefits
        – Beliefs concerning enforcement style
        Degree of staff professionalism
```

Figure 4.2 [Table 2] Factors affecting regulatory enforcement style.

Both the 'legal/task environment' and the 'political environment' explanations treat regulatory officials as fungible actors, responding to outside stimuli. In most social science studies, the political attitudes and personal characteristics of regulatory officials play no independent explanatory role; the agency's internal ethos, it is assumed, is shaped by the legal, social and political winds that buffet the agency. Sprinkled through the case study literature, however, and pervading regulatory folk-lore, are signs that agency officials at all levels frequently have minds (and interests) of their own, and that intra-agency commitment and competence (or lack thereof) significantly affect regulatory enforcement style. Agency officials sometimes resist external political and economic pressures, or actively seek to influence their environment. In short, regulatory behaviour can also be affected by variations in agency leadership and its effect on 'agency culture'.

All four sets of explanatory factors – regulatory legal design, the agency's social and economic task environment, its political environment, and its internal leadership – can simultaneously influence agency action. The intellectual problem is to analyse the relative weight of each under varying conditions.

Although most socio-legal studies of the behaviour of regulatory enforcement officials have focused either on a single agency or on a pair of agencies, a handful of more ambitious, multi-agency studies have sought to identify whether, and if so why, a particular style of enforcement prevails on a nation-wide scale. In the following extract, Vogel contrasts the adversarial, legalistic approach which he claims has characterised the American experience of regulatory enforcement with the British approach which he characterises as flexible and discretionary.

D. Vogel, 'National styles of regulation' (1986)

In sum, each nation does exhibit a distinctive regulatory style, one that transcends any given policy area. The British government regulates the impact of business decisions on the environment in much the same way it attempts to control a variety of dimensions of corporate conduct. Regulation of industry tends to be more infor-mal in Britain than in the United States, more flexible, and more private. Regulatory officials are able to exercise considerable discretion and tend to make policy on a case-by-case basis rather than through the application of general rules and stan-dards. Little use is made of prosecution and much reliance is placed on securing compliance through informal mechanisms of social control, including, in many instances, self-regulation. Regulatory officials tend to have close working relation-ships with the members of those industries whose conduct they are responsible for supervising; the latter are closely consulted before rules are issued and regulations enforced. In America, on the other hand, regulation tends to be highly formalized: it proceeds on the basis of the application of broad rules that are made and enforced in accordance with strictly defined procedures. The entire regulatory process is subject to close scrutiny by the courts, the legislature, and the public as a whole. Fines are levied for violations relatively frequently and little reliance is placed on industry self-regulation.

Participation by nonindustry constituencies does vary widely across regulatory areas in both countries. The Alkali Inspectorate and the system of land-use planning, for example, represent virtually polar opposites in terms of the opportunities they extend for participation by nonindustry constituencies. On the other hand, the American system of regulation does not invariably provide more opportunity for nonindustry participation than the British: trade unions are more directly involved in the making and enforcement of occupational health and safety regulation in Britain than in the United States. The critical distinction between the British and American approaches to regulation has to do with the terms in which nonindustry participation takes place.

In America there are numerous points of access to the regulatory process: interest groups can lobby Congress, participate in agency rule-making procedures, attempt to influence the regulatory review process at the White House, and challenge particular regulations in the courts. If state and local governmental units are also affected, the opportunities for intervention are multiplied still further. In Britain the number of forums at which the public can intervene in the regulatory process is more limited; to the extent that public participation takes place at all, it is generally restricted to a handful of arenas. An important reason why government regulation of industry has created so much less overt political conflict in Britain than in the United States is that the relationship among the interest groups involved in particular policy areas tends to be relatively structured. This is clearly true in the case of industry, whose inter-action with government officials usually takes place through trade associations, though large companies generally negotiate with the government directly. But to a significant extent it is also true of nonbusiness constituencies: both by controlling access and by using private organizations to implement various regulatory policies, the British government has played an important role in shaping both the number and scope of the political pressures placed upon it. Alternatively, it is in part the relative openness of the American regulatory process that makes it so contentious.

There are exceptions to each of these generalizations. The making of British land-use policies takes place in highly visible forums and the procedures governing the "large public inquiries" are highly legalistic. In addition, over the last decade the regulation of both ethical drugs and the City has come to resemble more closely the more formal approach adopted earlier by the United States. Nor are the politics of British regulation invariably less contentious: the four case studies of British environmental policy described in [an earlier chapter] demonstrate the extent to which disputes over various policies have spilled over from the forums originally established to contain them and become highly public, involving both Parliament and the cabinet. Yet if one compares policies in any particular area of regulation, significant differences remain. Particularly over the last fifteen years, a significantly larger proportion of regulatory policies have been formulated and implemented through relatively informal and private negotiations between regulatory officials and interest groups in Britain than in the United States. On the whole, the regulatory process has been far more public — and therefore more politicized — in the United States than in Great Britain. It has not, however, been notably more effective.

This conclusion does not, however, unequivocally support the position of political scientists who contend that policy process and outcomes are primarily the result of factors peculiar to the countries where they are developed, that is, that "politics matters." For the agenda of regulatory policy itself does appear to be shaped by socioeconomic factors that transcend any particular political system. It is not merely that the issues of environmental quality and of worker and consumer health and safety in general have become more salient in both Great Britain and the United States over the last two decades. Rather the specific ways in which these issues have been defined are strikingly similar. Consider the following examples of issue convergence: the construction and expansion of airport facilities, highways, and offshore energy facilities (i.e., LNG), the safety of nuclear power (Windscale and Three Mile Island), the health impact of exhaust from the internal combustion engine (i.e., lead), the effects of pesticide use on the health of both birds and agricultural workers (DDT, dieldrin, 2,4,5-T), the environmental impact of energy production (the North Sea and the North Slope), the pollution produced by the burning of coal in power plants (acid rain), offshore oil spills (Santa Barbara and *Torrey Canyon*), the disposal of toxic wastes (Love Canal, Nuneaton), health hazards to workers (asbestos and vinyl chloride), the safety of ethical drugs (thalidomide, Oraflex).

This convergence of regulatory agendas appears to be due to two factors. One is the similar levels of industrial development in the two nations. The economies of both Britain and the United States are dominated by many of the same industries — indeed, in many cases, the very same multinational companies. Obviously these firms — and their products — produce many of the same externalities. Moreover, because significant segments of their populations are both affluent and highly educated, they have similar expectations: they are in a position to demand — and to pay for — less hazardous working conditions, safer products, and a more scenic and healthful physical environment. Industrial growth in a democratic society thus simultaneously creates environmental problems and places pressures on policy makers to ameliorate them. It is certainly not coincidental that public interest in these policy areas increased in both countries in the late 1960s and early 1970s, following two decades of relatively sustained and rapid economic growth.

There is a second explanation for the convergence of the regulatory agendas of Great Britain and the United States in the postwar period: international communication. The media have played an important role in disseminating information about various regulatory issues to interested citizens on both sides of the Atlantic. The London "killer fog" of 1952, the blowout at Santa Barbara in 1966, the wreck of the *Torrey Canyon* in 1965, the publication of *Silent Spring* in 1962, Love Canal in 1977 — all received considerable press coverage in both countries. Policy makers and scientists have also communicated extensively: they attend the same conferences, read the same journals, and regularly exchange technical information. While on occasion scientists in Great Britain and the United States disagree about the hazards associated with particular products, chemicals, or technologies, these differences are far outweighed by their areas of agreement. This scientific consensus has played an important role in shaping the regulatory agendas of both nations. As a result, whenever one nation has identified a particular product, chemical, or production process as hazardous, officials on the other side of the Atlantic invariably find themselves under pressure from both activists and scientists in their own country to do likewise.

Since the early 1970s, activists in both countries have developed increasingly close ties: both Greenpeace and Friends of the Earth have British and American chapters, and Ralph Nader provided some of the initial funding for the investigatory journalism of the *Social Audit*. The German Marshall Fund regularly sends American environmentalists to European countries, including Britain. British environmental organizations, with fewer resources and with less access to government documents, have come to rely on their counterparts in the United States for information, and so raise in Britain many of the issues that have recently appeared on the political agenda in the United States.

Why do regulatory outcomes appear relatively similar in the two countries? Why have they been only marginally affected by the substantial differences in the ways in which policies have been made and enforced? One reason is that policy makers in both capitalist democracies operate under a similar set of constraints. For while economic growth both creates externalities and provides the available resources to ameliorate them, it also constrains the amount of resources that can be committed to such efforts. Obviously, national priorities do differ somewhat and there can be legitimate disagreements about what a nation or a particular industry, firm, or plant can "afford." But in the long run, the severity of enforcement is strongly influenced by the interests of policy makers, industrial workers, and the public as a whole in keeping their nation's industries internationally competitive. Again, it is not coincidental that enforcement efforts in both nations slackened somewhat following the increase in oil prices in late 1973. Moreover, as I have previously argued, regulation is only one factor among many that affect either environmental quality or public health and safety. To the extent that the actual quality of the environment varies in Great Britain and the United States, the difference appears to be due less to their systems of regulation than to geographical conditions and industrial and technical factors.

Yet at the same time, the ways in which regulatory decisions are made vary substantially in Great Britain and the United States. In this context, the importance of each nation's political system remains decisive: these are distinctive national styles of regulation. Compared to both the regulatory agenda and regulatory outcomes, the way in which each political system has gone about making and implementing regulatory controls remains highly distinctive. The latter dimension appears to have been much less affected by technological or socioeconomic factors than the former two. The evidence presented [here] does not of course resolve the debate over the relative importance of political and structural factors in shaping public policies across national boundaries. Their conclusion is valid only for the two countries and the limited numbers of issues they have addressed. At the same time, the body of scholarly literature on this subject does suggest that these generalizations can be applied to other industrialized democracies as well . . . .

[Several other] studies and my own analysis suggest that at least among the advanced capitalist democracies, the politics and administration of amenity and health and safety regulation vary much more than either actual regulatory outcomes or the political agenda itself.

4.3.2 Normative approaches to enforcement

4.3.2.1 Normative prescriptions developed from empirical observation

When considering observational studies of the behaviour of enforcement officials, it is important to note that their aim is to identify, document and understand observed enforcement practices. In pursuit of this objective, they adopt an empirical, rather than a normative, methodological approach. There is, however, a growing body of academic scholarship that is normative in outlook, aimed at prescribing and evaluating the desirability of particular enforcement strategies and styles. But although these two forms of inquiry are methodologically distinct, some scholars have combined them, by drawing from the findings of empirical research to develop a series of prescriptions which they argue should be used to guide regulatory design and practice. One of the most well-known attempts to prescribe the kind of enforcement strategies which regulators should adopt is that of Ayres and Braithwaite, whose work on tripartism we have already considered in the previous chapter. Their approach is based on both empirical observations and normative prescriptions derived from economic game theory, sociological inquiries into shaming and political theory exploring republican conceptions of community. In so doing, their object is to construct a normative model that prescribes strategies to guide enforcement officials in responding to suspected regulatory violations.

I. Ayres and J. Braithwaite, '*Responsive regulation*' (1992)
Mixed motives and Tit-for-Tat
Deterrence versus compliance models of regulation
The first step on the road to our conclusions is to understand that there is a long history of barren disputation within regulatory agencies, and more recently among scholars of regulation, between those who think that corporations will comply with the law only when confronted with tough sanctions and those who believe that gentle persuasion works in securing business compliance with the law . . . .

Happily, this era of crude polarization of the regulatory enforcement debate between staunch advocates of deterrence and defenders of the compliance model is beginning to pass. Increasingly within both scholarly and regulatory communities there is a feeling that the regulatory agencies that do best at achieving their goals are those that strike some sort of sophisticated balance between the two models. The crucial question has become: When to punish; when to persuade?

The game theorist's answer
The game theory literature stood ready with some answers to this question. . .

Scholz models regulation as a prisoner's dilemma game wherein the motivation of the firm is to minimize regulatory costs and the motivation of the regulator is to maximize compliance outcomes. He shows that a TFT [Tit-For-Tat] enforcement strategy will most likely establish mutually beneficial cooperation, under assumptions he believes will be met in many regulatory contexts. TFT means that the regulator refrains from a deterrent response as long as the firm is cooperating; but when the firm yields to the temptation to exploit the cooperative posture of the regulator and cheats on compliance, then the regulator shifts from a cooperative to a deterrent response. Confronted with the matrix of payoffs typical in the enforcement dilemma, the optimal strategy is for both the firm and the regulator to cooperate until the other defects from cooperation. Then the rational player should retaliate (the state to deterrence regulation; the firm to a law evasion strategy). If and only if the retaliation secures a return to cooperation by the other player, then the retaliator should be forgiving, restoring the benefits of mutual cooperation in place of the lower payoffs of mutual defection.

As a "nice" strategy (one that does not use deterrence until after the firm defects), TFT gains the full advantage of mutual cooperation with all firms pursuing nice strategies. As a vengeful strategy which retaliates immediately, it gets stuck with the sucker payoff only once against firms that evade in every round. Yet as a forgiving strategy it responds almost immediately if a previous evader begins to comply, thereby restoring the benefit of mutual cooperation rather than the lower payoffs of mutual defection. Furthermore, the simplicity of TFT makes it easily recognized by an opponent.

Alternative motivational accounts

The TFT policy prescription is for the regulator to try cooperation first. This conclusion is not grounded in any assumption that business people are cooperative in nature; rather, the payoffs in the regulation game make cooperation rational until the other player defects from cooperation. The motivational account of the firm is of a unitary actor concerned only with maximizing profit. Braithwaite's empirical work on corporate offending has led him to posit some alternative motivational accounts...

... We argue that a strong case for TFT can be made from the alternative motivational accounts revealed from these studies. The first stage of our argument is, therefore, that TFT is an unusually robust policy idea because radically divergent accounts of regulation converge on the efficacy of TFT . . . Braithwaite concluded in *To Punish or Persuade* that you could not develop a sound regulatory enforcement policy unless you understood the fact that sometimes business actors were powerfully motivated by making money and sometimes they were powerfully motivated by a sense of social responsibility. He, therefore, rejected a regulatory strategy based totally on persuasion and a strategy based totally on punishment. He concluded that business actors exploit a strategy of persuasion and self-regulation when they are motivated by economic rationality. But a strategy based mostly on punishment will undermine the good will of actors when they are motivated by a sense of responsibility. This will be true of any version of responsibility that is construed by actors as a more noble calling than making money. When actors see themselves as pursuing a higher calling, to treat them as driven by what they see as baser motivation insults them, demotivates them...

...A crucial danger of a punitive posture that projects negative expectations of the regulated actor is that it inhibits self-regulation... When punishment rather than dialogue is in the foreground of regulatory encounters, it is basic to human psychology that people will find this humiliating, will resent and resist in ways that include abandoning self-regulation. The point is not new; it is made in a passage from Confucius that every educated Chinese used to know by heart: "If people be led by laws and uniformity is sought to be given them by punishments, they will try to avoid punishments but have no sense of shame"... To reject punitive regulation is naive; to be totally committed to it is to lead a charge of the Light Brigade. The trick of successful regulation is to establish a synergy between punishment and persuasion. Strategic punishment underwrites regulatory persuasion as something that ought to be attended to. Persuasion legitimates punishment as reasonable, fair, and even something that might elicit remorse or repentance... Going in with punishment as a strategy of first choice is counterproductive in a number of ways. First, punishment is expensive; persuasion is cheap. Therefore, if persuasion is tried first and works, more resources are left to expand regulatory coverage. In contrast, a mining inspectorate with a first preference for punitive enforcement will spend more time in court than in mines. Second, punitive enforcement engenders a game of regulatory cat-and-mouse whereby firms defy the spirit of the law by exploiting loopholes, and the state writes more and more specific rules to cover the loopholes. The result can be: (1) rule making by accretion that gives no coherence to the rules as a package, and (2) a barren legalism concentrating on specific, simple, visible violations to the neglect of underlying systemic problems. Third, heavy reliance must be placed on persuasion rather than on punishment in industries where technological and environmental realities change so quickly that the regulations that give detailed content to the law cannot keep up to date.

Given these problems of punitive enforcement, and given that large numbers of corporate actors in many contexts do fit the responsible citizen model, *To Punish or Persuade* argued that persuasion is preferable to punishment as the strategy of first choice. To adopt punishment as a strategy of first choice is unaffordable, unworkable, and counterproductive in undermining the good will of those with a commitment to compliance. However, when firms which are not responsible corporate citizens exploit the privilege of persuasion, the regulator should switch to a tough punitive response.

...TFT is the best strategy for Scholz because, in maximizing the difference between the punishment payoff and the cooperation payoff, it makes cooperation the most economically rational response. TFT is the best strategy in *To Punish or Persuade* because it holds out the best hope of nurturing the noneconomic motivations of firms to be responsible and law abiding. Paradoxically, diametrically opposed motivational accounts of business can converge on the same enforcement prescription.

...In all of these ways analyses of what makes compliance rational and what builds business cultures of social responsibility can converge on the conclusion that compliance is optimized by regulation that is contingently ferocious and forgiving. . . .

Pyramid strategies of responsive regulation

The enforcement pyramid

... In this section we take this suggestion of the need for a range of sanctions a radical step further. This step was taken in Braithwaite's *To Punish or Persuade* where the argument was first made that compliance is most likely when an agency displays an explicit enforcement pyramid. An example of an enforcement pyramid appears in Figure 2.1[4.3].

Most regulatory action occurs at the base of the pyramid where attempts are initially made to coax compliance by persuasion. The next phase of enforcement escalation is a warning letter; if this fails to secure compliance, imposition of civil monetary penalties; if this fails, criminal prosecution; if this fails, plant shutdown or temporary suspension of a license to operate; if this fails, permanent revocation of license. This particular enforcement pyramid might be applicable to occupational health and safety, environment or nursing home regulation, but inapplicable to banking or affirmative action regulation. It is not the content of the enforcement pyramid on which we wish to focus during this discussion, but its form. Different kinds of sanctioning are appropriate to different regulatory arenas.

Defection from cooperation is likely to be a less attractive proposition for business when it faces a regulator with an enforcement pyramid than when confronted with a regulator having only one deterrence option. This is true even where the deterrence option available to the regulator is maximally potent. Actually, it is especially true

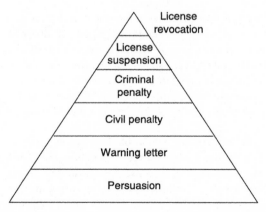

Figure 4.3 [Figure 2.1] Example of an enforcement pyramid. The proportion of space at each layer represents the proportion of enforcement activity at that level.

where the single deterrence option is cataclysmic. It is not uncommon for regulatory agencies to have the power to withdraw or suspend licenses as the only effective power at their disposal. The problem is that the sanction is such a drastic one (e.g., putting a television station off the air) that it is politically impossible and morally unacceptable to use it with any but the most extraordinary offenses. Hence, such agencies often find themselves in the situation where their implied plea to "cooperate or else" has little credibility. This is one case of how we can get the paradox of extremely stringent regulatory laws causing underregulation. Regulatory agencies have maximum capacity to lever cooperation when they can escalate deterrence in a way that is responsive to the degree of uncooperativeness of the firm, and to the moral and political acceptability of the response. It is the same point as in strategic deterrence in international affairs; a country with a nuclear deterrent but no conventional forces may be more vulnerable than one that can bargain with a limited range of conventional escalations. And it is the same point that has been demonstrated empirically in the domain of criminal justice: if death is the sentence for rape, juries that think this excessive will not convict rapists; if mandatory imprisonment is provided for drunk drivers, many police officers will decline to arrest them.

A regulatory agency with only a sanction that cannot politically or legally be used in a particular situation is unable to deliver a punishment payoff. When a regulatory agency has a number of weapons in its armory, for any particular offense the rational offending firm will calculate that the regulatory agency will in practical terms be unable to use some of the weapons theoretically at its disposal. For those sanctions that can practically be used, it will calculate that the regulator can choose sanctions ranging in severity from s_1 to s_n with probabilities that these sanctions can actually be delivered ranging from p_1 to p_n. But the information costs of calculating these probabilities will be high even for a large company with the best legal advice. These information costs imply that the regulator with an enforcement pyramid may have superior resources with which it can bargain and bluff.

The pyramid of regulatory strategies

The pyramid of sanctions in Figure 2.1[4.3] is pitched at the target of the single regulated firm. But there is a more fundamental enforcement pyramid pitched at the entire industry. This is a pyramid of regulatory strategies.

To Punish or Persuade argued that governments are most likely to achieve their goals by communicating to industry that in any regulatory arena the preferred strategy is industry self-regulation. When self-regulation works well, it is the least burdensome approach from the point of view of both taxpayers and the regulated industry. When the state negotiates the substantive regulatory goal with industry, leaving the industry discretion and responsibility of how to achieve this goal, then there is the best chance of an optimal strategy that trades off maximum goal attainment at least cost to productive efficiency. But given that an industry will be tempted to exploit the privilege of self-regulation by socially suboptimal compliance with regulatory goals, the state must also communicate its willingness to escalate its regulatory strategy up another pyramid of interventionism. The pyramid suggested was from self-regulation to enforced self-regulation to command regulation with discretionary punishment to command regulation with nondiscretionary punishment (Fig 2.3[4.4]). Command regulation with nondiscretionary punishment has its military analogue in the burning of bridges. If the bridges that are an army's only route of retreat are burned, the enemy knows that it must fight a bloody battle if it advances beyond a certain point. Burning bridges and enacting a policy of nondiscretionary punishment both have the effect of demonstrating commitment — of communicating to an adversary an intention never to give in.

Again, this is just one example of the particular strategies that might be installed at different layers of the strategy pyramid. One could conceive of another pyramid that might escalate from self-regulation to negative licensing, to positive licensing, to taxes on harm. . . .

Escalation up this pyramid gives the state greater capacity to enforce compliance but at the cost of increasingly inflexible and adversarial regulation. Clear communication in advance of willingness by the state to escalate up the pyramid gives incentives to both the industry and regulatory agents to make regulation work at lower levels of interventionism. The key contention of this regulatory theory is that the existence of the gradients and peaks of the two enforcement pyramids channels most of the regulatory action to the base of the pyramid — in the realms of persuasion and self-regulation. The irony proposed was that the existence and signaling of the capacity to get as tough as needed can usher in a regulatory climate that is more voluntaristic and nonlitigious than is possible when the state rules out adversariness and punitiveness as an option. Lop the tops off the enforcement pyramids and there is less prospect of self-regulation, less prospect of persuasion as an alternative to punishment . . .

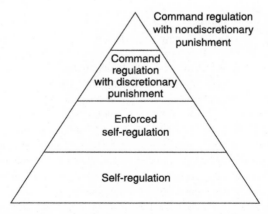

Figure 4.4 [Figure 2.3] Example of a pyramid of enforcement strategies.

... The idea of the pyramid of regulatory strategies underlines the importance of transcending models of regulation as games played with single firms. The importance of business subcultures of resistance to regulation means that we must understand the significance of industry-wide forces beyond the agency of the single firm. In some respects industry associations can be more important regulatory players than single firms. For example, individual firms will often follow the advice of the industry association to cooperate on a particular regulatory requirement because if the industry does not make this requirement work, it will confront a political backlash that may lead to a more interventionist regulatory regime. Hence, the importance of the pyramid of regulatory strategies (Fig 2.3[4.4]) as well as the pyramid of sanctions (Fig 2.1[4.3]). Regulatory cultures can be transformed by clever signaling by regulatory agencies, public interest groups, and political leaders that an escalation of the interventionism of regulatory strategy may be in the offing. As even bigger costs and more unfathomable probabilities are involved in such threats, the potential for bluff is even greater. So much so that industry associations can often be coopted into disciplining and bluffing individual firms that free ride on the regulatory future of the industry.

The benign big gun
The possibility that the range and the nature of the sanctions and strategies at the disposal of regulators may matter is suggested from the application [by Grabosky and Braithwaite] of a variety of multivariate techniques to taxonomize ninety-six Australian regulatory agencies according to patterns of enforcement behavior. A "benign big gun" cluster of agencies emerged from this research. The benign big guns were agencies that spoke softly while carrying very big sticks. The agencies in the benign big gun cluster were distinguished by having enormous powers: the power of the Reserve Bank to take over banks, seize gold, increase reserve deposit ratios; the power of the Australian Broadcasting Tribunal or the Life Insurance Commissioner to shut down business completely by revoking licenses; the power of oil and gas regulators to stop production on rigs at extraordinary cost; the power of drug and motor vehicle safety regulators to refuse to allow a product on the market that has cost a fortune in development. The core members of this cluster of agencies had such enormous powers but never, or hardly ever, used them. They also never or hardly ever used the lesser power of criminal prosecution. Commentators in the past have described the Australian Broadcasting Tribunal's strategy as "regulation by raised eyebrows," and the Reserve Bank strategy as "regulation by vice-regal suasion."

The data from this study are not adequate to measure the relative effectiveness of these ninety-six agencies in achieving their regulatory goals. Nevertheless, the very empirical association of speaking softly and carrying big sticks is an interesting basis for theoretical speculation. The pyramid of enforcement idea suggests that the greater the heights of punitiveness to which an agency can escalate, the greater its capacity to push regulation down to the cooperative base of the pyramid. Graduated response up to draconian final solutions can make passive deterrence formidable (even if the final solution has never been used, as in nuclear deterrence) and can give active (escalated) deterrence room to maneuver. Thus, the theory would be that the successful pursuit of cooperative regulation is predicted by:

(1) Use of a tit-for-tat strategy;
(2) Access to a hierarchical range of sanctions and a hierarchy of interventionism in regulatory style (the enforcement pyramids); and
(3) Height of the pyramid (the punitiveness of the most severe sanction).

4.3.2.2 Value-based critiques of enforcement practices and prescriptions

The preceding extract from Ayres and Braithwaite exemplifies attempts to pre-scribe the conditions under which policy-makers and enforcement officials should adopt particular strategies in securing compliance with regulatory goals. These can be distinguished from another strand of normative scholarship, one that illustrates variation in the expressive dimension of the law's role in regula-tion. It does so by evaluating the strategies adopted or advocated by regulators, academics and policymakers on the basis of a particular value or set of values considered necessary for legitimating the enforcement process and, in turn, the regulatory regime more generally. For example, the following extract from Ashworth considers the criminal law's expression of censure and the principle of equal treatment in making the decision to prosecute.

A. Ashworth, 'Is the criminal law a lost cause' (2000)

[A] deep difference between Braithwaite and me concerns the function of the crim-inal law and the role of prevention. For Braithwaite, the prevention of harm is a primary goal of social policy, and the criminal law is regarded as one among a number of mechanisms for bringing this about. It should therefore be used as and when it is efficient, and replaced by other mechanisms when it is not efficient and/or cost-effective. This view underlies the idea of responsive regulation, as a means of dealing with the varying contexts in which regulatory agencies have to operate. My conception of the criminal law gives primary place to its censuring function, a public function with possibly severe consequences for citizens, which should be exercised in as fair and non-discriminatory a manner as possible. In this context the principle of equal treatment is assigned a high priority. This is not to suggest that the prevention of harm is irrelevant to criminal law: it remains significant as a fundamental justi-fication for having a criminal law with sanctions attached. But to invoke it as a reason for shaping the criminal law in particular ways would lead to an unacceptably distorted system in which the prospects of effectiveness and prevention, not the seriousness of the wrongdoing, would determine decisions to criminalise, decisions to prosecute and decisions about the appropriate penalty. In principle, the preven-tion of harm should be pursued through a range of initiatives in social, criminal and environmental policy. In practice, there is no shortage of examples of governments either repeatedly over-estimating the preventive efficacy of the criminal law or deliberately ignoring the poor prospects of prevention in favour of the politically symbolic effect of creating a new crime. The aim should be to produce a set of criminal laws that penalise substantial wrongdoing and only substantial wrongdoing, enforcing those fairly and dealing with them proportionately. There is no justification for differential enforcement systems that detract grossly from the principle of equal treatment and the sense of fairness about proportionate responses to wrongdoing.

Ashworth's concern that the enforcement of the criminal law should give expression to the principle of equal treatment directs our attention to the role of the law in institutionalising moral principles of fairness in the distribution of punishment. Principles of this kind may also be associated with constitutional values and the rule of law. The following extract subjects the prescriptive strategies advocated by Ayres and Braithwaite to critical scrutiny by reference to their conformity with constitutional values more generally.

K. Yeung, 'Securing compliance' (2004)

... Ayres and Braithwaite's dynamic model suffers from a ... potentially ... dangerous weakness . . . .

The essence of the Ayres and Braithwaite strategy is that co-operation with the regulator should be rewarded, whilst failure to co-operate should be punished. Where, in such a strategy, is consideration given to the notion of freedom under the law in which all citizens may act as they wish provided that they do not contravene the law? In the absence of specific legislative proscription, it is not unlawful to decline to co-operate with state authorities, be it the police or commercial regulators. On this basis, Ayres and Braithwaite seem to ignore the implications of their model for a liberal constitutional democracy, failing to accord due respect to individual rights. Even more worrying is the pivotal importance placed on the firm's co-operation as the primary guide to regulatory enforcement action. There is something seriously suspicious about a strategy in which very serious regulatory infractions causing widespread harm are not treated with the appropriate level of severity because the suspect chose at all times to co-operate fully with the regulator, whilst minor infractions are dealt with in a punitive and severe manner because the suspect refused to co-operate with the regulator in its investigations. These examples illustrate the risks of unthinking adherence to the Ayres and Braithwaite model without an awareness of its constitutional shortcomings. In particular, their model overlooks the constitutional values of proportionality and consistency, which are themselves rooted in the right to fair and equal treatment.

As we saw in [an earlier chapter], the proportionality principle requires that state action must be commensurate to the seriousness of the issue at hand. The concept of proportionality involves the evaluation of three factors: the suitability of the measure for the attainment of the desired objective, the necessity of the measure (in the sense that the state has no other option at its disposal which is less restrictive of the citizen's freedom) and the proportionality of the measure to the restrictions which are thereby involved, including the burdens imposed on affected persons. In other words, proportionality entails some idea of balance, and of proper relationship between ends and means. The proportionality principle may, however, be inherently difficulty to apply because it is not an independent principle of review. Rather, it refers to the relationship between other specific and possibly competing substantive interests, requiring an articulation of the relevant benchmark for evaluating proportionality. Given that the focus of the present inquiry is to identify the level of punitiveness that ought to inform the regulator's response to a suspected contravention, the relevant benchmark is the nature and seriousness of the suspected wrongdoing which . . . may be defined in terms of harm and culpability. Thus the seriousness of a contravention will be determined by a multiplicity of factors, including the degree of harm caused by the contravention, the deliberateness of the breach, the duration of the contravention, and the existence of prior contravening conduct by the firm concerned.

While Ayres and Braithwaite invoke a form of proportionality in applying what they refer to as the 'minimal sufficiency' principle, they adopt as their reference point the goal of effective future compliance, rather than the nature and seriousness of the defendant's violation. In other words, their proportionality assessment is largely functional and prospective in its orientation, rather than grounded in a concern for restraints on state power that are rooted in respecting individual rights. Their approach seems to suggest that a suspect who fails to co-operate with the regulator in response to a trivial contravention ought to be severely punished, whilst those who commit grave violations of the law but co-operate fully with the regulator should be left unpunished. The relentless quest for effective compliance pervades their policy prescriptions, reflected in their claim that:

'The trick of successful regulation is to establish a synergy between punishment and persuasion. Strategic punishment underwrites regulatory persuasion as something that ought to be attended to. Persuasion legitimates punishment as reasonable, fair, and even something that might elicit remorse or repentance.'

In liberal democratic societies, punishment is legitimated not by persuasion, as Ayres and Braithwaite suggest, but by a finding of guilt determined in accordance with the requirements of procedural fairness, and by proportionality between the severity of punishment imposed upon the offender and the seriousness of the offence. By failing to acknowledge the importance of offence seriousness as a matter properly informing the regulator's enforcement strategy, relying instead on the co-operation of the regulated as the determining factor, Ayres and Braithwaite neglect several essential constitutional values implicated in the enforcement process.

In short, Ayres and Braithwaite's pyramid of enforcement fails to live up to the [important constitutional values] . . . that inform and constrain the enforcement authority's powers. Although I do not deny that it may be effective in promoting the overriding goals of regulation in securing its collective goals . . . it largely overlooks the constitutional values of proportionality and consistency which should restrict the extent to which regulation's instrumentalist enterprise may legitimately be pursued. These latter values suggest that, while regulatory officials should employ the enforcement tool most likely to be effective in securing compliance, that choice should also be informed by the desired social purpose(s) sought to be promoted, subject to the requirement that the choice of instrument constitutes a fair and proportionate response to the seriousness of the alleged offence.

By pointing to a potential clash between constitutional values and Ayres and Braithwaite's prescriptions for effective enforcement, the above extract draws attention to possible conflict between the law's expressive and facilitative roles. Whether or not the resolution of such conflicts is possible or legitimate will ultimately be dependent upon some underlying political vision and upon the specific empirical context in which a potential conflict arises.

4.3.3 Discussion questions

1. To what extent are 'regulatory conversations' likely to occur where a regulatory agency employs a 'sanctioning' rather than a 'compliance' strategy in enforcing regulatory standards?
2. Is it possible to identify how variation in enforcement styles affects regulatory outcomes? Why or why not?
3. Are variations in compliance style likely to emerge within regulatory regimes that do not employ command-based techniques of control?
4. What is the relationship between Black's 'regulatory conversations' and the implementation of regulatory policy?
5. What is the appropriate role of persuasion and negotiation in enforcing regulatory standards?
6. Should regulatory enforcement officials seek to prevent harm or censure violations of the law?
7. What, if any, role should principles of due process and equal treatment play in the enforcement of regulatory standards?

4.4 Public and private enforcement

Both the 'pyramid of enforcement strategies' and the 'pyramid of regulatory sanctions' advocated by Ayres and Braithwaite in the preceding section are intended to apply to a regulatory regime which imposes penal sanctions against law-breakers. They also assume a regulatory framework in which a public official is responsible for enforcing regulatory rules, and a hierarchical ordering of sanctions according to the level of 'punitiveness', in which criminal liability and criminal sanctions are ranked at higher levels up the pyramid than civil liability and civil sanctions. Two further features arising from their policy prescriptions are worth exploring: firstly, the standard of liability for regulatory violation and secondly, the role of public and private enforcement.

4.4.1 Civil and criminal liability

Within common law systems, every legal rule can be classified as either civil or criminal in nature. Although these labels are familiar to lawyers and may appear readily distinguishable, the distinction between the civil and criminal law is far from clear-cut in both the design and application of legal standards. In the following extract, Coffee explains the nub of the distinction between the civil and criminal law, identifying their 'paradigm' or classic forms by reference to their level of intent, evidentiary requirements, degree of reliance on a public official to bring enforcement action and social purpose. In paradigmatic form, the criminal law places more emphasis on the actor's subjective intent, imposes higher evidentiary requirements in order to prove that a violation has occurred, involves enforcement by a public official and is intended to censure and punish those who violate the law. By contrast, the civil law traditionally involves less emphasis on the actor's subjective intent, imposes lower evidentiary requirements in order to establish a contravention, may be enforced through litigation between private parties and aims to compensate or restore the damage caused by the legal contravention.

Although the civil and criminal law can be readily portrayed in paradigmatic form, the practice of western legal systems often blurs the distinction, particularly in the regulatory context. In the previous chapter, Neiman lamented the growing popularity of market-based tools within policy literature, and the dangers associated with eroding the law's expressive function. While Neiman focuses on the choice between, and substitutability of, command-based and competition-based tools, similar questions arise *within* a command-based framework, in relation to the choice of liability standards and sanctions for violation. For example, what social purpose should be pursued in sanctioning violations (i.e. to provide compensation, to punish for wrongdoing or to deter future violations) and, depending upon the chosen social purpose, should those sanctions be civil or criminal in nature? Just as tools have been creatively combined to generate hybrid policy instruments, legal forms have also been combined to generate hybrid legal forms. For example, one hybrid form is the 'punitive civil sanction'. These are sanctions imposed for violations of a statutory prohibition which are formally classified as civil, but are punitive in nature. They often take the form of a monetary penalty payable to the state, such as financial penalties for breach of EC competition law.

Hybrid legal sanctions such as the punitive civil sanction can be regarded as imaginative and socially valuable attempts to extend the range of sanctions available to enforcement officials. Although they have become popular devices for sanctioning regulatory violations, their utility, impact and the appropriate constraints that should limit their use are contested. As the following extract demonstrates, they raise concerns that relate to the law's expressive dimension.

J. C. Coffee Jr, 'Paradigms lost: The blurring of the criminal and civil law models – and what can be done about it' (1992)

Ken Mann's professed goal is to "shrink" the criminal law. To realize this worthy end, he advocates punitive civil sanctions that would largely parallel criminal sanctions, thereby reducing the need to use criminal law in order to achieve punitive purposes. I agree (heartily) with the end he seeks and even more with his general precept that "the criminal law should be reserved for the most damaging wrongs and the most culpable defendants." But I believe that the means he proposes would be counterproductive — and would probably expand, rather than contract, the operative scope of the criminal law as an engine of regulation and social control. The differences in our analyses follow from differences in our perspectives. Professor Mann's focus is largely doctrinal and basically centers on the question of whether courts will accept candidly punitive civil penalties. My perspective is more behavioral and focuses on incentives: what would regulators and private enforcers do under a legal system that largely overlaid punitive civil sanctions on top of criminal penalties? We also begin from different starting points. Although we both agree that the line between civil and criminal penalties is rapidly collapsing, Professor Mann sees (and favors) the encroachment of the civil law upon the criminal law. I see more of the reverse trend: the encroachment of the criminal law into areas previously thought to be civil or "regulatory" in character. Thus, I want to resist encroachment, while he wishes to encourage it in order to give enforcement authorities the less drastic remedy of civil penalties . . . .

The paradigms blur: The encroachment of the criminal law on the civil law
Most commentators acknowledge that the following attributes tend to distinguish the criminal law from the civil law: (1) the greater role of intent in the criminal law, with its emphasis on subjective awareness rather than objective reasonableness; (2) the criminal law's focus on risk creation, rather than actual harm; (3) its insistence on greater evidentiary certainty and its lesser tolerance for procedural informality; (4) its reliance on public enforcement, tempered by prosecutorial discretion; and (5) its deliberate intent to inflict punishment in a manner that maximizes stigma and censure. In contrast, tort law usually seeks only to force defendants to internalize the social costs that their conduct imposes on others. Its focus then is on harm, not blame. Professor Mann mentions most of these points (and others), and his discussion is instructive.

But there is one important difference that he largely ignores: criminal laws are legislative acts, while the civil law is largely judge-made. Early in the legal history of the United States, the separation of powers doctrine was interpreted to bar federal judges from creating common law crimes (as they did in Great Britain). But even apart from our unique constitutional context, in all common law countries, advance legislative specification today constitutes a fundamental prerequisite to a criminal prosecution.

In contrast, the civil law is always developing through judicial enlargement, often in surprising ways. American courts create new torts on a daily basis, and new substantive legal principles are regularly applied retroactively . . . The question in such a context is not whether to impose a substantial penalty on the defendant, but rather how to divide losses actually incurred between plaintiff and defendant. In any event, the important point is that if a legal prohibition were enacted as both a criminal and a civil rule, there is a greater likelihood that it would experience judicial expansion

— first in its civil law setting, but eventually (on a catchup basis) in its criminal setting. Moreover, judicial lawmaking inevitably tends to result in standards with a decidedly soft-edged, fuzzy quality. This imprecision is consistent with the natural desire of judges to leave themselves discretion and flexibility in future cases . . . .

A recurring pattern emerges. Public concern about a newly perceived social problem — the environment, worker safety, spousal abuse — triggers a societal reflex in the United States: the adoption of new criminal legislation that typically elevates any knowing or willful violation of the statutory regime to the status of an indictable felony. No doubt these social problems are serious (and no attempt to minimize the injuries from them is intended). But as this process of reflexive criminalization continues, its little-noticed consequence is to expose a significant portion of the population of the United States to potential entanglement with the criminal law during the ordinary course of their professional and personal lives. Actual use of the criminal sanction might remain rare, but it is the threat of its use that must be chiefly considered in evaluating the degree of freedom within a society. To be sure, some may justify pervasive use of the criminal sanction based on simple cost/benefit reasoning: the loss to those imprisoned is less than the harm thereby averted through specific and general deterrence. Yet this analysis depends on a myopic social cost accounting. Even if the deterrent effect gained under such a system of enforcement exceeded the penalties actually imposed, additional costs need to be considered, including the fear and anxiety imposed on risk-averse individuals forced to live under the constant threat of draconian penalties. These citizens would bear not only the risks of false accusation and erroneous conviction, but also the constant fear that they might commit an unintentional violation. Ultimately, if we measure the success of the criminal law exclusively in terms of the number of crimes prevented, we could wind up, in Herbert Packer's memorable phrase, "creating an environment in which all are safe but none is free." Yet, if the threat of the criminal law's use should be curtailed, Professor Mann's proposals do little or nothing to reduce that threat. . . .

A policy appraisal: The problems with overlapping criminal and civil penalties
. . .Why is it important to distinguish civil from criminal penalties when we could instead, as Professor Mann suggests, adopt a "middleground jurisprudence" applicable to all more-than-compensatory penalties? A partial answer lies in the incentive effects of overlapping civil and criminal penalties. The first and most obvious incentive for regulators confronting parallel civil and criminal penalties is to use the civil option for cases in which either the evidence or the legal merits are weak. Procedural informality benefits the prosecution. The prosecution obtains a decided advantage when it can try its case in an extrajudicial proceeding before an administrative law judge operating under informal rules of procedure and evidence. Indeed, the one common denominator in the Securities and Exchange Commission experience with administrative law judges is familiar: the Commission always seems to win before its in-house judges. Beyond the home court advantage, public enforcers also gain the ability to prove their cases simply by a preponderance of the evidence, rather

than beyond a reasonable doubt, and to evade the jury's ability to nullify an overly harsh law. As a result, civil penalties, particularly when administratively imposed, could provide the means for evading constitutional safeguards.

A less obvious reason why overlapping criminal and civil penalties may not "shrink" the criminal law involves two less visible facts of governmental life: the inevitability of bureaucratic competition and the struggle for credit. An implicit assumption underlying proposals to expand civil penalties is that federal criminal cases involving regulatory violations result primarily from criminal referrals made by administrative agencies to federal prosecutors. On this premise, if administrative enforcers were armed with powerful civil penalties, Professor Mann reasons that they might refer less of their enforcement cases to federal prosecutors, retaining for in-house discipline all but the most egregious violations. Although this reasoning may have some validity, it is naive in at least two important respects. First, many cases involving regulatory violations originate within the U.S. Attorney's office. They arise not from an external agency referral, but spontaneously, through the predictable dynamics of plea bargaining. Because the principal currencies in plea bargaining are information and cooperation, a defendant desiring favorable treatment needs as a practical matter to implicate someone else, preferably someone more important. The resulting parade of falling dominoes can move in unanticipated directions, leapfrogging over jurisdictional and subject matter boundaries. Thus, a bribery investigation might suddenly branch out into a regulatory crime, or a fraud case could become a criminal tax case as well. Authorizing enhanced civil penalties will not "shrink" these cases, because federal prosecutors want credit for the cases they have uncovered.

Predictions that the criminal law will "shrink" in the wake of enhanced civil penalties also seem unrealistic in light of the bureaucratic incentives to bring criminal cases. Even if enhanced civil penalties could be assessed more quickly at lower cost and with a lower reversal rate on appeal, the agency loses the publicity and public drama that uniquely attends the criminal process. Public attention is important to an agency for a variety of reasons. Public visibility may help the agency communicate its self-image as a tough, "no-nonsense" enforcer. That image may in turn assist the agency in obtaining its desired budgetary allocation, in recruiting new personnel, or simply in maintaining morale among its officials. In addition, such an image may generate greater general deterrence than a substantial number of low-visibility civil penalties, even if the aggregate amount of the civil penalties imposed were higher.

Still, a deeper reason explains why agencies are likely to persist in seeking criminal sanctions even if parallel civil penalties were available. No agency believes that violations of its rules are simply regulatory offenses that lack inherent moral culpability. Whatever the agency − [whether environmental, securities, health and safety, or food and drugs regulation] − it is a safe bet that its staffers believe that their agency's rules protect vital public interests. To communicate this view, the agency needs the public morality drama that only the criminal law affords. Indeed, the limited empirical evidence on public attitudes toward white-collar crimes suggests that the public learns what is criminal from what is punished, not vice versa. That is, the use of the criminal sanction changes public perceptions of the severity of an offense, increasing the public's estimate of its inherent culpability. Such evidence underscores the socializing power of the criminal law, but also explains in turn why there are pressures for its overuse. From the agency's perspective, any legislative failure to authorize criminal penalties for violations of its rules and regulations depreciates its mission — particularly in contrast to other agencies enjoying access to criminal penalties.

A predictable reply to these assertions is that prosecutors have no incentive to bring petty or technical cases, in part because they may incur judicial displeasure. This is a partial truth, but one offset by a corresponding perverse incentive. White-collar investigations take time, typically extending a year or more from when a U.S. Attorney's office commences a formal investigation to indictment. Such lengthy investigations require a substantial commitment of resources. The personal commitment of Assistant U.S. Attorneys actually conducting the investigation may be even more costly since most of them anticipate spending only a limited period of time in the office. Suppose, for example, that a two-year investigation into a suspected "traditional" crime (such as bribery or fraud) fails to turn up sufficient evidence for an indictment. But assume further that, as is almost invariably the case, some breach of an agency's rules and regulations surfaces. At the outset of the investigation, such evidence of a low-gravity violation would not have interested the prosecutors; but now, having sunk years of time into what is otherwise a dry well, the temptation arises for them to justify their efforts by indicting on the technical violations. Good prosecutors resist this urge to produce an indictment at all costs, but not all prosecutors live up to this standard. In short, technical violations may be criminally prosecuted because they provide a face-saving way of rationalizing failure. In addition, they allow the prosecutor who needs cooperation from a critical witness to pressure the witness to provide the necessary evidence. Whatever the reason, the bottom line is that bureaucratic and careerist incentives exist for prosecutors to use technical violations as a basis for criminal prosecutions. No doubt their chosen tool serves them well, but the cost to society involves tolerating a heightened potential for selective prosecutions.

Finally, a structure of overlapping civil and criminal penalties as proposed by Professor Mann might have unintended effects on judicial behavior. It is far easier to expand precedents and make new law in civil cases than in criminal ones. If enforcers could choose at their discretion between civil and criminal penalties, they might use the civil route as a vehicle by which to advance novel theories, hoping to impose criminal penalties later, after establishing the new theory of liability. In addition, to the extent that there is a "first mover" advantage and decisions by administrative law judges can influence courts, this technique might be a very effective means for enlarging the scope of the criminal law. Take, for example, the persistent problem of defining "insider trading." Had the Securities and Exchange Commission been able at the outset to develop a body of expansive administrative precedents defining this term, it is likely that courts would have deferred to the Commission, given their lesser familiarity with the field. If so, overlapping civil and criminal penalties should expand, not contract, the criminal law.

4.4.2 Enforcement rights

In the regulatory context, there is a tendency to associate the enforcement of legal standards with a system of public enforcement whereby a state official (typically an administrative agency) is responsible for monitoring compliance with standards, investigating suspected non-compliance and taking action against violators. This model is adopted in modern democratic legal systems to enforce violations of the criminal law, and reflects the criminal law in its paradigmatic form: a state prosecutor possesses the exclusive right to enforce violations of the criminal law and, in so doing, is regarded as acting for and on behalf of the victim and community in general. By contrast, in paradigmatic form, the civil law enables private persons who have been harmed by a violation of civil law standards to bring court action against the alleged perpetrator, seeking compensation for the harm so caused.

Rather than rely on a public official to take enforcement action against suspected violators, it is possible to construct a regulatory scheme in which private actors are allowed to litigate to enforce violations of regulatory norms. Within a private scheme of enforcement, the state's enforcement role would be limited to providing a court system to adjudicate private claims. Alternatively, public and private enforcement may co-exist within a regulatory regime, generating further questions concerning the relationship between them. Perhaps the most well-known approaches to such questions employ economic analysis to evaluate whether an 'optimal' level and division of enforcement responsibilities between public and private enforcers can be identified.

4.4.2.1 Economic analysis of public and private enforcement

According to the economic analysis of law, the level of law enforcement which will occur is a product of the cost of enforcement, the level of fine imposed for legal violation following successful enforcement action, and the probability of detection. An increase in the fine will lead to an increase in the expected cost of an offence, generating a higher level of enforcement and, consequently, a higher level of deterrence. In a well-known paper, Gary Becker and George Stigler, two leading exponents of the economic analysis of law, advocate a scheme in which all law enforcement, including the criminal law, is privatised. They propose that private individuals and firms would investigate violations, apprehend violators (including criminal offenders) and conduct legal proceedings (including criminal prosecutions) to redress violation. If successful, the private enforcer (who need not be the victim of the violation) would be entitled to retain the entire proceeds of suit (i.e. the fine paid by the offender in a criminal case); but if unsuccessful, the private enforcer would be required to reimburse the defendant's legal expenses. Landes and Posner refine the economic model proposed by Becker and Stigler, to assert that the area in which private enforcement is clearly preferable to public enforcement on efficiency grounds is more restricted than Becker and Stigler believe. The intuitive explanation for their conclusions is extracted next. The formal economic modelling has been removed from the extract.

W. Landes and R. Posner, 'The private enforcement of law' (1975)

The intuitive explanation for the overenforcement theorem is straightforward. If the[re was 100%] probability of apprehension and conviction..., the optimal fine would be set equal to the social costs of illegal activity — ie. to the value of crime prevention. If the value of crime prevention rose because the harm from crime was increasing, the optimum fine would rise by the same amount. This would be perceived by enforcers as an upward shift in the demand curve facing them, and would have the effect of increasing the resources devoted to crime prevention, as in the case of an ordinary product the demand for which increases. The difficulty arises because in the design of an optimum system of penalties where the probability of apprehension and conviction is less than [100%], the fine is set higher than the social cost of the illegal activity, not as a signal that additional resources should be devoted to the activity because its value has increased relative to other activities, but rather as a device for attempting to minimise those resources. A fine so set communicates the wrong signal, from a social standpoint, to the private enforcer. In the case of public enforcement, the high fine need not be taken as a signal to invest greater resources in crime prevention, since the public enforcer is not constrained to act as a private profit maximizer.

In showing that private enforcement is less efficient than optimum public enforcement, we have not established a case for preferring public to private enforcement. That would require a comparison between private and actual, not optimal, public enforcement, a comparison very difficult to make without a theory of behaviour of public enterprises. The overenforcement theorem is nonetheless useful... in explaining policies designed to limit the scale of law enforcement activities.

4.4.2.2 Public discretion and private rights

While the economic analysis of law enforcement seeks to identify the optimal quantity of enforcement, other scholars have considered the relative strengths and shortcomings of public and private enforcement in qualitative terms. They have typically examined enforcement decision-making structures, purposes and processes, rather than focusing on their relative contribution to achieving an economically efficient level of enforcement. The following extract compares the advantages and disadvantages of private enforcement to those of public enforcement, pointing to the attractions of a mixed regime and the challenges of combining forms of enforcement.

K. Yeung, '*Privatising competition regulation*' (1998)

1. Enforcing competition law

    ...

The use of judicial adjudication within a regulatory framework provides scope for private enforcement. The absence of effective private rights of action in UK competition law has been heavily criticised. Indeed, one of the features of the Competition Bill is the introduction of private rights of action where a breach of competition legislation occurs. . . .

Private enforcement and effective regulation
. . . Financial penalties for infringing the law serve as a powerful deterrent against infringement, provided that firms are faced with a real risk that infringements will be detected and actively enforced so that the threat of financial penalties is a real one. Similarly, the obligation to pay civil damages following a successful private action can have a strong deterrent effect. In other words, private actions can be instrumentally valuable. By discouraging anti-competitive commercial behaviour, private actions promote the substantive goals of competition regulation. Procedural and substantive rules can be structured so as to create economic incentives to act in a particular way. Individual behaviour is affected by altering the costs of targeted activities. The availability of treble damages in US anti-trust suits . . . so as to encourage private suits is a striking example of this technique. The aim is to devise a regulatory framework in which the incentives to take private action are aligned with the public objectives which justify the need for regulation.

Not only is private enforcement instrumentally valuable in that it may promote the substantive goals of competition regulation, it can also be regarded as intrinsically valuable. Private actions may have a legitimate role in ensuring that those who harm others by their unlawful conduct should be legally responsible to make reparation to those so harmed. The obligation to pay damages also serves to punish offenders for unlawful action. If the objectives of compensation and punishment are regarded as independent values which should be reflected in the law, then entitling private litigants to seek damages can further these subsidiary goals. Private enforcement can also be regarded as a participatory activity which allows individuals and groups to compete over increasingly pluralistic understandings of the public interest. It allows those with a direct sense of grievance a direct opportunity to make enforcement claims in court.

Private enforcement and efficient regulation
Whilst effectiveness concerns the extent to which stated goals are achieved, efficiency is concerned with how cost-effectively they are achieved. Private actions enhance the efficiency of the enforcement scheme if they facilitate the substantive goals of competition regulation at a reduced cost.

Governments may favour private enforcement because actions are funded by private individuals rather than the public purse. The efficiency imperative is not, however, concerned with the source of funding but the overall cost of enforcement. In a purely private scheme, the overall cost of enforcement of the system itself is an externality which individual litigants cannot be expected to factor into their calculation when deciding whether to litigate. Litigation involves considerable transaction costs. Therefore, excessive litigation arising from over-enforcement is undesirable. That said, public agencies charged with the responsibility of monitoring and enforcing regulatory policy are in practice often unable effectively to fulfil their duties due to inadequate funding, generating an 'enforcement gap'. Thus even if private enforcement is more expensive overall than public enforcement, it may nonetheless provide a second-best solution to fill the enforcement gap which would otherwise arise.

Litigation, whether public or private, also serves a variety of functions beyond that of conflict resolution. Litigation (particularly where it results in the imposition of a financial penalty for unlawful activity) also has a wider deterrent effect: indicating to firms the type of behaviour which the law does not tolerate in the broader public interest. Where actions are pursued to judgement, then litigation also contributes to the elucidation of the law and the reinforcement of social values. Private actions can raise issues of importance which benefit the general public. In other words, private litigation has the capacity to generate a positive externality. That is, when one person confers a benefit upon another without receiving a reward, the social benefit of the activity is greater than the private return. Private rights of action can also enhance the accountability of public enforcement authorities by providing a check on their integrity, assiduousness and competence. Finally, private enforcers enjoy certain practical advantages which are not shared by public enforcers: personal motivation, first-hand knowledge of the relevant industry, diverse outlooks and (in some cases) access to litigation budgets.

The limitations of private enforcement
But private enforcement suffers from certain limitations which are outlined below . . .

The free rider problem
Competition regulation which relies entirely on private enforcement is unlikely to prove wholly effective nor efficient because such a scheme is likely to generate an incentive gap due to the problem of the free rider. The free rider problem stems from the fact that court judgements display many of the characteristics of 'public goods'. This means that the benefit of court precedents (and indeed success in an individual case) is not enjoyed by the successful individual litigant alone, but by others who cannot be excluded from such enjoyment. Collective action problems (or 'co-ordination problems') are likely to arise where the harm arising from certain anti-competitive conduct has a diffuse impact. No rational individual litigant will be sufficiently motivated to proceed on the basis of recoverable compensation damages. Individual victims may be unwilling to incur the costs and risks involved in litigation in anticipation of being able to free-ride on the successful action of another. Accordingly, under-enforcement of competition law is likely to result. The [proscribed] conduct may be permitted to continue to an extent which exceeds the level which would prevail under a scheme of efficient enforcement.

Fine-tuning and over-enforcement
Private actions can potentially create problems of over-enforcement and excessive litigation. If efficient enforcement is one aim of regulation, then this requires that the

sum of the cost of enforcing the law and the cost of harmful conduct which is permitted to occur is minimised. If, however, the level of recoverable damages is set too high thereby providing powerful incentives for private actions, then the total cost of litigation may not justify the overall public benefit. . . .

The task of setting damages awards at an efficient level is made particularly difficult where private enforcement is contemplated because such awards serve a dual function. Not only does the level of damages affect the extent to which potential offenders are deterred, but it also provides potential plaintiffs with incentives to sue. Thus, if enforcement costs rise then pursuing enforcement action in marginal cases should be avoided. This can be achieved by modifying the regulatory framework in one of two ways: either by increasing deterrence or reducing incentives to sue. If deterrence is strengthened by raising the level of recoverable damages, this automatically has the unwanted effect of increasing the incentives to sue. But if the incentives to sue are reduced by decreasing the level of recoverable damages this weakens the deterrence effect. This generates a regulatory dilemma.

The role of public enforcement
Public enforcement can be used to overcome the above problems when used in conjunction with private enforcement. A public enforcer is not motivated by the prospect of recovering compensation damages in deciding whether to pursue enforcement action against an alleged violator and can therefore take action to fill the enforcement gap which is likely to arise within a wholly private enforcement scheme. For the same reason, a public enforcer can more readily adjust its enforcement strategy to achieve the desired level of deterrence. Within a system of public enforcement, deterrence can be achieved by imposing penalties for infringement. Thus by decoupling the link between the incentive to sue and the deterrence impact of private damages awards, the amount of penalty imposed on a violator following successful public action can be adjusted without affecting the intensity of enforcement effort by the public enforcer . . .

A public enforcer may also enjoy certain advantages which are not present in a private enforcement system. For example, public enforcers may also enjoy stronger information gathering powers than those available to private litigants by way of civil procedure. In addition, the public enforcer may also possess an element of discretion in developing an enforcement strategy enabling it to take into account the underlying rationale for . . . regulation in prioritising cases. Such flexibility also allows the public enforcer to adjust for error due, for example, to an under- or overinclusive legal standard. Private litigants, on the other hand, are motivated by self-interest and are rationally unconcerned with the broader public interest.

The practical benefits of public enforcement can also be supported on more theoretical grounds. Private litigation is primarily concerned to settle disputes between private parties [or citizens] about private rights and interests. If the aim of [regulation] is to protect individual firms, then private enforcement is a simple and logical means by which firms can safeguard their position. But [regulation is more often] . . . regarded as a form of public law.

Because [regulation] is a form of public law which seeks to protect the public interest . . . , this may suggest that a public official is the most appropriate means by which [regulation] should be enforced. Not only can a public official be expected to take a more global view of the economic system and give paramount concern to the policy goals which [it] is designed to promote, the public official may be placed under a legal duty to do so.

That said, private rights may be conferred on individuals in order to implement the objectives of public law. Thus, for example, the public interest in promoting the objective of gender equality may be furthered by conferring private rights on those discriminated against on the basis of gender. The same is true of competition law. It may be possible to confer private rights on those injured by the anti-competitive conduct of others so that the assertion of such rights by private litigants also serves the public interest of promoting and protecting the competitive process. Put simply, private actions can provide the means of vindicating public policy. Although the inability directly to control private actions in order to pursue a given set of enforcement priorities may be considered to be a shortcoming of private enforcement, some indirect control can be exerted over private actions by shaping the legal regime to provide appropriate incentives for private enforcement.

2. Combining public and private enforcement

Within a regulatory scheme which utilises both public and private enforcement, the challenge is to determine how both types of enforcement can be appropriately aggregated. Two broad issues can be identified. First, what is the appropriate level and mix of public and private enforcement? In other words, how should the overall intensity of enforcement be determined? In order to bring about the desired overall behaviour in the system it is necessary to establish appropriate incentives for both private and public enforcers. Secondly, the relationship between the public and private enforcer needs to be clearly prescribed. The procedural dimensions of the relationship may be of considerable significance to both public and private enforcers in deciding whether to take action against a suspected infringement, thereby affecting the overall operation of the regulatory scheme . . . .

. . . In summary, a regulatory regime which combines both public and private enforcement must clearly define the relationship between them. In order to generate the efficient level of aggregate enforcement and deterrence, the public enforcer should pursue an enforcement strategy which accords priority to cases which significantly harm and distort the [public interest] but where private actions are unlikely to be instituted. In principle, private actions should be available where successful public actions have been brought and, conversely, a public enforcer should be entitled to seek penal sanctions against a defendant found liable at the suit of a private plaintiff. The availability of such follow-on actions may, however, render the courts' task of setting the appropriate levels of penalty and damages awards very difficult.

Both the preceding extracts focus on the capacity for involving private actors in the enforcement process through civil litigation. It is important to emphasise, however, that private actors can play a wide range of roles, of varying levels of formality, in helping to provide oversight, monitoring, and in promoting compliance with regulatory rules. Mechanisms such as third party auditing, inspection, verification, judicial review, ombudsman and many other complaints-handling procedures all enrol the capacities of private actors in the overall enforcement effort. The law's role here is to provide avenues through which private and non-state actors can participate in the enforcement process, reflecting the umpiring dimension of its facilitative role by making private participation possible, but also by expressing a commitment to community-wide participation in shaping the content and contours of the public interest in regulation through participatory processes.

4.4.3 Discussion questions

1. Why does Coffee refer to a law and economics approach to law enforcement as a form of 'myopic social cost accounting'? How might law and economics scholars respond?
2. What factors should influence the design and choice of regulatory sanctions and liability standards for regulatory rules?
3. What are the appropriate roles for the civil law and criminal law in regulatory enforcement?
4. Is it possible to identify the conditions under which private enforcement may be more appropriate than public enforcement or vice versa?
5. What are the advantages and shortcomings of involving courts in the implementation of regulatory regimes?

4.5 Conclusion

In the previous chapter, we observed that the image of law as threat, as well as that of law as umpire, help to depict the way in which law is embedded in regulatory tools and techniques. The literature extracted in this chapter highlights the socially contextual, complex and sometimes contradictory nature of each of these images. It also reveals both the facilitative and expressive dimensions of law's role in regulatory enforcement and compliance. Studies of regulatory enforcement have focused primarily on the enforcement of rule-based legal norms enforced by a public official and, as a consequence, it is the law's threatening face that appears most prominently. In this context, the law's threat is problematic in at least two senses. Firstly, its scope and content are indeterminate, owing to the inescapable indeterminacy of language in which the law's command is couched. The difficulties and challenges associated with formulating, interpreting and applying rules preclude the law's threat from being deployed in a simple and straightforward manner. Secondly, the findings arising from observational studies of the behaviour of regulatory enforcement officials reveal the incompleteness of the law's threat. Human agency complicates the process of bringing the law's threatening force directly to bear upon a particular actor. In addition, ethnographic studies show that the law's threat, couched in terms of formal prosecution, is rarely invoked, typically held in abeyance by enforcement officials for use only as a 'last resort' in exceptional circumstances. This is not to say that the law's threat is necessarily neutralised in the process of human inter-mediation. Rather, regulatory enforcement officials invoke the law's threat in various ways, often with considerable subtlety and sensitivity, such that its visibility and strength vary in accordance with the official's perception of the surrounding social context. Nor does the need for human agency to enforce regulatory norms imply that enforcement is random or unpredictable. On the contrary, socio-legal studies of the behaviour of regulatory enforcement officials demonstrate that the exercise of enforcement discretion by public offi-cials is socially patterned, highlighting the limits of the law's formal threats and the pervasiveness of informal practices. While one could regard the reluc-tance of enforcement officials to prosecute suspected regulatory violations as indicative of regulatory capture, observational studies suggest that this is better explained by the officials' perception that invoking the law's threat is likely to be counter-productive in securing lasting compliance with the collective goals of a regulatory regime.

The scholarly focus on the enforcement of legal rules within the context of command and control regimes means that the law's umpiring role in facilitating interactions between citizens has not occupied centre stage within compliance literature. But the law's facilitative dimension is nevertheless evident in at least four guises. Firstly, the economic analysis of public and private enforcement rests on a set of assumptions in which the law's threat, in the form of prohibitive commands, merely provides a framework of incentives that seeks to shape behaviour through deterrence. The law's incentive structures appear from this perspective as pliable, capable of being moulded to achieve the desired behavioural outcomes. Secondly, the emergence of 'alternative' and 'hybrid' civil/criminal sanctions reflects an essentially facilitative view of the law in its umpiring role, enabling policy-makers and public officials to establish and employ sanctions creatively in shaping social behaviour. Thirdly, scholars have drawn attention to the potential to harness the resources and motivations of private actors to enforce regulation by litigation. When the legal framework is structured to provide a direct right of action to private parties to seek redress from alleged violators, the law acts as umpire in ensuring adherence to regulatory requirements. Finally, prescriptive models of strategic enforcement developed by academics to guide the enforcement decisions of regulatory officials assume the law's role is that of both threat and umpire, facilitating compliance with regulatory objectives in the most effective and efficient manner.

But although the facilitative dimension of the law's role is evident throughout this chapter, arguably it is the law's expressive dimension that is brought to the fore in the enforcement and compliance literature. It is the law's moral face that socio-legal scholars have highlighted here, demonstrating the importance of perceptions of fairness, both by regulatory enforcement officials and those they regulate, in determining the way regulatory actors behave. So, for example, the decision to prosecute and bring the force of the law's threat to bear on those suspected to have violated regulatory rules is strongly influenced by the extent to which the enforcement authority seeks to enlist the law's expressive dimension in publicly condemning the activity in question. Here, the exercise of prosecutorial discretion is shaped by the law's role in expressing principles of fairness or in giving effect to the community's general understandings of the kind of conduct that is worthy of public censure. Furthermore, the perceived moral ambivalence associated with regulatory violations leads to the predominance of a 'compliance' rather than a 'sanctioning' style of enforcement. But the law's expressive dimension is also reflected in normative critiques which appeal to rule-of-law values such as proportionality, equality and fair treatment in order to critique the models of strategic enforcement adopted or advocated by regulators, policy-makers and academics. These critiques draw on such values as constraints on the use of the law's facilitative capacity. So, for example, the imposition of criminal sanctions for violating legal standards publicly condemns and censures violators, thus embodying the expressive dimension of the law's threat. Finally, conferring enforcement rights on private actors not only facilitates the attainment of regulatory goals, but also provides a legal avenue through which citizens may participate in increasingly pluralistic understandings of the public interest served by regulation. In this way, the legal framework gives expression to the values of participation and restoration, reflecting the image of law as umpire. This expressive umpiring role of law is explored more fully in the following chapter.

References

Ashworth, A. 2000. 'Is The criminal law a lost cause?', *Law Quarterly Review* 116: 225–256.

Ayres, I. and Braithwaite, J. 1992. *Responsive Regulation: Transcending the regulation debate*, New York: Oxford University Press, 19–53.

Bardach, E. and Kagan, R. 1982. *Going by the Book: The Problem of Regulatory Unreasonableness*, Philadelphia: Temple University Press.

Becker, G. and Stigler, G. 1974. 'Law enforcement, malfeasance, and compensation of enforcers', *Journal of Legal Studies* 3: 1–18.

Bevan, G. and Hood, C. 2005. 'What's measured is what matters: targets and gaming in the English public health care system', *ESRC Discussion Paper Series: No. 0501.*

Black, J. 1997. *Rules and Regulators*, Oxford: Clarendon Press, 5–45.

1998. 'Talking about regulation', *Public Law*, 77–105.

Braithwaite, J. 1985. *To Punish or Persuade: Enforcement of Coal Mine* Safety, Albany: State University of New York Press.

Braithwaite, J., Grabosky, P. and Walker, J. 1987. 'An enforcement taxonomy of regulatory agencies', *Law and Policy* 9: 323–351.

Coffee Jr, J. C. 1992. 'Paradigms lost: The blurring of the criminal and civil law models – and what can be done about it', *Yale Law Journal* 101: 1875–1893.

Diver, C. 1983. 'The optimal precision of administrative rules', *Yale Law Journal* 93: 65–109.

Edelman, L. E., Petterson, S., Chambliss, E. and Howard, S. E. 1991. 'Legal ambiguity and the politics of compliance: affirmative action officers' dilemma', *Law and Policy* 13: 73–97.

Edelman, M. 1964. *The Symbolic Uses of Politics*, Urbana Ill.: University of Illinois Press.

Fish, S. 1980. *Is There a Text in This Class?: The Authority of Interpretive Communities*, Cambridge, MA: Harvard University Press.

    1989. *Doing What Comes Naturally: Change, Rhetoric and the Practice of Theory in Literary and Legal Studies*, Oxford: Clarendon Press.

Goodhart, C. A. E. 1984. *Monetary Theory and Practice: The UK Experience*, London: Macmillan.

Gouldner, A. W. 1954. *Patterns of Industrial Bureaucracy*, New York: Free Press.

Grabosky, P. and Braithwaite, J. 1986. *Of Manners Gentle: Enforcement Strategies of Australian Business Regulatory Agencies*, Melbourne: Oxford University Press.

Hart, H. L. A. 1994. *The Concept of Law*, Oxford: Clarendon Press, 2nd ed.

Hawkins, K. 1984. *Environment and Enforcement*, Oxford: Clarendon Press.

Hutter, B. 1997. *Compliance: Regulation and Environment*, Oxford: Oxford University Press.

Kagan, R. 1994. 'Regulatory enforcement' in Schwartz and Rosenbloom, (eds.) *Handbook of Regulation and Administrative Law*, New York: Marcel Dekker.

Landes, W. and Posner, R. 1975. 'The private enforcement of law', *Journal of Legal Studies* 4: 1–46.

LeGrand, J. 2003. *Motivation, Agency and Public Policy*, Oxford: Oxford University Press.

Mann, K. 1992. 'Punitive civil sanctions: The middle ground between criminal and civil law', *Yale law journal* 101: 1795–1873.

McBarnet, D. and Whelan, C. 1991. 'The elusive spirit of the law: Formalism and the struggle for legal control', *Modern Law Review* 54: 848–873.

Packer, H. 1968. *The Limits of the Criminal Sanction*, Stanford: Stanford University Press.

Schauer, F. 1989. 'Formalism', *Yale Law Journal* 97: 509–548.

1991. *Playing by the Rules: A Philosophical Examination of Rule-Based Decision-Making in Law and Life*, Oxford: Clarendon Press.

Scholz, J. 1984. 'Deterrence, cooperation and the ecology of regulatory enforcement', *Law and Society Review* 18: 179–224.

Vogel, D. 1986. *National Styles of Regulation: Environmental Policy in Great Britain and the United States*, Ithaca: Cornell University Press.

Waismann, F. 1951. 'Verifiability' in A. G. N. Flew (ed.), *Logic and Language: First Series*, Blackwell: Oxford, 117–44.

Wittgenstein, L. (G. E. M. Anscombe, trans.) 1968. *Philosophical Investigations*, Oxford: Blackwell, 3rd ed.

Yeung, K. 1998. 'Privatising competition regulation', *Oxford Journal of Legal Studies* 18: 581–615.

2004. *Securing Compliance*, Oxford: Hart Publishing.

Suggested further reading

Baldwin, R. 1990. 'Why rules don't work', *Modern Law Review* 53: 321–337.

Bardach, E. and Kagan, R. 1982. *Going by the Book: The Problem of Regulatory Unreasonableness*, Philadelphia: Temple University Press.

Black, D. 1976. *The Behavior of Law*, New York: Academic Press.

Cabinet Office, 1999. *Modernizing Government* (Cm 4310), London: The Stationery Office. http://www.archive.official-documents.co.uk/document/cm43/4310/4310.htm.

Campbell, D. 2000. 'Of coase and corn: A (sort of) defence of private nuisance', *Modern Law Review* 63: 197–215.

Cowan, D. and Marsh, A. 2001. 'There's regulatory crime, and then there's landlord crime: From "Rachmanites" to "Partners", *Modern Law Review* 64: 855–874.

Hampton, P. 2004. *Reducing Administrative Burdens: Effective Inspection and Enforcement*, London: HM Treasury.

Hawkins, K. 2003. *Law as Last Resort*, Oxford: Oxford University Press.

Hopkins, A. 1994. 'Compliance with what? The fundamental regulatory question', *British Journal of Criminology* 34: 431–441.

Kagan, R. 1991. 'Adversarial legalism and American government', *Journal of Policy Analysis and Management* 10: 369–406.

Kagan, R. and Scholtz, J. 1984. 'The "Criminology of the corporation" and regulatory enforcement strategies' in Hawkins and Thomas (eds.) *Enforcing Regulation*, Massachusetts: Kluwer Nijhoff, 67–95.

Klein, S. 1999. 'Redrawing the civil-criminal boundary', *Buffalo Criminal Law Review* 2: 679–722.

Lofstedt, R. E. and Vogel, D. 2001. 'The changing character of regulation: A comparison of Europe and the United States', *Risk Analysis* 21: 399–415.

Marshall, M., Shekelle, P., Brook, R. and Leatherman, S. 2000. *Dying to Know: Public Release of Information about Quality of Care*, London: The Nuffield Trust.

Mnookin, R. and Kornhauser, L. 1979. 'Bargaining in the shadow of the law: The case of divorce', *Yale Law Journal* 88: 950–97.

Parker, C. 1999. 'Compliance professionalism and regulatory community: The Australian trade practices regime', *Journal of Law and Society* 26: 215–39.

Polinsky, A. and Shavell, S. (in press). 'The theory of public enforcement of law', in Polinsky and Shavell (eds.), *Handbook of Law and Economics*, *Handbooks in Economices*, Vol 1.

Pontin, B. 1998. 'Tort law and Victorian government growth: The historiographical significance of tort in the shadow of chemical pollution and factory safety regulation', *Oxford Journal of Legal Studies* 18: 661–680.

Richardson, G. 1987. 'Strict liability for regulatory crime', *Criminal Law Review* 295–306.

Richardson, G., Ogus, A. and Burrows, P. 1984. *Policing Pollution*, Oxford: Clarendon Press.

Rowan-Robinson, J., Watchman, P. and Barker, C. 1990. *Crime and Regulation: a Study of the Enforcement of Regulatory Codes*, Edinburgh: TandT Clarke.

Scott, C. 2002. 'Private regulation of the public sector: A neglected facet of contemporary governance', *Journal of Law and Society* 29: 56–76.

Shavell, S. 1993. 'The optimal structure of law enforcement', *Journal of Law and Economics* 36: 255–87.

Stewart, R. B. and Sunstein, C. R. 1982. 'Public programs and private rights', *Harvard Law Review* 95: 1193–1322.

Sparrow, M. 2000. *The Regulatory Craft*, Washington: Brookings Institution Press.

Reiss Jr, A. J. 1984. 'Selecting strategies of social control over organisational life', in Hawkins and Thomas (eds.), *Enforcing Regulation*, Boston: Kluwer-Nijhoff (1984) 23–35.

Steele, J. 1995. 'Private law and the environment: Nuisance in context', *Legal Studies* 15: 236–259.

Zimring, F. E. 1992. 'The multiple middlegrounds between civil and criminal law', *Yale Law Journal* 101: 1901–1908.

5

Regulatory accountability and legitimacy

5.1 Introduction

The previous chapters have explored how and why regulation emerges, how it is deployed and how it works on the ground. They have established that the scope of regulation both conceptually and practically goes substantially beyond a narrow view of formal legal control of private actors. The expansion of the meaning of regulation and its practical impact is closely associated with a flourishing debate about regulatory legitimacy and accountability. Legitimacy, according to Jody Freeman, is when the public accepts decisions without having to be coerced (Freeman 1999), or as Rob Baldwin puts it, the legitimacy of an administrative process can be seen in terms of the persuasive power of the arguments made in its favour (Baldwin 1995). Accountability is, more concretely, 'the duty to give account for one's actions to some other persons or body', in Colin Scott's words (Scott 2000). The changes in the scope of regulation that the preceding chapters have charted have led to significant challenges to acceptance of regulatory regimes and calls for those who control them to account for decisions made under them. Indeed, commentators often refer to a 'crisis' in the regulatory state, as the myriad complex forms of controlling behaviour which it has developed make it increasingly difficult to trace the lines of responsibility for public decision-making, especially when things go wrong. Moreover, regulatory regimes often create institutions that are at least partially independent from directly elected political decision-makers, yet make politically sensitive decisions. Independent regulatory agencies are a common example of this, and a claim that these agencies lack legitimacy is often the focus of challenges to regulation. The purpose of this chapter is to map different approaches to questions of regulatory legitimacy and accountability.

There are two important constraints on this mapping exercise. Firstly, while we take a more in-depth look at the normative dimension of regulatory regimes than has been the case in previous chapters, we will not venture too far into the terrain of philosophical analysis, or make any sustained attempt to provide an objective valuation of particular types of regulatory regimes, instruments or enforcement practices. Indeed, one might say that we are more concerned here with studying patterns in the *legitimation* of regulatory regimes than with their legitimacy. Our focus is on mapping the sorts of reasons that persuade people to accept regulatory decisions, rather than on conducting an exercise in moral reasoning in order to evaluate whether a decision is morally correct. Secondly, while this chapter discusses the implications for legitimacy and accountability of the trend towards 'decentred' regulation, it does so in general terms rather than by linking directly back to every aspect of the topics already discussed. Apart from limitations of space, we have confined the focus of this chapter because the expansive direction of literature about regulation comes close to collapsing the distinction between regulation as a *subset* of government activities, and governing as a whole. But if an exploration of regulatory legitimacy comes too close to a task as expansive as justifying government itself, it would be too large for a book of this nature. For this reason, the structure of this chapter differs from other chapters, although all aspects of those chapters could be seen as generating questions about the legitimation of regulation and the accountability of regulatory regimes.

The remainder of this chapter proceeds in five sections. In the next section, we briefly touch upon what would be involved in justifying regulatory legitimacy at a philosophical level and explain why we will not pursue this level of analysis any further. We then explore regulatory *accountability*, which is more concrete than an exploration of patterns of legitimation, because it involves looking at the concrete practical details of different institutional designs that help different actors in a regulatory space to account for what they are doing to other actors in that space. Legitimation, the question of whether these accounts might be persuasive ones that have some claim to being accepted, is more diffuse, and it is helpful to consider it through the lens of what is sometimes called 'middle-level' theory. We will explain what we mean by 'middle-level' theorising in the next section, but we use it to provide two perspectives from which to consider regulatory legitimation. One is to understand it as a question of *different logics of justification*, and the second is to understand it in terms of *different visions of democracy*. Different (and sometimes competing) logics of justification have arisen implicitly in the preceding chapters: for example, the potential tensions between economic and political conceptions of the public interest, different assumptions about human motivations underpinning public and private interest theories, the ideological aspects of instrument choice or the moral dimensions involved in the 'human face' of regulatory enforcement. Considerations of democracy provide an ideal foil for taking account of the apparently counter-majoritarian nature of regulatory institutions, which often lies at the heart of legitimation challenges in regulation. In particular, different versions of democracy link to one or other side of a common cleavage in debates about legitimation between, on the one hand, appeals to expertise and appeals to pluralism on the other.

Both the idea of varying logics of justification and the linkage to democracy make it possible to explore regulatory legitimation in a general fashion without losing all specificity or resorting to a fall-back reliance on context. In the final section, we link the discussion back to one enduring theme of the book and foreshadow the penultimate chapter's discussion of supranational regulation. Looking backwards, we consider the implications of 'decentred' regulation: when so much of what is important in regulation takes place *beyond* the state, involving non-state actors, what does this mean for regulatory legitimation? Looking forwards, we ask the same question when regulation moves *above* the state: a topic which we return to in Chapter 6 and tie it more tightly to the different components of our regulatory map.

Finally, it is worth emphasising that this chapter more than any other poses more questions than answers. The study of this topic in combination with specific contextually situated case study materials about a particular policy area is the only fruitful way to make concrete evaluations of whether a particular regulatory regime is an accountable one that can lay claim to public acceptance. That is a task beyond the scope of this book, although we do make some general observations regarding the expressive and facilitative dimensions of law's role in legitimating regulation. These observations will be developed incrementally in the following sections and summarised in the conclusion.

5.2   Levels of theorising

Our emphasis on the need for contextual evaluation as the preferred ground for patterns of legitimation in regulation reflects our intention to engage only very lightly with philosophical explorations of this topic. We aim instead, as mentioned above, to engage with the topic in a manner that is sometimes referred to as 'middle-level' theorising. By this term, we mean a strategy that works inductively from a 'thick descriptive' understanding of the regulatory world towards an elaboration of 'models' or 'paradigms' that express, at a medium level of abstraction, why the relevant strategies help to persuade people to accept the regime in question. This is why, in subsequent sections, we focus initially on descriptive accounts of accountability, then move to accounts of the varied and sometimes competing *logics* of justification that arise in debates about legitimating regulation, and finally discuss linkages with different ideas of democracy. Although democracy can of course be analysed as a philosophical concept, it can also be approached in more concrete, institutional terms. Accordingly, our aim in that section is to craft a bridge between the abstract and the concrete.

A more fully fledged philosophical defence of the regulatory state entails considerable abstraction, and this is what the extract that follows aims to demonstrate. In that extract, Sunstein makes a brief foray into philosophical justifications of regulatory goals, exploring whether the values of 'welfare' and 'autonomy' can provide a foundation for justifying regulation. He focuses on regulation that fully endorses substantive collective intervention by the state. In other words, the assumption underpinning this extract is that law plays the role in regulation of facilitative threat. Whether a conception of law as umpire, implicit in regulation that supports only the narrower liberal goal of facilitating maximum individual freedom, would change the reasoning offered in this extract is not clear. But in this extract, we get a glimpse of the level of theoretical abstraction that would be required to answer such a question. Valuable as such work is, this level of theoretical abstraction extends beyond this book's aims and length. We include this one brief glimpse as a counter-foil to the more empirically grounded conceptions we seek to derive from 'middle-level' theoretical literature on regulatory legitimacy.

Cass Sunstein, 'After the rights revolution: Reconceiving the regulatory state' (1990)

[Arguments grounded on welfare and autonomy] provide solid reasons for a presumption in favour of protecting voluntary agreements and behaviour from collective control. They help to explain the increasing disenchantment with collectivism in socialist and communist countries and supply reasons to understand and approve aspects of the movement toward deregulation in the liberal democracies as well. They do not, however, prove nearly as much as they purport to do.

An initial set of responses would point to the possibility that both liberty and welfare might be promoted, not undermined, by government action. The most conventional example here involves the problem of market failures of harms to third parties — a point to which we will return. But a more general response would begin by suggesting that governmental rules are implicated in, indeed constitute, the distribution of wealth and entitlements in the first instance. A system that required unanimous consent for redistribution would be understandable only if the existing distribution seemed prepolitical, or just, or supported by unanimous consent at some privileged earlier stage not later disturbed by injustice. If the existing distribution is in fact none of these, Buchanan's notion that something called "constitutionalism" should be designed to bar redistribution that does not have unanimous consent seems exceedingly peculiar.

In short, market outcomes — including prices and wages pursuant to a system of freedom of contract — are affected by a wide range of factors that are morally arbitrary. They include, for example, supply and demand at any particular place and time, unequally distributed opportunities before people become traders at all, existing tastes, the sheer number of purchasers and sellers, and even the unequal distributions of skills. There is no good reason for government to take these factors as natural or fixed, or to allow them to be turned into social and legal advantages, when it is deciding on the appropriate scope of regulation. If this is so, governmental efforts to interfere with market outcomes, at least if they can be made to accomplish their intended purposes (an important qualification), would seem to be required rather than proscribed.

This problem infects considerable work in public choice theory. In its normative capacity, and in the hands of some of its proponents, the field seems built on the (implicit and unjustified) assumption that the status quo itself is in no need of defence. The same point applies to Paretian criteria if they are presented as the exclusive reasons for social change. A Pareto improvement is generally a sufficient condition for change; but it is an altogether different thing to suggest that it is a necessary condition as well. A distribution in which one person owns everything, and everyone else nothing, is Pareto-optimal; but it would not for that reason be uncontroversial on moral grounds.

Moreover, the welfarist and non-welfarist arguments for freedom of contract and private ordering seem to depend on crude understandings of both liberty and welfare.

Liberty. The most obvious problem with the objection from liberty is that difficulties in coordinating the behaviour of many people, and problems of collective action, sometimes make private ordering coercive or unworkable. Here government regulation prevents coercion or chaos, and thus promotes liberty by making it easier for people to do or to get what they want. For example, the rules of the road, regulation of airplane traffic, controls on polluting behaviour, and governmental allocation of broadcast licenses do not interfere with freedom, rightly understood. I take up this point in more detail below.

Moreover, the satisfaction of private preferences, whatever their content, is an utterly implausible conception of liberty or autonomy. The notion of autonomy should be taken to refer instead to decisions reached with a full and vivid awareness of available opportunities, with all relevant information, or, most generally, without illegitimate constraints on the process of preference formation. When these conditions are not met, decisions might be described as unfree or non-autonomous.

Above all, the mistake here consists in taking all preferences as fixed and exogenous. This mistake is an extremely prominent one in welfare economics and in many contemporary challenges to regulation. If preferences are instead a product of available information, of existing consumption patterns, of social pressures, and of legal rules, it seems odd to suggest that individual freedom lies exclusively or by definition in preference satisfaction. It seems even odder to suggest that all preferences should be treated the same way, independently of their origins and the reasons offered in their support.

Consider, for example, a decision to purchase dangerous foods, consumer products, or cigarettes by someone unaware of the (serious) health risks; an employer's decision not to deal with blacks because of the background of public and private segregation or racial hostility in his community; a decision of a woman to adopt a traditional gender role because of the social stigma of refusing to do so; a decision not to purchase cars equipped with seatbelts or to wear motorcycle helmets because of the social pressures imposed by one's peer group; a lack of interest in environmental diversity resulting from personal experiences that are limited to industrialised urban areas; a decision not to employ blacks at a restaurant because of fear of violence from whites. In all of these cases, the interest in liberty or autonomy does not call for governmental inaction, even if that were an intelligible category. Indeed, in all of these cases regulation removes a kind of coercion.

One goal of a legal system, in short, is not merely to ensure autonomy by allowing satisfaction of preferences, but also and more fundamentally to promote autonomy in the processes of preference formation. The view that freedom requires an opportunity to choose among alternatives is supplemented by the view that people should not face unjustifiable constraints on the free development of their preferences and beliefs, although it is not altogether clear what such a view would require. At the very least, such a view would see a failure of autonomy, and a reason for collective response, in beliefs and preferences based on the absence of information or available opportunities - as, for example, in the case of members of disadvantaged groups who accept their subordinate position because the status quo seems intractable, or in the case of people who are indifferent to high quality broadcasting because they have experienced only banal situation comedies and dehumanising, violence-ridden police dramas.

The point suggests more fundamentally that it is incorrect to claim that something called the market, or respect for private arrangements, embodies governmental "neutrality". Private preferences are partly a product of available opportunities, which are a function of legal rules. Those rules allocate rights and entitlements; that function is simply unavoidable (short of anarchy). The allocation will in turn have a profound effect on and indeed help constitute the distribution of wealth and the content of private preferences.

Whether someone has a preference for a commodity, a right, or anything else is in part a function of whether the legal system has allocated it to him in the first instance. For example, a decision to give employees a right to organise, or women a right not to be subject to sexual harassment, will have a significant impact on social attitudes toward labour organisation and sexual harassment. The legal allocation helps to legitimate or delegitimate the relevant rights. It therefore has an effect on social attitudes toward them, and on their valuation by both current owners and would-be purchasers.

In addition, the government's allocation will affect the ways in which preferences are manifested in markets, which rely on the criterion of private willingness to pay. Willingness to pay is a function of ability to pay, and an actor's ability to pay is a function of the amount of goods that have been (legally) allocated to him. In these circumstances, it is hard to see neutrality in governmental respect for preferences, whatever their content and consequences.

To put the point most simply: when preferences are a function of legal rules, the rules cannot, without circularity, be justified by reference to the preferences. It should be a familiar point that government is responsible for the allocation of wealth and entitlements in the first instance. . . . The decision to permit market ordering pursuant to that allocation represents a controversial choice about competing values.

To say this is not to say that the government ought generally to be free to override preferences on the ground that they are a function of the existing social order. Such a view would be a licence for tyranny. It is to say, however, that the concept of autonomy will call not merely for the satisfaction of whatever preferences people currently have, but more generally, or instead, for protection of the processes of preference formation. . . . The discussion thus far suggests that if individual freedom is the goal, laissez-faire is not the solution.

Government action might also be justified on grounds of autonomy when the public seeks to implement, though democratic processes culminating in law, widely held social aspirations or collective "preferences about preferences". Individual consumption choices often diverge from collective considered judgments: people may seek, through law, to implement their reflective democratic decisions about what courses to pursue. If so, it is no violation of autonomy to allow those considered judgments to be vindicated by governmental action. Consider a law calling for protection of the environment or support of high-quality broadcasting, wanted by a majority of the population and creating opportunities insufficiently provided through market ordering. Ideas of this sort can be connected to the original constitutional belief in deliberative democracy, a belief that, as we have seen, grew out of republican conceptions of politics, which place a high premium on political deliberation. Collective aspirations or considered judgments, produced by a process of deliberation in which competing perspectives are brought to bear, reflect a conception of political freedom having deep roots in the American constitutional tradition.

Welfare. With respect to welfare, the response to the case for respecting voluntary agreements would begin by pointing to the existence of coordination and collective action problems, which make the ordinary model of contractual freedom, built on two-party transactions, far less attractive when large numbers of people are involved. Rules regulating automobile or airplane traffic are necessary to prevent chaos. Frequently, moreover, a group of people in a position to contract with one or many firms face a prisoner's dilemma: a situation in which market pressures, and sheer numbers, prevent them from obtaining their preferred solution, which will result only if all cooperate, and are indeed constrained to do so. It is in this sense that markets can be genuinely coercive. On utilitarian grounds, they are not the realm of freedom at all.

A simple case here is that of littering in a park. It may well be in everyone's self-interest to litter, since the individual benefits may outweigh the individual costs. But if everyone litters, the aggregate costs may dwarf the aggregate benefits. If this is so, the preferred outcome, for most or all citizens, is a situation in which everyone can be assured that no one will litter. It is possible that this solution may be obtained through social norms, which sometimes solve dilemmas of this sort, but when such norms are absent or weak, legal controls are the only solution. Here the force of law is necessary to allow people to obtain what they want. The example of pollution is a clear one, but the need for legal coercion to ensure the satisfaction of individual preferences comes up in more surprising contexts.

Consider, for example, laws prohibiting employers from refusing to hire or discharging workers who have declined to sign a pledge not to join labour unions. It may be individually rational for each worker to sign such a pledge. Each worker may be better off with the job and the pledge than without either. But laws prohibiting an employer from requiring the pledge are in the interest of employees as a whole, since they bar the employer from taking advantage of the employees' need to compete among themselves. That competition works to the collective detriment of employees. Regulation is the solution. . . .

To make these claims is emphatically not to deny that democratic societies should make much room for private property, freedom of contract, and other voluntary arrangements. Indeed, a system having all of these has the crucial advantage of respecting and fostering diverse conceptions of the good, an important part of individual freedom; it will promote economic productivity as well. A presumption in favour of a system of voluntary arrangements, operated within the basic institutions of private property, tort, and contract, thus emerges quite naturally from the guiding criteria of autonomy and welfare. The presumption is, however, only that, and it hardly provides a decisive reason to reject a wide array of regulatory initiatives. In many cases, considerations of autonomy and welfare will argue for rather than against such initiatives.

The above extract shows how arguments about regulatory legitimacy might proceed if one were to try to justify the decision to regulate in a particular instance by philosophical reference to basic political values such as liberty and welfare. As foreshadowed, the remainder of this chapter takes a much more empirically grounded approach, beginning with questions of who is accountable, to whom and for what.

5.3   Regulatory accountability

As stated at the outset, Colin Scott, whose work we extract here (Scott 2000), defines accountability as, 'the duty to give account for one's actions to some other persons or body', and we adopt this as our working definition of accountability. Arguably, accountability is one avenue for securing legitimacy. There could be other avenues — for example, success in achieving particular substantive outcomes such as efficiency or equality, fidelity to legal procedures, or charismatic leadership. Usually, however, achieving legitimacy for a regulatory regime will require some form of demonstrable accountability. Broadly speaking, the fulfilment of accountability generally involves ex-post oversight of the actions of one person or institution by another person or institution. Implicit in this is a notion of simultaneous communication and justification that can be concretely described by answering the questions 'who is accountable, to whom and for what'.

Traditionally, debates about accountability in a regulatory regime have revolved around different strategies of employing public power, particularly the choice between political avenues of accountability to ministers or parliament on the one hand, and legal avenues to the courts through judicial review on the other hand. The following extract, however, extends these traditional views to argue that *multiple strategies* of accountability typically exist in relation to regulatory regimes, involving both public and private actors in both horizontal and vertical relationship with public decision-makers. Thus, in addition to the role of state institutions (legislatures, regulators, courts), Scott stresses the role of downward accountability (i.e. accountability mechanisms that operate from the bottom upwards through markets, grievance mechanisms or consultations with users) and of horizontal checks and balances (e.g. via auditors, third party accreditation of standards or supervision by public interest groups). This perspective on accountability recognises the increasingly decentred nature of regulation and builds that recognition into designing strategies for holding regulators accountable.

Colin Scott, *'Accountability in the regulatory state'* (2000)

This article deploys a concept of 'extended accountability' to argue that the fragmentation of the public sector associated with public sector reforms, loosely referred to under the rubric of 'the regulatory state', has made more transparent the existing dense networks of accountability associated with both public and private actors concerned with the delivery of public services. Traditional accountability mechanisms are part, but only part of these complex networks, which have the potential to ensure that service providers may be effectively required to account for their activities. . . .

Accountability is the duty to give account for one's actions to some other person or body. Normanton once offered a somewhat more expansive definition: a liability to reveal, to explain, and to justify what one does; how one discharges responsibilities, financial or other, whose several origins may be political, constitutional, hierarchical or contractual.

The concept of accountability has traditionally been drawn somewhat narrowly by public lawyers, to encompass the formal duties of public bodies to account for their actions to ministers, Parliament, and to courts. Changes in accountability structures since the Second World War have resulted in a recognition of some extended forms of accountability, as courts have been supplemented by a growing number of tribunals (for example, in the immigration and social security domains) and new or revamped administrative agencies such as grievance-handlers and public audit institutions have played a greater role in calling public bodies to account. Simultaneously Parliament has enhanced its capacity for holding ministers and officials to account through the development of select committee structures, in some cases linked to new oversight bodies such as the Parliamentary Ombudsman and the National Audit Office. It is helpful to keep distinct the three sets of accountability questions: 'who is accountable?'; 'to whom?'; and 'for what?'. With the 'who is accountable?' question, the courts have been willing to review all decisions involving the exercise of public power, even where exercised by bodies in private ownership.

The 'to whom?' question has often been mingled with the 'for what?' question, for example in the distinction between legal accountability (to the courts in respect of the juridical values of fairness, rationality and legality) and political accountability (to ministers and to Parliament or other elected bodies such as local authorities and via these institutions ultimately to the electorate). Furthermore, while it might be helpful to think of 'administrative accountability' as accountability to administrative bodies such as grievance holders and auditors, in fact these mechanisms for accountability have conventionally been distinguished, with administrative accountability only indicating the former, while financial accountability is used for the latter.

Separating the 'to whom?' and 'for what?' we find three broad classes within each category. Thus accountability may be rendered to a higher authority ('upwards accountability'), to a broadly parallel institution ('horizontal accountability') or to lower level institutions and groups (such as consumers) ('downwards accountability'). The range of values for which accountability is rendered can be placed in three categories: economic values (including financial probity and value for money (VFM)); social and procedural values (such as fairness, equality, and legality); continuity/security values (such as social cohesion, universal service, and safety). Figure 1[5.1] sets out the possible configurations of the 'to whom?' and 'for what?' questions, producing nine possible pairs of co-ordinates.

The final remark to be made about traditional approaches to accountability mechanisms is that public lawyers almost universally regard them as inadequate. This dissatisfaction exists notwithstanding the remarkable expansion of accountability mechanisms applied to the United Kingdom public sector in recent years. It is rarely possible to discern how adequacy is actually being assessed. In its narrowest form, an adequate accountability system would ensure that all public bodies act in ways which correspond with the core juridical value of legality, and thus correspond with the democratic will. Such a Diceyan conception of accountability was already in severe difficulty within Dicey's lifetime as discretionary authority was more widely dispersed with the growth of the welfare state. Even with the extension of juridical concerns to encompass rationality and fairness in decision making, and thus concerns to improve the quality of discretionary decisions, this narrow model is also very weak at holding public bodies to account for decisions which affect the collectivity, but have little bearing on the welfare of any individual. A broader approach might look for correspondence with a range of other values, such as value for money or openness. But such substantive tests of the effectiveness of accountability mechanisms create difficulties of measurement and do not indicate any appropriate way to recognise the conflict between desired values which is inevitable within particular domains.

For what? To whom?	Economic Values	Social/Procedural Values	Continuity/ Security Values
'Upwards' accountability	Of departments to treasury for expenditure	Of administrative decision-makers to courts/tribunals	Of utility companies to regulators
'Horizontal' accountability	Of public bodies to external and internal audit for Probity and VFM	Review of decisions by grievance-handlers	*Third-party accreditation of safety standards*
'Downwards' accountability	Of utility companies to financial markets	Of public/privatised service providers to users	Consultation requirements re: universal service requirement

Figure 5.1 [Figure 1] Examples of linkages between values and accountability institutions.

We are said to live in the age of the regulatory state. This refers to a shift in the style of governance away from the direct provision of public services, associated with the welfare state, and towards oversight of provision of public services by others. This shift is, in part, a response to the recognition that 'total control' models of state activity fail to deliver desired outcomes. The problem can be expressed in a number of ways: the limited capacity of central-state institutions to know what is best provided by state intervention; the tendency of highly active states towards fiscal crisis; the risk that state actors will be diverted from pursuit of public interest outcomes to the exercise of public power for the pursuit of narrower private interests; and the limited capacity of the instruments of state activity (and notably law) to effect change in social and economic systems. The response to these disparate concerns has been a withdrawal of central-state institutions from much 'operational' activity (a trend mirrored in local government, and to a lesser extent in other public institutions such as the National Health Service), with the reservation to the centre of certain policy tasks, and a marked expansion in central oversight mechanisms. In Osborne and Gaebler's phrase, this is a shift from rowing to steering. Figure 2[5.2] identifies the main characteristics of regulatory state governance and offers examples.

We return to the analysis of prisons and telecommunications [later] to show how the (inadequate and possibly diminishing) traditional accountability mechanisms are being supplemented by new forms which enable us to conceive of an 'extended accountability' applying to actors within these policy domains. . . .[But] we need to be clear that the extended accountability structures identified [here], while they do not correspond to a traditional public law model, equally are not simply the product of an alternative neo-liberal model. To be sure, the neo-liberal model of accountability through market mechanisms has been important. We need only think of the creation of internal markets (for example in the National Health Service), the changes to accountability for local service provision through the introduction

Characteristics	Examples
Separation of policy from operation	NHS internal market Next Steps agencies Contracting out/market testing Utilities privatization
Creation of fee-standing regulatory institutions	Utilities regulator (for example, OFTEL, OFGEM, OFWAT, OFREG) National Audit Office Audit Commission Prisons Inspectorate Social Sendees Inspectorate Service First Unit Better Regulation Unit Financial Services Authority
Increased formality/shift from discretion to rules	Financial Services Service First (formerly Citizen's Charter)

Figure 5.2 [Figure 2] Main characteristics of regulatory state.

of Compulsory Competitive Tendering (CCT), encouraging users to hold service providers to account through league tables and enforceable quality standards, and the introduction of capital market disciplines through privatization. Such market or 'downwards accountability' structures are often characterised by a lack of distinctive normative content, effectively leaving the 'for what?' question to be filled in by the 'discovery procedure' of competition. But the development of 'downwards accountability' mechanisms has not displaced the more traditional accountability mechanisms described above. Market accountability forms have frequently been laid over hierarchical structures. The investigation of any particular policy domain reveals complex structures of extended accountability, best characterised as hybrid in character.

The extended mechanisms of accountability in the regulatory state are not linear in the way anticipated either by the public law literature or neo-liberal prescription. Rather, they are premised on the existence of complex networks of accountability and functional equivalents within the British state structure. Close exploration of the structures of extended accountability in the United Kingdom reveals at least two different models which have developed which feature overlapping and fuzzy responsibility and accountability: interdependence and redundancy. No domain is likely to precisely correspond to one or other of these models. There are likely to be elements of both identifiable in many policy domains but, for reasons of clarity, the examples used in the following sections are presented in somewhat simplified and ideal-type form.

Interdependence

The identification and mapping out of relationships of interdependence within policy domains has been one of the key contributions of the recent pluralist literature in public policy. The identification of interdependence has important implications for accountability structures. Interdependence provides a model of accountability in which the formal parliamentary, judicial, and administrative methods of traditional accountability are supplemented by an extended accountability. Interdependent actors are dependent on each other in their actions because of the dispersal of key resources of authority (formal and informal), information, expertise, and capacity to bestow legitimacy such that each of the principal actors has constantly to account for at least some of its actions to others within the space, as a precondition to action. The executive generally, and the Treasury in particular, has long had a central role in calling public bodies to account over a range of values, in a way that is often less transparent in the case of the more dignified, but arguably less efficient parliamentary mechanisms of accountability. But these less formal and more hidden accountability mechanisms extend well beyond the capacities of central government, extending potentially to any actors, public or private, within a domain with the practical capacity to make another actor, public or private, account for its actions. Within the pluralist political science literature this conception is sometimes referred to as 'constituency relations' or 'mutual accountability'. Indeed it may be that the simple monolithic structures presented as the welfare state model are too simple, that they disguise intricate internal and opaque webs of control and accountability that are functionally equivalent to the new instruments of the regulatory state, but are less formal and transparent. Among the more obvious examples were the consumer committees established for the nationalised industries with a brief to hold those public corporations to account from a collective consumer viewpoint.

This model is exemplified by the United Kingdom telecommunications sector (Figure 4[5.3]). Figure 4[5.3] shows that though BT is subject to diminished upwards accountability to parliament and courts (noted above), it has a new forms of accountability in each dimension − upwards to a new regulator, horizontally to the mechanisms of corporate governance, and downwards to shareholders (and possibly also the market for corporate control) and users. The financial markets arguably provide a more rigorous form of financial accountability than applies to public bodies because there are so many individual and institutional actors with a stake in scrutinizing BT's financial performance.

The accountability of BT to the regulator, OFTEL, is also more focused, in the sense that OFTEL has a considerable stake in getting its regulatory scrutiny right, being itself scrutinised closely by BT, by other licensees, and by ministers, in additional to the more traditional scrutiny by the courts and by public audit institutions. OFTEL's quest for legitimacy has caused it to develop novel consultative procedures, and to publish a very wide range of documents on such matters as competition investigations and enforcement practices. Each of these other actors has powers or capacities which constrain the capacities of the others and require a day-to-day accounting for actions, more intense in character than the accountability typically applied within traditional upwards accountability mechanisms. This form of accountability, premised upon interdependence, is not linear, but more like a

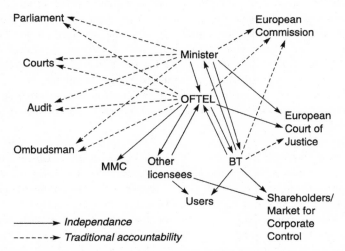

Figure 5.3 [Figure 4] Accountability for provision of telecoms services 2. Interdependence model.

servo-mechanism holding the regime in a broadly acceptable place through the opposing tensions and forces generated. Such a model creates the potential to use the shifting of balances in order to change the way the model works in any particular case.

Redundancy

A second extended accountability model is that of redundancy, in which overlapping (and ostensibly superfluous) accountability mechanisms reduce the centrality of any one of them. In common parlance, redundancy is represented by the 'belt and braces' approach, within which two independent mechanisms are deployed to ensure the system does not fail, both of which are capable of working on their own. Where one fails the other will still prevent disaster. Redundancy in failsafe mechanisms is a common characteristic of public sector activities generally, and can be threatened by privatization. Equally explicit concern about risks associated with change may cause redundancy to be built in to oversight structures. Redundancy can be an unintended effect of certain institutional configurations. In practice, examples of redundancy in accountability regimes appear to be a product of a mixture of design and contingency.

There are at least two forms to the redundancy model: traditional and multi-level governance. The traditional redundancy model is exemplified by the accountability mechanisms for contracted-out prisons in the United Kingdom. Directors of contracted-out prisons are subject to all the forms of accountability directed at publicly operated prisons: upwards (legal, to the courts); financial (to the National Audit Office); and horizontal (to the Prisons Inspectorate, the Prisons Ombudsman, and prison visitors). But, contracted-out prisons are additionally subject to a further form of horizontal accountability with a requirement to account, day-to-day to an on-site regulator (called a controller), appointed by the Prison Service to monitor compliance with contract specification. Unusually within the prisons sector, controllers wield the capacity to levy formal sanctions for breach of contract. Some commentators have suggested that there is a structural risk with on-site regulators of capture by the director, in the sense of controllers over-identifying with the needs and limits to the capacities of those they are supposed to regulate. However, with the redundancy model of accountability were such capture to occur it would likely be identified by one or more of the others holding the director to account.

The challenge for public lawyers is to know when, where, and how to make appropriate strategic interventions in complex accountability networks to secure appropriate normative structures and outcomes. What I have in mind here is something like process of 'collibration' described by Andew Dunsire. Dunsire sees collibration as a stratagem common to a wide variety of processes by which balances are shifted to change the nature of the way that control systems (such as account-ability mechanisms) work. Such interventions may be applied to any of the three accountability parameters: who is accountable? for what? to whom? This offers the possibility of meeting Martin Loughlin's challenge for public law to 'adopt as its principal focus the examination of the manner in which the normative structures of law can contribute to the guidance, control and evaluation in government.' The value of such changes may lie not directly in the development of a single accountability mechanism, but rather in the effects on the overall balance within the regime. The logic of the argument presented here is that conflict and tension are inevitable within the complex accountability webs within any particular domain, and that the objective should not be to iron out conflict, but to exploit it to hold regimes in appropriate tension.

To take an example, within a redundancy model of accountability for contracted-out prisons, how do we ensure proper accountability for the range of values, such as humanity, efficiency, and security which might be deemed appropriate desiderata for a prisons regime? The orthodox answer would be to say that we have an inspector with a specific mandate to check on the humanity of prison regimes, and auditors to assess efficiency, and security people overseeing security. But this is only a partial answer. Within the redundancy model we have other mechanisms which directly or indirectly check on each of these values — the controller, company management, the Prisons Ombudsman, the European Committee for the Prevention of Torture, and the courts. These mechanisms are in tension with another, in the sense of having different concerns, powers, procedures, and culture, which generate competing agendas and capacities. Within contracted-out prisons, corporate governance structures will hold directors to account for the expenditure of money, so that within an efficient redundancy system enough money but no more than is necessary to provide a humane regime will be spent. We might expect periodically that value for money norms or security norms might inhibit the achievement of humanity norms. The solution would not necessarily be to crank up the humanity regime, but rather to apply techniques of selective inhibition to the other norm structures so that their pull on the overall system was diminished somewhat. This might, for example, be through changing financial incentives or oversight structures, or through enhancing access of prisoners to grievance-handlers or judicial review.

There are some rather obvious problems with relying on dense webs of accountability or functional equivalents to secure the achievement of key public law objectives in respect of governance regimes. Chief among these is a marked lack of transparency in the traditional informal arrangements of government, and in many of the new mechanisms such as contracting out, and a lack of scope for broad participation in decision making. . . .

Each of the two models of extended accountability discussed in this article presents difficulties for public lawyers and more generally. Neither model is directly 'programmable' with the public law norms (fairness, legality, rationality, and so on). Interventions to secure appropriate normative outcomes must necessarily be indirect and unpredictable in their effects. The interdependence model carries with it the risk that special interests, such as those of a particular firm or group of firms, may capture the regime through their overall weighting of power within it. The redundancy model presents particular problems. If redundancy *per se* is a good characteristic for an accountability regime, it is difficult to calculate how much redundancy is sufficient and how to know when an additional layer of accountability is inefficient and to be removed. Equally, there is also the risk within a redundancy model of simultaneous failure of different parts of the system for the same reason. Where, for example, information is successfully hidden from more than one part of the accountability network, there is a risk of complete failure in respect of the matters for which that information is relevant.

In the above extract, law continues to play a role in many of the extended accountability mechanisms discussed by Scott. In all the dimensions of accountability which Scott maps, law has both a facilitative and an expressive role. Law is, in other words, a tool for shaping social behaviour, but in so doing it institutionalises the values that Scott categorises as economic, social/procedural and security values. This is a common feature of the role of law when considering regulatory legitimation. This is because the topic is necessarily linked to evaluative claims, even when we ourselves are not going so far as to engage directly in moral reasoning. As a result, the law's expressive dimension in institutionalising values is ever-present, just as its instrumental dimension in shaping social behaviour is an aspect common to all theories of regulation. We will still find, however, that aspects of the topic we discuss distinguish between the various dimensions and images of law's role. For example, the contrasts drawn by Scott between downwards, horizontal and upwards accountability are loosely linked to the difference between law as threat (present in upwards accountability and in the background in horizontal accountability) and law as umpire (encompassed by downwards accountability and at the forefront of horizontal accountability).

5.3.1 Discussion questions

1. What is the relationship between the regulatory techniques discussed in Chapter 3 and the array of accountability mechanisms identified by Scott?
2. Is accountability in a regulatory regime more than just the combination of an array of different regulatory techniques employed to ensure that the outcomes and goals of the regulatory regime are actually secured?
3. Does the role of the law in 'bottom-up' mechanisms mirror the role of the law in competition-based regulatory techniques discussed in Chapter 3?
4. What is the relationship between mechanisms for enforcing regulatory standards (some of which were explored in Chapter 4) and mechanisms for securing regulatory accountability?
5. Can you think of situations in which accountability mechanisms that are intended to operate interdependently actually 'cancel each other out', or at least operate in tension with each other? Consider, when you have read the next section, whether identifying the different logics that underpin regulatory legitimation helps to identify and critically examine such circumstances.

5.4   Varying logics of regulatory legitimation

The detailed description of strategies of accountability provided by Scott is a useful springboard for engaging in concrete discussions of regulatory legitimation, without the need for high levels of theoretical abstraction. But in order to assess fully why such strategies may (or may not) amount to a persuasive case for accepting a particular regulatory regime inevitably requires some link to substantive values or normative ideals. Certain constellations of ideals or values tend to reoccur in real-life debates about the legitimacy of regulatory affairs. For example, Scott articulates three sets of values that a regulatory regime will typically be held to account for: (1) economic values, (2) social and procedural values and (3) values related to continuity and security. But Scott also emphasises the degree to which contemporary strategies and mechanisms of accountability blur and mix different institutional structures that have previously been thought of as distinct paradigms of accountability. For example, he gathers under the single heading of 'strategies that promote social and procedural values', two mechanisms that have often been *contrasted*, particularly in traditional approaches that distinguish between public and private actors. The accountability of administrative decision-makers to courts is a traditional public law mechanism linking the legal and political systems, whereas the accountability of public service providers to users through customer complaints is a private process typical of the economic system. For Scott, however, they both contribute to the promotion of social and procedural values (although one is upwards and the other downwards in design and operation).

The preceding example demonstrates that relationships between mechanisms of accountability and the values promoted by those mechanisms may be complex, particularly within decentred regulatory environments. It is here that the middle-level theorising mentioned above plays an important and helpful role. Much writing on regulatory legitimacy can be considered as classifying thick, descriptive detail about mechanisms and strategies of accountability into one or more 'models' or 'paradigms' of legitimacy, models that capture at a medium level of abstraction something about why the relevant strategies help to persuade people to accept the regime in question. We have seen in previous chapters how theories, techniques and enforcement strategies in regulation increasingly depart from keeping private and public spheres separate, relying on hybrid or 'networked' mixes of interest group influence, techniques and actors in achieving their ends. However, it is generally easier to see how 'network' views of regulation and toolboxes of techniques are linked to greater effectiveness in instrumentally changing behaviour, than to offer a clear account of why they should be accepted as legitimate by the people whose lives it affects. Without denying that effectiveness in achieving regulatory goals is an important component of such legitimation, it is widely accepted that it is not the only dimension of legitimation. Indeed, debates over legitimation often revolve around multiple and often competing logics of justification.

The following extract from Baldwin suggests five potential dimensions of legitimation. In the extract, he uses the term legitimacy, but he stresses that he is mapping the kind of claims that lead people, at least in Britain and the US, to *regard* a particular regime as legitimate. This is what we are interpreting as legitimation. According to Baldwin, governmental processes (which we would extend here to include regulatory and governance processes) will be regarded as legitimate if they can claim to fulfil one or more of five claims: the legislative mandate claim (the regulatory system is based on clear orders from the main democratic organ of the state), the accountability claim (accountability of the system to democratic institutions), the due process claim (the system is based on fair and open procedures), the expertise claim (the system involves 'objective' expertise) and the efficiency claim (the system and/or the produced results are efficient). Baldwin concludes that, if the ratings of a particularly regulatory regime according to these five claims are improved, the overall legitimation of the regime increases.

Robert Baldwin, 'Rules and Government' (1995)

How . . . can one evaluate the acceptability of governmental processes involving the exercise of discretionary power? . . . To separate law from political considerations gives an unduly narrow approach. The task is to identify the set of political values that is to serve as the basis for developing legal principles relevant to the control of discretion. . . . Values play a role in justifying and legitimating particular governmental procedures. The legitimacy of an administrative process can . . . be seen in terms of the persuasive power of the arguments made in its favour [but] the offer of the different bench-marks for administration is of limited utility if one is not told which benchmarks are appropriate and when. An explanation can be offered, however, which explores the nature of legitimacy claims or attributions and employs the notion of a discourse of justification within which certain values operate. Such a notion holds that evaluations of procedures are, as a matter of practice, argued out with reference to certain recognised values. Language users, on this view, distinguish between claims that bureaucratic processes are justifiable or appropriate (let us call these 'legitimacy claims') and claims that processes are constitutionally correct, legal, or morally praiseworthy. When legitimacy claims are made, those involved can recognise both relevant and irrelevant arguments and can see that relevant arguments invoke certain understood values and only these. Thus different persons may employ different models of the optimal democracy but each is able to recognise the basis of the arguments as to legitimacy being made by the other. They may each place different emphasis on the furtherance of certain values but they share a common recognition that certain values are relevant.

When there is talk of this or that process being legitimate or illegitimate, in the sense that certain values are argued to be satisfied or left unsatisfied, reference is made to a limited set of values or justificatory arguments. Thus Gerald Frug argues that in justifying bureaucracy: 'we have adopted only a limited number of ways to reassure ourselves about these institutions.' These justifications are all problematic in some respects but, as will be argued, it is their cumulative force that justifies. The types of claim can be outlined as follows:

(i) The legislative mandate claim

This claim attributes value to achieving objectives that are set out in legislative form (it echoes Mashaw's 'bureaucratic rationality' model [extracted below]). Thus in Britain a support claim would point to existence of an authorizing mandate from Parliament. The proponent of the claim is in effect stating: 'Support what is done because that is what Parliament, the fountain of democratic authority, has ordered.'

There are, of course, problems with this rationale as were pointed out by Stewart in his attack on the traditional model of administrative law. The claim is weakened in so far as the legislature has provided administrators with broad discretions ('what did Parliament order?') Implementation of the mandate demands interpretation and, accordingly, legitimacy claims become problematic. Nor is it usually feasible for the legislature to overcome such problems by setting down precise standards and objectives. Parliament has neither the time nor the expertise to solve all problems in advance and, indeed, it may deliberately decline to do so and give, say a regulatory agency, a set of discretionary powers so as to allow it to make judgements on policies and implementing strategies.

(ii) Accountability or control claim

Like the legislative mandate claim this model seeks justification in the assent of the people but, instead of relying on the people's voice as expressed in Parliament, it looks to more narrowly-defined groupings as conduits for the democratic voice. Thus, where a particular interpretation of the mandate is put into effect, the implementer(s) may claim that they are accountable for that interpretation to a representative body and that this oversight renders the chosen mode of implementation acceptable. Rights of participation and consultation are valued, as is openness. This claim is not unproblematic. Deciding to whom the bureaucrat is to be made accountable is controversial. In so far as a system of accountability or control is not exercised by Parliament or elected persons, it may be open to criticism as unrepresentative. Where control is exercised by means of certain institutions (e.g. courts) then the competence of those institutions in a specialist area may be called into question.

(iii) The due process claim

This claim values the use of certain procedures which imply a respect for individuals and fairness or even-handedness in government. Support claims are based on the level of consideration that has been shown, not to the broad public will, but to the interests of those persons affected by the process, decision, policy, or action. As a complete claim this is again limited. There is no guarantee that maximizing the recognition of individuals' rights will deal with collective or social issues or will produce an efficient decision (it may lead to stagnation and indecision). The dictates of such a claim may not correspond with the legislative mandate and to pay heed to process rights beyond a certain point may not be consistent with the development and exercise of necessary expertise and judgement.

(iv) The expertise claim

Many governmental, and particularly regulatory, functions require that expert judgements be made and applied. In such cases the issues are often polycentric and the decision- or policy-maker has to consider a number of competing options and values so as to form a balanced judgement on incomplete and shifting information. Where this is so, it is inappropriate to demand either that rules or guidelines be set out in advance so as to govern the matter or that, beyond a certain point, reasons and justifications can be given. The expertise claim urges that the expert will take the most appropriate action when given an area of freedom in which to operate and that his/her performance will improve over time. As Mashaw put it in relation to his 'professional treatment' model: 'The basis for the legitimacy of professional treatment is that the professional is master of an arcane body of knowledge and supports his judgement by appealing to expertise. But whereas the bureaucrat displays his or her knowledge through instrumentally rational routines designed to render transparent the connection between concrete decisions and legislatively validated policy, the professional's art remains opaque to the lay man.'

This comment points to the problems of making claims to expertise. Lay observers find it difficult to understand the bases for expert judgements and often impossible to assess the success with which the expertise has been applied. The patient who is not a surgeon tends not to know if the operation was as successful as it might have been. The observer may not know what would have happened if alternative strategies had been adopted. It is, moreover, difficult for the expert to explain why this issue demands expert judgement. Attacks on the competence and independence of experts serve further to undermine claims. Such attacks are fostered by an instinctive distrust of those who claim to 'know best', who fail to give full reasons, or who pursue a specialist or arcane mode of analysis. Where expert opinions conflict within a field or between disciplines, this again undermines legitimacy claims.

(V) The efficiency claim

Two kinds of claim can potentially be made on the basis of efficiency. First, that stated objectives are being achieved in an effective manner, and second, that economically efficient actions are being taken. The first kind of claim can be considered a version of the legislative mandate claim and, accordingly, problems arise in so far as it is difficult to define the content of the given objectives. Even if objectives are clear, the absence of comparators usually makes it difficult to demonstrate that the most effective approach is being taken at any one time — what might have happened had another approach been adopted is often impossible to judge.

The second form of claim — that efficient results are produced — is highly contentious, indeed it is the most dubious form of claim discussed here. It is difficult to see efficiency as a value independent of distributional considerations and, unless there is legislative authority for taking 'efficient' action there is liable to be a degree of conflict between the dictates of efficiency and the distributional implications of a statute. An efficiency claim may have a role, however, in so far as support may be claimed according to a particular efficiency-based interpretation of a legislative mandate.

How are the above claims made and how can they be identified? The contention here is that there is a language of justification that invokes certain values. These values are recognised and given meaning according to a discourse of justification (or legitimacy) which attributes relevance to certain forms of argument in discussions of legitimacy and which distinguishes these from other forms of argument. Thus if I were to argue that the Director General of OFTEL should be supported because he wears elegant suits, this argument would be recognised by my listener as not bearing on the issue of legitimacy. Language-users are able to separate legitimacy claims from moral, legal, constitutional, or even aesthetic assertions.

Why the five rationales or values described? The answer is these are the rationales that are employed and have currency: that an analysis of justificatory arguments will reveal a consistent resort to these rationales — at least in Britain and North America.

What, then, is involved when a critic assesses the legitimacy of an institution or process? A distinction should be drawn at this point between assessing the legitimacy of a state or regime and assessing the legitimacy of an institution or process that operates within a regime or governmental system whose broad legitimacy is accepted. This [argument] is concerned with the second form of legitimacy assessment. A second distinction should also be drawn between normative *judgements* as to legitimacy and *descriptions* of legitimacy. A judgement as to legitimacy involves the critic's making an assessment of the legitimacy that an institution or process deserves to be attributed evaluated according to commonly recognised criteria. A description of legitimacy outlines the legitimacy that the public or a section of it in fact accords to the institution or process. If a description of legitimacy is offered then recognition will be given to legitimacy which is gained by mystification, or deception, of the public. If a judgement as to legitimacy is made, an opinion is offered on the *merits* of any legitimacy claims. (The opinion is personal but the criteria for assessing merits are established impersonally). It is on the basis of such judgements that is appropriate to go about designing rules or evaluating governmental processes. In David Beetham's words: 'The social scientist, in concluding that a given power relationship is legitimate, is making a judgement, not delivering a report; about people's beliefs in legitimacy.'

... [M]y argument has sought to identify the benchmarks for legitimacy claims by referring to a language of legitimacy. Such an account may explain how people go about legitimacy claiming, but how can the critic make a judgement on legitimacy (as judged with reference to the five claims) without explaining how the different claims interact, without justifying a particular weighting of the claims?

In the first instance, it can be responded that when an argument is made in support of a process, act, or institution of government what matters is the collective justificatory power of the five forms of claim. A claim under one head may be weak but may be compensated for by a strong claim under another. Where strong claims can be made under all heads (a rare event) then a high level of legitimacy is assured; where only weak claims can be made under each heading then the power to justify will be low. Where a claim under one head can be improved by a reform that does not weaken claims under other heads then a convincing case for such a reform can be made. What, however, of the mass of cases in the middle? How can one say whether a trade-off between different kinds of claim is desirable? [One strategy is to] disentangle legitimacy claiming from the positing of a political theory or vision.... Such an uncoupling bears in mind Niklas Luhmann's point that the complexity of social systems requires different levels of generalization to be distinguished: 'It is no longer possible to find a point for man's highest fulfilment that is equidistant from all values and is at the same time an ethical maxim for action. We have to think in a more differentiated manner – we have to separate the levels of values, norms and goals from one another.'

A first step in the process of disentangling is to examine what normative political theories and legitimacy assessments do. The former, it can be argued, aim to make statements about the way that society or government ought to be organised and will commonly attempt to derive such statements from premises allegedly immune from contention. To assess legitimacy can be seen, however, as engaging in a distinct activity that operates at a different level. It involves, as noted, making judgements as to the merits of legitimacy claims but constitutes what might be termed an intermediate discourse. It is intermediate because it allows a discussion of legitimacy to take place without immediate linkage to any particular vision of democracy. To assert this does not imply that those individuals who are engaged in a discourse on the legitimacy of a governmental process will at heart possess no personal belief in a particular balancing of rationales or values. An individual's own preferences or vision of the optimal society will suggest such a balancing. The point is that it is possible to converse on legitimacy with another individual (perhaps one of a very different political persuasion) by making reference to rationales or that have unspecified weight or ranking but are nevertheless commonly recognised. It has to be acknowledged, that in theoretical terms this is a discourse within limits and that these limits may be reached (at which stage preferred political visions may be referred to). This does not mean, however, that justificatory discourse on legitimacy is not possible or useful. In practical terms such discourse is the general currency of debates concerning governmental processes.

How, on this view, should the critic or the designer of a governmental process judge the legitimacy of that process? First, he or she should assess the merits of the claims under the individual five headings while having an eye to cumulative claims. This will ensure that where action can be taken to improve a claim under one heading (e.g. to efficiency) the case for the action will be recognised as legitimacy maximizing where other claims are not prejudiced. Given the resource and informational constraints usual in government, such relatively uncontentious assessments will often be as far as it is feasible to pursue analysis. An approach that recognises the five forms of justification avoids both the narrowness and the lack of realism associated with, for example, legalistic analyses. Moreover, it accords more fully with the breadth of justificatory argument employed and recognised by the public.

Second, where it is necessary to consider a trade-off between two or more types of claim (e.g. a step that increases efficiency and diminishes accountability) the critic should recognise that, although choosing between different distributions of legitimacy claim does at root demand reference to some notion of the optimal model of state or democracy, it may make no sense to base such a choice on a purely personal vision. This is because the strength of a legitimacy claim made under one heading may be affected by the willingness of a variety of persons to attribute legitimacy under other headings. Thus, for instance, I might, because of my personal vision of democracy, be inclined to design or change a process so as to trade off lower accountability for greater efficiency. Without further thought, I might judge the process I propose as highly legitimate on that basis. In the real world, however, the greater efficiency I envisage may not be realizable because other persons may attack the process (or its operating institution) for lack of accountability, and such attacks may detract from the achievement of results. Thus, if I set up a process in which (in the interests of efficiency) a regulator acts in an unaccountable fashion, objectors to that lack of accountability (e.g. the regulated industry or consumer groups) may be so hostile and uncooperative that hoped-for efficiency is not realised.

In judging a governmental process, therefore, it is appropriate to consider how the merits of some legitimacy claims (e.g. the efficiency and expertise claims in particular) stand to be affected by anticipated reactions to claims under other headings (notably under the accountability and due process heads). This is not to argue that what is legitimate is what seems legitimate to other people (or to people generally), it is to recognise that claims are made in the real world, that, even within the terms of a particular person's judgement as to legitimacy, it may be necessary to take on board the potential attributions of legitimacy of other persons. The personal judgement has to be placed in the context of the anticipated reactions of others and a position of tempered idealism adopted. The implication is that the critic or designer of processes may be on unsure ground in seeking to argue for extreme trade-offs of legitimacy claims by making reference to a personal vision. Such a critic/designer should, accordingly, be wary of endorsing processes which score conspicuously badly on any of the five headings since those poor scores may tend to undermine the higher scores anticipated under other headings. (Non-extreme trade-offs may, of course, be more safely made on the basis of impersonal vision.)

. . .[Overall], debates concerning governmental processes are unduly confined if conducted with reference solely to what might be called 'traditional legal values'. In order to break out of the straitjacket of the legal paradigm it is necessary to consider the wide range of values being served by governmental processes and it is necessary also to explore the nature of disputes concerning legitimacy. The notion of a discourse of legitimacy makes it possible to explain the role of five rationales for legitimacy claims. The same notion involves a degree of indeterminacy in so far as the weighting of rationales is flexible, but the five rationales can be identified and the values appealed to are not open-ended in nature. The idea of a particular discourse of legitimacy also allows a distinction to be drawn between assessing legitimacy and the assertion of prescriptive political theories. It sees assessing legitimacy as an intermediate level of argument which has significance and offers practical guidance in a way that an immediate appeal to a normative theory of democracy does not.

Although Baldwin does not directly discuss the role of law in laying out his five benchmarks for legitimacy claims, it is plausible that the first three claims accord a significant role to law. The legislative mandate claim fits well with the image of law as expressive threat: the coercive directions issued by the state in legal form legitimate the exercise of regulatory power. The accountability claim implies more of an image of law as facilitative umpire — the legal framework specifies a narrow group or institution to whom regulatory officials must account for their decisions, and this framework instrumentally secures the goal of disciplining the regulator. Finally the due process claim resonates with the role of law as expressive umpire, because constitutional values traditionally include the notions of fair and consistent treatment embodied in the ideal of due process. As for the expertise and efficiency claims, law is much more in the background, at least in Baldwin's formulation. (We shall later explore linkages between efficiency and the role of law when we turn to the extract from Majone.)

While Baldwin's schema is readily applicable to situations where the state regulates private enterprise, Jerry Mashaw (Marshaw 1983) articulates an alternative set of logics for the justification of regulatory legitimation patterns *internal* to public administration. In the extract that follows, Mashaw distinguishes three different conceptions of administrative justice: bureaucratic rationality, professional treatment and moral judgment. These capture three distinct and possibly competing bases for legitimating administrative action: rule-based proceduralism, professional knowledge or expertise and notions of moral fairness. Mashaw talks of administrative justice rather than of a regulatory regime, but arguably this makes little difference to the analytical usefulness of the models he sketches. Each model captures the normative dimensions of oversight, monitoring and supervision that typically characterise regulatory regimes, locating them within state programmes such as the administration of social security benefits (the subject of the book from which we here extract). Social security systems, like regulatory regimes, address social risk, market failure or equitable aims by means of governmental processes. Although there are similarities between these contexts, there is also one significant difference. Models of legitimation generated by looking *within* the arena of the state, as Mashaw does, emerge from a context that does not employ the public/private divide that dominates traditional approaches to regulatory accountability and legitimacy. They might therefore be of greater assistance in identifying the bases of legitimacy for hybrid regulatory regimes than Baldwin's approach. The following extract should therefore be read by considering whether the argument it makes applies equally well to 'regulators' and 'regulatory legitimation' as it does to 'administrators' and 'administrative justice' (the terms employed by Mashaw).

Jerry Mashaw, 'Bureaucratic justice: Managing social security disability claims' (1983)

We begin...by conceding the legal realists' insight. The legally required means of agency implementation, as developed by courts and legislatures, may sometimes inform but cannot control administration...The...legal realist challenge is to admit the limitations of an externally oriented administrative law and yet to affirm a vision of administration that is subject to the normative evaluation and improvement that is the promise of legal discourse; to view the administrative process, like the judicial and legislative processes, as somehow in pursuit of justice and the general welfare; to see "administration," like "democracy" and "the rule of law," as a motivating ideal.

In part the disposition to construct such a vision is a pragmatic response to my personal inability to move firmly into the camp of the cynics. But even if the effort is in some sense a working out of individual psychic need, the exploration seems to have a broader utility. That society has collective needs, at least collective wants, seems inescapable. And, since we lack the altruistic genetic programming of the social insect, these needs and wants can be satisfied only through a bureaucratised application of collective authority. We need somehow to come to terms with our constant demand for institutions — bureaucracies — that once created we then excoriate.

If a set of external controls called administrative law no longer comforts us as we seek to manage our love-hate relationship with bureaucracy, perhaps we can see more clearly what needs to be done by turning to look inside the bureau, while retaining a normative perspective. Might there not be an internal law of administration that guides the conduct of administrators? And might not that law be capable of generalization, critique, improvement; even of producing a sense of satisfaction, acceptance, and justice quite apart from its connection to external legal institutions? Might there be in bureaucratic operation not merely the pure play of ambition, self-interest, or inertia that confounds our collective ideals but also a striving for normative goodness — complex and compromised perhaps, but only sometimes absent?

The search for such a vision inside the bureaucracy is, indeed, reminiscent of the realist technique. The purpose of this quest, however, is not to describe power but to structure responsibility. For the task of improving the quality of administrative justice is one that must be carried forward primarily by administrators. The task is too complex for the nonexpert, too time and resource consuming for outside institutions with competing interests. Moreover, the task requires a positive commitment to maintaining and balancing the full range of values that impinge on the system's functioning. The twists and turns of political-agendas, the episodic and random interests of courts and of outside commentators provide information on social perceptions and expectations and shed some light on the ultimate effects of bureaucratic routines. But the job of evaluating the significance of these external communications and, having thus evaluated them, responding with appropriate action can reside only with the bureaucracy itself.

The central position of the bureaucracy thus implies a correlative central responsibility for the quality of administrative justice. The bureau is not a mere receptacle for the perspective and preferences of institutions, a vector sum of contending external forces that impinge on its functioning. It is a focus for political initiative combined with technical competence, for the assertion of values beyond the time horizon of most other political actors. An externally oriented administrative law may be adequate when defined in terms of constraints and abstract ideals; an internal perspective would be inadequate without a more instrumental vision of the particular system of administrative justice that is sought to be produced.

For the line administrator this should be obvious. He or she continually faces decisions for which external standards provide no binding, perhaps no relevant, guidelines. Administration goes on, not just in terms of technical rules and bureaucratic routines but within some structure of guiding norms or salient images of the appropriate means for wielding legal power. And, like the actors in the external legal order, the administrator confronts conflicting modes of conceptualizing the normative "goodness" of the administrative system that is to be constructed. What are the images of "good administration" that guide bureaucratic behavior, that permit evaluation and hierarchical control? How can this internal law be conceptualised in terms of its ideal types, and to what degree do these ideals conflict? What are the techniques by which administrative ideals are concretely realised, reinforced, and sanctioned? How are they connected to or influenced by the norms of the external law of administration? If one could answer these questions, at least a partial description of administrative law from an internal perspective would emerge... The pages that follow make but a necessary beginning.

My attempt, obviously, is to reorient discussion. I will concentrate on a particular administrative system — the adjudication of claims for social security disability benefits. Descriptively, I will explain the administrative mission; how the system is structured and managed; what the effects of structure and management are on the definition and redefinition of goals and on the output of implementing decisions. Instead of describing and analyzing the top of the pyramid of administrative decisionmaking, judicial review, or even administrative "hearings," I will be concerned primarily with the system for managing routine administrative action by low-level administrators. For it is here that 100 percent of bureaucratic implementation begins, and most of it ends.

Second, I will generate and elaborate some conceptions of administrative justice and evaluate my exemplary bureaucracy's performance against those conceptions. The technique for developing these conceptions, or "models," of justice is in part empirical and in part intuitive and analytic. By examining patterns of criticism of the performance of the disability decision process we will observe the types of claims for legitimation that are made on the system. These claims seem to imply distinctive visions of how disability decisionmaking *ought* to be organised, visions that the history and structure of the program support. Although the patterns of claims and the relevant statutory provisions project these visions as relatively unformed images, we can develop a clearer picture of the characteristics of each model of justice – what gives each its distinctive structure and justificatory appeal.

Third, we will be forced to recognise that the models of justice suggested by the structure and the critics of the program are competitive. Implementing decisions will at critical points exalt one vision while suppressing others. The administrative system must choose which model of justice to employ. [The] dominant approach [is] the model of bureaucratic rationality.

...Assume, therefore, a disability program:...a program whose statutory standard for income support payments harnesses medical, personal, and vocational criteria to the task of determining whether an individual can work. In the language of the [US] Social Security Act:

...an individual shall be determined to be under a disability only if his physical or mental impairment or impairments are of such severity that he is not only unable to do his previous work but cannot, considering his age, education and work experience, engage in any other kind of substantial gainful work which exists in the national economy, regardless of whether such work exists in the immediate area in which he lives, or whether a specific job vacancy exists for him, or whether he would be hired if he applied for work. For purposes of the preceding sentence (with respect to any individual), "work which exists in the national economy" means work which exists in significant numbers either in the region where such individual lives or in several regions of the country.

Qualification under that standard entitles the recipient both to income support and, after a waiting period, to medical benefits. The eligibility determination also includes an analysis of the applicant's fitness for referral to a vocational rehabilitation program and a judgment concerning the scheduling of a "continuing disability investigation" to redetermine eligibility at some future date. The problematic nature of recovery is cushioned by trial work periods during which time a return to beneficiary status requires no waiting periods or reapplication. The statute also gives some guidance concerning the administrative structure for making disability determinations. Claims are to be processed by state agencies, preferably state vocational rehabilitation services. Disappointed claimants are entitled to hearings before a federal administrative law judge and, thereafter, to judicial review in federal district courts. How should [an administration or regulatory agency] flesh out this substantive and procedural skeleton? What is administrative justice to mean in the disability program?

The *justice* of an administrative system, as I shall employ the term, means simply this: those qualities of a decision process that provide arguments for the acceptability of its decisions. I do not mean to suggest, of course, that all arguments – moral, legal, or political – are the same or that to be just a process must avoid all complaint or even all assertions of illegitimacy. I am here merely developing some distinct structures of justificatory argument. For present purposes we need not strongly distinguish among the possible sources of other claims to acceptability. Nor shall I attempt to demonstrate that everyone is powerfully attached to one or more of the arguments suggested. These justificatory structures, once identified, should appear to be ubiquitous in the legal structure of public institutions and in ordinary experience.

The three strands in the critical literature on the disability program suggest three types of justice arguments: (1) that decisions should be accurate and efficient concrete realizations of the legislative will; (2) that decisions should provide appropriate support or therapy from the perspective of relevant professional cultures; and (3) that decisions should be fairly arrived at when assessed in the light of traditional processes for determining individual entitlements. Elaboration of these arguments in the context of the disability program produces three distinct models of administrative justice; models that I shall denominate *bureaucratic rationality, professional treatment, and moral judgment.*

Bureaucratic rationality

Given the democratically (legislatively) approved task — to pay disability benefits to eligible persons — the administrative goal in the ideal conception of bureaucratic rationality is to develop, at the least possible cost, a system for distinguishing between true and false claims. Adjudicating should be both accurate (the legislatively specified goal) and cost-effective. This approach can be stated more broadly by introducing trade-offs between error, administrative, and other "process" costs such that the goal becomes "minimise the sum of error and other associated costs." A system focused on correctness defines the questions presented to it by implementing decisions in essentially factual and technocratic terms. Individual adjudicators must be concerned about the facts in the real world that relate to the truth or falsity of the claimed disability. At a managerial level the question becomes technocratic: What is the least-cost methodology for collecting and combining those facts about claims that will reveal the proper decision? To illustrate by contrast, this model would exclude questions of value or preference as obviously irrelevant to the administrative task, and it would view reliance on nonreplicable, nonreviewable *judgment* or *intuition* as a singularly unattractive methodology for decision. The legislature should have previously decided the value questions; and decision on the basis of intuition would cause authority to devolve from the bureau to individuals, thereby preventing a supervisory determination of whether any adjudicative action taken corresponded to a true state of the world.

The general decisional technique, then, is information retrieval and processing. In Weber's words, "Bureaucratic administration means fundamentally domination through knowledge." And, of course, this application of knowledge must in any large-scale program be structured through the usual bureaucratic routines: selection and training of personnel, detailed specification of administrative tasks, specialization and division of labour, coordination via rules and hierarchical lines of authority, and hierarchical review of the accuracy and efficiency of decisionmaking. In the disability program, for example, decisionmaking goes on not in one head but, initially, in the heads of thousands of state agency examiners.

From the perspective of bureaucratic rationality, administrative justice is accurate decisionmaking carried on through processes appropriately rationalised to take account of costs. The legitimating force of this conception flows both from its claim to correct implementation of otherwise legitimate social decisions and from its attempt to realise society's preestablished goals in some particular substantive domain while conserving social resources for the pursuit of other valuable ends. No program, after all, exhausts our conception of good government, much less of a good society or a good life.

Professional treatment

The goal of the professional is to serve the client. The service delivery goal or ideal is most obvious, perhaps, in the queen of the professions, medicine; but it is also a defining characteristic of law and the ministry and of newer professions such as social work. Although one might view medicine, for example, as principally oriented toward science and therefore knowledge, such a view is fundamentally mistaken. The scientific side of medicine, its disease and pathology constructs, are generated by an attempt to treat complaints relating to biological and psychological functioning, pain, or deformity. Characterization and explanation are important to treatment but not necessary. The physician is committed to treatment even if the patient's complaints cannot be characterised or explained within current scientific modes of conceptualizing medical problems. The value to be served by the professional is the elimination of the health complaints presented to him or her by patients. Curing a patient by eliminating a physically identifiable pathology may be good science, but if the patient still feels sick it is not good medicine. The objective is to wield the science so that it produces good as defined by the patient. This entails interpersonal and diagnostic intuition − clinical intelligence − as well as scientific knowledge.

An administrative system for disability decisionmaking based on professional treatment would, therefore, be client-oriented. It would seek to provide those services − income support, medical care, vocational rehabilitation, and counseling − that the client needed to improve his well-being and perhaps regain self-sufficiency. Such services, of course, would be constrained by cost. The professional must at least tailor advice or treatment to his or her own resources: some clients must be rejected or given less in order that others, who are needier, may be helped more. But the constraints on professional service tend to be conceptualised by professionals in terms of competing service modalities for or among clients, not as trade-offs between professional services and other social values.

Like bureaucratic rationality, professional judgment requires the collection of information that may be manipulated in accordance with standardised procedures. But in the professional treatment model the incompleteness of facts, the singularity of individual contexts, and the ultimately intuitive nature of judgment are recognised, if not exalted. Disability decisions would be viewed not as attempts to establish the truth or falsity of some state of the world, but rather as prognoses of the likely effects of disease or trauma on functioning, and as efforts to support the client while pursuing therapeutic and vocational prospects.

The basic techniques of professional treatment are personal examination and counseling. There is some specialization of functions-delegation to other professions or subprofessionals — but the judgment of what is to be done is holistic. The professional combines the information of others with his or her own observations and experience to reach conclusions that are as much art as science. Moreover, judgment is always subject to revision as conditions change, as attempted therapy proves unsatisfactory or therapeutic successes emerge. The application of clinical judgment entails a relationship and may involve repeated instances of service-oriented decisionmaking.

An administrative system for providing professional treatment would thus have characteristics rather different from those of the system supporting bureaucratic rationality. The basic idea would be to apply the appropriate profession to the problem at hand. And since these allocation decisions, decisions about needs or ability to help, are themselves professional judgments, they would be made best by the relevant professionals in conjunction with claimants. The administrative structure need, for example, only funnel claimant-clients to multi-professional centers where they would be examined and counseled. Administration would include the facilitation of these contacts, coordination of multiprofessional teams, and implementation of professional judgments concerning particular cases. Substantive and procedural rules, hierarchical controls, and efficiency considerations would all be subordinated to the norms of the professional culture. The organization would be more a lateral network than a hierarchical command structure.

The basis for the legitimacy of professional treatment is in one respect similar to that of bureaucratic decisionmaking: the professional is master of an arcane body of knowledge and supports his judgment by appeals to expertise. But whereas the bureaucrat displays his or her knowledge through instrumentally rational routines designed to render transparent the connection between concrete decisions and legislatively validated policy, the professional's art remains opaque to the layman. The mystery of professional judgment is, nevertheless, acceptable because of the service ideal of professionalism. The element of mystery and charisma in the office of physician, priest, or lawyer is combined with the trusteeship implicit in professional-client relations. Justice lies in having the appropriate professional judgment applied to one's particular situation *in the context of a service relationship*.

Moral judgment

The traditional goal of the adjudicatory process is to resolve disputes about rights, about the allocation of benefits and burdens. The paradigm adjudicatory situations are those of civil and criminal trial. In the former, the context generally concerns competing claims to property or the mutual responsibilities of the litigants. Property claims of "It has been in my family for generations" confront counterclaims of "I bought it from a dealer" or "I have made productive use of it"; "The smell of turkey farm is driving me mad" confronts "I was here first." In the latter, accused murderers claim self-defense or diminished responsibility. The goal in individual adjudications is to decide who deserves what.

To some degree these traditional notions of justice in adjudicatory process merely imply getting the facts right in order to apply existing legal rules. So conceived, the goal of a moral judgment model of justice is the same as that of a bureaucratic rationality model — factually correct realization of previously validated legal norms. If this conception exhausted the notion of adjudicatory fairness, moral judgment's competition with bureaucratic rationality would entail merely a technical dispute about the most efficient way to find facts. But there is more to the competition than that.

The moral judgment model views decisionmaking as value defining. The turkey farmer's neighbor makes a valid appeal not to be burdened by "noisome" smells, *provided* his conduct in locating nearby is "reasonable" and he is not being "overly sensitive." The turkey farmer also has a valid claim to carry on a legitimate business, *provided* he does so in ways that will not unreasonably burden his neighbors. The question is not just who did what, but who is to be preferred, all things considered, when interests and the values to which they can be relevantly connected conflict. Similarly, the criminal trial seeks to establish not just whether a harmful and proscribed act took place but also whether or to what extent the actor is culpable.

This entitlement-awarding goal of the moral judgment model gives an obvious and distinctive cast to the basic issue for adjudicatory resolution. The issue is the deservingness of some or all of the parties in the context of certain events, transactions, or relationships that give rise to a claim. This issue, in turn, seems to imply certain things about a just process of proof and decision. For example, fair disposition of charges of culpability or lack of desert requires that claims be specifically stated and that any affected party be given an opportunity to rebut or explain allegations. And in order for this contextualised exploration of individual deservingness to be meaningful the decisionmaker must be neutral — that is, not previously connected with the relevant parties or events in ways that would impair the exercise of independent judgment on the evidence and arguments presented.

Moreover, given the generally threatening nature of an inquiry into moral desert, parties should be able to exclude from the decisional context information not directly related to the entitlements issue that gives rise to the disputed claim. This power of exclusion may take the form of pleading rules, of notions of standing or proper-parties, and, more importantly, may permit total exclusion of directive judgment where claims are abandoned or disputants come to some mutually satisfactory agreement concerning the relevant allocation. The goal is limited: to resolve particular claims of entitlement in a way that fairly allocates certain benefits and burdens, not to allocate benefits and burdens in general in accordance with the relative deservingness of individuals or groups. The decider is to a degree passive. The parties control how much of their lives or relationships is put at issue and what factual and normative arguments are brought to bear on the resolution of the dispute.

While the traditional examples of entitlements-oriented individualised adjudication involve adversary process, this feature is not critical. Claims to publicly provided benefits via nonadversary hearing processes may also conform to the model. . . . The goals of this most traditional model of justice may suggest additional decisional

Dimension/ Model	Legitimating Values	Primary Goal	Structure or Organisation	Cognitive Technique
Bureaucratic rationality	Accuracy and Efficiency	Programme Implementation	Hierarchical	Information Processing
Professional treatment	Service	Client satisfaction	Interpersonal	Clinical Application of Knowledge
Moral judgement	Fairness	Conflict resolution	Independent	Contextual interpretation

Figure 5.4 Features of the three justice models.

techniques and routines designed to preserve party equality and control, promote agreed allocations, and protect the authority of the decider. But these are details that need not detain us. The important point is that the "justice" of this model inheres in its promise of a full and equal opportunity to obtain one's entitlements. Its authority rests on the neutral development and application of common moral principles within the contexts giving rise to entitlement claims.

As we have described them, each justice model is composed of distinctive goals, specific approaches to framing the questions for administrative determination, basic techniques for resolving those questions, and subsidiary decision processes and routines that functionally describe the model. The distinctive features of the three models are outlined in the accompanying chart. These features are, of course, meant to indicate the central tendencies, not to suggest that features, and whole models, do not shade one into another at the margins....[T]he paradigm examples of our models contain internal tensions that reflect alternative justice perspectives. My intuition is that this is generally the case.

The table above (Figure 5.4) that concludes the extract clearly identifies the connection between Mashaw's various logics of justification and the institutionalisation of values. But this does not necessarily mean that law simply plays an expressive role in each model. Rather, if we consider the key practices that Mashaw identifies as central to each of his three models of legitimation, we can see that law continues to play both an expressive and a facilitative role and that these are distinct. Where information retrieval is a key technique for achieving this, as in the bureaucratic rationality model, law functions as facilitative threat, creating a hierarchical set of rules for processing and collecting crucial information, and backing that function with the threat of coercion. Where personal examination and counseling are at the centre of the legitimation process, as in the professional treatment model, the role of law is much more muted, acting as facilitative umpire in providing a space within which professional discretion can be flexibly applied. The moral judgment model, however, is explicitly 'value-defining', in Mashaw's terms, and echoes both the constitutional values of due process articulated by Baldwin and possibly even a more substantive claim to moral correctness, in his discussion of 'deservingness'.

5.4.1 Discussion questions

1. Mashaw and Baldwin both claim to move beyond 'traditional legal' notions of accountability and legitimacy. Compare and contrast their reasons for doing so.
2. Mashaw's models articulate three distinct and possibly competing bases for legitimacy: technical expertise, rules-based procedures and notions of moral fairness. Do these encompass, overlap with, or exist in parallel to, Baldwin's five dimensions of regulatory legitimation?
3. What tensions exist between Mashaw's three models? Can you think of specific examples where the use of one model would preclude the use of the others? Alternatively can you think of specific examples where they could be productively interdependent in the manner Scott suggests?
4. Mashaw's models are derived from looking inside public administration rather than from situations where the state regulates private actors. Does this make them more or less applicable than Baldwin's five dimensions of legitimation to the kind of situations emphasised by Scott, i.e. where public and private actors are mutually interdependent?

5.5 Regulatory legitimacy and democracy: Between expertise and pluralism

As we saw earlier, no single one of Baldwin's five dimensions is exhaustive of legitimacy and he explicitly acknowledges that overlapping claims are inevitable and necessary. The same is true of Mashaw's three models of administrative justice. This of course leaves unanswered the question of which bench-mark is appropriate and when, and of knowing how best to combine different mechanisms. To use Baldwin's array of logics, for example, even if we assume that it is possible to evaluate precisely whether a regulatory goal is efficiently achieved in particular contexts, the enquiry into legitimation would not thereby be exhausted. If the regulatory goal was to improve the treatment of prisoners, an accurate comparative cost-effectiveness analysis of the following options would not tell us which is the right choice: more aggressive prisons inspections, greater prisoner access to judicial review, or changes in audit regimes that decreased financial pressures. Answers to such questions are inevitably contextual, but all such explorations must deal with the unavoidable tensions between different models. While all the extracts so far have emphasised a need to move beyond traditional ideas of the rule of law to encompass market-based, professional and other mechanisms for securing both accountability and legitimation, the next extract, by Giandomenico Majone, articulates one influential way of prioritising competing logics of justification. Drawing upon the economic theory underpinning private interest theories of regulation, this approach relies partly on expertise and partly on a claim to be enhancing democracy.

Majone's core argument is that regulatory institutions are legitimated when they are designed as expert sites that pursue efficiency goals and deliberately partition off redistributive goals from the regulatory endeavour. His vision of expertise-grounded regulatory legitimacy is analytically underpinned by a private interest theory of regulation insofar as he regards regulatory institutions as susceptible to capture by narrow interest groups, which would lead them to make decisions skewing the distribution of overall wealth to those groups. To cure this, he restricts the legitimate goal for regulation to that of pursuing efficiency, aided by the application of economic expertise. The redistributive facets of regulatory policy should be decided by political institutions and majoritarian vote. This argument presents the use of economic expertise by independent regulatory agencies as a way of promoting 'non-majoritarian democracy'.

All the writers in this chapter so far have touched upon democracy, albeit lightly, from Baldwin's pragmatic and concrete discussion (Baldwin 1995) through to Sunstein's venture (Sunstein 1990) into more theoretically abstract philosophical terrain. The three extracts included in this section develop this linkage between regulatory legitimation further, while nevertheless remaining at a 'middle' level of theoretical abstraction. In other words, although the various conceptions of democracy discussed in these extracts are implicitly underpinned by different philosophical commitments, the extracts present varying conceptions of democracy in outline form, connecting them to institutional design. Majone's approach will be complemented by different versions of democracy emerging in the extracts which follow (Shapiro 1988; Cuéllar 2005; Slaughter 2003). What is perhaps most distinctive about Majone's approach is that he develops a *substantive* conception of legitimacy linked to the maximisation of aggregate welfare, and links this to democracy. Most other writers adopt more procedural conceptions of democracy, as we shall see (Cuéllar 2005; Slaughter 2003).

Giandomenico Majone, *'Regulatory legitimacy'* (1996)

Regulators wield enormous power, yet they are neither elected nor directly responsible to elected officials. How is their exercise of that power to be controlled? This, in a nutshell, is the question before us; the answer, we argue in this chapter, ultimately depends on the model of democracy one adopts. According to the majoritarian model, the main if not the only source of legitimacy is accountability to voters or to their elected representatives. Measured by this standard, independent agencies can be seen only as 'constitutional anomalies which do not fit well into the traditional framework of controls, checks and balances' [as Veljanovski terms them], even as challenges to the basic principles of constitutionalism and of democratic theory. . . .

Those who favour a non-majoritarian model of democracy agree that a problem of regulatory legitimacy exists at both the national and the European levels, but deny that a higher level of politicization of the regulatory process is the correct answer. The non-majoritarian model is particularly concerned with protecting minorities from the 'tyranny of the majority', and the judicial, the executive and the administrative functions from representative assemblies and from fickle mass opinion . . . . Hence, instead of concentrating power in the hands of the majority, it aims to limit and to disperse power among different institutions. Delegation of policy-making responsibilities to independent bodies, whether at the national or supranational level, is viewed favourably as one important means of diffusing power. Such diffusion, according to the model, may be a more effective form of democratic control than direct accountability to voters or to elected officials.

Most democratic polities rely extensively on non-majoritarian principles and institutions. In fact, Lijphart (1984, 1991...) has produced massive empirical evidence that majoritarian democracy is the exception rather than the rule, being mainly limited to the United Kingdom and to countries strongly influenced by the British tradition. In spite of this, the assumption that majority rule is the only source of democratic legitimacy is still generally accepted. This paradox may be explained in part by historical and cultural factors, such as the weight of British practices and traditions, but the following pages suggest a more general explanation. For reasons to be discussed below, but which are at any rate fairly obvious, in a democracy redistributive policies can only be legitimated by majority vote. Such policies have been central to the modern welfare state, and their overwhelming importance in the past explains the tendency to apply majoritarian standards of legitimacy to all policy types.

The crisis of the welfare state has reduced the political significance of redistribution relative to policies which aim to increase aggregate welfare, but the normative standards have not been set accordingly . . . [U]ntil this is done regulatory legitimacy will remain an elusive concept both at the national and the EC levels, impeding the search for suitable mechanisms of public accountability and political control . . . .

Independent regulatory bodies, like independent central banks, courts of law, administrative tribunals or the European Commission, belong to the genus 'non-majoritarian institutions', that is, public institutions which, by design, are not directly accountable either to voters or to elected officials. The growing importance of such institutions in all democratic countries shows that for many purposes reliance upon qualities such as expertise, professional discretion, policy consistency, fairness or independence of judgement is considered to be more important than reliance upon direct political accountability.

At the same time, however, doubts as to the legitimacy of non-majoritarian institutions persist, and indeed increase, in direct proportion to the expanding role of these institutions. Probably the most important reason why the debate tends to be inconclusive is the failure to realise that a normative appraisal of non-majoritarian mechanisms — blatant violation of democratic principles or legitimate instruments of democratic governance — depends crucially on the model of democracy one adopts.

Democratic theorists distinguish two different conceptions of democracy, both compatible with Abraham Lincoln's notion of 'government of the people, by the people, for the people'. The first, represented by the majoritarian or populistic model of democracy, tends to concentrate all political power in the hands of the majority. According to this conception, majorities should be able to control all of government—legislative, executive and, if they have a mind to, judicial — and thus to control everything politics can touch. Nothing clarifies the total sway of majorities more than their ability to alter and adjust the standards of legitimacy.... Although majority rule is viewed here as the very essence of democracy, in practice it is usually admitted that the will of the majority must be restrained by minority rights. In a strict formulation of the majoritarian model, however, these restraints should be informal — a matter of historical tradition and political culture — rather than of a formal-constitutional nature which cannot be changed by bare majorities. The model also implies that the governmental system should be unitary and centralised in order to ensure that there are no geographical or policy areas which the Cabinet and its parliamentary majority fail to control.

By contrast, the non-majoritarian ... model of democracy aims to share, disperse, delegate and limit power in a variety of ways. The overriding objective is, to use Madisonian language, to protect minorities against the 'tyranny of the majority', and to create safeguards against 'factionalism' — the usurpation of government by powerful and self-interested groups — and the threat which factionalism poses to the republican belief in deliberative democracy. In particular, delegation — a non-majoritarian strategy... attempts to restrain majority rule by placing public authority in the hands of officials who have limited or no direct accountability to either political majorities or minorities....

Recent empirical research provides additional evidence in favour of the thesis that non-majoritarian decision-making mechanisms are more suitable for complex, plural societies than are mechanisms that concentrate power in the hands of the political majority. Lijphart defines plural societies as those which are 'sharply divided along religious, ideological, linguistic, cultural, ethnic, or racial lines into virtually separate sub-societies with their own political parties, interest groups, and media of communication' (Lijphart 1984: 22). The evidence collected by Lijphart and other scholars concerning the relationship between the needs of cleavage management in these societies and non-majoritarian mechanisms is quite strong ...[M]any non-majoritarian features of [political] ... systems are best explained as strategies of cleavage management [which], however imperfect, ... have been essential to the progress of [political] integration, while a strict application of majoritarian principles could produce only deadlock and possibly even disintegration.

[R]eliance upon qualities such as expertise, credibility, fairness or independence has always been considered more important than reliance upon direct political accountability — but only for some purposes. The substantive legitimacy of non-majoritarian institutions depends crucially on how precisely those purposes are defined. In essence, this is because accountability by results cannot be enforced when the objectives of an organization are either too vague or too broad. In this section, I argue that the . . . distinction between efficiency and redistribution . . . provides a sound conceptual basis for deciding whether the delegation of policy-making authority to an independent regulatory body has at least *prima facie* legitimacy.

. . . In a democracy, public decisions concerning the redistribution of income and wealth can be taken only by a majority vote since any issue over which there is unavoidable conflict is defeated under a unanimity rule. Redistribution is a zero-sum game since the gain of one group in society is the loss of another group. Efficiency issues, on the other hand, may be thought of as positive-sum games where everybody can gain, provided the right solution is discovered. Hence, such issues could be settled, in principle, by unanimity. The unanimity rule guarantees that the result of collective choice is efficient in the Pareto sense, since anybody adversely affected by the collective decision can veto it.

Naturally, unanimity is practically impossible in a large polity, but there are second-best alternatives. These include various non-majoritarian mechanisms such as consociational strategies, which encourage bargaining among elites of relatively well-organised cleavage segments, supermajorities and, of particular interest in the present context, delegation of problem-solving tasks to independent expert agencies. . . . The main task delegated to regulatory agencies is to correct market failures so as to increase aggregate welfare. It is important to note that the adoption of efficiency as the standard by which the regulators are to be evaluated implies, *inter alia*, that regulatory instruments should not be used for redistributive purposes. Regulatory policies, like all public policies, have redistributive consequences; but for the regulator such consequences should represent potential policy constraints rather than policy objectives. Only a commitment to efficiency, that is, to the maximization of aggregate welfare, and to accountability by results, can substantively legitimise the political independence of regulators. By the same token, decisions involving significant redistribution of resources from one social group to another cannot be legitimately taken by independent experts, but only by elected officials or by administrators directly responsible to elected officials.

A criticism frequently raised against these normative arguments is that efficiency and redistribution . . . cannot be separated in practice. Were this the case, [the] analytic distinction would in fact have limited policy relevance. Indeed, the two issues *can* be separated under conditions which economists have succeeded in specifying with sufficient precision . . . : the main condition is that of 'no wealth effects', meaning that every decision-maker regards each possible outcome as being completely equivalent to receiving or paying some amount of money, and that he or she has sufficient resources to be able to absorb any wealth reduction necessary to pay for a switch from the less preferred to the more preferred alternative.

When there are no wealth effects, 'value creation' and 'value claiming' can be treated as distinct and separable processes . . . . In other words, decisions about resource allocations or about institutional arrangements are unaffected by the wealth, assets or bargaining power of the parties: efficiency alone determines the outcome. Only the decision of how benefits and costs are to be distributed is affected by the resources or power of the parties.

It is easy to think of situations where the condition of no wealth effects does not hold, that is, where the choice actually made depends on the decision-maker's wealth. For example, a poor person or a poor country may not have the resources to pursue some course of action that a richer one would. When the decision-makers are large organizations or governments of rich countries, however, the assumption of no wealth effect, and hence the possibility of separating efficiency from redistributive considerations, is often plausible. The history of European integration shows that such a separation is both possible and useful. A striking feature of the integration process is that all major efficiency-increasing strategies – from the creation of the Common Market to Economic and Monetary Union – were accompanied by separate redistributive measures in favour of the poorer member states: the Social Fund, the European Investment Bank, the European Regional Development Fund, the Structural Funds and finally the Cohesion Fund which the Maastricht Treaty explicitly ties to the adjustments made necessary by monetary union. By this method it has been possible to achieve a remarkable level of economic integration, in which the richer member states are particularly interested, while distributing the benefits so as to induce all the members to participate in such projects.

I have insisted on the possibility of separating efficiency and redistributive concerns because such a separation is crucial to the substantive legitimacy of regulatory policies. To repeat, the delegation of important policy-making powers to independent institutions is democratically justified only in the sphere of efficiency issues, where reliance on expertise and on a problem-solving style of decision-making is more important than reliance on direct political accountability. Where redistributive concerns prevail, legitimacy can be ensured only by majoritarian means....

To conclude... Non-majoritarian institutions are bound to play an increasingly important role in Europe. The multiplication of regulatory bodies at the national and EC levels is a clear indication of this trend, but equally revealing are the growth of judicial review and the expanding role of courts in the policy-making process. The latter find their policy-making role enlarged by the public perception of them as guarantors of the substantive, as well as procedural, ideals of democracy when electoral accountability in the traditional spheres of government seems to be on the wane (Volcansek 1992). Similarly, the rise of independent agencies has been facilitated by the widespread perception that governmental powers are too concentrated, that public policies lack credibility, and that accountability by results is not sufficiently developed in the public sector.

In country after country, voters have expressed their opposition to an uncontrolled expansion of the welfare state, thus questioning the legitimacy of a model of democracy which has reduced politics to a zero-sum game among redistributive coalitions. What the majority of voters seem to demand, however, is less a general retreat of the state than a redefinition of its functions and modes of operation – greater transparency and accountability, more emphasis on efficiency and a clearer separation of policy and politics. Because of their insulation from partisan politics, their expertise, and their commitment to a problem-solving style of decision-making, independent regulatory bodies and other specialised agencies would seem to be in a better position than government departments to satisfy the new demands of the electorate.

Unlike judges, however, regulators cannot rely on a firm foundation of legitimacy. Regulatory agencies tend to be treated as constitutional anomalies in countries where the delegation of state power to independent institutions is viewed as a serious threat to democracy, parliamentary sovereignty and the hallowed principle that public policy ought to be subject to control only by persons directly accountable to the electorate. These traditional principles are used to justify ministerial interference in agency decision-making, and the retention of important regulatory powers by government departments.

Against these attempts to establish political control by means which contradict the very *raison d'etre* of the agencies we must restate [a] central theme: ... the root problem of regulatory legitimacy in Europe today is not an excess of independence but, on the contrary, the constant threat of politically motivated interference. With greater independence would go greater accountability.

The real question ... is how agency independence and public accountability can be made complementary and mutually reinforcing rather than antithetical values. Our arguments, and the century-old experience of the American regulatory state, indicate that independence and accountability can be reconciled by a combination of control mechanisms rather than by oversight exercised from any fixed place in the political spectrum: clear and limited statutory objectives to provide unambiguous performance standards; reason-giving and transparency requirements to facilitate judicial review and public participation; due process provisions to ensure fairness among the inevitable winners and losers from regulatory decisions; and professionalism to withstand external interference and reduce the risk of an arbitrary use of agency discretion. ... [W]when such a system of multiple control works properly, no one controls an agency, yet the agency is 'under control'. At that point the problem of regulatory legitimacy will have been largely solved.

Majone's approach to substantive legitimation via the pursuit of efficiency goals tends to sideline the role of law, although it implicitly assumes law's facilitative role, functioning as an umpire of the interactions of regulatory actors. The extract ends by suggesting a raft of mechanisms that help to balance the use of opaque expertise against the demands of public accountability, and in these law plays a more prominent role: transparency, detailed rules, due process, judicial review and public participation. These correlate with the role of law as expressive umpire: institutionalising constitutional values for 'fair play' in decision-making based on an underlying vision of − in Majone's case − non-majoritarian democratic governance imposing conditions on the exercise of the state's power.

This procedural dimension of Majone's theory is relevant to a core tension between pluralism and expertise that characterises many examples of 'middle-level' theorising linking regulation and democracy. The pluralism/

expertise cleavage differs from the models articulated by Baldwin and Mashaw, although it does imply competing logics of justification, and at least some of Baldwin's five dimensions could arguably be organised around it. Pluralism implies that legitimation occurs by following procedures which may be either laid down in advance (whether by legal fiat or political mandate) or are sufficiently inclusive to guarantee the adequate representation of affected interests. This is a very different basis from expertise, which rests on substantive knowledge, often of a technical and allegedly 'objective', or at least disinterested, nature.

Pluralism plays an important role in the next extract from Martin Shapiro. It is drawn from a book which considers the question of regulatory legitimation, for our purposes, as a question of what counts as a 'good' or 'bad' government action. The extract included here charts the waxing and waning influence of (procedural) pluralism on the one hand, and (substantive) expertise on the other. Shapiro charts a rough progression over a chronological period in the US context through three phases. An initial reliance on pluralism leads to disenchantment and a search for substance, grounded in moral rightness or economic efficiency. After a second phase of disenchantment, the debate attempts to *blend* economic rationality and expertise with a reinvigorated proceduralism: one closer to deliberation (as exemplified by the Prosser extract in Chapter 2) than to pluralism. The extract is long, but deliberately so, because it makes unusually clear linkages between questions of legitimation (what counts as a good or bad government action, sufficient for it to be generally accepted) and the assumptions underpinning public and private interest theories that we explored in Chapter 2. The extract also connects these questions to different visions of democracy. One vision of democracy accepts pluralism and the relative moral arbitrariness of outcomes reached through representative politics. Another vision of democracy seeks to institutionalise values and to reconnect democracy with moral virtue. Like Majone, Shapiro also charts a link between this substantive turn and non-majoritarian democracy. Unlike Majone's reliance on the neutral, economically-based expertise of independent regulators, however, Shapiro places more emphasis (and betrays a good deal of skepticism about) the neutral, philosophically-based expertise of judges – those who guard the (regulatory) guardians.

Martin Shapiro, 'Who guards the guardians? Judicial control of administration' (1988)

Answers to questions about the goodness or badness of a particular government action ultimately depend on whether we believe that political life in general ought to be devoted to the satisfaction of individual preferences or the attainment of moral principles. The current body of writing on judicial review of administrative action – what lawyers call "administrative law" – is clearly, directly, and often self-consciously linked to current developments in moral and political philosophy.

So before we get to the judges themselves, we must look at these issues of preferences and principles.

Let us suppose for the moment that we believe it is impossible to discover a set of fundamental moral principles or values that can be used to guide and evaluate political action in a democracy. We might come to such a belief for a number of reasons. A review of the past efforts of moral philosophers might lead us to the conclusion that the discovery or formulation of a coherent set of such principles is beyond human capacity, or that many such sets of principles had been formulated by various persons at various times but none had achieved sufficient consensus to serve as a basis for governance. Yet another possibility is that the only such principles to achieve a sufficient consensus were necessarily so general that even those who agreed upon the principle could not agree whether a particular public policy was required, allowed, or forbidden by the principle. (We all believe in the principle that equals should be treated equally, but that does not lead to a moral consensus on affirmative action, for instance.) In short we might conclude that, at least as far as political life was concerned, we ought to think of every individual as having his or her own moral values which we ought to treat as nothing more than personal preferences. Whether a particular government policy was right or wrong would depend on how many people preferred it to some alternative policy.

Such a position is not identical to the claim that in politics every person is an entirely selfish being seeking only to maximise his or her "power" or material benefits. Indeed, this "preference" stance toward politics does not depend upon any particular vision of human nature as selfish or altruistic or even of the universe as a cosmos governed by rules or a chaos. It rests only on an interpretation of human history that sees humans as unable to generate an agreed set of basic principles from which indisputably correct public policies can be deduced. As a result we treat politics as having to do with aggregating or choosing among individual preferences, rather than finding and following moral principles.

An alternative view of the moral history of mankind and an alternative approach to ethics teaches that human values are not mere preferences, mere statements that "I like vanilla" and "You like chocolate". Instead, there are objective values in the sense of some ultimate goal of the good person in the good state and/or in the sense of some do's and don'ts that are morally binding at all times. If a particular public policy leads us away from our ultimate vision of the good, or if it violates one of our do's and don'ts, then it is a bad public policy. The goodness or badness of a law or other government action does not depend on how many people want it but on whether it is objectively right or wrong.

From about 1930 to 1970 most Americans who devoted themselves to thinking and writing about law and politics relied upon the former, or "preference", vision. The dominant school of moral philosophy was utilitarianism, drawn from the writings of Jeremy Bentham. Bentham sought to derive a moral philosophy by what he though of as a purely empirical and scientific mode of inquiry. He began from a purely factual premise of human behaviour or psychology – all people seek pleasure and shun pain. From that premise he derived a moral premise: every act is good to the degree that it increases the sum of human pleasure and bad to the degree that it increases the sum of pain. From there it is but a step to a political morality. A government action is good or bad depending upon whether or not it achieves the greatest good for the greatest number of persons. Or to put the matter in slightly different words, every act is to be judged by its consequences in terms of how many benefits it will bring at what costs.

In a sense, utilitarianism, too, offered an objective moral standard, "the greatest good of the greatest number". To the utilitarian, however, no act or government policy was good in and of itself but was good only on the basis of its consequences in creating more or less of what they wanted for more or fewer people. And any action, no matter how adverse to a particular individual, might be justified on the basis that the detriment to some individuals was outweighed by the advantages to others. The objective ethical principle that utilitarianism offered was that there were no such principles except satisfying the preferences of individuals. So the only right thing to do was to give as many people what they wanted as you could. Modern economics is a branch of utilitarianism, and it offers an especially precise formulation of the basic utilitarian principle called "Paretan optimality". Paretan optimality is a distribution of whatever is valued by individuals in such a way that any change in the distribution would make fewer people better off than it would make worse off.

Utilitarianism and American democracy appear to be compatible in many ways. Every voter can be seen as having a set of preferences. Elections are mechanisms for summating these preferences and giving the majority what they want. Any government and any government action approved by majority vote must, almost by definition, be right because it will give the greater number what they prefer.

Pluralist political theory
In the period immediately preceding and following World War II, political scientist began to stress that democratic politics was centred less in individual voting than in group political activity. Politics consisted of interest groups struggling with one another for access to the levers of power. This pluralist, or "polyarchical", vision of politics was compatible with utilitarianism. What defined a set of individuals as an interest group was that they shared a particular set of preferences. The process of making public policy consisted of groups competing with one another for what legislators, administrative agencies, and courts had to offer. The result of this group struggle would be an aggregation or summating of group preferences in the way that elections summated individual preferences. Any government action achieved by a group struggle in which all the relevant groups participated would be right almost by definition, because it would reflect the interests of the greater number of groups.

The group theory of politics is today offered in two slightly different forms, one derived from political science and the other from economics. The political theorists who propounded pluralist or polyarchical views did not necessarily imply that there was no such thing as the common good or public interest as opposed to the sum of individual or group interests. They did not explicitly argue that there was no ideal of the good person in the good state toward which public policy should be directed or that there were no absolute or deontological rights or wrongs. They did argue, however, that there was no universally accepted logical or scientific procedure for determining the good and relatively little consensus on what the good was. Each group would have its own necessarily incomplete and somewhat distorted vision of the public good. Given these realities, and as a second-best solution in the absence of universally agreed right policies, the pluralists were driven toward a proceduralist criterion as a working standard for public policy. Those public policies were to be considered correct that were arrived at by a process in which all relevant groups had actively participated, each with enough political clout to ensure that its views had to be taken into account by the ultimate decision makers.

Such a pluralist, procedural criterion could be taken in one of two ways. It could mean that, in the absence of any more objective way of determining political truth, the clash and compromise of various groups, each with its own vision of the public good, was the best available means of approximating that good. Taken in this way, pluralism is not a denial that there are good and bad, or at least better and worse, public policies, perhaps even quite apart from the greatest good for the greatest number. The pluralist need not be taken as saying that politics is merely the aggregation of group preferences devoid of any component of a more absolute or general good. He may be insisting only that the best political process for achieving the good is one that allows for the clash of competing visions of the good.

Pluralism may be viewed another way, however, as in the case of many economists who have turned it into a theory of "public choice [discussed in Chapter Two of this book]...[I]n this economic vision, most legislation, particularly when it regulates economic activity, is essentially a matter of creating and allocating "rents.".... Most group politics will consist of groups exchanging their political support for votes from legislators on bills that will get them more than they could get in a free market in the absence of legislation. Thus, while in theory leaving some room for the pursuit of the common good, group politics as presented by economists is even more oriented to partial and selfish interests than is the pluralism of political scientists.

Political theories of pluralism are usually expressed in terms of access and influence. Those groups that can gain access to policymakers use that access to seek to persuade them that the policies favoured by the group should be adopted by the government. Some of this access and influence is pure exchange. The group gains the ear of the policymaker by saying, "if you will listen to us and then do what we say, we will vote for you, or contribute to your campaign or support some policy you want." Often, however, access and influence may be based on the perception of policymakers that they and an interest group share a desire to achieve the common good and can achieve that good by cooperation. Thus a "Union of Concerned Scientists' may gain access to a Senate committee by saying", "We both want to solve the problem of nuclear waste, and we scientists have the expertise to tell you how. So listen to us." And the union of scientists may actually influence the committee's decision because the senators believe that the scientists have the expert knowledge to solve the common problem.

Economic group theories tend to emphasise pure exchange elements. Government policymakers are thought to pursue their own selfish interest, such as getting reelected, and interest groups are regarded in the same way. The policymakers will give the groups the policies they want if, in exchange, the groups give the policy-makers the political support they need in order to get reelected or keep their administrative agencies going. More politically oriented group theories leave more room for collaboration between groups and government decision makers to achieve shared visions of the public good.

It is not difficult to imagine the first set of objections to be made to group theories of politics. In free markets, goods are allocated to individuals on the basis of what price they will pay. Prices are set by supply and demand under competitive conditions. Such markets do a perfect job of satisfying everyone's preferences so long as everyone starts with the same amount of money with which to pay the prices. Even if life is merely individual preferences, the free market, viewed only as a distribution mechanism, is not fair or just if some people have a lot more money than others. Similarly, even where government policy is seen as only the satisfaction of group interests that compete freely for government favour, the result will not be considered fair and just if some groups have a great deal more political power than others. If some groups control a large number of votes, or can make large campaign contributions, or have other political resources, they can "pay" more and thus wield more access and influence than other groups. So they will get more of their preferences enacted into law or other government policy.

The first critical response to pluralism was, therefore, an emphasis on the fact that the group struggle would yield public policies that favoured some groups over others simply because some groups were more politically influential than others. The result might be quite at odds with the preferences of a majority of the individual citizens and not in accord with the greatest good of the greatest number.

...[The] first response was a whole set of devices designed to equalise the position in the policy "market" of the competing interests. In many instances, large numbers of people shared an interest but had not organised into groups that could compete effectively, [for example]...organiz[ing] neighborhood residents, the elderly, the poor, consumers, nature lovers, members of racial and linguistic minorities, and others into effective political groups. Simply organizing often gave these groups considerable political influence because, once organised, they could call on their members for votes, money, and personal action in support of group political goals.

Various efforts have also been made to increase group access to administrative agencies and courts by providing some of them with government-funded legal services and other kinds of support funded by government and private foundations. The Freedom of Information Act and various "sunshine" acts were passed to make it easier for groups that do not have good "inside" contacts to find out what is happening in government. Then they are in a better position to present their cases to the right government decision makers at the right time.

All of these are attempts to level up, to give more access and influence to the weaker groups. There have also been attempts to level down. For instance, the sunshine acts that require government bodies to make their decisions in public do provide more needed information for groups without government friends to tell them what is going on. In addition, these acts are designed to limit the influence of the most powerful groups by exposing their dealings with government agencies to public scrutiny. The Campaign Financing Act and other statutes that limit campaign contributions and spending and provide government funds to candidates are designed to reduce the power of big money groups.

In spite of all the tinkerings of the last three decades, however, there remains great discontent with a pluralist political process. Some groups are obviously far more equal than others. Above all is the fear that certain powerful groups will "capture" administrative agencies or congressional committees or courts and run the government. A part of government that constantly hears form one powerful group that offers to help the agency if the agency will just do what the group defines as right is likely, over the years, to take on the group's point of view as its own.

Some allegedly captured agencies are sometimes "liberated". Ecologists now have a major voice in Forest Service decisions that once appeared to be dominated by timber-cutting interests. Deregulation has tried to solve the problem of capture of certain agencies by simply doing away with the agency's power to help those who might have held it captive. The Civil Aeronautics Board may have been the captive of the airlines. Airline deregulation means that no federal agency can any longer grant airlines exclusive routes and high rates. Many of the new agencies, such as the Environmental Protection Agency and the Occupational Safety and Health Administration, regulate all industries rather than a particular one. Agencies like the Civil Aeronautics Board that regulated a single industry were obvious targets for capture; that industry would work very hard to influence the agency. An agency that regulates all industries is not easily captured by any one of them. . . .

For a time it seemed that the only response to the perceived inequalities of pluralism—the picture of powerful groups capturing agencies in order to help themselves against less powerful rival group − would be more pluralism. We would undertake the organization of more groups and the assignment of more resources to the weaker ones. The competition of relatively equal rival groups for influence over a given part of government would prevent any one of them from achieving capture.

It seems unlikely that such superpluralist moves would have fully satisfied the antipluralist critiques no matter what else was happening. Something else, however, was happening. Pluralism was highly compatible with the brand of ethics that conceived of values as essentially matters of personal preference. The critique of pluralism might have been regarded as only making the point that group processes . . . did not result in government policies that accurately aggregated the preferences of all groups. The more politically powerful groups got too much of what they preferred and the weaker ones too little. If that had been the only ethical basis of the attack on pluralism, the response from pluralists would have been, "Group processes may not perfectly aggregate preferences but they are the best way we've got to aggregate preferences." Something of a standoff would have been reached.

Just at the time when attacks on pluralism reached their peak, however, a new development in ethics was occurring that allowed antipluralists to make out a far more positive case for an alternative to pluralism than simply that pluralism did not work perfectly because of group inequality. Beginning in the 1960s, a major movement has occurred in moral philosophy that has been labelled "postconsequentialist" ethics. It rejects utilitarianism in favour of an emphasis on the value of an act quite apart from its consequences .... This alternative or postconsequentialist ethics may insist that acts are good and bad in and of themselves because they are in accordance with or violate moral rules like 'Thou Shalt Not Kill.' These moral rules are taken to be valid quite apart from their consequences. Such an ethic is said to assert "deontological" values. Or postconsequentialist ethics may be based on the notion that political life is informed by a vision of what the good life would ultimately be in the good society or the good state. The goodness or badness of a particular act depends upon whether it moves us toward or away from that vision. Such an ethics is said to be "teleological." Of course, it is not purely nonconsequentialist. It does look to the consequences of an act to determine its rightness or wrongness. It is asking about consequences, however, not in terms of giving most people what they immediately prefer but in terms of an ultimate goal. That ultimate goal of the good person leading the good life in the good state is not a matter of personal preferences. The teleologist is actually measuring current acts against some ideal and the content of that ideal is determined in some way other than aggregating preferences. Moral persons must think out what the ideal society would look like and measure the ethical quality of current acts in accordance with their contribution to that ideal. Both varieties of nonconsequentialist ethics are antiutilitarian.

They refuse to accept "the greatest good for the greatest number" particularly in the form "the greatest preferences of the greatest number" as the central tenant of public ethics. When these sorts of antiutilitarian ethics are added to the initial attack on pluralism, they provide a much more positive thrust to that attack.

Basing themselves on the interest in reviving deontological and teleological ethics to be found in the new breed of postutilitarian or postconsequentialist philosophers, antipluralists could now move to a new position. They could argue that even if group struggle were the best available way in an imperfect world to aggregate personal preferences, the goodness or badness of a government action ought not to be solely a question of aggregate personal preferences or the greatest good for the greatest number. We also ought to ask whether proposed government actions are right or wrong in the deontological sense. Do they or do they not violate basic moral rules? And we ought to ask of every government action whether it contributes merely to the immediate selfish interests of some or many or to the common good or the general welfare in the sense of moving us toward a better society for everyone? In short, the key public policy question is not how many groups want it but whether it is right or wrong. If that is the question, then mere tinkering with the groups to even them up is not the route to political virtue.

Thus, increasingly, we are coming to believe that government policy should be judged not only as to its process but as to its substance. We are no longer content to say that, because everyone has his or her own ideas of right and wrong, the only good public policy is one which every relevant group participated in forming. If all the groups took part in the ecological plan, but all the fish in the river died, we are not prepared to say that the plan was right. But what criteria of substantive, as opposed to procedural, right and wrong are we to use? And what procedures are we to use for establishing such substantive criteria of right and wrong? These are the questions that have begun to beckon to the critics of pluralism. Perhaps they provide a way out of the frustration of being able to propose no cure for the pathologies of pluralism except more pluralism — that is, the creation of more groups and more equalization of group resources.

... Not surprisingly, one of the very first routes chosen for establishing substantive criteria of right and wrong for government policy was utilitarianism itself. It may appear something of a paradox that one of the first vehicles of postconsequentialist urges should be an appeal to that most preference-oriented and most consequentialist philosophy. The greatest good for the greatest number, however, particularly as translated by economists into the concept of economic efficiency, is a very useful tool lying ready to hand for the critics of pluralism. If the processes of group politics at any given moment yield public policies that are not economically efficient, such as subsidies to tobacco farmers, then those policies are substantively wrong even if the groups all struggled vigorously.

Economists have both optimistic and pessimistic readings of the phenomenon. Some say that over time the competition and logrolling of the groups will lead to economically efficient policies, that is, policies that provide optimum satisfaction for the preferences that actually exist in the society. Groups that want something badly enough will keep fighting until they get it and will give in to other groups on things the other groups want the most. Other economists are prone to argue that such efficiency would result only if there were perfectly free and equal group competition in a political market perfectly structured to respond accurately to all expressions of group preference. Many of them argue that, in fact, existing political processes and institutions tend to heavily overweight some groups and their preferences and underweigh others. Even the optimists agree that no matter what the long term overall outcome, many public policies proposed or in place today are substantively wrong in the sense of being economically inefficient ...

One solution, therefore, for many of those dissatisfied with group struggle is to turn to rationality or efficiency as criteria for public policy and rational or synoptic decision-making processes as the best decision-making processes. By synoptic we simply mean a process that gathers all the facts, considers all alternative policies and all the possible consequences of each, and chooses those policies with the highest probability of achieving agreed goals at least cost. Such procedures have been widely adopted as reforms designed to give us better public policies. "Program," "zero-based," and other budgeting techniques, environmental and regulatory impact statements and regulatory analyses, and statutes that specify that agencies make rules on the basis of "the best available evidence" or "substantial evidence on the rule-making record as a whole" are examples of recent tendencies to move away from group struggle and toward "rational" decision making. In these instances it is not the product of group struggle but the product of rational economic and technical analysis is, by definition, good policy.

This renewed confidence in rationality is only a very partial solution to most pluralist problems, however, because it retains the weakness of utilitarianism at the ultimate ethical level. Synoptic decision processes can work only if we can agree on precisely what goals or values the policy we are seeking is to serve and exactly what the priority among those goals is if there are more than one. So the ultimate ethical problem of specifying basic values remains .... To many persons concerned with ethics, it seems unlikely that deontological or teleological moral truth is to be found by the majority vote of people who have not thought seriously about value questions. Voting and other methods of simply aggregating preferences entail asking value questions in a rapid and casual way that appears unlikely to lead to moral truth, because moral truth is not ultimately a matter of unexamined personal preference.

[So] what procedures would postconsequentialist philosophers and the postpluralists who look to those philosophers find appropriate for discovering the values that are to guide government decisions about public policy? To find out, we must first discover what procedures they believe philosophers themselves ought to employ in discovering ethical truth. For anyone not a professional philosopher, it is quite difficult to understand how the new moral philosophers do what they do. It is even more difficult to convey the spirit and style of what they do to other nonprofessionals. We must try to understand, however, because there is really a very substantial contemporary push to get this style inserted into governmental decision-making processes. And ... many descriptions of the style suggest that judges would be particularly good at it.

The central feature of the new ethics appears to be discourse. Philosophers arrive at postconsequentialist values by speaking and writing to one another. This communication is not usually conceived of as some sort of formal debate. Rather it should be a collective, collaborative discussion among philosophers that proposes and tests moral propositions. Its outstanding feature is that everyone must speak carefully and precisely .... Most importantly, when dealing with moral questions, discourse aims at persuasion rather than proof. The new moral philosophers believe that those who reject the notion that there are true moral values do so because of a fundamental error. Just because one cannot prove a moral value the way one proves a theorem in geometry or a fact ought not to mean that we abandon the search for values. We cannot conclude that, because no value is absolutely true or can be proved with total certainty, we should treat values as mere personal preferences. The new moral discourse seeks to arrive at an agreement that certain moral positions are more true than other propositions. The talk is not ended by a vote on which propositions discussed are truest, nor does consensus prove that the proposition that has achieved consensus is true. As soon as one of the talkers can offer a persuasive objection to a principle on which consensus appears to have been reached, talk will begin again, aimed at a more persuasive formulation. It is extremely difficult to convey the style of this talk, but it is a curious and wonderful mixture of appeals to logic, to experience, and above all, to very carefully examined and criticised, but nonetheless deeply held convictions that certain ways of treating human beings are revolting to our deepest moral senses. A process of careful, logical reasoning together is central to the ethical enterprise.

Having said all this, we cannot quite have captured the essence of the postconsequentialist movement. Some of us might suppose that ten philosophers might speak together carefully for ten years and not come up with a set of moral values that were self-evidently true. What happens when the philosophers reach a disagreement about a value question that cannot be resolved simply by clearing up linguistic misunderstandings and logical flaws? The postconsequentialists forbid us to call them intuitionist. Intuitionism is an earlier and now outmoded approach to philosophy. Nevertheless, it is difficult for outsiders not to say that when postconsequentialists have cleared away misunderstandings and reached a real moral issue, they decide the issue by responding to their moral intuitions.

Postconsequentialists say otherwise. They say that when true moral issues are uncovered and carefully stated, the participants in moral discourse are able to discern some moral resolutions that are far more persuasive, appealing or correct than others. The participants in such discourse insist that they do not simply add up or try for a consensus about their moral hunches. Instead, by the very process of discourse itself, they arrive at statements of moral values that are persuasive even if they cannot be proven to be absolutely correct. These statements might take the form of general moral rules to guide individual and political life. Or they might take the form of a conclusion that, in a particular situation, it would be right to do one thing and wrong to do another.

Again, to outsiders, it may appear that, for all the discourse, these ultimate conclusions of right and wrong rest on purely personal, subjective feelings or hunches or instincts or intuitions about right and wrong. When a postconsequentialist discourse leads the discoursers to agree about moral principles, it may be simply because they happened to be a set of persons who already had roughly the same personal moralities before the discourse began. The discoursers claim otherwise. They believe that they have arrived at statements of moral truth that are more objective than a mere collective statement of their individual moral preferences.

If the claims of the postconsequentialists are correct, it would follow that there could be public values that were not simply the greatest value preferences of the greatest number. Such values might take the form of overarching general rules that particular public policies would have to obey in order to be legitimate. They might take the form of individual moral rights that no public policy might legitimately impinge. They might enter in the form of a judgment that in a particular situation, a particular public policy was not merely effective or expedient, or the product of group struggle, or capable of yielding the greatest good for the greatest number, but was right or wrong.

What procedures would we use for arriving at such public values and injecting them as governing elements in public policy making? The key to understanding the most recent tendencies of thought about administrative procedure is to be found in observing the tension between the way postconsequentialists do moral philosophy and the demand for wide public participation that marks democratic political theory.

Those who believe that there are statements of right and wrong that go beyond mere personal preference must, of course, have some method or procedure of arriving at such statements....[There is a] preference of many contemporary moral philosophers for discourse among a number of persons, rather than introspection, as the best procedure for arriving at truer statements of right and wrong.... Moral discourse promises the production of moral values or truths that are far more persuasive than those arrived at by mere individual thought and assertion. [But] ... in a democracy, political or public policy decisions ought to be made in a democratic way. As practiced by moral philosophers, discourse appears to be a highly elitist enterprise — the very antithesis of democracy. Such a careful and critical discussion with so much give-and-take can only be undertaken by a small group of persons. ...[Moreover]... the "people" or the "voters" can hardly be expected to become ethical discoursers in the style of the philosophers. It is not that postconsequentialist philosophers are asserting that the nation should be run by philosopher-kings. Neither they nor anyone else, however, could expect the vast majority of [ordinary citizens] to do much discourse or the vast majority of public decisions to be arrived at by discourse of this sort.

For those who believe that public policy decisions should be right, rather than merely the product of group struggle, how is the kind of discourse necessary to arrive at right decisions to be introduced into democratic public policy-making? A number of schools of thought are now emerging on this subject. One is that of legal proceduralists. Lawyers, particularly constitutional lawyers, are always looking for special defenses of judicial policy-making. Such defenses are necessary precisely because public policy-making by nonelected, "independent" judges always appears to be antidemocratic. One such defense runs as follows.

Particularly in the appeal of cases with major public policy implications, the litigational process consists of a very careful dialogue between two persons highly trained in a particular mode of discourse. That dialogue between opposing counsel is constrained by a set of legal rules and professional traditions. It is aimed at persuading a set of third persons, the judges. The judges are trained in the same mode of discourse. They are anxious to reach public policy decisions that are justifiable in terms of neutral principles of law which are themselves the product of this same mode of discourse. Molière's "would-be gentleman" was astounded at the discovery that he had been speaking "prose" all along when he thought he had just been speaking. These lawyers discover that litigating lawyers and judges all along have been engaging in the ethical discourse prescribed by the philosophers when what they had thought they were doing was trying a law suit ...[C]onstitutional and other policy-laden litigation ... can be seen as a continuous discourse about public values engaged in by the set of people best trained in discourse about public values, those who have graduated from the best law schools. The public-value conclusions from this discourse are to be drawn by neutral, principled, independent judges who themselves are, of course, lawyers from the same law schools.

Not all of us are equally charmed by the discovery that a set of Ivy League lawyers are the ideal medium for introducing ethical discourse into public affairs and creating and enforcing our public values. Nor are all of us equally charmed that courts, as opposed to legislatures, or executives, or political parties, or voters are to be the seat of the principles of right and wrong that are to replace group struggle as the criteria for public policy. Yet the alliance between postconsequentialist ethics and the "jurisprudence of values" is becoming an increasingly powerful and persuasive one. It sees judicial processes as a, or even the, principal mode of arriving at public values which will then be used by judges to uphold good public policies and strike down bad ones. . . .

Judicial policy-making becomes democratic because now it is the way in which public values come to direct public policy. Yet public values in this sense are not values declared by the public but values declared by the lawyers. Simply attaching the word public to the values discovered in litigation is not enough to make them democratic values. [And]. . . . most public policy is not made through litigation. Most of it is made through the legislative and administrative processes. We will focus on the administrative process. How can the method of ethical moral discourse be introduced into the administrative process? The major symptom of this effort is the increasing fashionableness of using the word deliberation in conjunction with prescriptions for and descriptions of the administrative process. For those who want administrative decisions to be right, rather than merely the product of group struggle, there is increasing interest in administrative deliberation and the use of judicial review to require administrators to deliberate.

It is not entirely clear exactly what administrative deliberation would look like. Some main outlines and some big do's and don'ts are discernable. The administrator is neither to be captured by a particular interest nor to be a mere neutral aggregator of the preferences of the various groups that vie for the agencies' favours. Instead, administrators must seek for and arrive at good public policies, that is, policies that are in accord with deontological standards of right and wrong and/or serve the public interest.

Of course, there have always been notorious difficulties with defining the public interest, but those favouring administrative deliberation seem to mix and match a number of approaches. Some public policy areas involve nothing more than government distribution of a relatively scarce resource on which no one has any particular moral claim, for example, campsites in [national parks] in the summer. In such policy areas, the public interest may be the utilitarian greatest good for the greatest number. Few public policy areas are purely distributive in this sense. In most areas, the proponents of administrative deliberation appear to mean by public interest something like Rousseau's General Will as opposed to the will of all. Administrators should adopt those policies which a fully informed and attentive public itself would have adopted after engaging in serious public debate.

Or alternatively, administrators ought to discover true values, either deontological or teleological or both, and apply them to a fully developed understanding of the facts so as to arrive at correct public policies. Such policies would, of course, be in the public interest both in the sense of achieving the general good and in the sense of meriting public approval, for surely the people would approve the good either tacitly or actively once it was pointed out to them.

The jurisprudence of values has focused on judges, and particularly on judges in constitutional interpretation. . . . [But] administrators do not hold lawyers' séances with the common law . . . From whence and how are mere administrators to derive their values?

One answer is that they are to derive them just as judges do, through a process of litigation that serves as the equivalent of the moral discourse conducted by philosophers . . . [T]here has been an increasing tendency toward turning administrative decision making into a quasi-judicial process in which policy emerges from trial-like administrative hearings. The administrators become lawyer-like moral discoursers.

A second answer is simply that administrative deliberation ought to be like philosophic discourse. *Deliberation* comes to signify a process in which administrators seek to identify the public interest or common good by engaging in discourse among themselves and with relevant groups. That discourse is to be explicitly aimed at arriving at deontological and or teleological statements of basic values that serve as guides to policy outcomes. The administrators become moral philosophers.

A third answer is that administrators are not free moral actors. They administer, that is implement or carry out, statutes. Statutes prescribe the organization and duties of administrative agencies. They create the programs that the administrators are to carry out. Therefore those administering a program ought to adopt the values and goals that the legislature puts into the statute creating it. Administrative deliberation becomes a process of statutory interpretation. The administrator seeks to discover the true values in the statute, a task that is not as easy as it sounds . . . [later developments have led to] one of the major elements in postpluralist, postconsequentialist prescriptions for administrative deliberation [which is that] the administrator should engage in synoptic decision making . . . Synopticism demands that, within reasonable cost and time constraints, the agencies do, not a perfect, but the best possible job of gathering facts and identifying alternatives. Within the same constraints, they should articulate the values that have led to their choices among alternatives. . . . The demand is that administrators do the best possible job, not the least that will "satisfice" the interest groups . . . .

The vision of agency deliberation has been built up to oppose the vision of administrators as mere incremental aggregators of group preferences and captives of dominant groups. It is not that groups are to be excluded from the deliberations conducted by administrators. They are to be allowed a voice. Ultimately, however, administrators are to conduct an ethical discourse quite comparable to that conducted by philosophers and judges. The purpose of this discourse is to identify true public values.

Administrators are to add to this discourse a technical expertise that, within reasonable time and cost constraints, allows them to discover all the facts and consider all the alternative policies. Putting values, facts, and alternatives together, they are to arrive at correct public policies — policies that accord with the deontological values of the society and move it toward its vision of the good person in the good state.

There is a sense in which democracy is not at issue. Surely the people want right administrative decisions, so as long as the administrators arrive at policies by careful deliberation, the people will approve their policies. Many of those who espouse administrative deliberation, however, add a series of democratic controls. All interest groups are to have as nearly as possible equal access to the deliberators. There is to be a public record of the deliberation. The deliberators are to provide the public a reasoned explanation of their decision. In their search for values, administrators are to take the values incorporated into the governing statutes by the democratically elected legislature as crucial. Courts will engage in judicial review of administrative decisions to insure that they are in accord with the values and goals of the democratically elected legislature. Administrative deliberation somehow manages to combine ethical discourse, technological expertise and democratic responsiveness.

The key bridge between deliberation and democracy is the notion of a deliberative community which has its origins in the Greek idea of the polis. The polis is the Greek city state in which all the citizens participate in making decisions about all matters of public concern. A central aspect of postconsequential concepts of deliberation is the call for a political community in which all aspects of government, including administration, would be embedded.

To sum up, those in revolt against the pluralist, incrementalist theory of politics and administration did not have to content themselves with negative carping at the unfairness of the group struggle. Instead, they found in postconsequentialist ethical discourse a model for postpluralist administration. Such administration was to combine ethical discourse and technical expertise to achieve synoptic policy decisions that are intrinsically correct and democratic. Postconsequentialist philosophy and postpluralist political theory are thus central to the current fascination of administrative lawyers and administrative theorists with deliberation.

The above extract concludes with a strong connection between the creation of a deliberative community and the role of judges. What Shapiro labels 'postpluralist administration' is strongly resonant with according law a role of expressive umpire. In this context, courts and judges are central fora for structuring dialogue to ensure proper deliberation in collective policy making. His account stresses how those who advocate this approach regard judges' interpretations of legal rules as arriving at morally correct decisions.

In the next extract, Mariano-Florentino Cuéllar links democracy once again to processes of regulatory legitimation, this time in a far more institutionally detailed context than Shapiro. Cuéllar maps different visions of democracy by contrasting representative and participatory democracy. As with the other classifications of democratic traditions depicted in previous extracts, Cuéllar's vision also reflects a tension between pluralism and expertise. His extract explores the possibility of regulatory democracy, developing a proposal to inject democratic energy directly into regulatory agencies. Although the institutional context in this extract is the US, similar emphases on participatory versus representative visions of democracy embodied in concrete mechanisms of regulatory accountability could legitimate regulatory agency decisions in other contexts.

Mariano-Florentino Cuéllar, 'Rethinking regulatory democracy' (2005)

Regulatory agencies write ten to twenty times as many new public laws in a year as does the federal legislature, and in the process make an overwhelming number of the nation's public policy decisions. Agencies regulate privacy, political competition, parks, pollution, ports, power plants, pork belly prices and political "pork" among other things. Not surprisingly, scholars, judges, and lawyers have consumed enormous energy debating agencies' legal and philosophical status. This outpouring of theoretical attention is matched, however, by the gaps in our knowledge about the actual workings of what we might call *regulatory democracy*, or how the public participates in those decisions of the regulatory state that so dramatically affect them under existing law.

The basic legal requirements built into [the US] system are clear enough: agencies get statutory authority to regulate from the legislature. They must ordinarily provide notice of proposed regulations, accept comments about them, and give clear reasons for their actions. Clear, too, are the theoretical insights gleaned from social scientists about the purported difficulty of mobilizing individual members of the public with diffuse interests to affect regulations, the powerful role of the legislature in overseeing the regulatory state, and the incentives of agency officials to pay disproportionate heed to the concerns of certain players in the regulatory process. Less clear is who might be concerned enough to actually comment on regulations, what they say, and how agencies react to those concerns in practice.

My own concern here is to [use empirical evidence] . . . to offer a new perspective on current regulatory democracy and how it can be reformed. [I have elsewhere] examine[d] three quite different regulations, from the Treasury Department, the Nuclear Regulatory Commission, and the Federal Election Commission. Each regulation was crafted from statutes giving the agency massive discretion over a substantively important issue. None provoked any discernible legislative response either before or since the regulation was finalised. My analysis show[ed], among other things, that comments from individual members of the public account for the lion's share of total input received about these regulations. Those individual comments, moreover, raise different concerns from those of organised interests. While those concerns raised by individual commenters are nearly always relevant to the agency's legal mandate, they lack the legal and policy sophistication of the comments to which the agencies paid the most heed. In fact this "sophistication deficit" appears to have some effect on the agency's probability of accepting a commenter suggestion, even when controlling for the commenter's status as a regulated entity. Yet agencies and existing law have no systematic means of assimilating unsophisticated comments or gleaning any other sort of public insights from among the tens of millions of people who lack either the knowledge of a regulation's existence or the ability to advance their opinion about it in a sophisicated way.... My data belie the notion that organised interests raise the full range of concerns relevant to writing regulations. Surprisingly, my data also belie the notion that agencies disproportionately respond to the concerns of the companies and entities they regulate, which would make it largely pointless to reform regulatory democracy. Instead my data suggest agencies will heed comments from individual members of the public if they are presented in a more sophisticated fashion. Along with other research on political behavior, my data also raise questions about whether the larger public's sophistication and interest in regulatory policy are stuck in the "low" positions. In short, my data and discussion emphasise the gap between current regulatory democracy and the sort of arrangement that many plausible normative accounts of democracy would consider desirable.

If one still believes in compromise acceptance in the face of these data, it is likely because no alternative arrangement appears reasonable. How exactly does one motivate the larger public to think carefully about the regulations that so profoundly affect their lives? Surely the prospect of having a referendum on campaign finance or nuclear licensing regulations is as ludicrous as mass opinions are devoid of any useful content on these technical arguments. But under scrutiny the feasibility argument favouring the current system turns brittle, too. I show this by pursuing... an extended thought experiment in the institutional design of a new arrangement for regulatory democracy. The reformed procedures preserve some of the strengths of the status quo. They also yield a trove of valuable information about public attitudes that the status quo can never provide. The key elements of that design include the creation of a specialised participation agency. The agency would then select random voter samples (or stratified samples, if the goal is to represent key interests rather than to foster majoritarian deliberation) and provide them with time and balanced information about the regulation, as well as a "regulatory public defender" to articulate views to the agency writing the regulation. This approach not only yields richer information about how and when the public might want to comply with regulations, but also treats the regulatory state as a fertile setting for democratic experimentation ....

There is no way to move beyond current regulatory democracy (or even to judge whether such a move is advisable) without addressing the persistent view that no viable changes are practically feasible. Though I dismiss most of the "feasibility" problems in the pages that follow, it's best to start by proposing a reasonable definition of feasibility. It would be hard to accept such a definition if it did not include some of the following elements. Any mechanism for consulting the public should not dramatically raise the financial cost of developing regulations. Neither should it disrupt the regulatory state's existing capacity to analyze complicated technical and scientific information. A feasible alternative, moreover, should incorporate some way to mitigate the drawbacks associated with most versions of direct democracy, where apparently unsophisticated voters to little to enrich the policymaking process. Finally, reforms in regulatory democracy should not weigh down the regulatory process by just adding veto players.

The proposals that follow live up to this definition . . . They take advantage of the regulatory state's existing institutions without disrupting the capacity of analysts, economists, scientists, and lawyers to develop sophisticated technical analyses of regulatory programs. The costs are manageable when compared to other costs borne in the development of regulations, such as economic analysis or enforcement costs. Moreover, the costs are scalable, so if only scarce resources are available the techniques I describe could be used to focus on particularly important regulations. Regardless of whether the proposals end up applying to only a small subset of regulations at first or to most of them, my proposals don't simply add veto players that would further paralyze the regulatory process. Instead they add to the rulemaking record that can be used by agencies to support regulations and by courts to review agencies' work. Most crucially, these approaches solve the problems associated with the more quotidian versions of direct democracy by obtaining a manageable number of participants who can be coaxed toward thinking about regulatory problems in a more sophisticated way.

Corrective interest representation: Suppose one believes that people should take part in regulatory decisions when they will be materially affected. This is not an unreasonable premise in the regulatory state. Practices like negotiated rulemaking occasionally involve agencies in figuring out *who* might be affected by a particular rulemaking proceeding. Through negotiated rulemaking, the agency determines who might be interested in participating in the rulemaking proceeding in order to reach an early consensus on the proposed rule. But the point of negotiated rulemaking is not explicitly to identify people or constituencies who might have a particular interest and yet run the risk of being unrepresented. Instead, the major purpose of negotiated rulemaking is to enhance rules, reduce litigation, and shorten the rulemaking process by providing a mechanism for consensus rulemaking proposals.

Imagine extending just one aspect of the agency's mandate during a negotiated rulemaking procedure, identifying interests that are likely to be particularly affected by the regulation, and transferring this mandate to a specialised agency charged with selecting participants who will be affected by the regulation but are unlikely to speak up on their own. The goal here would not be to speed up the regulatory process but instead to do something that might seem to go in precisely the opposite direction: including people who will clearly be impacted by the regulation but may lack the sophistication to gracefully articulate their concerns, and giving those people a chance to constructively voice their interests. The process would involve at least three components: (1) selecting a *"corrective" sample* of people, (2) providing a setting in which they could *voice their concerns* in a way that corrects for deficiencies in sophistication (i.e., through assistance from counsel or a facilitator), and (3) devising a process through which an agency would be nudged to take seriously the *resulting opinions*. A lawyer from the agency or an independent agency might then be charged with advocating for the group's ideas.

Imagine how this could work in the context of [a] financial privacy regulation. The agency charged with issuing the regulations (i.e., Treasury), perhaps along with a separate specialised agency focused on public engagement (call it a *participation agency*), make an initial determination about who is likely to be particularly affected by the regulations but unlikely to represent themselves — including, among others, smaller banks and credit unions, bank employees, or legitimate customers particularly likely to be concerned about privacy. No doubt that it would be difficult to design a defensible system for choosing "who will be especially affected yet unlikely to adequately represent themselves."

The participation agency would break down the task into a few different pieces. One is to define the kinds of benefits and burdens that could be caused by the proposed regulation if it went into effect (i.e., privacy intrusions that could result in unauthorised disclosure, changes in the probability of being subjected to time-consuming, costly, or harrowing investigation, new tasks for financial institution employees). Another is to make some considered judgment about who among members of the general population may disproportionately bear the preceding benefits and costs.... Finally, once the agency has made this determination, it might consider whether the constituencies disproportionately affected are constructively represented in the process. This might include considering the sophistication (or even existence) of comments from some of the impacted constituencies. The agency would then select a small number of people in the "underrepresented" constituencies to take part in the rulemaking process.

How exactly would the selected participants take part in the regulatory process?... At least two possibilities are worth considering here. One is to provide people with a sort of deliberative forum. Some group of people numbering between 7 and 15 might be chosen to receive information, with the chance to deliberate. They would all get balanced materials explaining the arguments for and against the proposed regulation. Then they would get the chance to talk to each other and question experts from the agency about the possible alternatives. The agency would use the existing proposed regulations as a basis for discussion. The goal of the deliberation would not be to subject the regulations to an up-or-down vote but rather to elicit concerns, observations, and ideas about how the regulation should evolve.

Part of what the process would have to accomplish is to separate the factual issues best resolved through expert analysis from interpretation of an ambiguous statute and policy judgments. The deliberation group would be in a position to inform what to do about the latter but not necessarily the former. The corrective sample's discussions then inform the rulemaking process and become part of the record. Accordingly, the public can raise valid concerns given the statutory scheme, and these in turn can become a basis for litigation....[T]he most important point is that the corrective sample's deliberations would have some legal effect — for example, by creating a presumption in favour of a particular regulatory strategy, such as the issuance of .... regulations with a remedy for unauthorised disclosure of sensitive financial information.

Public defenders: It takes special knowledge to run a new means of infusing agencies with public participation. The new "participation agency" could handle a panoply of functions supporting the process of public participation in the regulatory process. A separate agency would have a specific mandate to enhance decision making across agencies, without having to concern itself with competing tasks involving civil servants and political appointees who get invested with a specific point of view. Its leadership might consist of a board of appointees with fixed, staggered terms. Their job would be to supervise the staff in discharging a few interrelated functions. First, the agency would promulgate rules for how members of the public would be selected to participate in deliberation groups. Second, the agency would prepare risk and cost-benefit analysis materials that would be presented to corrective deliberation groups. These analyses would be designed to complement those of the agency with direct responsibility for the regulatory program. Deliberation groups would therefore get more than one point of view about the risks, costs, and benefits associated with any given proposal.

Third, the participation agency would provide trained moderators to facilitate the discussion among either the corrective or the majoritarian deliberation groups. Finally, the agency would provide the lawyers to take the contributions of participants and turn these into more sophisticated comments that would become part of the administrative record. . . . The defining features of reforms would be to get participants as close to the actual decision as possible, instead of keeping their input general. The more specific the feedback, transmitted through a moderator or legal representative, the more possible it would be for the implementing agency to grapple directly with public input about specific proposals.

The agency would develop mechanisms to select the relevant sample and structure discussions among people (in a manner that mitigated any potential adverse effects to decision-making arising from collective discussions and from distinctions in the degree to which some members of the public consider risk-related probabilistic information). For the corrective approach, the external agency could empanel groups of unaffiliated experts who would identify stakeholders for consultation.

The agency would then structure discussions among the selected participants. The main goal of structuring the discussion is not necessarily to realise some deliberative ideal. It is [more] to have the public react to a specific agency policy proposal . . . rather than some vague generality. That is what makes virtually any version of this reformed regulatory democracy different from proposals to hold deliberation days or deliberative polls. All that may be fine, but it still requires a regulatory state to translate ambiguous legal commands into regulatory rules and enforcement patterns, and therefore the question remains (even with deliberative polls and deliberation days) regarding how the regulatory agencies themselves should function.

The agency's role would further encompass the provision of regulatory public defenders — teams of lawyers whose role would be to promote the perspective of the group constituted to consider the regulatory proposal in question. The agency could also leverage resources such as the Internet to promote and facilitate forms of participation consistent with the corrective deliberation approach. A reasonable oversight structure...would be a critical ingredient of all this, to preserve the agency's ability to act and appear in a manner that would be perceived as legitimate and politically unbiased. The agency would also have to be at least somewhat insulated from interference from the president's administration and the legislature's ...

The point of all these changes is as simple as it is profound: a redesigned system of regulatory democracy can achieve things – in particular, three – that the present system cannot. The new system can leverage the existing structure of the regulatory state to experiment with alternative democratic arrangements involving the representation of interested constituencies. That sort of experimentation can also extend to encompass the methods used to combine democratic participation with rigorous technical analyses of costs, benefits, and risk. All of this can also yield valuable information about how the electorate views specific regulations – including some that depend on public support.

Reforms in regulatory democracy would be most attractive in the following [three] situation[s]. First, if there is both] a high enough probability that a low-importance issue might skyrocket in importance later on; and [legislators] ... cannot guess what a voter would think once circumstances forced her to reflect more about it ...[Second], if reforms in regulatory democracy were politically valuable to legislators but faced bureaucratic resistance, outside interest groups might fund corrective deliberation proceedings and then funnel the results to agencies through the existing notice-and-comment process...The corrective or deliberative proceedings themselves might be conducted by companies or not-forprofit organizations with a reputation interest in the integrity of the results. [Third], reforms in regulatory democracy [might be] ... promoted by political entrepreneurs ... to resolve statutory ambiguities in areas where the interest group context is not strong enough to pre-determine the result [and] legislators might see a political payoff in telling the electorate that the public will be more involved in these decisions ...

The kind of participation that conventional regulatory democracy produces may serve the practical designs of legislators and organised interests. It lets politically powerful interest groups get what they want from government. It helps representative politicians align the outputs of the regulatory state with the concerns of those who can most obviously affect the politicians' careers. It allows regulators to forestall the wrath of critical constituencies. ...[M]y ... analysis ... has discussed the possibility of a far richer conception of regulatory democracy – one that allows for correcting gaps in representation and deficits in sophistication ...[S]uch a conception is legally feasible, administrable, and desirable. Without it, the regulatory state will remain shackled to the imperfections of representative democracy and pluralist politics, unable to serve as a stimulating setting for practical experimentation on how to integrate democratic participation with expert technical knowledge.

5.5.1   Discussion questions

1. Can you think of any examples of the kind of redistributive purposes that Majone argues should be excluded from the remit of regulators?

2. Majone claims that, as an empirical matter, the crisis of the welfare state means that 'policies which aim to increase aggregate welfare' are more politically significant than redistributive policies. Does his argument about the implications for the design of regulatory institutions depend upon this claim? Is it an implicit normative claim that undermines the neutrality of his approach, or is some kind of normative commitment a necessary and inevitable part of any discussion of legitimacy or legitimation?

3. For Majone, the disadvantages of substantively legitimating regulation through independent agencies and economic expertise can be mitigated by the advantages of procedural mechanisms of accountability. Does Shapiro view expertise and pluralism as equally complementary?

4. What might be examples of the 'pathologies of pluralism' to which Shapiro refers to?

5. Cuéllar distinguishes his proposal for regulatory democracy from attempts to realise 'deliberative ideals'. What then, distinguishes his approach from (i) pluralism as Shapiro describes it? (ii) Majone's expertise-based proposals for achieving substantive regulatory legitimacy? Does Cuéllar's approach meet Majone's concerns about the problems that majoritarian decision-making creates in regulatory regimes?

6. Is there a trade-off between an 'accountability deficit' and an 'effectiveness deficit' in the degree of autonomy regulatory agencies have from the legislature and executive?

7. Independent regulators are common in utilities regulation but less common in the regulation of health professionals. Is there any reason why an independent regulator might be more important for regulatory legitimacy in one instance than in the other? Does your answer depend on whether 'independent' means independent from the industry itself or from ministerial intervention?

8. Evaluate the claim that institutionalist approaches to regulation do not provide a theory of regulation so much as a theory of regulatory accountability (refer back to Chapter 2).

5.6.   Decentred regulatory legitimacy: Beyond and above the state

While Cuéllar's extract opens up space for connecting ideas about democracy to the practical operation of regulatory institutions and rule-making procedures, it remains state-centred. As the earlier chapters of the book have emphasised, current understanding of regulatory dynamics urge us to go beyond traditional assumptions about the institutional context in which regulation takes place, and respond to both the horizontal and vertical decentring of the state. In the next extract, Jody Freeman's exploration of legitimation addresses the horizontal decentring of the state, taking full cognisance of the degree to which private actors are, as a matter of empirical fact, deeply embedded in the regulatory landscape. Her picture of this landscape challenges readers to look beyond legislative mandates, professional bureaucratic expertise and judicial review as avenues of legitimation, towards the contributions of non-state actors such as the regulated, those who benefit from regulation and third-party monitors (banks, public interest groups, etc).

Freeman calls for extending traditional public mechanisms of accountability to private actors performing public functions, but stresses the necessity of avoiding an overly legalistic approach to such an extension. She argues that even in traditional command-and-control regulation, compliance requires considerable informal interdependence between public and private actors, and goes on to suggest that private actors are in fact constrained by existing accountability mechanisms, understood in the extended sense advocated by Colin Scott's extract (Scott 2000).

While private interest and institutionalist theories of regulation have often been viewed as a challenge to effective accountability and successful legitimation in traditional analyses of regulation, Freeman's argument effectively extends the implications of these theories through to the domain of accountability. The result is a much more optimistic assessment of the hybrid ways in which public and private actors depend upon each other in regulatory spaces. It also challenges idealised ways of envisioning democracy and participation in public life (hence the tart reference to 'real' democracy in her title).

Jody Freeman, *'Private parties, public function and the real democracy problem in the new administrative law?'* (1999)

[P]ersistent attempts to solve [the democratic deficit of the bureaucratic administrative state] . . . have obscured a phenomenon with . . . [significant] . . . implications for democracy: the role of non-government actors in the exercise of administrative authority. An *exclusive* focus on agency discretion prevents us from appreciating the extent of private participation in governance. Although legal scholars have long acknowledged some forms of private engagement with public agencies, such as lobbying and litigation, non-government actors remain marginal in a field dominated by agency action. And yet, non-government actors are involved in all stages of the regulatory and administrative process, sometimes assuming or sharing roles that we think either are, or ought to be, reserved for public actors. To the extent that it has been discussed in legal scholarship, the participation of private actors in the administrative-process is framed either as a delegation issue or an illustration of public choice theory. Models of the administrative process, whether pluralist, civic republican or 'expertocratic' continue to focus primarily on agencies as decision makers.

In fact, many private actors participate in governance in ways that are rarely recognised by the public, acknowledged by politicians or carefully analyzed by legal scholars. The contributions of private individuals, private firms, financial institutions, public interest organizations, domestic and international standard-setting bodies, professional associations, labour unions, business networks, advisory boards, expert panels, self-regulating organizations and non-profit groups belie administrative law's pre-occupation with agency discretion. Private individuals serve on influential government boards; "expert" private committees exercise important powers of accreditation; private producer groups formulate regulations and set prices that bind dissenters; private groups may directly negotiate regulations together with other interested parties and the agency; non-profit and for-profit organizations contract to provide a variety of government services and perform public functions ranging from garbage collection to prison operation; individuals and organizations act as private attorneys general in prosecuting statutory violations; trade associations generate and enforce industrial codes that may become de facto regulatory standards; private standard setting organizations generate health and safety standards that agencies automatically adopt. Contemporary governance might be best described then, as a regime of "mixed administration" in which private and public actors share responsibility for both regulation and service provision . . .

The agency emphasis in administrative law makes it difficult to imagine the appropriate legal and institutional response to the essentially shared nature of governance. It threatens to misdirect political and scholarly energy toward imposing ever more marginally effective controls on agencies when in fact agencies are part of a richer institutional environment of public and private activity. Many scholars believe that private actors exacerbate the lack of accountability that makes the exercise of agency discretion so problematic. Like administrators, private actors are unelected. Unlike agencies, however, they are not generally *expected* to serve the public interest, nor are they subject to institutional norms of professionalism and public service that might mitigate against the pursuit of mere self-interest or capitulation to narrow private interests.

Moreover, private actors remain relatively insulated from legislative, executive and judicial oversight. To the extent that private actors increasingly perform traditionally public functions unfettered by the scrutiny that normally accompanies the exercise of public power, private participation may indeed raise accountability concerns that dwarf the problem of unchecked agency discretion. In this view, private actors do not raise a *new* democracy problem; they simply make the traditional one even worse because they are considerably more unaccountable than agencies. In addition, private actors may threaten other public law values that are arguably as important as accountability. Their participation in governance may undermine features of decision making that administrative law demands of public actors, such as openness, fairness, participation, consistency, rationality and impartiality.

Concern about how private actors compromise public law values has only intensified in an era of widespread privatization and contracting out of government functions. To defend against the threats posed by increased private activity, some scholars propose that we extend to private actors the oversight mechanisms and procedural controls that apply to agencies, effectively treating them as if they were "public." . . . I argue that we ought to resist the impulse to constrain private actors as we would agencies in the absence of a careful consideration of the advantages they offer and the threats they pose. Importantly, private actors are often *already* constrained by alternative accountability mechanisms that go largely unrecognised in administrative law. A private decision maker's internal procedural rules, market pressures, informal norms of compliance, third party oversight and the background threat of agency enforcement might hold private actors to account for their performance, even in what seem to be voluntary self-regulatory systems. Although these forms of accountability may not satisfy the traditional administrative law demand for accountability to an elected body, they nonetheless may play an important role in *legitimizing*, or rendering acceptable, a particular regulatory regime. Before we can assess whether alternative accountability mechanisms might be appropriate substitutes for, or complements to, traditional forms of oversight we must, at a minimum, recognise that they exist.

A deeper understanding of the private role in governance . . . help[s] clarify both the dangers that private parties represent and the accountability mechanisms, both traditional and non-traditional, with which administrative law might respond.

Viewing governance as a shared enterprise allows us to separate the mechanisms that *produce* accountability from the public or private *nature* of the decision maker. This in turn helps to cast private parties in a more realistic and balanced light. Private actors are not just rational, self-interested rent-seekers that exacerbate the traditional democracy problem in administrative law; they are also *regulatory resources* capable of contributing to the efficacy and legitimacy of administration . . . .

An emerging literature in administrative law suggests that the pressing challenge for the field is to determine when and how to extend legal requirements to private actors performing public functions. In this view, privatization and contracting out disrupt the traditional administrative law project of turning discretion into rules. The trend away from government shifts the administrative law terrain so much that the failure to constrain discretion is decidedly *not* the crucial problem in the field. Instead, the challenge is ensuring that privatization, contracting out, and other measures designed to yield authority to private parties, do not eviscerate the public law norms of accountability, procedural regularity and substantive rationality that administrative law has laboured so hard to provide. Viewed in this light, a continued emphasis on constraining agency discretion is like shuffling the deck chairs on the *Titanic*. That such concerns have arisen first and most forcefully in the United Kingdom, Australia and in New Zealand, countries that already impose far fewer legal and procedural constraints [than the US] on ministerial discretion, and which have witnessed very significant degrees of public sector re-structuring in the last two decades, should not be surprising. Although laudable for its focus on private actors and its bold assertion that agency discretion is no longer the central issue in the field, the emerging privatization literature in administrative law does not go far enough. First, the private role in regulation is even more pervasive and longstanding than the literature suggests. Even traditional command and control regulation − a hierarchical arrangement in which the agency dictates and enforces standards − is characterised by significant informal interdependence between government and private actors. Widespread contracting out of public functions and greater reliance on self-regulation might seem to increase the private role, but every aspect of administration is deeply and inevitably interdependent.

The new privatization literature in administrative law is marked by debates over whether judicial review will subside or intensify as the private role in administration increases. Some scholars argue that a proliferation of private activity will weaken the executive and legislative capacity to exert control over public decisions, which will invite greater judicial oversight. Courts may then choose to regulate private actors either by expanding the state action doctrine or by infusing common law doctrines with public law norms, such as good faith obligations in contract.

[In relation to these issues], scholars [may] . . . consider the extent to which the benefits of private participation in governance, including expertise, innovation and efficiency, may be frustrated by the imposition of traditional constraints such as compliance with legal procedures and formal accountability to an elected body. Greater participation of private actors in the administrative process may help to produce superior regulatory decisions and facilitate their implementation. Indeed, opportunities for greater participation in governance may have an independent, democracy-enhancing value. There might be circumstances in which we are willing to trade some degree of formal accountability for these other benefits. [But] . . . the impulse to respond to private activity by constraining private actors merely shifts the focus to the private side of the equation rather than re-orienting the administrative law inquiry to the public-private regime as a new entity. Acknowledging the shared nature of governance invites us to explore more fully what we mean when we say that regulation is "unaccountable." What interests lay behind the traditional concern about accountability and how would we weight those concerns in the context of a specific decision making regime that offers some benefits at the cost of other things? The public acceptability or legitimacy of a decision making regime turns in part upon our expectations of how the actors in that regime *ought* to behave when they play certain kinds of roles. For example, when private actors function in an advisory capacity in which they purport to be neutral, we might rightly expect disinterested decision making. Disinterest might matter less, however, in a process like regulatory negotiation, where we might expect parties to pursue their interests (which might, nonetheless facilitate problem-solving that is in the public interest). In this context we might place a premium on participation and adequate representation rather than neutrality. When a private actor plays an enforcement role either through independent oversight or by exercising a private right of action, we might expect it to behave differently than when it acts in a standard-setting capacity. In the former case, we might worry about private motivations that threaten to derail a rational enforcement agenda. In the latter case, we might want to minimise, self-dealing and anti-competitive behavior by ensuring adequate representation on the standard-setting committee of all affected interests.

The imposition of rigorous legal procedures, together with oversight by an elected body that is itself accountable to the electorate, is not the only way to ensure the legitimacy of public-private arrangements. A mixed administrative,-regime might rely on numerous *informed* accountability mechanisms and *nongovernmental* actors to control the dangers posed by public-private arrangements.... Sometimes the legitimacy of a regulatory initiative depends in part on trust and shared norms. Public-private arrangements can be more accountable because of the presence of powerful independent professionals within private organizations or because the agency's threat of regulation provides the necessary motivation for effective and credible self-regulation which itself involves non-government actors. Sometimes the two principal partners in a regulatory enterprise (the agency and the regulated firm) might rely on independent third parties to set standards and oversee enforcement. Even the absence of a direct government role does not mean a seemingly private regime is free of regulation or oversight. Informal regulatory regimes can emerge in a context where there is no formal government participation

The [chemical industry's] Responsible Care programme... demonstrates how informal mechanisms can be essential to the effectiveness of self-regulation and at the same time provide some assurance of accountability ...[This consists of a set of industry codes that integrate environmental considerations into every aspect of the manufacture and distribution of chemical products but without imposing quantitative performance standards. Compliance is monitored by the industry trade association, which can expel non-compliant member firms, and which audits management practices]. The [trade association's] formal power to enforce Responsible Care may be less important to the programme's success than informal disciplinary mechanisms such as peer pressure and institutional norms of compliance. Empirical studies reveal that executives from leading firms pressure their non-compliant counterparts at industry meetings to adopt and adhere to the industrial codes. Publication of the codes has also given leverage to professionals and managers within the industry who wish to take a leadership role in environmental performance.

Responsible Care models how self-regulation can provide an opportunity for experimenting with the most innovative and environmentally protective regulatory strategies. Most self-regulatory systems designed to address environmental problems emphasise technological innovation, life-cycle assessment, benchmarking, continuous improvement and pollution prevention. Indeed, proponents of self-regulation argue that these strategies, which in theory seek to integrate environmental concerns into both every stage of product development (design, distribution and sale) and every business relationship (between firms, suppliers, distributors and customers), have flourished precisely because they were developed by *private* industry. On this view, private actors are sources of innovative regulation – an unsurprising conclusion if true, but one that militates toward harnessing self-regulatory efforts rather than prematurely dismissing them as fundamentally unaccountable.

Perhaps most importantly, the example illustrates the perils of generalizing about the threat to accountability posed by self-regulatory initiatives, given the extent to which their features turn on the internal structure of the industry itself and the institutional background against which the self-regulation arises. Responsible Care is widely regarded as the most far-reaching and successful example of a self-regulatory regime. Its success depends, however, on the unique features of the chemical industry, including its relative maturity and stability, its vulnerability to poor publicity and the unusually strong influence of its peak level trade association. As a result, the program may be hard to replicate without a similar convergence of circumstances, structures and relationships.

It would, of course, significantly enhance Responsible Care's credibility were the auditing process independently performed by, or at least subject to, third party verification. In turn, a supervising regulatory agency could play a role overseeing the independent auditors. Third party verification is an increasingly popular tool for ensuring that private firms live up to their voluntary obligations, at least in the environmental arena.... Financial institutions − lenders and insurance companies − might also be helpful third party regulators. Again, environmental regulation provides a useful illustration. Until recently, lenders faced potentially massive liability for any toxic waste contamination for which their clients were potentially responsible parties .... The threat of exposure motivated lenders to demand stricter environmental compliance from their clients. Along with insurance companies, lenders developed programs to help clients adopt environmental management systems and to train employees. The principal objection to reliance on financial institutions instead of public agencies is that they will only discipline private actors to the extent that they are themselves exposed to liability. As the risk subsides ..., lenders and insurers will likely retreat from their role as regulators. Moreover, even when they do play an active role in disciplining private firms, the standard of performance demanded will be dictated by the lender or insurer's calculation of risk, rather than a determination of what level of performance would adequately protect the public health. Reliance on private institutions to play such a role raises additional accountability problems to the extent that their processes for determining performance standards are not themselves subject to oversight.

The growth of "informational regulation" could also function as a form of third party monitoring. In environmental regulation, mandatory disclosure requires firms to monitor quantity and quality of emissions and disclose that information to the public and/or public agencies. In some cases, agencies demand that firms provide warnings to the public of toxic exposure or other risks. In the context of contracting out services, greater transparency in the tendering process and better publication of contractual terms between agencies and providers could assist the beneficiaries of the those services in seeking redress for injuries suffered due to breach. To the extent that the informed public encounters high transaction costs and other impediments to collective action (both organizational and cognitive), however, informational regulation may not be an adequate accountability mechanism in the absence of additional, complementary measures. Like the other market measures described here, informational regulation not subject to adequate oversight would likely pose accountability problems itself because of the potential for industry manipulation of the information disclosure process.

Many of these informal, market or other accountability mechanisms might be used simultaneously. The rich institutional context of private prison operation suggests that in addition to public actors (the agency, the legislature and courts), private parties and non-traditional mechanisms may play useful oversight roles. For example, lending institutions motivated to protect their investment and insurers wishing to minimise risk may act as third-party regulators over private prison operators. As a condition of the loan or policy, for example, they might require that guards and officials submit to training or that prisons officials develop detailed management plans. As the Supreme Court recently observed, market forces should play at least some role in ensuring that private guards are neither too timid nor too aggressive.

Either the legislature or the supervising agency might facilitate third party participation in oversight by requiring independent monitoring or auditing of prisons by certified professionals. A statute or regulation might stipulate that the prison hire only guards certified by independent training programs. Professionals within the prison (say, medical personnel) might have sufficient institutional power and independence to perform a critical role in maintaining health standards; to insulate them from the wrath of the private employer, such personnel might be hired directly by the state agency. States might also enlist the help of independent prisoner's rights groups by granting them standing to sue for violations of any requirements stipulated in the statute or contract.

In sum, a mix of measures and actors can contribute to the effectiveness and legitimacy of public-private arrangements while minimizing the particular dangers they pose. By the same token, simply because a public entity (the agency) retains ultimate authority over a decision making process may not make that process acceptable or legitimate. When an agency adopts without deliberation a private standard-setting organization's safety standards, for example, we may rightly doubt that the mere fact of agency incorporation ensures the legitimacy of the standards. Formal legal procedures and agency oversight may provide the appearance of adequate accountability, but informal mechanisms and private parties play an important and undervalued role legitimizing public-private arrangements.

Conceptually, as in reality, agencies are hard to dislodge. The centrality of the agency in scholarly discussion derives from the most basic theoretical and doctrinal understandings in public law. Perhaps most fundamental among these understandings is that regulatory power is public power. This stems, in part, from the state-centrism of public law. [Though some] doctrinal innovations [enable courts] . . . to impose public law constraints on private actors, [they] . . . continue to rely heavily on the formalistic and conceptually dubious characterization of activity as *essentially* public or private. Indeed, this divide remains resilient in the face of withering attacks from critical legal studies, feminist legal theory, legal postmodernism and outsider legal scholarship. . . . No matter how blurred the line between public and private and no matter how difficult to design an intellectually defensible test to distinguish them, most scholars agree that there *ought to be a* meaningful difference between the two and that constitutional constraints should apply *only* to the former . . . Focusing on private actors as potential partners in governance attracts a visceral skepticism in administrative law. Even if most private delegations survive constitutional scrutiny, there remains significant *cultural* resistance to private bodies playing a formal role in regulation, particularly in the performance of quintessentially public functions, such as standard setting. Any attempt to formally delegate such regulatory powers to private actors would likely encounter significant opposition from those concerned about the potential of private participation to undermine congressional intent or to benefit powerful interest groups at the expense of the larger public interest. Already, rather modest attempts to bring stakeholders more directly into the standard setting and implementation process, have met with a storm of controversy, despite numerous procedural checks on such processes, including the reservation of the ultimate decision making authority in the agency.

It would be naive to quarrel with the concern about agency capture. Chastened by practical experience with powerful regulated industries and influenced by public choice theory, administrative law has grown sensitive to the excesses of pluralism. Public choice theory presumes that private interests (be they firms or "public interest" organizations, labour unions, trade associations or consumer groups) are rent-seekers bent on pursing their interests at the expense of the larger public interest. Indeed, the strongest version of the public choice claim resists altogether the notion of a public interest. Rather, regulation is the product of deal-making between private actors able to provide rewards to legislators and bureaucrats motivated by the desire for job security or other forms of personal gain. Of course, the public choice account of agency action competes with alternative explanations in which, for example, the agency acts as a neutral expert or reaches decision only after engaging in "public-regarding" deliberation over the public interest. Nonetheless, much legislation and many regulations can be explained in public choice terms. Although it strikes some commentators as a cynical theory with potentially corrosive effects, public choice is grounded in powerful economic models and offers a compelling thesis.

Whether or not one subscribes to the public choice view of legislators, administrators and interest groups, the assumptions about private behavior that characterise public choice theory exemplify the relatively truncated view of private participation that dominates administrative law. Even those who resist public choice explanations as too extreme tend to think that private parties play a narrow and mostly rent-seeking role in governance. Given the weaknesses of the extreme public choice explanation, however, the extent to which administrative law conceives of private actors *exclusively* in this light is surprising. While private actors undoubtedly pursue their interests, this hardly captures the nuances of their pervasive role in governance. A more complete description of private participation in the administrative process might temper or add new dimensions to the public choice view of private groups. Instead of orienting administrative law *solely* toward erecting barriers to private participation in order to insulate legislators and administrators from influence, we might explore how to harness private capacity in the service of public goals.... Recognizing the deep roots of the [regulatory] agency emphasis [suggests that] ... shifting the inquiry to shared governance and its implications might prove challenging indeed.

In the final extract of this chapter, Anne-Marie Slaughter confronts the vertical decentring of the state, moving towards an analysis of what a legitimate regulatory regime might look like in a global context. Her discussion is included here as a bridge to the next chapter. On the one hand, she makes clear links between regulatory legitimation, different theories of democracy, and tensions between pluralism and expertise, all key themes of this chapter. But she also explicitly considers strategies of network governance beyond the context of the national state, which is the topic of our next chapter. Her analysis of some key tensions sparked by this move beyond the national context provides a helpful base for moving onto detailed discussion of that topic. In particular, she suggests that network forms of governance will be more likely to promote expertise-based forms of regulatory legitimacy, an issue with significant implications for the changing role of law which we explore more fully in Chapter 6.

Anne-Marie Slaughter, 'Global government networks, global information agencies and disaggregated democracies' (2003)

Proponents of global governance, particularly through multiple parallel networks of public and private actors, must offer at least a partial response to the problems of democracy as traditionally defined, before redefining it. After all, in true post-modern fashion, post-modernity cannot displace modernity, but only exist alongside it.

I propose in this essay to ground the discussion ... by developing a typology of more concrete and prosaic accountability problems connected with a rapidly growing form of global governance – transgovernmental regulatory networks, or, more generally, "government networks." These are networks of national government officials exchanging information, coordinating national policies, and working together to address common problems. For some, they herald a new and attractive form of global governance, enhancing the ability of states to work together to address common problems without the centralised bureaucracy of formal international institutions. For others, however, these networks portend a vast technocratic conspiracy, a shadowy world of regulators bent on "de-politicizing" global issues in ways that will inevitably benefit the rich and powerful at the expense of the poor and weak.

This essay seeks to broaden our understanding of government networks by placing them in more historical context and by elaborating different types of government networks within and without traditional international institutions. After a brief overview of ... a typology of three different categories of government networks, I ... [build on] the ... similarity between global government networks and a number of EU governance structures, primarily the "comitology" system and related transgovernmental and public-private networks ... [to survey some of the more fundamental reconceptualizations of democracy ... and distil ... various elements of these visions that could be useful in strengthening the democratic pedigree of government networks.

... It is possible to identify three different types of transnational regulatory networks, based on the different contexts in which they arise and operate. First are those networks of national regulators that develop within the context of established international organizations. Second are networks of national regulators that develop under the umbrella of an overall agreement negotiated by heads of state. And third are the networks that have attracted the most attention over the past decade – networks of national regulators that develop outside any formal framework. These networks arise spontaneously from a need to work together to address common problems; in some cases members interact sufficiently autonomously to require the institutionalization of their activities in their own transgovernmental regulatory organizations. These three types are inter-linked in many ways; some may seem such a standard part of the international furniture as to be beneath notice; others compete directly with actual or possible international organizations . . . .

[T]he EU offers a deceptively simple source of analogies and potential institutional solutions to the general problem of enhancing the accountability of government networks. Lawyers and political scientists studying the EU have spent much of the past decade grappling with the growing phenomenon of "comitology" – the extraordinarily complex web of committees that play advisory, management, and regulatory functions in between the European Commission and the Council of Ministers. Although the leading scholars in these debates have different positive understandings and normative evaluations of comitology, they all agree that it is a critical and distinctive dimension of EU governance that must be addressed in any effort to promote constitutionalism and democracy within the EU as an institution and/or an emerging polity.

. . . [D]ebates over comitology [have larger implications] for arguments over the accountability of global government networks. To understand the relevance of these debates, however, it is first necessary to delve a bit deeper into the distinctions between different types of EU institutions and government networks as defined here. The European Community (EC), one of the pillars of the EU, has a number of different types of committees – scientific committees, interest committees, and policy-making/implementation committees. Many of these committees must be consulted as part of the Community legislative process. The policy-making/implementation committees are the most powerful of these committees; they are composed of representatives of the Member States from the different issue-areas under consideration – agriculture, transport, health, etc. In terms of membership and structure, these committees most resemble networks of national government officials charged with responsibility for a particular issue-area. However, as the semantic distinction between "committee" and "network" suggests, the committees are more tightly structured and have a specific charge and function within a larger governance structure – specifically, mediating between a supranational entity, the Commission, and an inter-governmental one, the Council. They are theoretically responsible for ensuring that the views of the different EC member states are fully and powerfully represented in the legislative process.

The EC also has agencies and more informal networks of both public and private actors. Agencies are entities with legal personality and their own administrative structure. Networks, as used in EC parlance, typically describe the looser and more informal interactions between national government officials that are increasingly necessary to implement EC policies. According to two prominent EU scholars, Giandomenico Majone (1997a; 1997b) and Renaud Dehousse (1997), the relationship between these two types of governance structures is the wave of the future in the EC. Together they are best poised to exploit the potential of "regulation by information." This conception of both the substance and form of governance within the EU parallels many of the perceptions and insights that animate the description of government networks as an emerging form of global governance .... Eight new agencies were created at European level between 1990 and 1997 as a way of facilitating further harmonization. Four of these – the European Environmental Agency, the Lisbon Drug Monitoring Centre, the European Agency for Health and Safety at Work, and the European Agency for the Evaluation of Medicinal Products – are best described as "information agencies." Their job is to collect, coordinate, and disseminate information needed by policymakers. They lack decision-making authority, much less coercive enforcement power. Both Majone and Dehousse describe these agencies as easy to underestimate but actually likely to play an important and powerful role. Majone sees them as the quintessential example of regulation by information.... Dehousse also sees the European information agencies as network creators and coordinators ... Another important virtue of these regulatory agencies, understood as convenors and coordinators, derives from their projected impact on the democratic legitimacy of EU regulatory processes. First, they enhance transparency, [both in that] several agencies are explicitly required to make accessible to the public the data they collect [and in that] the provision of information has generally been broadly construed; it often encompasses policy analysis and the preparation of measures and legislation in their field of activity ... Second, and equally important, they are often able to expand the transgovernmental network to include private actors in a particular policy area. This activity need not be merely inviting comment from NGOs of various types as well as regulated entities, but can also include bringing together all relevant actors and inviting them to pool information ...

Why not create global information agencies? In many ways, the secretariats or technical committees of existing transgovernmental regulatory organizations such as the Basle Committee or International Organization of Securities Commissions (IOSCO) perform some of the same functions. But these are essentially ad hoc, organic entities, created and empowered by networks of national officials to serve various needs as they arise. Suppose national governments were to come together to create a global securities agency, or a global environmental agency, but with the express charge not of arrogating power from national officials, but rather of providing information to such officials and helping to coordinate relations among them. Further, these agencies would service not only transgovernmental networks, but also transnational networks within their issue areas, working to bring together both private and public actors in a particular policy sector.

Equating a "global agency," of any kind, with enhancing the democratic legitimacy of global regulatory processes may seem oxymoronic. "Agency" conjures automatic images of bureaucratic technocrats and technocratic bureaucrats. Beyond the stereotypes, however, the proposal has a number of potential advantages.

First, convening heads of state to establish an international institution, even one with only informational powers, would highlight the existence and importance of current transgovernmental networks, helping to legitimate them by acknowledging them as key elements of a system of global governance. The purpose of the agency would be to facilitate the functioning of these networks and to expand them both to other governments and to private actors as necessary. Notice and approval by heads of state would also help allay charges of transgovernmental policy collusion to strengthen the hands of particular national officials in domestic bureaucratic infighting.

Second, and perhaps paradoxically, the creation of a *global* entity would emphasise the *national* identity of network participants. The existence of even a small group of international bureaucrats to meet the needs of national officials can only emphasise the location of actual decision-making power in national hands. Even if those national officials are networking with one another to plug growing gaps in national jurisdiction and to solve common problems, they remain national officials answerable only to national legislatures and chief executives. In this regard, it is interesting to note that the European information agencies have actually resisted an increase in their power over national officials, perhaps because "instilling a degree of (vertical) hierarchical control in structures created to promote (horizontal) co-operation among peers may result in the undermining of the basis of consensus, which is indispensable for the smooth and efficient operation of the network."

Third, the appellation "information agency" would focus attention on whether the collection and cross-fertilization of information is in fact problematic. How could it be wrong or even worrisome to know more about what other countries are doing? For many, however, even to pose the question this way, however, betrays an academic or even technocratic bias. If, as many critical scholars maintain, "technical" decisions are but a convenient way of depoliticizing political decisions with distributional implications, then models and ideas borrowed helter-skelter from different political contexts are likely to prove at best useless and at worst dangerous. On the other side of the political spectrum, as Justice Scalia has argued vehemently with regard to the question of whether the U.S. Supreme Court should take account of ideas and decisions from foreign courts, foreign transplants contravene basic notions of local democracy.

In the increasingly borderless "information age," where citizens of many countries have access to a literal world wide web of information, this debate seems archaic and almost preposterous. But it should be had — openly and directly. If the objections are real and resonate with a wider public, then existing government networks are on much weaker ground than previously imagined. But even well short of such a scenario of willful ignorance, questions of how the information collected from foreign counterparts is used and disseminated are not only legitimate but also necessary. ...

Fourth, as in the European context, the existence of an information agency charged with convening and supporting networks of national officials immediately invites expansion of the network to a host of private actors. U.N. Secretary General

Kofi Annan has recognised the importance of this function by positioning the U.N. as the convener of "global policy networks," designed precisely to bring together all public and private actors on issues critical to the global public interest. Transgovernmental and transnational networks currently parallel each other in many cases and intersect in all sorts of ways, such as the NGO conferences held together with major inter-governmental conferences on issues ranging from the environment to women's rights. Nevertheless, the process is haphazard and in some cases chaotic. Information agencies could provide focus and a minimum degree of organization.

Beyond these minimal functions, it is imaginable that information agencies could become the focal points for dispute resolution processes designed to disseminate information and mobilise public participation to check and correct government performance ... If the basic paradigm for global regulatory processes is the promulgation of performance standards, codes of best practices, and other aspirational models based on compiled comparative information, together with national legislation taking account of global practice but tailored to individual national circumstance, then why should citizens not have some means of shaming their governments into complying with their own rules? The entity charged with hearing the dispute would have the power only to issue some kind of informational record − backed by its legitimacy and credibility. It would be up to national and transnational citizen groups to do the rest.

These may seem fanciful visions. But the European Union has in fact pioneered the paradigm of transgovernmental networks as governance structures within a community of states that have come together for a set of specific purposes. It has also run aground on the questions of the democratic legitimacy of these structures. To the extent that European information agencies offer at least a partial solution to these problems, they merit examination on a global scale.

Disaggregated democracy: Adding another type and even layer of institutions to the existing patchwork of inter-governmental, transgovernmental, and transnational global governance structures still seems a rather patchwork approach to addressing a fundamental democracy deficit above the level of the nation state. As Keohane and Nye observe, it cannot address the more fundamental democratic problem, which they identify as a lack of intermediating politicians directly responsive to the electorate. It is possible to do better, but only in the context of a rethinking of the elements of democratic legitimacy. Here it is helpful to return to ... broader frameworks for democratic governance ...[S]ome of the strongest claims of a democratic deficit in the EU focus precisely on the phenomenon of comitology. ... [T]he debates about comitology as either a source of or a solution to the democracy deficit in the EU ... creates a catalyst for rethinking more fundamental ideas of democracy in the face of problems and institutions whose scope and scale seem to defy popular participation or control.

This section offers a brief and sharply simplified overview of some of the most important positions staked out in the European debate. A longer-term effort to develop a framework within which to understand and justify the distinctive contribution of global transgovernmental networks to global governance is likely to be most successful if it can synthesise a number of different arguments about the relationship between government networks and democratic values. As a first step, it is possible to isolate some of the most important legitimating arguments about transgovernmentalism (or infranationalism, in Weiler's parlance) in the EU, including arguments about delegation to independent agencies, the possibilities of deliberative supranationalism, a reimagination of the essential possibilities of individual self-governance in a heterarchical society, and democratic experimentalism.

At a very deep level, these different arguments proceed from different conceptions of democracy. Arguments about delegation to non-majoritarian institutions and deliberative supranationalism, although often at loggerheads with one another, nevertheless all proceed from a fairly traditional conception of vertical representative government, in which the principal question is how to design state institutions "above" the citizens they represent to represent them as well as possible. "Postmodern" arguments about individuals with multiple selves operating in multiple parallel forums to advance their interests and develop their identities rest on a more horizontal conception of democracy, a challenging yet empirically grounded division of the ways in which self-government can take place in settings that are neither public nor private and that exist in a space between hierarchy and anarchy.

In a world in which the basic unit of operation is not a unitary state but a disaggregated state, meaning that the elements of both government within the state and governance between and above states are different government institutions, both conceptions are important. No amount of post-modern theorizing and prostration before the gods of technology is likely to displace the very basic concept of electoral accountability on as small a scale as possible consistent with a minimum level of government effectiveness. On the other hand, the impossibility of fully "reaggregating" the state in a tidy democratic package will ultimately require a much more sophisticated understanding of networks and the interaction of nodes in a network with each other – whether individual or institutional. A successful synthesis of these two approaches – at least for the purposes of reconciling many of the functional and ideational needs of global governance – will be a vision of disaggregated democracy.

A. Vertical democracy: A first and familiar effort to legitimate transgovernmental networks is through an appeal to the desirability of de-politicization. In this view, politics means rent-seeking and deal-making, messy processes that prevent adoption of the "optimal" policy. Insulating specific policy areas by delegation to independent technical experts will produce much better outcomes for the society as a whole, reflecting the supposed choices of a hypothetical median voter ... [This view is present in Majone's approach, in] his assumption that independence (insulation from ordinary politics) and public accountability are mutually reinforcing ... as well as the more general presupposition of "the possibility of a clear separation between efficiency-oriented and re-distributive politics." Implicit in Majone's mode of argument is the assumption of a "right answer" that the public trusts experts to adopt. In addition to this democratic justification, Majone also advances an argument from effectiveness, suggesting that today the main reason for delegating powers is the need to make credible policy commitments.

A second alternative is an updated model of deliberative democracy, in Habermasian more than Madisonian terms. Christian Joerges and Juergen Neyer (Georges and Neyer 1997a; 1997b) originally advanced the concept of "deliberative supranationalism" as both a normative and a positive paradigm of EU governance, based on extensive research into the formation of European foodstuffs policy. Empirically, they found that government representatives on the various foodstuffs committees do not bargain on the basis of national positions. Rather, they: "not only learn to reduce differences between national legal provisions but also to develop converging definitions of problems and philosophies for their solution. They slowly proceed from being representatives from national interests to being representatives of a Europeanised inter-administrative discourse characterised by mutual learning and an understanding of each other's difficulties in the implementation of specific solutions."

Normatively, Joerges and Neyer argued that the EU committee system "must be based upon, and controlled by, constitutional provisions favouring a 'deliberative' style of problem solving." The result will be a "vision of a law of transnational governance which would avoid both the pitfalls of intergovernmentalism and of building up a centralised technocratic governance structure."

Two years later ... Joerges tempered his original optimism but nevertheless continued to insist on at least the possibility of "good governance through comitology." Here he offers deliberative supranationalism as a "normative yardstick" by which to evaluate the legitimacy of the EU as a multi-level governance system. Although he recognises many problems with the existing comitology system, he nevertheless insists on the *possibility* of designing rules and procedures to establish deliberative politics within transgovernmental networks. The architects of such a system should seek to structure "*national* decision-making processes by the imposition of supranational standards," particularly designed to check "parochial interests" and ensure that "foreign concerns" be given equal consideration. They should also seek to establish "transnational 'regimes'" that would be structured to encourage "deliberative problem-solving procedures" instead of intergovernmental bargaining.

Joseph Weiler, among others, remains unconvinced (Weiler 1999). He recognises the force of Joerges and Neyer's data as supporting a major paradigm shift ... He accepts that infranational decision-making has its own particular characteristics, including a remarkable degree of autonomy, polycentricity, administrative and managerial orientation rather than constitutional and diplomatic, and "a *modus operandi* which is less by negotiation and more by deliberation." But in his view, it is definitely not democratic. It "is a microcosm of the problems of democracy, not a microcosm of the solution." It is fatally flawed by the inevitably elitist identity of the participants in these networks, their corresponding biases in making vitally important public decisions and their unawareness of these biases, and the impossibility of creating equal access to these networks without destroying the very conditions that make them work as deliberative bodies.

Note that Joerges never claims that transgovernmental deliberation is "apolitical" in any way. On the contrary, he rejects the idea of delegation to "technical" experts on both empirical and theoretical grounds, noting that "no national constitutional state has ever given *carte blanche* to expert committees" and denying the possibility of a "dichotomy between a-political social regulation and political distributive politics." Unlike Majone, he does not champion comitology networks as insulated from redistributors or rent-seekers, but rather as places where genuine persuasion is possible on the basis of a wider consideration of interests than purely national ones — a critical element, he argues, for democracy in a multinational space.

Further, Joerges insists that comitology is not separate from supranationalism, but rather an unavoidable part of it. It flows ineluctably from the dependency of the hierarchical elements of the EU system on decentralised implementation systems. The participants in these systems must come together in networks to coordinate, cooperate, and solve common problems. Without a "supranational central implementation machinery headed by the Commission," national governments in the EU are forced into a "co-operative venture." Thus deliberation within transgovernmental networks is the flipside of a decision not to displace national officials with a layer of bureaucracy one step further away from the individuals they regulate.

This last point makes it easier to see how, notwithstanding their differences, both Joerges and Majone, as well as Dehousse and others in a more intermediate position, all assume a basic vertical relationship between the governors and the governed, the regulators and the regulated entities. The European level of governance still exists "above" the national level in some conceptual space; the national level in turn exists "above" individuals and groups in domestic and transnational society. The result is a two-tiered representative system in which the fundamental mechanism of self-government is the election or selection of officials who formulate and adopt rules that are then transposed back down a level in their application to the "people."

B. Horizontal democracy: A sharply contrasting and much more radical vision is an emerging horizontal conception of democracy, which imagines self-government as the product of a much richer set of interactions among individuals and groups in both private and public fora. It begins from the empirical fact of mushrooming "private governance regimes" in which individuals, groups, and corporate entities in domestic and transnational society generate the rules, norms and principles they are prepared to live by. It also takes account of important innovations in national and international administrative regulation, in which the elaboration of formal rules is increasingly giving way to "rolling best practices rule-making." The challenge is to integrate these regimes into a revised understanding of public governance. Many different scholars are elaborating this vision in different ways and are engaged in a lively debate with one another. At this juncture, however, it is possible to identify three more or less distinct elements of this type of analysis.

First is a different conception of individual identity, premised not on a single self but on plural selves. This is a post-modern concept of the self, in which individuals define different parts of themselves by differentiating themselves from others in multiple contexts.

The second essential element is a conception of how in fact individuals organise themselves to flourish and solve problems both as autonomous beings and as members of society. The labels here proliferate — heterarchy, polyarchy, polycontexturality — but the fundamental idea is the same. Individuals are able to organise themselves in multiple networks or even communities that are "disembedded" from traditional state structures but that are nevertheless "communicatively interdependent" in the sense of being able to compile and cumulate knowledge, problem-solving capacity, and normative frameworks. They are self-organizing, self-transforming, and de-territorialised. A fundamental dimension of this vision is the perception that the traditional separation between the formulation and application of rules is being dissolved by technology, a development that is in turn undermining "a shared common knowledge basis of practical experience." Instead, public and private actors are coming together to develop new ways of "decision-making under conditions of complexity."

The third element is a revised conception of the state. Participants in these multiple, parallel networks, both domestic and transnational, face a continuous stream of problems and require a continuous stream of knowledge both about each another and about their counterparts in other networks. The state's function is not to regulate directly, but rather to manage these processes by facilitating problem solving and information pooling. It must also devise norms and enforcement mechanisms for assuring the widest possible participation within each network, consistent with its effectiveness. To complicate matters even further, states themselves should be viewed "as co-operative networks of networks and not as sovereign units."

These ideas, even as compressed and over-simplified as they are here, are all valuable in helping to explain, justify, and amplify the functions of global transgovernmental regulatory networks. They also provide a much richer context for introducing the idea of global information agencies. The ultimate task is to integrate ideas of delegation, transgovernmental deliberation, and horizontal democracy in ways that recognise the continuing existence of the territorial state and designated "public" officials but that takes full and central account of the possibilities and actuality of "private" self-organization.

C. Legislative networks: Even assuming a completely integrated concept of post-modern democracy, however, a key element would be missing. Elected representatives are surely not obsolete. Popular perceptions of democracy are likely to remain relatively impervious to theoretical redefinition. Dahl's very simple concept of democracy — the control of the elite by the mass — will still resonate. Government by elected representatives will still approximate this ideal in important ways.

It is thus vital to add legislative networks to the existing networks of regulators and judges currently operating as an informal global governance system. Many worthy organizations exist designed to bring together the world's parliamentarians. A number of inter-governmental institutions, from the [Organization for Security and Co-Operation in Europe] OSCE to [the North Atlantic Treaty Organization] NATO, have parliamentary assemblies composed of national legislators, many of which play a more important role than is often realised. Nevertheless, with all the summits of heads of government, central bankers, finance ministers, justice ministers, environmental ministers, and even judges, the absence of meetings among powerful national legislators is striking.

Former senator Jesse Helms, then-chair of the U.S. Foreign Relations Committee, finally went to the U.N. to meet the assembled ambassadors. He did not go, however, to meet his counterparts in control of foreign relations committees in legislatures around the world. With the advent of President Vincente Fox in Mexico, however, Senator Helms has agreed on a meeting between his committee members and their counterparts in the Mexican legislature. Groups of legislators from around the world have also met to share ideas and initiatives on legislation in specific issue areas, such as human rights and the environment. But before entertaining any more ideas for a global parliament, national policymakers should focus on creating global or at least regional legislative networks.

[To conclude], . . . [g]lobal governance is taking place through global networks of national government officials. These networks can exist within international institutions, within the framework of inter-governmental agreements of various kinds, and on their own as spontaneous responses to the need to interact to coordinate policy and address common problems. This typology is hardly the only way to identify and categorise different types of transgovernmental networks . . . [but it] helps illuminate different types of accountability concerns. It appears to reflect varying degrees of democratic input and control, depending on the extent to which the elected representatives of the people were ever consulted as to the desirability of establishing such networks, much less their actual operation. It also allows us to see international institutions as just another framework for the operation of transgovernmental networks, at least in many cases. Genuine supranational bureaucracies certainly exist, but they are far smaller than might be supposed.

Here also is the parallel to the EU. The networks of national government officials who comprise the comitology system exhibit many of the same characteristics of transgovernmental networks more generally, including perceptions of their lack of legitimacy. It is thus possible to borrow specific solutions from the EU context, such as the creation of global information agencies.

In the final analysis, however, disaggregated decision-making by national government officials who have a loyalty both to their national constituents and to the need to solve a larger problem in the interests of people beyond national borders requires a more sophisticated concept of disaggregated democracy. Developing such a concept is likely to require a synthesis of anti-majoritarian rationales, deliberative politics, and self-actualization through networks of every kind. The task ahead is to develop such a synthesis in such a way that it can be both operationalised and actually communicated to the people it is supposed to serve.

5.6.1 Discussion questions

1. To what extent are Cuéllar's proposals for regulatory democracy transferable to contexts outside of the United States?

2. Does Jody Freeman's defence of private actors' involvement in regulatory governance rest on any particular theory of regulation? In particular, what assumptions about private interest theories of regulation does her approach implicitly challenge?
3. Jody Freeman suggests that a normative theory of the state's role would rest on 'facilitating the intervention of the public—private arrangement likely to most maximise benefits and minimise dangers'. Can you think of real-world examples that might meet this goal?
4. What are the relative roles of pluralism and expertise in Slaughter's defence of regulatory legitimacy achieved by networks?
5. Would Anne-Marie Slaughter's account of regulatory legitimacy achieved by networks apply in the same way within the national arena, or is it dependent on a global governance context? In particular, how would the role of representative political institutions interact with her approach if applied in a national context?

5.7 Conclusion

This chapter has mapped a variety of approaches that help us understand processes of regulatory legitimation. After contrasting a highly theoretical philosophical approach to legitimation with concrete descriptions of mechanisms for securing accountability, this chapter has built a bridge between these two extremes. We have done so from two directions: first, by referring to the varying logics of justification that underpin legitimation processes, and secondly, by drawing links with different visions of democracy. The relationship between these two forms of 'middle-level' theorising is reflected in the cleavage between pluralism and expertise. Many of the varying logics of justification explored in the extracts from Baldwin (Baldwin 1995) and Majone (Majone 1996) could be classified as either pluralist or expertise based. But this cleavage also captures the characteristics that Majone, Shapiro and Cuéllar emphasise in linking different visions of democracy to regulatory legitimation. Even when we move beyond and above the state, the theme has resonance: Freeman's exploration of regulatory legitimation in a decentred state (Freeman 1999) could be viewed as an elaboration of pluralism while Anne-Marie Slaughter focuses more on expertise (Slaughter 2003).

Pluralism and expertise also shape the role that law plays in legitimating regulatory regimes. Where pluralism is relied upon to inject legitimacy into regulatory processes, the law's role is one of expressive umpire: structuring dialogue between those involved in, or affected by, regulation to ensure proper deliberation. On the other hand, where expertise is emphasised as the basis for legitimating regulatory decisions, the law's role is largely facilitative. It creates a decision-making framework that fosters expert input, fashioning a space for the relatively unfettered exercise of discretion informed by expert technical knowledge. Nonetheless, the role of law in regulatory legitimation overall centres on law's expressive dimension in institutionalising values. This is because the topic is necessarily linked to evaluative claims based on normative values, although we have avoided engaging directly in abstract moral reasoning. The degree to which these claims are contestable is evident in their sheer diversity and the sensitivity of their relationship to democracy, even without exploring the legitimacy of specific policy arenas characterised by a high degree of political contestation. Much that is written in this more contextual vein reflects the 'crisis' in regulatory legitimacy, and much of the preceding discussion points towards sources of that crisis in the national context. Troubled as these issues are at the national level, they are intensified further once we consider regulation above and beyond the state. It is to the supranational context that we turn in the following chapter.

References

Baldwin, R. 1995. *Rules and Government*, Oxford: Clarendon Press.

Cuéllar, M. 2005. 'Rethinking regulatory democracy', http://papers.ssrn.com/sol3/papers.cfm?abstract_id=595181, later published in a slightly different form in *Administrative Law Review* 57(2): 411–500.

Dehousse, R. 1997. 'Regulation by networks in the European community: The role of European agencies', *Journal of European Public Policy* 4: 246–61.

Dunsire, A. 1996. 'Tipping the balance: Autopoiesis and governance', *Administration and Society* 28(3): 299–334.

Freeman, J. 1999. 'Private parties, public function and the real democracy problem in the new administrative law?', in D. Dyzenhaus (ed.), *Recrafting the Rule of Law*, Oxford: Hart Publishing, 331–70.

Frug, G. 1984. 'The ideology of bureacracy in American law', *Harvard Law Review* 97: 1277–1378.

Joerges, C. and Neyer, J. 1997a. 'From intergovernmental bargaining to deliberative political processes: The constitutionalisation of comitology', *European Law Journal* 3: 273–99.

1997b. 'Transforming strategic interaction into deliberative problem-solving: European comitology in the foodstuffs sector', *Journal of European Public Policy* 4: 609–25.

Lijphart, A. 1984. *Democracies: Patterns of Majoritarian and Consensus Government in Twenty-One Democracies*, New Haven: Yale University Press.

Lijphart, A. 1991. 'Constitutional choices for new democracies', *Journal of Democracy* 2: 72–84.

Luhmann, N. 1982. *The Differentiation of Society*, New York: Columbia University Press.

Majone, G. D. 1996. 'Regulatory legitimacy', in G. D. Majone (ed.), *Regulating Europe*, London: Routledge, 284–301.

1997a. 'From the positive to the regulatory state: Causes and consequences of changes in the mode of governance', *Journal of Public Policy* 17(2): 139–167.

1997b. 'The new European agencies: Regulation by information', *Journal of European Public Policy* 4: 262–275.

Mashaw, J. L. 1983. *Bureaucratic Justice: Managing Social Security Disability Claims*, New Haven: Yale University Press.

Scott, C. 2000. 'Accountability in the regulatory state', *Journal of Law and Society* 27(1): 38–60.

Shapiro, M. 1988. *Who Guards the Guardians? Judicial Control of Administration*, Athens: Georgia University Press.

Slaughter, A.-M. 2003. 'Global government networks, global information agencies and disaggregated democracies', *Michigan Journal of International Law* 24: 1041–1074.

Stewart, R. B. 1975. 'The reformation of American administrative law', *Harvard Law Review* 88(8): 1669–1813.

Sunstein, C. 1990. *After the Rights Revolution: Reconceiving the Regulatory State*, Cambridge: Harvard University Press.

Volcansek, M. (ed.) 1992. *Judicial Politics and Policymaking in Western Europe*, London: Frank Cass.

Weiler, J. H. H. 1999. 'Comitology' as revolution – infranationalism, constitutionalism and democracy', in C. Joerges and E. Vos (eds.), *EU Committees: Social Regulation, Law and Politics*, Oxford: Hart Publishing.

Suggested further reading

Breyer, S. 1982. *Regulation and its Reform*, Cambridge: Harvard University Press.

Feintuck, M. 2004. *The Public Interest in Regulation*, Oxford: Oxford University Press.

Meidinger, E. 1999–2000. 'Private environmental regulation, human rights, and community', *Buffalo Environmental Law Journal* 7: 125–236.

Morgan, B. 2003. 'The economisation of politics: Meta-regulation as a form of nonjudicial legality', *Social and Legal Studies* 12: 489–523.

Pierre, J. (ed.) 2000. *Debating Governance: Authority, Steering and Democracy*, Oxford: Oxford University Press.

Prosser, T. 2004. 'Regulation, markets and legitimacy' in D. Oliver and J. Jowell (eds.), *The Changing Constitution*, 5th edition, Oxford: Oxford University Press.

Salter, L. 1993. 'Capture or co-management: Democracy and accountability in regulatory agencies' in G., Albo, D. Langille and L. Panich (eds.), *A Different Kind of State? Popular Power and Democratic Administration*, Toronto: Oxford University Press.

Steele, J. 2001. 'Participation and deliberation in environmental law: Exploring a problem-solving approach', *Oxford Journal of Legal Studies* 21: 415–442.

6

Regulation above and beyond the state

6.1 Overview

The preceding chapters have identified and developed a series of analytical tools and framing devices that assist in mapping the growing field of regulation scholarship. As we made clear in the introductory chapter, our focus has hitherto assumed that regulation takes place within a nation-state. The explosion of interest in, and literature about, globalisation since the early 1990s reflects the changing regulatory landscapes and calls for examination of this assumption. Accordingly, this chapter will explore the degree to which the analytical tools and framing devices used throughout the preceding chapters can be applied to the supranational context, building directly upon the conceptual structure developed throughout the book. Although each field of social science is developing a voluminous literature on globalisation, broadly understood in various different terminologies, we will consciously avoid any attempt to map these terrains, although we occasionally cite some literature by way of brief example. Thus, unlike the earlier chapters, we are not integrating existing literatures into our mapping exercise, and as a result this chapter does not include extracts from selected texts. Rather, this chapter does two things. Firstly, we explore whether theories and techniques of regulation, as well as issues of regulatory enforcement and legitimacy, can be transposed to the supranational context. Secondly, we consider the role of law in regulation above and beyond the state. The essence of our argument will be that the conceptual apparatus adopted in the earlier chapters transposes with relative ease into a supranational frame, but the role and contribution of law shifts significantly. Our argument is analytically dependent upon the earlier chapters, and therefore this chapter is less freestanding than the other chapters. It can, however, be read in combination with Chapter 1, although the nuance of the argument is best fleshed out by reading the earlier chapters first.

Before outlining the elements of our argument, it is helpful first to clarify what we mean by 'law' and 'supranational' in this chapter. In keeping with the preceding chapters, we will continue to adopt a state-centric definition of law: that is, a conception of law as authoritative rules backed by coercive force, exercised at the national level by a legitimately constituted (democratic) nation-state, and constituted in the supranational context by binding commitments voluntarily entered into between sovereign states (that is, typified by public international law). Our references to a supranational context aim to capture purposive attempts to regulate behaviour that draws upon multiple sources of norms and rules arising at more than one level. In particular, our interest in this chapter is in the relationship between these multiple sources of authoritative norms. While the nature of networked relationships resonates with 'decentred' approaches to regulation (referred to in earlier chapters) and challenges hierarchical conceptions of these relationships, our emphasis on state-centric law in a supranational context highlights questions of national sovereignty with which a decentred analysis does not necessarily engage. With these questions in mind, our examination encompasses transnational regulation of the kind that occurs in the European Union (EU) and the World Trade Organisation (WTO), as well as through cross-border voluntary initiatives.

Since our primary goal is to explore the transposability of our conceptual framework on regulation, including considerations of the role of law, it is not necessary to have a detailed understanding of the complex and contested legal, institutional and political contexts of the EU, WTO or specific voluntary initiatives concerned. For our purposes, it is sufficient to note that all three may be understood as forms of supranational regulation.

The EU is the most ambitious and highly developed system of supranational law, in which membership of the EU obliges member states to implement EU law. For this purpose, each member entrenches EU law domestically such that it overrides inconsistent national law. The EU also has distinct supranational institutions performing executive, legislative and judicial functions: the European Commission, the European Parliament, the European Council and the European Court of Justice. The comparatively strong institutional dimension of the EU and the unique way in which national and EU law interact make the EU something of a special case, and its distinctive features will be noted as we develop the argument.

By contrast with the EU, the international trading agreements established under the WTO are more typical of binding international commitments entered into by nation-states through international treaties. But what sets the WTO agreements apart from other international agreements is the dispute resolution mechanism which it establishes. This provides for a process of supranational adjudication administered by the WTO Appellate Body, a quasi-judicial body which is empowered to issue binding determinations to resolve disputes brought before it by member states alleging a contravention of WTO rules.

Finally, there are many cross-border regulatory initiatives that have developed in the context of globalisation which do not conform to state-centric conceptions of law but are often referred to as 'soft' forms of control. Ranging from administrative cooperation between regulatory bodies to codes developed by non-state actors, these measures are not legally binding on states, yet they may nonetheless have great practical significance.

The argument developed in the following four sections is focused around two ideas: transposability of our conceptual framework and the role of law. First, we will suggest that theories of regulation and of regulatory legitimacy can be applied to the supranational regulatory context with little conceptual difficulty, and that examples of the regulatory techniques surveyed and many of the challenges associated with enforcement can readily be found. However, the *practical salience* of particular subsets of theories, techniques, enforcement and legitimacy is sometimes diluted, other times enhanced. Very broadly, the following patterns emerge: institutionalist theories of regulation predominate; consensus and communication techniques take centre stage; informal dimensions of enforcement are strongly accentuated, leading to aggravation of political tensions; and expertise-based models of regulatory legitimacy acquire greater prominence.

Secondly, we claim that the role of law in the context of supranational regulation alters. At the national level, the law plays a central facilitative role (both by threatening coercive sanctions to deter violation of its commands and in constituting the democratic market order which may be harnessed in order to shape behaviour in aid of collective goals). It also plays an expressive role, by legitimating the coercive role of the state and institutionalising the values which a particular democratic community or constitutional order may demand. The law's facilitative and expressive contributions to domestic regulation are challenged by the pressures resulting from the co-existence of supranational regulatory regimes and from competition between domestic regulatory regimes. When we illustrate shifts in the role of law in the remainder of this chapter, we refer in some contexts to law operating at the national level, and in other contexts to law operating at the supranational level. Within the scope of this chapter, it is not possible to provide a full survey of the implications of supranational pressures on every aspect of law's contribution to regulation at all levels. In particular, we do not explore in any detail ways in which national and supranational law operate in *combination* with each other. For clarity's sake, this chapter simply highlights selected aspects of the pressures on the role that law plays in regulation either at the national level, or at the supranational level.

The nub of our argument is this: although the law is capable of playing a facilitative role, its effectiveness may vary, and it is especially difficult for law to fulfil the kind of expressive role that it occupies at the national level. We suggest that these consequences may be attributed to three related features of the supranational regulatory context: firstly, the absence of a single homogeneous 'community' whose values are embodied in the content and contours of the law; secondly, the absence of democratically legitimate coercive supranational institutions that enable policy trade-offs to be made transparently, authoritatively and in a manner which is responsive to the community; and thirdly, the sector-specificity and policy fragmentation that tends to characterise the focus of supranational regulation. Although issues of policy trade-off arise in a supranational context (and are often fiercely contested), there is no overarching institution for mediating and authoritatively and democratically resolving these trade-offs *across* policy sectors. And although supranational law can sometimes regulate transborder issues more effectively than national institutions, they rarely (with the possible exception of the EU) provide an institutional framework that clearly defines the scope of the community to which they are accountable above and beyond the state.

6.2   Theories of regulation

Theories of regulation developed in relation to national regulation may be readily translated to the supranational context. In this context, national law continues to play an essential role, particularly in facilitative terms, but its expressive role is complex. Our method of cumulatively introducing the various facets of law's role in regulation throughout the book means that there was no sustained attention paid to law's *expressive* role in the discussion of theories of regulation in Chapter 2. We can now draw out both law's facilitative and expressive roles in relation to theories of regulation, albeit very briefly, within the limited confines of this chapter. In relation to public interest theories, for example, national law continues to function as a mechanism for providing the general framework for implementing collective goals, but because the goals are now supranational, the link between national law and the values and desires of the national community is now much more attenuated. In relation to private interest theories, the role of domestic law is radically altered – domestic law is no longer the object fought for by private actors, but merely one feature that influences private supranational actors in selecting between competing domestic regulatory regimes. Within institutionalist theories of regulation, law continues to serve, albeit on an expanded level, the same 'co-ordinating' function it performs at national level, but since the reflexive process of influence and change in which it participates crosses national borders, the connection between law's coordinating role and the community values it promotes is much less clear.

6.2.1   Public interest theories

The translation of welfare economic versions of public interest theories of regulation to a supranational level is evident in the developments surrounding global regulatory regimes such as the international trade law regime administered by the WTO. Here, and arguably in highly developed areas of EU law, such as competition law, the conceptual structure of welfare economics, and the idea of an ordered global market as the appropriate goal of regulation, increasingly animate the way in which these developments are conceptualised. Veijo Heiskanen, for example, argues that the principal function of international trade agreements is not to promote free international trade by eliminating discriminatory domestic regulations, but to establish a global regulatory infrastructure by harmonising

00

existing domestic regulations on the basis of international standards or by introducing a more adequate and effective global regulatory regime (Heiskanen
2004:14). He stresses the interdependent nature of markets and regulation
from this perspective, acknowledging that views about the appropriate minimum
level and substance are bitterly contested.

Contestation over the appropriate minimum level and substance of regulation
is partly played out in the range of perspectives on the public interest promoted
by regulatory intervention at the supranational level, which can encompass
political perspectives as well as economic ones. Once international trade law is
understood as establishing a global regulatory infrastructure by harmonising
domestic regulations on the basis of international standards, there is no conceptual bar to including the sorts of regulatory goals explored in Chapter 2 in
the extract from Sunstein. Indeed, tensions between efficiency and redistributive
goals in this particular instance of supranational law are arguably at the heart
of broader debates about globalisation, especially those global regulatory projects such as fair trade, international labour laws or socio-economic human
rights. Moreover, procedural ideas about deliberation, rooted in the kind of
Habermasian theory that Chapter 2 surveyed in its extract from Prosser's work,
is an increasingly pervasive lens for framing the legitimacy of supranational law,
especially EU law with its elaborate structures of committee-based decision-
making procedures.

While this chapter is not the place for exploring the substance of these debates
in any detail, here we emphasise only that this substance is the contested terrain
of what constitutes the 'public interest' promoted by supranational regulatory
intervention. We also want to consider the implications of this contestation
for the role that law plays in supranational regulation. This role is shaped by
the organisational implications for identifying how, where and by whom the content of the public interest is determined. Traditional public international law
(i.e. binding treaties) is established through bargaining between high-level
officials representing nation-state interests. As Heiskanen says, however, when
regulatory harmonisation becomes integral to international trade law, the
bargaining process is not well suited to the complex balancing required, not
only between trade interests and non-trade concerns, but also between non-
trade interests and concerns (Heiskanen 2004:18). He then argues that in this
situation, regulatory effectiveness and legitimacy are enhanced when the drafting
process, and even the right to initiate new agreements, is delegated to international economic, legal and technical experts, who, unlike government officials,
have no vested interest in the substance of the regulations and thus no conflict
of interests.

Some supranational orders rely more extensively on technical expertise than
others, particularly the EU where functional separation and formal oversight
institutions are much more extensive and elaborate than in other supranational regulatory regimes. The critical point here is the displacement of detailed

decision-making power, particularly the task of balancing competing interests, from representatives of nation-state governments to international experts. Whereas, in a national context, contested dialogues over the content of the public interest are ultimately fought out in the arena of state law, in a supranational context, public interest theories of regulation *harness* national state law to contribute to a supranational substantive or procedural conception of the public interest — one defined by reference to a global or regional transnational community. This creates a disjunction between the idea of the 'public interest' or collective welfare, and the territorial scope of a national community. Indeed, Heiskanen's formulation actually emphasises the *necessity* of stripping out the national perspective, casting it as a vested interest that creates conflicts of interest. National law will still be present instrumentally, as a mechanism for providing the general framework for the implementation of collective goals. Supranational regulation may even provide an effective tool for addressing the interests of some groups within national borders whose interests may have been marginalised by national law. But those collective goals will no longer be solely or even significantly defined by the political institutions at national level. National law's *expressive* dimension will thus be more limited than its facilitative role in a supranational context: in effect, national law becomes either a tool for or an obstacle against achieving a public interest defined by a post-national (usually larger) community. Whether supranational regulation re-establishes a link between the expressive dimension of national law and national community values is a separate question which we do not here pursue.

6.2.2   Private interest theories

Private interest theories of regulation remain conceptually applicable in a supranational context and have a purchase on current debates, most notably in theories of regulatory competition. In particular, the descriptive explanatory facet of private interest theories may be readily transposed to the supranational level, explaining how and why particular phenomena occur in the dynamics of supranational regulation. It is probably no accident that theories of regulatory competition, which provide the most well known account of supranational regulatory dynamics are built upon the assumptions of private interest theories of regulation. Regulatory competition defines itself *against* the positive harmonisation vision that we associated above with *public* interest accounts of supranational regulation. As Esty and Geradin argue (Esty and Geradin 2000:2−6), the positive harmonisation vision has tended to justify regulatory expansion in areas such as environmental regulation, consumer protection, health and safety and labour protection. By contrast, scholars who praise the virtues of regulatory competition draw the kind of analogy between product markets and competition among jurisdictions that we drew in Chapter 2 when we introduced private interest theories of regulation. Applying this logic to supranational regulation, private interest theory (which takes for granted the notion that legislators are self-interested actors seeking re-election) argues that regulatory competition leads to the adoption of standards of varying stringency that efficiently match the needs and desires of each jurisdiction. To the extent that there is a 'race to the bottom', it is seen as generating welfare *gains* (Esty and Geradin 2000:5).

Just as the private interest theory of regulation at national level suggested a corrective to optimistic assumptions about the motivations and effects of 'public interested' regulators, so too private interest approaches in the supra-national contexts suggest that the policy implications of regulatory competition force regulators and their collaborators in industry to abandon the manipu-lation of regulatory mechanisms for private gain ('capture') and to adopt deci-sions better aligned with the preferences of their citizens (Esty and Geradin 2000: 5). The basic idea of treating law as, in a sense, the 'product' of a political market is equally at work in the national and in the supranational context. Crucially, however, the supranational context itself shifts the characteristic of that good — law — from being a monopoly good to a competitive market good. In that context, the argument is even extended, as Esty and Geradin do, to a claim that 'centralised systems of standard setting' (which are, in the case of national law, democratically legitimate coercive institutions) are a form of collusion between competitors whose activities should be eliminated or narrowed to the greatest extent possible, due to their negative effects on economic efficiency.

In the supranational context, this approach has specific implications for the expressive role of national law. In particular, the content of national law is no longer an arena of political contestation explicable only in terms of the supply and demand of domestic electoral support; rather national law is a product competing with other comparable regulatory norms. This means that those sub-ject to national regulatory norms which they oppose have an additional option over and above participating in national political contestation over those norms: they can exit the jurisdiction altogether. The ability of regulated entities to use exit rather than voice has implications for the role of national law, to the extent that national law-makers respond to these pressures by shaping national law in ways that will attract regulated entities to the jurisdiction. When private interest theories are applied at the national level, laws promulgated by national legis-latures are seen as expressing political bargains resulting from contestation between rent-seeking groups at the national level. But when private interest theories are applied at the supranational level, laws promulgated by national legislatures are seen as expressing outcomes arising from the interplay of market forces: between 'demand' for regulation by regulated entities seeking a regulatory framework that best suits their needs, and the 'supply' of regulation by national legislatures seeking to attract regulated entities to their jurisdiction. Thus, national law may continue to play a facilitative role as an instrument shaping the coordination of social action. But its expressive role of institutionalising values and legitimating coercion is muddied, due to the ill 'fit' between national law and the values (whether moral, constitutional or democratically chosen) of a national community. Even granted that national law's expressive dimension may fall short in this regard for a variety of entirely domestic reasons, the expressive role that national law plays in making authoritative decisions on *trade-offs between competing values* is especially difficult to reproduce. In short, national democracy is far from perfect at representing all the local interests and values within its borders, but regulatory pressures at the supranational level further undercut its role in so doing, without providing an overarching alternative for making policy trade-offs across different sectors. Although public interest theories may be troubled by the absence of strong supranational democratic political processes to make these trade-offs, private interest theories regard supranational regulatory competition as a superior mechanism for making such trade-offs.

6.2.3   Institutionalist approaches

Of the three broad families of theories of regulation surveyed in Chapter 2, institutionalist approaches apply most comfortably in the supranational context. Indeed, the effects of supranational governance have arguably been one of the key pressures on the national regulatory arena which have fostered and shaped the growth of institutionalist theories in the first place. The emphasis on 'decentring' which, we have highlighted, presupposes that the state plays a significant role but is supplemented by a range of non-state mechanisms and actors. Institutionalist theories can therefore readily accommodate the supranational context. In both contexts, national law plays a key role as a *coordinating mechanism*. For example, as we saw in Chapter 2 from the survey on Teubner's work, the self-referential legal system plays a coordinating role, facilitating communication in systematic ways between semi-autonomous social subsystems.

At the supranational level, the law's co-ordinating function is also embedded in a reflexive process of influence and change but because that process crosses borders, the connection between law's coordinating role and the community desires and values it promotes is much less clear. Perhaps this explains why it is more common at present to find institutionalist approaches to supranational regulatory dynamics using rational actor models resembling the network approach of Ayres and Braithwaite more closely than the more sociologically 'thick' regulatory space and systems theory approaches. Karen Alter and Sophie Meunier, for example (Alter and Meunier 2006), argue that where regulatory regimes overlap with each other, and particularly when they are nested within each other, a distinctive kind of politics results. Groups and actors subject to regulation tend to 'forum-shop' between the overlapping regulatory regimes, searching for the forum that is most likely to promote their interests. In supranational contexts where there are no clear answers to the question of which forum, being hierarchically superior, will prevail, political decision-makers may take very different positions from those they would take in a national context. In order to outwit the forum shoppers, they may keep their own options open in order to maximise their bargaining power (Alter and Meunier 2006).

This type of approach emphasises the strategic and gaming behaviour of national legislators. Within a supranational context, cross-border regulatory networks create pressures and opportunities for external regulatory norms to influence domestic law and vice versa. When national law is embedded in this reflexive relationship with supranational dynamics, its strategic instrumental significance comes to the fore, intensifying the facilitative dimension of national law's role and complicating its expressive dimension. Accounts of this process, which stress power dynamics between strong and weak states, suggest that the expressive role of law is enhanced for powerful states but only at the expense of weaker states. 'Rule-taker' states find their national regulatory regimes reshaped by forces that are separate and distinct from the collective political institutions that produce their national laws. As Raustiala argues, for example, networks of government officials that cooperate on regulatory enforcement issues become conduits for the diffusion of regulatory rules and practices, thus exporting regulatory regimes in the process (Raustiala 2002). His account of what drives this export process encompasses a range of motivations that fits both public and private interest accounts of regulation, but Raustiala places particular emphasis on the organisational form of networks and the way in which they provide or enhance incentives for convergence and cooperation.

The well-known example of the eclipse of Betamax videotapes by VHS standards illustrates 'network effects', which occur in non-physical contexts when increasing the number of members increases the utility of other members, even though a single item or member is not useless. Raustiala argues (Raustiala 2002) that the adoption of regulatory standards follows a logic of network effects, creating incentives for weak jurisdictions to import regulatory models in line with the emerging international "standards" in regulation, and for powerful jurisdictions to try to export their standards. For weak states, the import of regulation can be thought of as "a price of admission" to the fullest range of benefits provided by the network − which includes international recognition, lowered regulatory costs, technical assistance and so on. His analysis mixes power relations, organisational dynamics and rational self-interest in ways that echo a regulatory space analysis in a national context. Furthermore, the analysis illustrates how complicated it becomes to identify the shared values or desires of a particular community in the context of supranational regulatory dynamics. This suggests that at the very least the capacity of national law to institutionalise such values is complex, if not diluted. In short, institutionalist types of approach to theories of regulation can be conceptually transposed to the supranational context, but not without implications for the role of national law.

6.2.4   Conclusion

It is perhaps no accident that Majone argues that the EU is turning towards a 'regulatory state' as its supranational governance framework deepens. The US regulatory state is famous for its relatively pronounced reliance on law as a means of structuring regulatory dialogues. As national member states increasingly find the market infrastructure framework provided by European law operating as a constraint upon the use of political discretion and national law as social democratic tools for promoting the public interest and expressing shared values, they increasingly place reliance on supranational law to express such values. It is, however, debatable whether *supranational* law has the capacity both to facilitate the promotion of collective welfare in an instrumental sense and to express community values. Although we think there is a greater possibility that EU law has this capacity, in comparison with either WTO law or self-regulatory supranational regimes, it is not a question we pursue further here. Rather, confining our consideration of the transposability of theories of regulation to the supranational context and its implications for the role of *national* law, we suggest there is a strongly arguable link between large-scale, supranational governance, an absence of homogeneous community, and the use of law as a tool for coordination. This link manifests itself in the following way.

Overall, theories of regulation developed in relation to national regulation may be readily translated to the supranational context. Economic versions of public interest theory conceive of collective welfare at the global level while political versions of public interest theory emphasise collective dialogue and deliberation occurring at the supranational level. Private interest theory influences are evident in theories of regulatory competition that posit national legislatures as self-interested bureaucrats, whose self-seeking impulses are disciplined by the possibility of competition between legislatures to attract foreign investors. Institutionalist theories may be applied directly, virtually without any need for transposition, to the supranational context. Although the role of law within institutionalist theories continues to serve a 'co-ordinating' function, it has a more expansive reach which crosses national borders, thus weakening the connection between law's coordinating role and its capacity to express or institutionalise community values. Law's role also shifts in a similar manner within public interest theories of regulation: here, national law may implement collective goals, but the underlying goals are supranational, so the link between national law and national community values and desires is now more attenuated. The role of domestic law from a private interest theory perspective is radically altered by the supranational context − domestic law is no longer the object fought for, but a product to be offered for sale, competing with other national legal regimes.

6.3   Techniques of regulation

In Chapter 3, we identified five distinct modalities of control that may be employed to regulate social behaviour at the national level: command, competition, consensus, communication and code. In theory, each of these modalities may be utilised to regulate behaviour at the supranational level. However, the absence of a robust, democratically legitimate supranational system of governance, including established supranational institutions empowered to make and implement legally binding rules, means that, in practice, non-coercive techniques acquire greater practical salience. In particular, incentive-based techniques which appeal to the self-interest of firms and nation-states seeking to profit from access to offshore markets, and complex hybrid (or 'network-based') techniques that seek to harness multiple sources of influence, are commonly employed in the supranational context. The relatively under-developed nature of supranational legal institutions also appears to alter the contribution of law as an instrument of control. The coercive power of the law, and its associated image of law as *threat* is only weakly present in the supranational context, and while the facilitative capacity of the law, reflected in the image of law as *umpire* remains present, it may not be strongly visible. The EU appears to be a notable exception, where the image of law as threat is reflected in extensive hard-edged rules at the supranational level in some policy sectors such as the regulation of competition; nor is the law entirely absent in less-developed supranational regulatory regimes. The consensual and networked techniques of control which often predominate at the supranational level may be buttressed in various ways by the coercive force of law, be it in the form of binding obligations arising from bilateral or multi-lateral agreements between nation states or the coercive force of domestic law within specific national contexts. Finally, while the ideological and political dimensions of tool choice may be rather opaque and hidden at the domestic level, issues concerning their political and ideological legitimacy tend to surface much more sharply at the supranational level, arguably in response to the highly visible inequalities in political power between nation-states.

6.3.1   Command

The possibility of utilising command-based techniques of control runs into an obvious hurdle once we move to the supranational level: the absence of democratic rule-making institutions that can legitimately establish and enforce legally binding commands across and within nation-states. In the WTO, for example, attempts to promulgate binding legal standards are frequently characterised by highly visible political conflict, blocking the path towards agreement on the content, scope and purpose of command-based prohibitions to regulate and deter particular behaviour. As the size of the supranational community participating in these institutions expands, these political conflicts widen and deepen, further eroding their practical capacity to establish legally binding supranational rules.

Thus, disagreement in standard setting at the WTO level appears to be even more entrenched and acute than political disagreement arising at the EU standard-setting level, given that the WTO system involves a greater number of states and a more heterogenous range of national communities characterised in part by strongly conflicting local values and conditions. Of course, the EU's capacity to secure agreement on hard-edged rules in some policy sectors arises from its unique and legal institutional structure as much as from any relative homogeneity across EU member states. Indeed the EU experience indicates that the obstacles to command-based techniques in the supranational context are not insurmountable. More typically, variation in the local conditions, needs and interests of national communities means that supranational community consensus is rarely forthcoming in practice due to different conceptions of national political self-interest. But although this has tended to preclude the articulation of hard-edged commands by emerging law-making institutions, policy stasis appears to have been avoided by at least two strategies. Firstly, by utilising broad framework principles for the regulation of activity, rather than detailed commands, in relation to which broad political consensus may be achievable. Secondly, by infusing the policy-making process with scope for an iterative process of mutual discussion and dialogue between national administrations assisted and supplemented by a network of expert committees. The goals of regulation may be specified as provisional, to be continually refined and amended through a process of on-going deliberation, policy learning and experience.

Procedures of this latter kind may be found in the Open Method of Co-ordination (the OMC) increasingly adopted in various areas of EU policy-making. The OMC varies widely from one policy domain to another but is defined by four common elements, described by Sabel and Zeitlin as involving (1) Joint definition by the member states of initial objectives (general and specific), indicators and in some cases guidelines; (2) National reports or action plans which assess performance in light of the objectives and metrics, and propose reforms accordingly; (3) Peer review of these plans, including mutual criticism and exchange of good practices, backed up by recommendations in some cases; (4) Re-elaboration of the individual plans and, at less-frequent intervals, of the broader objectives and metrics in light of the experience gained in their implementation (Sabel and Zeitlin 2003). Interestingly, these kinds of soft law-making techniques have emerged even within the EU, which has had greater success than other supranational regimes in producing detailed, command-based rules. Sabel and Zeitlin observe that the OMC procedures have been adopted in domestically sensitive policy areas where the legal basis for EU action is weak, where inaction is politically unacceptable and where diversity among member states precludes harmonisation. Thus, even in a supranational regime of the institutional strength that the EU has, there is likely to be a tendency to develop soft-law making procedures, exemplified by the OMC.

Strategies such as the OMC may be understood as allowing space for policy development without resort to the threatening, deterrent-based nature of the law's commands. It is true that supranational institutions resembling the functional equivalent of national coercive legislatures have been established (such as the EU and WTO), with the capacity to employ sanctions to deter states from violating regulatory standards. But within these regimes coercive sanctions are considered to be a last resort and their effectiveness depends heavily on visiting significant financial detriment on the violating state. So, for example, under the EU Treaties, states may be fined for failing to comply with their Treaty obligations, but the procedures for imposing such fines strongly emphasise the resolution of disputes concerning alleged violation through negotiation and agreement rather than through the imposition of fines. Conscientious efforts to avoid using sanctions and resort to looser framework principles rather than detailed, precisely formulated standards conveys an image of law that is soft edged, at least in comparison to legal commands and sanctions employed at the national level. Not only is the law's threatening face generally avoided, but the use of vague, framework principles may not be a reliable indicator of strong cross-national political or moral consensus, so that the law's expressive face is much less visible, if at all, in supranational 'commands'.

6.3.2 Competition

Unlike command-based techniques, competition-based techniques such as tradeable permits, pollution taxes and pollution activity charges to regulate environmental harm and encourage sustainable development appear to be capable of easy transposition to the supranational context. These mechanisms seek to harness the financial self-interest of market actors, an impulse which readily transcends national borders. Yet such techniques ultimately rest on the existence of an established legal infrastructure within which the market can operate and within which the security of transactions can be guaranteed. Although the law's role in constituting markets may be less visible than the threatening role embodied in its commands, its contribution is equally vital because it provides the foundational framework within which the techniques of competition may be employed. Not only is a legal infrastructure guaranteeing security of transactions between competing units an essential prerequisite, but the establishment of such a framework entails many of the functional tasks that are inherent in command-based regimes. Examples include the qualitative specification of the conduct falling within the scope of the regime, the determination of the quantity or level of regulated activity considered permissible within the regime, the allocation or recognition of entitlements to members of the regulated community and the guaranteed enforcement of transactions undertaken on the market. In order to achieve these tasks, some degree of coercive power is required. In short, the implementation challenges associated with command-based techniques arising at the supranational may apply with equal force to the use of market-based regulatory schemes. So, for example, the global emissions trading regime established under the Kyoto Protocol framework depends critically on the commitment of participating member states to ensure that emission reduction targets are met within their jurisdiction, and in which the allocation of such targets is decided upon the basis of political negotiation rather than determined by competitive auction. Similarly, the allocation of emission allowances under the EU Emissions Trading Scheme was based upon quantities proposed by member states (although subject to approval by the EU Commission) and hence based upon political rather than competitive forces. In both of these examples, the structure and dynamics of the resulting 'market' are heavily dominated by intergovernmental politics in which nation states (rather than polluting firms) remain the primary actors. The market can at best be regarded as partial and incomplete.

In other words, though command-based techniques appear to face the most significant obstacles to deployment beyond the national level, the possibility of utilising competition techniques in a purposive manner to shape behaviour faces similarly large, if not larger, challenges. By seeking to impose a competitive system of market discipline on activities where a competitive market system has not developed spontaneously, some kind of coercive infrastructure is required in order to guarantee compliance with the market allocation mechanism thereby imposed. Ultimately, it is the law which acts as market umpire, providing the means by which the 'rules of the game' are established and enforced.

6.3.3 Consensus

Unlike techniques based on command or competition, the absence of democratically legitimate supranational law-making institutions does not preclude the creation and implementation of consensual regulatory forms. Accordingly, it is not surprising that consensual, self-regulatory modes of governance have proliferated in this context, due to their reliance on voluntary participation rather than coercion to promote behavioural change. But while political conflict has not precluded the use of consensual techniques at the supranational level, these conflicts may resurface once the resulting agreements have been implemented. The avoidance of overt political conflict at the level of standard-setting may be achievable through the use of consensus-based techniques by narrowing the focus of activity to a highly specific level. But as soon as the effects of consensual techniques of regulation are felt beyond their narrowly circumscribed origins, political conflict may emerge, generating acute legitimacy challenges. These consensual forms of regulation appear to have been forthcoming in many contexts. For example, where participants recognise that they constitute a 'community of shared fate', such that the failure of one participant may have catastrophic effects on the entire community and thereby threaten the well-being of each individual participant, voluntary consensual mechanisms of regulating against the potential harms from the targeted activity have emerged. This high degree of interdependence between supranational participants characterises international financial systems, in which the failure of one national financial system may generate contagion effects and seriously jeopardise the stability of the entire system. For example, the Basel Committee on banking supervision, comprised of central bank governors from ten states, does not possess any formal supranational supervisory authority, and its conclusions do not have legal force. Rather, it formulates broad supervisory standards and guidelines, recommending statements of best practice in the expectation that individual authorities will take steps to implement them through detailed arrangements best suited to their own national systems, thereby encouraging convergence towards common approaches and common standards.

In addition, technical expert-based forums with a narrow sector-specific focus have succeeded in developing precisely formulated standards intended to apply to specific sectoral activity, often made available for voluntary adoption by states, rather than being coercively imposed. Broadly cohesive discourse within expert communities (for example, 'comitology' procedures in the EU), enhances the political feasibility of achieving agreement on detailed technical standards, unlike overtly political supranational forums, in which national political self-interest typically prevents agreement on detailed rules and standards from being achieved. Moreover, these expert communities may be highly informal in nature, comprised by a loose association of administrative officials and other technical experts who meet together on a regular basis to share knowledge and exchange practical advice and experience, rather than being formally constituted under the auspices of established supranational standard-setting institutions.

Consensual techniques for shaping behaviour at the supernational level also occur through agreement between two parties rather than through multi-party consensus. The establishment of a network of bilateral agreements between the regulator and members of the regulated community can be used to shape behaviour in the supranational context. We referred to similar networks of bilateral agreements at the national level in Chapter 3. For example, developing states may agree to implement regulatory reforms at the local level in return for financial aid. For example, the International Monetary Fund (IMF) provides loan financing to developing states pursuant to loan agreements that impose a range of behavioural conditions on the borrowing state. The mechanism through which behavioural change is intended to be effected is consensual in form: the IMF agrees to provide funding in exchange for the state's agreement to undertake various economic reforms. The motive, however, is essentially economic: the developing state requires funding to meet immediate local needs, while the IMF seeks to effect more long-term structural reform to national state economic systems in order to shore up the stability of the global monetary system, thereby serving the interests of 'lending' states. By establishing a network of these conditional loan agreements with developing states in receipt of IMF financial aid, the IMF's intention is to bring about the gradual transformation of developing economies across the globe. Yet, in the discussion of consensual negotiation between a public enforcement official and a member of the regulated community who is believed to have violated regulatory law in Chapter 3, we observed that the integrity of the underlying consent might be cast into question where there is considerable disparity in bargaining power between the state official and member of the regulated community consenting to the agreement. In the same way, it is questionable whether the consent of the developing state to abide by IMF conditions can truly be regarded as voluntary and informed, in light of the acute need in which the state in receipt of aid finds itself.

While there may be less reason to doubt the validity of consensus underlying consensus-based techniques involving multiple participants, such techniques are accompanied by challenges that resonate with the challenges to law's role in the national setting. That is, the possibility of drawing upon consensus-based techniques appear to be allied with narrow, expert-based communities. By narrowing the focus of discussions over which consensus is forged to a given policy sector, and by recognising the 'shared fate' of the participants in a highly interdependent network of institutions, it is possible to achieve some degree of consensus. But the resulting voluntary mechanisms may serve to conceal deeper political consequences that flow from the agreed regulatory response. Once the consequences of these agreed standards are felt beyond that narrow community, political division may be brought to the surface. In particular, it may become apparent that the consensus underlying the voluntary regimes is not shared beyond those involved in the policy-specific expert community (i.e. no longer reflect homogeneity).

Even where it is possible to identify broader community consensus in support of the collective goals lying at the heart of a voluntary regime, this does not prevent the emergence of competing priorities to collective well-being. Yet the possibility of such conflict demands the making of political trade-offs which the limited expert community cannot claim to make on behalf of the broader global community affected by the relevant activity. Moreover, the legitimacy of expert-based consensus is called further into question in circumstances where the community of experts establishing consensual standards does not rest on any strong formalised institutional foundation with associated mechanisms for ensuring transparency and accountability. In other words, even in circumstances where the law's facilitative capacities are enrolled to provide binding force to the consensual basis of supranational regulatory structures, underlying political tensions may remain unresolved, so that the social and political cohesion that the law's expressive force may contribute to national regulation is not reflected in the role which it plays within the supranational context.

6.3.4   Communication

As we saw in Chapter 3, communication techniques seek to effect behavioural change by enriching the information available to those whose behaviour is targeted (e.g. consumers, bureaucrats, citizens), sometimes with the aim of bringing indirect pressure to bear on the ultimate targets of communication-based strategies of influence (e.g. multi-national firms, nation-states). Although communication techniques may be mandated by law in the national context, such techniques may also be employed on a non-coercive basis, and, as such, they are readily employed in the supranational context. For example, the compilation and publication of official 'league tables' or performance indices by national governments to impose a form of discipline on members of a regulated community may be seen as directly analogous to the publication of global performance indices, be they sponsored by formal supranational institutions such as the OECD, or promulgated by civil society groups (of varying degrees of formal organisation). Supranational performance indices have been compiled and published on a wide range of issues, motivated by a variety of aims. These aims may include a deliberate attempt to regulate, seeking to effect behavioural change through multiple influences: guiding the resource allocation or investment decisions of donor institutions or private investors, by attracting acclaim or shame in the minds of the global community or by fostering technical debate as a means for raising standards. Yet their use as a regulatory tool appears to be plagued by similar kinds of problems that arise when published performance indicators are employed at the national level, including difficulties in defining the sphere of activity subject to assessment. Difficulties also arise in evaluating and measuring the quality of performance and translating those evaluations into ranked quantitative indicators, casting doubt on the validity and reliability of the resulting measures.

Communication-based techniques do not always take the form of widespread public dissemination of information and may not, therefore, be conventionally understood as instruments of regulation. In particular, active support through capacity-building programmes, such as the provision of 'technical assistance' by supranational institutions or expert communities within powerful states, is frequently offered to developing states explicitly aimed at 'educating' the assisted state in the practices, understandings and policies of the assisting institution or donor state − in the hope and expectation that the latter will adopt those practices internally.

While the provision of technical assistance may be sympathetically understood as the provision of knowledge and expertise to recipient states where knowledge gaps may impede regulatory development, they might also be viewed more cynically as a disguised form of propaganda. Cast in these terms, critiques of technical assistance as a means for 'improving' local standards clearly resonate with critiques of 'public communications management' techniques discussed in Chapter 3. This is not to suggest that the donor state may be motivated by anything other than laudable aims: it may simply be that the technical or expert nature of such assistance conceals particular political and cultural values that may be unsuited, or not shared, by the 'assisted' state and thereby cast doubt on the legitimacy of the underlying assistance in so far as it meets local needs.

6.3.5   Code

As we saw in Chapter 3, the capacity to regulate behaviour using architectural controls depends critically upon the capacity of the regulator to mould and manipulate the physical environment in which the targeted behaviour takes place. Much of the impetus driving the move towards supranational regulation may be attributed to growing recognition that the behaviour taking place in one physical environment may have adverse consequences beyond the locality in which it originates. In particular, it is the adverse effects of activity taking place in another state that have formed the focal point of acute political conflict between states. Yet the capacity for one state to confine those adverse effects through architecture is currently restricted to the confines of its own geographic territory. Any attempt to impose architectural mechanisms within the physical territory of another state without the latter's permission would constitute an illegal and illegitimate invasion of the latter state's sovereignty. For this reason, the capacity of an individual state to legitimately deploy architectural mechanisms at the supranational level is severely restricted.

This point applies less to cyberspace than to real space, because the boundaries of cyberspace are not delineated by reference to the right to exert control over physical territory associated with national sovereignty. Rather, the capacity to assert control in cyberspace through code arises from the nature of cyberspace, which, owing to its 'virtual' nature, transcends national boundaries. For this reason, control of cyberspace through code has attracted considerable scholarly attention and appears, at least to cyber-paternalists, to hold the most promise (and hence poses the gravest dangers) for the imposition of effective controls on cyberspace. But the experience of utilising code-based controls as a means for regulating cyberspace to date indicates that such controls are not inviolable, particularly in the face of successful attempts by the hacking community to find ways for circumventing them (Lessig 1999). Although it is the global reach of cyberspace that enables the effective deployment of code-based control, it is the same capacity of cyberspace to transcend national borders that makes hacking so difficult to eliminate. Attempts to regulate hacking through traditional, command-based, anti-circumvention laws appear to have been severely constrained because the capacity to enforce such laws is subject to the jurisdictional limits of national sovereignty.

6.3.6   Complex hybrids and the role of law

Despite the absence of a robust, democratically legitimate supranational system of governance, programmes with the capacity to exert regulatory influence have not only emerged but appear to have flourished, particularly through the establishment and development of networks of actors, be it in the form of expert communities, civil society activists or national administrative officials. The resulting patterns of influence are complex and non-hierarchical, comprised of mechanisms that, taken together, utilise a hybrid range of techniques that seek to regulate conduct. The possibility of exerting pressure on supranational behaviour through multiple points of access has been harnessed within individual regulatory programmes. These programmes rely heavily on voluntarism and competitive market forces to provide the impetus for behavioural change, but from which the law is rarely absent altogether.

Although these programmes utilise a wide variety of forms, they may be divided into two broad groups: those which are entirely voluntary in nature (such as codes of conduct voluntarily adopted by individual firms) and those which are ultimately buttressed by a coercive, albeit largely hidden, legal framework. An example of the former kind of programme includes voluntary 'codes of conduct' adopted by commercial enterprises that are claimed to bring about an improvement in the treatment of workers within industrial production processes, described by Redmond as a form of 'human rights entrepreneurialism' (Redmond 2003:87). These programmes, commonly referred to collectively under the banner of 'corporate social responsibility', entail efforts by firms to compete for consumers or investors by means of signalled respect for human rights standards in their operations. They rely upon the voluntary assumption of corporate responsibility and self-regulation, sometimes with external monitoring and verification, representing a focus for development of corporate responsibility and civil society. The source of norms upon which these codes rest varies. Many take the form of individual codes adopted by the firms' own initiative, a smaller proportion adopt codes established by an industry or trade association or are constructed from agreement between stakeholders in the industry such as unions, NGOs, firms and industry associations; a very small proportion are constructed upon codes of conduct developed by international organisations (Redmond 2003). Accordingly, these programmes rely upon multiple influences to generate behavioural change, involving consent, communication and competition.

A widely known example of a hybrid regulatory programme that entails partial reliance on the coercive force of law may be found in the technical food safety standards promulgated by Codex Alimentarius, an international standard-setting body set up as a subsidiary to the Food and Agriculture Organisation and the World Health Organisation with the aim of harmonising food standards so as to protect human health and to facilitate international trade. Although acceptance by nation-states with Codex standards is voluntary, participation is leveraged through the power of cross-national trade. The Sanitary and Phytosanitary Standards Agreement (the 'SPS Agreement') established under the WTO Agreement confers official recognition on Codex standards, so that compliance with Codex standards is presumed to comply with the requirements of the SPS Agreement. Thus, states wishing to benefit from the free trading system established under the WTO are effectively compelled to accept Codex standards, or run the risk that their local food safety standards may be regarded as contrary to the SPS Agreement and therefore in breach of WTO obligations, potentially jeopardising access to valuable foreign markets. Accordingly, the scheme of supranational regulation established under the Codex regime entails a complex mix of consent, competition and coercion, the latter arising from the obligations arising under the WTO Agreements to which nation-states have legally committed themselves to observing.

In sum, techniques of regulation developed in relation to national regulation can be readily transposed to the supranational context, but their relative practical salience changes. Although both command-based and competition-based techniques may be utilised by emerging supranational law-making institutions, their practical capacity to establish agreement on collective goals and the rules for their implementation is relatively limited due to national political conflict. Consequently, consensus-based and communication-based techniques have proliferated, for they do not require coercive mechanisms in order to shape and constrain behaviour. Despite the turn away from overtly coercive mechanisms of control, the law's coercive role does not disappear altogether. Rather, complex hybrids tend to predominate, in which the law's role is often enlisted as one source of influence for establishing a programme for regulating supranational behaviour. In particular, regulatory programmes that are underpinned by trade and investment agreements between sovereign states rely in part for their effectiveness on the coercive power of law at two levels: legally binding trade agreements between sovereign states and the power of states to introduce and enforce domestic laws imposing import restrictions on foreign products.

In other words, the law's facilitative role persists, both as threat and as umpire, but in a largely hidden and indirect fashion: either through national law or through public international law rendering agreements between states binding. By contrast, the law's expressive role (most clearly reflected in its imperative commands) is fairly thin: for it is seldom visible at the supranational level in terms of 'law as threat'. This is partly because the invocation of the law's expressive force must be underpinned by general community agreement or acceptance community – otherwise, the law's threats may be cast into disrepute (and potentially ignored). As we have seen, the political and ideological dimensions of tools arise much more starkly in supranational contexts when compared alongside national policy discussions, where discussion of the appropriate regulatory instruments tends to be cast as largely bureaucratic, technical choices.

6.4   Enforcement

The effectiveness of any regulatory regime in generating behavioural change will depend in large measure upon the ways in which its enforcement mechanisms operate in concrete social contexts. At the domestic level, we observed that a diverse range of factors affect the framework for enforcement of a given regulatory regime and the range of enforcement activities and practices. Although the domestic experience of enforcement practices powerfully illustrates their highly contextual nature, it was nonetheless possible to identify common areas of tension and difficulty encountered at the level of enforcement design, including problems with rules, the involvement of private actors and the legitimacy of particular kinds of practices. Similar tensions can be found when exploring the enforcement of supranational regulatory standards, although the focus of discussion tends to shift away from individual enforcement officials to individual states. This shift may be seen as a consequence of the invocation of national law as a *tool* of enforcement, rather than a regulatory framework, and — when contested — the legitimacy of the national law itself (rather than the actions of particular state officials) may be called into question.

6.4.1 Problems with rules

Our discussion of enforcement in Chapter 4 began with a discussion of the nature of rules, highlighting the inherent and unavoidable difficulties associated with the use of rules, particularly as instruments of control. In the preceding section, we observed that significant obstacles often lie in the path of utilising command-based techniques at the supranational level, largely due to difficulties in achieving consensus: both in identifying collective policy goals and, in turn, setting standards for achieving those goals. As a result, supranational norms are often drafted in vague, aspirational or framework terms. Although these broad generalised statements of principle may conceal underlying political disagreement concerning their scope and content, they pose considerable difficulties for those responsible for their implementation. As domestic enforcement studies demonstrate, vague and indeterminate rules do not translate easily into hard, practical norms for guiding behaviour and identifying contraventions.

Although the use of open-ended, framework regulation at the supranational level may succeed in concealing wide interpretative differences, they are not eliminated. Rather, the underlying political conflicts are often side-stepped — shifted to court-like adjudicatory institutions empowered to resolve those disputes authoritatively. While these authoritative judicial pronouncements may possess legally binding force arising from the terms of the supranational agreements under which they are established, they may fail effectively to defuse underlying political disagreement and, as a consequence, call into question the legitimacy of these adjudicatory determinations. Controversy over the legitimacy of the determinations of the WTO Appellate Body exemplifies the challenges associated with reliance upon adjudicative fora for resolving interpretive disparities in the implementation of supranational legal norms. While many have applauded the success of the WTO dispute resolution system, there have also been considerable criticisms. These criticisms include allegations that the Appellate Body engages in unwarranted judicial activism in making its determinations, particularly where they contradict the intention of the underlying WTO agreement.

The juridification of dispute settlement procedures under the WTO is increasingly depicted in terms of a paradigm shift away from the traditional diplomatic ethos of international politics in favour of the culture of law. The turn to legal institutions, processes and values as a means for filling out interpretive gaps in supranational norms may fail to resolve the deeply entrenched political disagreements concealed within the norms themselves. In the EU the unique legal and institutional context that establishes and mandates a structured dialogue between the European Court of Justice and member state institutions has arguably meant that juridification has been relatively successful in 'taming' politics (Menon and Weatherill 2002). However, where these legal mechanisms fail to 'tame' politics, as they do more frequently in broader intergovernmental contexts, this may serve to undermine the expressive dimension of supranational law: the persistence of disagreement about the proper interpretation of such rules may indicate that those rules are not accepted by the general body of persons within the supranational communities affected by those rules.

One way in which disparities in national conditions, values and practices might be overcome at the supranational level is through the development of expert policy networks in particular sectors, drawing upon expert knowledge as the basis for formulating generally applicable standards. The shared knowledge, culture and values embedded within the discourse adopted by such networks may be seen as establishing global epistemic communities in specific policy sectors. These epistemic communities have considerable potential to transcend local allegiances, especially where the appearance of universalistic, objective foundations for expert knowledge opens the possibility of depoliticising the rule-making process. It is therefore hardly surprising that international networks of experts have proliferated at the supranational level, accompanied by optimistic accounts of their potential role in global governance (Joerges and Vos 1999).

But although international epistemic communities may succeed in developing more detailed and specific rules than those developed through formal supranational institutions, they can experience legitimacy dilemmas not unlike those arising from the implementation of WTO adjudications, albeit of a different kind. Here the problem lies not with the indeterminacy of the standards, but with the need for the ensuing rules to be accepted and supported by citizens who experience the force of the rule's practical implications, and who may not share the same values, knowledge and outlook as experts. The potential for divergence between supranational standards developed on the basis of scientific expertise and moral acceptability of those standards to the community is well illustrated in the on-going 'hormone dispute' between the EU, on the one hand, and US, Canada and Argentina, on the other hand. This dispute concerns the EU's ban on hormone-treated meat which the US, Canada and Argentina claim is a disguised restriction on trade in breach of the SPS Agreement. Under that agreement, the obligation of member states to harmonise their regulations relating to sanitary and phytosanitary measures on the basis of international standards can only be departed from if there is scientific justification or if a scientific risk assessment has been conducted. The EU banned genetically modified products in response to widespread backlash expressed by consuming publics across a number of EU member states who feared potential long-term harm to both human and environmental health. But because the relevant international standard reflects current scientific knowledge, which suggests that genetically modified food is safe to eat, the WTO Appellate Body has indicated that the EU is prima facie in breach of its obligations.

6.4.2 Public enforcement of supranational norms

Despite criticisms of the dispute-resolution system established under the WTO agreements, the establishment and implementation of a legally binding supranational system of adjudication remains, at present, an exceptional development (exemplified by the EU, to whom the argument in this sub-section does not apply). It is true that there has been significant expansion in the number of supranational agreements establishing norms of conduct that bind states who accept and ratify those agreements. But the enforcement mechanisms established under those agreements are often weak or non-existent. In the absence of effective supranational mechanisms that operationalise supranational standards and translate them into social reality, it is typically left to member states themselves to implement their international commitments into domestic settings. Accordingly, the effectiveness of these standards in changing behaviour at the global level will depend in large measure on their effective implementation at the national level.

In the discussion of regulatory enforcement in Chapter 4, we considered a rich and fertile body of ethnographic studies of the behaviour of domestic enforcement officials. These studies demonstrate the patterned and sometimes profound ways in which human interpretation and interaction may temper, and sometimes appear to pervert, the clear language expressed in regulatory norms. In this respect, public enforcement officials provide the 'human face' of law: they operate as critical translators, acting as agents for change through which a practical life is breathed into the dry legal standards which they are called upon to enforce. At the supranational level, we might expect greater scope for variation across a range of the interpretations adopted by domestic officials in their attempts to translate global standards into domestic reality. But before these standards can be interpreted by domestic enforcement officials, there is a further hurdle to be overcome: the 'internalisation' of supranational standards into domestic law. While the domestic law of some states allows for international commitments to apply domestically consequent on acceptance and ratification, other national legal systems require the domestic legislature actively to incorporate those commitments into domestic legal standards. Yet because incorporation is dependent upon the political will of national governments, they may block the path to internalisation.

In other words, more pressing national political agendas may lead states to refuse to incorporate international commitments at the domestic level, despite having previously accepted these commitments as binding at the supranational level. For example, the Thatcher and Labour governments refused to honour their commitments to a significant number of ILO Conventions that earlier British governments had ratified because they were thought to obstruct Thatcher's neoliberal agenda (Hepple 1999). Although these measures clearly violated the UK's commitments under the ILO agreements, reflected in the significant number of complaints taken to the supervisory bodies in Geneva, and the adverse determinations made against it, these adverse rulings failed to alter domestic UK policy. Thus, even in areas such as human rights, where the universality of legal norms is asserted, uneven national commitment to these norms in practice may seriously erode their claimed universal application. As Picciotto observes, 'even a binding international standard may remain an empty aspiration unless it is supported by effective international procedures for monitoring practical implementation at the national and local levels, but these are often lacking or weak' (Picciotto 1999:21).

Studies of public enforcement of regulatory norms at the domestic level have highlighted the pervasiveness of informal practices and a strong emphasis on the resolution of suspected non-compliance through persuasion and negotiation rather than through punitive or deterrence-oriented styles of enforcement. In the supranational context, reliance on persuasion and negotiation is equally important, if not more so, where suspected non-compliance occurs. However, in the national enforcement context, negotiation and bargaining occurs 'in the shadow of the law' (Mnookin and Kornhauser 1979), where the law's facilitative functions are well established and largely taken for granted by those responsible for their implementation. In the terms used by Ayres and Braithwaite, the possibility of wielding the 'big stick' of the law at the top of the enforcement pyramid enhances the power of informal practices to generate behavioural change. When we move to the supranational context (excepting the EU, as noted above), there is no supranational 'big stick' and this may weaken the power of supranational norms to elicit the desired behavioural response. Moreover, when national governments are reluctant to internalise supranational regulatory norms into domestic law, there is simply no possibility for enrolling the facilitative capacity of *domestic* law in aid of global regulatory objectives.

6.4.3   Private and civil society enforcement

(a) Enforcement through law
When considering regulatory enforcement at the domestic level, we observed that there is a tendency within academic and policy literature to focus on the role of a public agency or other government official in taking action to secure compliance with regulatory norms. Nonetheless, it is not unusual to establish regulatory

regimes which empower private individuals (either as a substitute for, or complement to, action by public officials) to sue those suspected of violating regulatory norms to recover compensation for harm thereby caused. In a similar vein, enforcement at the supranational level has traditionally adopted a state-centric approach in which states are empowered to initiate and maintain action against those suspected of violating supranational standards. Unlike domestic enforcement regimes, however, supranational regulatory regimes only very rarely confer direct enforcement rights on private actors. So, for example, only states have standing before the WTO, in which trade complaints are formally raised by member state governments. Calls for greater openness within the WTO dispute resolution procedures have included calls to enable NGOs and civil society representatives to have greater access to WTO processes, perhaps through the use of amicus curiae briefs or even by giving standing to non-state actors to initiate complaints.

But, although private actors and other non-state organisations may lack standing before supranational adjudicatory fora, it may be possible in some circumstances for them to take formal enforcement action within *domestic* courts. This is what happens in the EU, arguably resulting in more extensive and effective enforcement than would otherwise be the case, and certainly preventing the kinds of failure to internalise supranational norms that we referred to above, exemplified in the Thatcher administration's failure to implement ILO norms. Even beyond the EU, limited use of domestic courts to secure compliance with supranational policy goals can be made when national legislation exists that applies to conduct occurring in foreign jurisdictions. Perhaps the most notable sphere in which private domestic legislation has been utilised in this manner concerns litigation under the US Alien Tort Claims Act 1789, which empowers US federal courts with jurisdiction over 'any civil action by an alien for a tort only, committed in violation of the law of nations.' Although the Act had largely lain dormant for most of its life, throughout the 1990s it began to be used as means by which NGOs sought damages from multi-national enterprises in response to alleged violations of internationally recognised human rights (Joseph 2004). More recently, the California Supreme Court entertained legal action against Nike for an alleged breach of domestic false advertising and unfair competition laws, challenging Nike's corporate publicity in which it claimed that a self-commissioned report on compliance with its corporate code by suppliers had found no evidence of illegal or unsafe working conditions at Nike factories in China, Vietnam and Indonesia (Kasky v Nike). While the Nike case was ultimately settled out of court, the settlement agreement included an undertaking by Nike to contribute to the Fair Labor Association (FLA) programmes for fostering education and economic opportunity for local workers, and may therefore be seen as a strategy by which private actors leverage formal enforcement actions in domestic courts to regulate off-shore conduct in aid of supranational policy goals.

Although these avenues for legal redress open up the possibility of enrolling the facilitative capacity of domestic law in the service of supranational goals, their contribution is limited by their narrow scope. Moreover, some have questioned their legitimacy, given that it falls to the courts of a single nation-state to act as the vehicle for enforcing and developing supranational legal norms, reflecting anxiety over the capacity of national law to give adequate expression to the views of a supranational community.

(b) Non-legal enforcement mechanisms

Although there are currently relatively few formal legal mechanisms which non-state actors can use to enforce supranational regulatory norms (with the exception of EU law), there has been considerable scope for private actors to participate in enforcement activity by using *non-legal* means. In particular, the use of techniques that combine consensus, communication and competition may help to facilitate compliance with voluntary norms. For example, voluntary codes of conduct incorporating the use of certification systems (discussed above) may be used together with internal monitoring and verification, third-party accredited auditors or NGO/independent monitors. Although the study of compliance monitoring within such voluntary codes remains considerably underdeveloped, doubts have been cast on their legitimacy, due to the claimed lack of competence or independence of auditors, particularly where they are paid by the firm being monitored (O'Rourke 2003). Sceptics fear that weak implementation of these voluntary initiatives, whose content is highly variable and uneven, is merely an exercise in corporate public relations, concealing the true effects of global corporate activity or co-opting well-meaning NGOs by 'changing them from watchdogs to "partners"' (Mayne 1999: 246). These sceptics also fear that such mechanisms may undermine traditional, sanction-based regulation which relies directly on the law's facilitative force to induce behavioural change. In other words, because voluntary initiatives lack the teeth accompanying the formal enforcement of legally binding regulatory norms, both their legitimacy and effectiveness are called into question. Legally binding norms are translated into practical, binding guidance via the formal enforcement process through the law's facilitative power. The expressive force of such norms may also institutionalise community values. In contrast, powerful commercial actors may invoke voluntary norms symbolically, portraying an ethos of social philanthropy which is devoid of substantive content.

Private actors have, however, achieved some notable successes in utilising informal action as a way of promoting global policy goals, particularly through the use of public communication techniques. Civil society groups have engaged in public advocacy and high profile media campaigning with the aim of mobilising public opinion to press for behavioural change, focusing the public spotlight on specific issues of concern, sometimes targeting individual firms. Well-publicised campaigns that have generated behavioural change in the desired direction include marketing of breast milk substitutes in developing companies, pesticides, pharmaceutical drugs and toxic waste dumping (Picciotto 1999). These campaigns tend to single out specific issues (on a relatively arbitrary basis) where the targeted behaviour is highly visible and perceived of as directly relevant to consuming publics. Accordingly, their capacity to achieve systematic, and generalised improvements is likely to be severely limited, although there are some well-known successes. Moreover, as we saw in Chapter 3 in considering the use of public communications techniques as a means for shaping behaviour, it is possible to interpret public communications management by national governments as attempts to engage in self-seeking propaganda rather than in enhancing the welfare of the national community. In a similar vein, it is possible to interpret media campaigning by civil society groups in a more sceptical light, questioning the extent to which they can claim a legitimate mandate to act as guardians of the global public interest, at least in terms of their representativeness, transparency and accountability.

6.4.4   Summary

The architecture for enforcing regulatory norms is vital to their successful implementation. Although the EU remains a persistent case of *sui generis* arrangements, we could otherwise broadly conclude that at the supranational level, it is nation-states, rather than human individuals, who tend to be the key drivers of formal enforcement action, responsible for translating supranational standards into domestic law, and in bringing formal enforcement action against contravening states before supranational bodies. Considerable reliance is placed on the good-will of individual nation-states to internalise supranational standards, thereby providing ample scope for national politics to thwart the implementation of supranational standards and undermine their effectiveness. Political tensions resurface at various points: in relation to problems with rules, public and private enforcement actions, and when formal and informal enforcement mechanisms are relied upon.

The role of formal law in the enforcement of supranational regulatory norms remains state-centric: states are the main access point for bringing disputes before supranational adjudicatory institutions and for implementing supranational norms into domestic systems. Techniques for avoiding political conflict in standard-setting by shifting to adjudicatory settings through law-like mechanisms often fail to dissolve political tension and call into question the legitimacy of law as a basis for dispute resolution. In the domestic context, the establishment and implementation of legal norms is partly legitimised through democratic processes where trade-offs between competing political values can be addressed directly. At the supranational level, however, even where regulatory norms can be established, they may fail to resolve underlying political tensions. Resort to vague, generalised norms, or the use of technical, expertise-based standards that disguise political disagreement, is likely to resurface once attempts are made to enforce those norms. This may erode the extent to which those norms may be seen as expressing the values and preferences of the community of citizens affected by their operation.

6.5   Legitimation

As we saw in Chapter 5, the expressive dimension of law's role is a pervasive aspect of regulatory legitimation. One of the core arguments of this chapter is that once we move to a supranational context, law does not currently play the kind of normative or expressive role that it occupies at the national level. For this reason, the different aspects of law's changing role already discussed in the preceding subsections bear directly upon questions of legitimation. In the supranational context, there is a continuation of law's facilitative role insofar as national law is enrolled as an instrument that assists in the pursuit of supranational goals. However, the supranational context poses significant challenges to law's expressive role, however. Chapter 5 foreshadowed these implications in two ways: firstly, by mapping a variety of often competing logics justifying regulatory legitimation, and secondly by linking regulatory legitimacy to differing visions of democracy that rely on various mixes of pluralism and expertise. Returning to both these perspectives in a supranational context demonstrates how national law's contribution to regulatory legitimation at the domestic level cannot necessarily be replicated.

6.5.1   Varying logics of regulatory legitimation

Chapter 5 explored a wide variety of logics underpinning the justification of regulatory regimes, which can be loosely organised around the cleavage of pluralism and expertise also discussed in that chapter. The logics identified at a national level that were strongly associated with law, such as Baldwin's legislative mandate, accountability and due process claims, are less prevalent in the absence of a supranational legislature. Expertise is non-territorial and easier to portray as apolitical and can more readily transcend intergovernmental conflict. As a result, it is more prevalent than pluralism in supranational regulatory dynamics. For example, Majone's work in Chapter 5 indicates that economic expertise is particularly dominant in European regulatory legitimacy. Where he considers that pluralism is appropriate, Majone separates political decision-making from regulatory decision-making, where he believes that economic expertise should reign. In a supranational context, where fora for political-making are underdeveloped, expertise often dominates decision-making at the supranational level, as Majone argues happens in the EU. Even if reliance upon expertise repairs certain defects in national democratic processes, the absence of institutions that structure pluralism at the supranational level deprives those affected by supranational decisions of an arena for participating in making political trade-offs.

Judicial knowledge, in contrast to economic knowledge, has a complex history of hybrid roots in both pluralism and expertise, at least in the extract by Shapiro provided in Chapter 5. Judges have often played a role in requiring the representation of a broad spectrum of affected interests in a regulatory dialogue: this is a role more akin to pluralism than expertise. But the more judges are called upon to provide right answers, the more the challenges of law's role in a supranational context rear their heads. Providing a right answer is difficult enough in national contexts with relative homogeneity and clear accountability lines to democratically legitimated coercive institutions that authoritatively resolve policy trade-offs across competing interests. In supranational contexts where these conditions do not obtain, the notion that judicial expertise can provide, of itself, a legitimate right answer is not easy to defend. It is no accident, perhaps, that in the arena most often cited as one where powerful quasi-judicial dynamics shape the regulatory trajectory − the WTO − legal knowledge is heavily embedded in economic expertise. Here too, as elsewhere, law's instrumental and facilitative role is preserved, but its cultural and expressive role is challenged.

6.5.2 Conceptions of democracy and the role of law

In the national context, there is an institutional infrastructure for democratic conceptions of regulatory legitimation, in which law can and does facilitate who has a right to contribute to a dialogue about the aggregate effect of multiple network influences in regulatory regimes. In other words, law structures conversations about regulation in national contexts. Sometimes the dialogue is one of traditional representative politics (Baldwin, 1995), at other times, one of a public participatory kind (Cuéllar, 2005); at still other times it is participatory but embedded more in networks of private actors (Freeman, 1999).

As we saw in Chapter 5, even at the national level, the different ways of defining democracy lead to different answers to the question of who can make authoritative critical evaluations in relation to regulatory trade-offs. Crossing national borders does not rule out democratic conceptions of regulatory legitimacy altogether, but intensifies the challenges poses by this decentred idea of regulation. Once again, however, we see that democracy differently defined shapes the answers. Anne-Marie Slaughter (Slaughter, 2003) appeals to representative participation through national public officials across borders, thus preserving the relevance of democratic procedures indirectly. Ronen Shamir and others argue that private sector litigation across borders is an additional form of legitimate pressure on public officials in areas as diverse as human rights and international trade law (Shamir, 2004). Just as at the national level, different conceptions of democracy play out in debates about regulatory legitimacy in a supranational context. But what of the role of legal institutions?

In the supranational context, as in the national context, there is a debate about how law should structure regulatory conversations. But there are two differences: firstly, law's facilitative role is markedly weaker. The contribution it makes to structuring regulatory conversations is either very thin (political and economic dynamics far more than law determine the question of who can bring disputes before the WTO) or highly unpredictable (who could have predicted that US judges would accept claims under the 1776 Alien Tort Claims Act for damages against foreign nationals committed beyond the borders of the US?). Secondly, in contexts in which the content of national law is powerfully shaped by supranational commitments, there is a disconnect, sometimes very marked, between national law and a national community. This disconnect dilutes the law's capacity to link coercive command to community consensus. In other words, the lack of an obvious transnational homogeneous community, together with the absence of global democratic institutions, means that even when law does play a practical role in structuring regulatory dialogue, the expressive implications of that role are unclear.

6.6   Conclusion: Law's role in regulation above and beyond the state

As we have seen, the conceptual framework for mapping regulation adopted in Chapters 2 to 5 transposes with relative ease to a supranational context, albeit with a shift in emphasis of the practical relevance of particular concepts. But the role and status of the law's contribution are markedly altered. Throughout the earlier chapters, we depicted the contribution of the law within national contexts in terms of its facilitative and expressive roles in domestic regulation. But under supranational regulatory pressure, although law is capable of playing a facilitative role (which may vary in strength and intensity), its expressive role shifts. In our opening comments to this chapter, we speculated that the shift in the law's contribution may be attributed to three related factors which have emerged throughout the preceding discussion of regulatory theories, techniques, enforcement and legitimacy at the supranational level. By drawing together the analysis for each of these three factors in the light of their relationship to law's facilitative and expressive dimensions, we can begin to make sense of the pressures influencing law's changing role in regulation above and beyond the state.

The first factor that we identified was the absence of a single homogeneous 'community' whose values are embodied in the content and contours of the law. The slippery nature of the supranational 'community' itself means that any attempt to suggest that supranational law reflects a shared political or moral consensus is problematic. So, drawing on examples already used in this chapter, the claim that international trade law might reflect a regulatory philosophy appropriate to a global community is highly contentious. Or, attempts to construct global rules as command-and-control regulatory tools are often thwarted by strong political resistance as a consequence of the absence of consensus on global goals. Similarly, even where some degree of global consensus can be reached, and is reflected in binding supranational commitments, their enforcement is patchy and uneven, often reflecting national political agendas. Finally, the move away from representative conceptions of democracy in discussions of regulatory legitimacy directly reflects this factor.

The above examples illustrate that the first factor entails a serious dilution of law's expressive dimension. The second, the absence of democratically legitimate coercive institutions that enable policy trade-offs to be made transparently, authoritatively and in a manner which is responsive to the community, is associated with a weakening of law's facilitative power. So, for example, institutionalist theories of regulation, which dominate supranational contexts, prioritise a coordinating function in which the image of law as threat plays little role. Competition-based techniques of regulation have difficulty flourishing at the supranational level in the absence of a stable coercive legal infrastructure upon which the global marketplace is founded. In enforcing supranational norms, the turn to adjudicatory institutions to resolve interpretive disparity may fail to eliminate political conflict, serving instead to cast doubt upon the legitimacy of the norms themselves. Finally, whereas in a national context, law could facilitate the pluralistic coexistence of multiple expert discourses, in a supranational context, the most law can do is encourage dialogue between different expert discourses. It cannot impose a solution should competing discources suggest different solutions to a regulatory dilemma.

The first set of examples illustrated challenges to law's expressive role in the supranational context, while the second set showed a weakening of the strength of law's facilitative role. The third factor helps explain the relationship between these two effects. That factor is the turn to sector-specificity governed by expertise that tends to characterise the focus of regulation beyond the state. This flows from the absence of overarching institutions for mediating and authoritatively and democratically resolving trade-offs *across* policy sectors: it is reflected in the lack of any annual budget which policy departments fight over. Of course, issues of policy trade-offs arise and are often fiercely contested. But regulatory conversations remain institutionally fragmented: that is, not systematically embedded in any formal institutions of global governance that are emerging. This means that it is possible to achieve consensus in narrow areas about the details of a desirable regulatory regime which can bolster law's facilitative role, but problems in implementation often illustrate that this does not necessarily reinvigorate law's expressive role.

The law's expressive role remains relatively weak. This is because reliance on expertise as the primary influence on regulatory dynamics in the supranational context, often improves regulatory efficacy within specific sectors. But shared understandings between experts often remain sector-specific and fragmented. While law may play a loose coordinating role across these sectors, it may be seen as an umpire of multiple different types of games, rather than providing oversight for a single league of teams playing more or less the same game.

Thus, the application of our analytical framework in the supranational context shows that the conceptual structure used in this book to explore national regulation can be readily transposed. In the EU, however, although transposition applies in some instances, its consequences are often different from those which arise in other supranational contexts, largely as a product of the EU's unique institutional arrangements for supranational regulation. The process of transposing our analytical framework has also helped to illuminate the nature and impact of the pressures exerted upon the law's contribution to regulation once we move beyond the confines of the nation-state. In the closing chapter, we summarise that contribution.

6.6.1 Discussion questions

Theories of regulation
1. What constitutes the 'public interest' in supranational regulation?
2. Are private interest theories more optimistic about the consequences of regulation in the supranational context than they are about regulation in the national context? Why or why not?
3. How might a regulatory space approach be applied to supranational regulation of a particular policy sector?

Techniques of regulation
4. If command-based techniques are the regarded as the 'classic' form of regulation at the national level, which (if any) technique occupies this role at the supranational level?
5. Compare and contrast the ease with which competition-based and communication-based techniques of control may be used to regulate behaviour above and beyond the state.
6. What factors might influence the choice of technique used in supranational regulation?

Enforcement
7. Consider the similarities and differences in law's role in enforcing regulatory rules at the national and supranational level.
8. To what extent have adjudicatory institutions successfully resolved conflict over the proper interpretation of supranational regulatory norms?
9. How important are non-state actors in supranational regulatory enforcement?

Accountability a Legitimacy
10. What are the principal challenges for securing accountability within supranational regulatory regimes?
11. In what ways can expert communities contribute to, or detract from, the legitimacy of supranational regulation?
12. How can the democratic legitimacy of a supranational regulatory regime be assessed?

References

Alter, K. and Meunier, S. 2006. 'Nested and overlapping regimes in transatlantic banana dispute', *European Journal of Public Policy* 13: 362–382.

Baldwin, R. 1995. *Rules and Government*, Oxford: Clarendon Press.

Cuéllar, M. 2005. 'Rethinking regulatory democracy', *Administrative Law Review* 57(2): 411–500.

Esty, D. and Geradin, D. 2000. 'Regulatory co-opetition', in D. Esty and D. Geradin (eds.), *Regulatory Competition and Economic Integration: Comparative Perspectives*, Oxford: Oxford University Press.

Freeman, J. (1999). 'Private parties, public function and the real democracy problem in the new administrative law?', in D. Dyzenhaus (ed.), *Recrafting the Rule of Law*, Oxford: Hart Publishing, 331–70.

Hepple, B. 1999. 'Labour regulation for internationalized markets' in S. Picciotto and R. Mayne (eds.), *Regulating International Business: Beyond Liberalisation*, Oxford: Macmillan Press, 183–202.

Heiskanen, V. 2004. 'The regulatory philosophy of international trade law', *Journal of World Trade* 38: 1–36.

Joerges, C. and Vos, E. (eds.) 1999. *EU Committees: Social Regulation, Law and Politics*, Oxford: Hart Publishing.

Joseph, S. 2004. *Corporations and Transnational Human Rights Litigation*, Oxford: Hart Publishing.

Kasky v. Nike. 2002. 02 - C.D.O.S. 3790.

Lessig, L. 1999. *Code and Other Laws of Cyberspace*, New York: Basic Books.

Menon, A. and Weatherill, S. 2002. 'Legitimacy, accountability and delegation in the European Union', in A. Arnull and D. Wincott (eds.), *accountability and legitimacy in the European Union*, New York: Oxford University Press, pp. 113–131.

Picciotto, S. 1999. 'What rules for the world economy?' in S. Picciotto and R. Mayne (eds.), *Regulating International Business: Beyond Liberalisation*, Oxford: Macmillan Press.

Majone, G. D. 1996. 'Regulatory legitimacy', in G. D. Majone (ed.), *Regulating Europe*, London: Routledge, pp. 284–301.

Mayne, R. 1999. 'Regulating TNCs: The role of voluntary and governmental approaches', in S. Picciotto and R. Mayne (eds.), *Regulating International Business: Beyond Liberalisation*, Oxford: Macmillan Press, pp. 235–254.

Mnookin, R. and Kornhauser, L. 1979. 'Bargaining in the shadow of the law: the case of divorce' *Yale Law Journal* 88: 950–997.

O'Rourke, D. (2003). 'Outsourcing regulation: Analyzing nongovernmental systems of labor standards and monitoring', *The Policy Studies Journal* 31(1): 1–29.

Raustiala, K. 2002. 'The architecture of international co-operation: transgovernmental networks and the future of international law', *Virginia Journal of
International Law* 43: 2–92.

Redmond, P. 2003. 'Transnational enterprise and human rights: Options
for standard setting and compliance', *The International Lawyer* 37: 69–102.

Sabel, C. and Zeitlin, J. 2003. 'Active welfare, experimental governance, pragmatic
constitutionalism: The new transformation of Europe', available at http://
eucenter.wisc.edu/OMC/Papers/EUC/zeitlinSabel3.pdf.

Shamir, R. 2004. 'Between self-regulation and the alien tort claims act: On the
contested concept of corporate social responsibility', *Law & Society Review*
38: 635–664.

Shapiro, M. 1988. *Who Guards the Guardians? Judicial Control of Administration*,
Athens: Georgia University Press.

Slaughter, A.-M. 2003. 'Global government networks, global information agencies
and disaggregated democracies', *Michigan Journal of International Law* 24:
1041–1074.

Suggested further reading

Bache, I. and Flinders, M. (eds.) 2004. *Multi-level Governance*, Oxford: Oxford
University Press.

Benner, T., Reinicke, W. H. and Witte, J. M. 2004. 'Multisectoral networks in
global governance: Towards a pluralistic system of accountability',
Government and Opposition 191–210.

Braithwaite, J. and Drahos, P. 2000. *Global Business Regulation*, Cambridge:
Cambridge University Press.

de Burca, G. 1996. 'The quest for legitimacy in the European Union', *Modern Law
Review* 59: 349–376.

Charny, D. 2000. 'Regulatory competition and the global coordination of labour
standards', *Journal of International Economic Law* 3(2): 281–302.

Held, D. 2000. 'Regulating globalization', in D. Held and A. McGrew (eds.),
*The Global Transformations Reader: An Introduction to the Globalisation
Debate*, Cambridge: Polity.

Kelsey, J. (ed.) 2003. *International Economic Regulation*, The Library of Essays in
International Law Series, Aldershot: Ashgate.

Kingsbury, B., Krisch, N. and Stewart, R. 2005. 'The emergence of global
administrative law', *Law and Contemporary Problems* 68: 15–58.

Picciotto, S. 2000. 'Liberalization and democratization: The forum and the hearth
in the era of cosmopolitan post-industrial capitalism', *Law & Contemporary
Problems* 63: 157–78.

McCahery, J., Bratton, W. W., Picciotto, S. and Scott, C. 1996. *Introduction:
Regulatory Competition and Insitutional Evolution*, Oxford: Clarendon
Press.

Volcansek, M. and Stack, J. (eds.) 2005. *Courts Crossing Borders: Blurring the Lines of Sovereignty*, Durham: Carolina Academic Press.

Weiler, J. 2001. 'The rule of lawyers and the ethos of diplomats: Reflections on the internal and external legitimacy of WTO dispute settlement', *Journal of World Trade* 35(2): 191–208.

Wiener, J. B. 1999. 'Global environmental regulation: Instrument choice in legal context', *Yale Law Journal* 108: 677–800.

7

Conclusion

In Chapter 6, we suggested that, although the conceptual frame around which our map of the regulatory terrain has been constructed transposes relatively easily to the supranational context, the law's contribution to regulation above and beyond the state alters significantly. In this concluding chapter, we offer some brief closing reflections on the conceptual frame for exploring regulation that we have developed throughout this book, and on how that frame may serve to illuminate the law's contribution to regulation. As we stated in the introductory chapter, one of our primary aims in writing this book was to provide a map of the diverse and wide-ranging terrain occupied by the flourishing literature on regulation that would help to orient relative newcomers to this field of intellectual inquiry. Our framework for examining regulatory literature is underpinned by four broad analytical constructs, forming the subject of Chapters 2 to 5: (i) theories of regulation; (ii) instruments and techniques of regulation; (iii) enforcement and compliance with regulation; and (iv) issues of accountability and legitimacy in regulation. Although our conceptual lens is developed in the context of national regulation, where regulatory scholarship has its origins, the analytical framework we construct is not inherently state-centric, as its application to regulation above and beyond the state context in Chapter 6 clearly demonstrates.

The primary aim of this text has been to demonstrate how the conceptual framework that we have used to map the regulatory literature provides a clear guide to a diverse terrain yet is flexible and durable enough to encompass a wide and varied range of scholarship. In the course of elaborating this conceptual framework, we have also observed a variety of roles that the law plays in the regulatory endeavour. Unlike some existing legal scholarship on regulation, which interrogates law's contribution to regulation by reference to the respective roles of the legislature, executive and judiciary as the constitutional organs of a democratic state, our analytical framework enables us to view the contribution of law in a more functional and contextual sense, locating its contribution in a broader socio-political environment. The result has generated two ways for organising the field: the first focusing on the conceptual structure or 'bones' of the subject, and the second drawing out the law's role as a thematic focus common to all domains of the map. While the conceptual structure offered here is largely descriptive and explanatory, the theme of law's role in regulation is developed as an argument. Readers need not accept our claims about the law's role in order to benefit from the guidance provided by our conceptual structure. Because our discussion of the law's role is a theme that appears periodically throughout the book in fragmented fashion, this concluding chapter draws together the threads of our argument about the role of law. This does not mean that the conceptual structure we have offered is less important: merely that its value lies in the cumulative unfolding of the preceding chapters.

Our argument concerning the role of law fleshes out a series of stylised concepts that we developed to summarise patterns of empirical variation, describing it in abstract, conceptual terms rather than as philosophical claims about the nature of law. The resulting account emphasises law's *facilitative* role as a potentially powerful instrument that may used to regulate behaviour, while highlighting its *expressive* role, the latter referring to the way in which the law may institutionalise and give expression to values of non-instrumental kind. At the level of national regulation, both the law's facilitative and expressive dimensions are reflected in its related but distinct contributions to regulation, encapsulated by two images: the *law as threat* and the *law as umpire*. These various facets were summarised in Chapter 1 in schematic form, reproduced in Figure 7.1, which we then developed incrementally as the book progressed.

Chapter 2 established what we mean by the law's facilitative role and introduced the umpiring facet of that role. Chapter 3 developed detailed examples of the difference between the image of law as threat and law as umpire and introduced the law's expressive dimension. Chapters 4 and 5 dealt with both images of law as threat and as umpire across the law's facilitative and expressive dimensions. In drawing together the threads of our argument about the law's role, we return to this schematic representation, rather than following the sequential discussion offered in preceding chapters.

Law's role	Law's image	
	Law as *threat*	Law as *umpire*
Law's *facilitative* role: law as an instrument for shaping social behaviour	Proscribing conduct and threatening sanctions for violation to deter that conduct	Creating and policing the boundaries of a space for free and secure interaction between participants
Law's *expressive* role: law institutionalising values	Legitimating coercion	Reflecting shared or agreed morality of the community of players

Figure 7.1. Law's image.

The facilitative dimension of the law's threat is most evident in regulatory scholarship concerned with understanding the mechanics of regulatory tools and techniques examined in Chapter 2. In particular, much of the literature that is described by its authors as 'regulatory scholarship' is concerned with identifying and prescribing the conditions under which various tools and techniques are likely to achieve defined social goals most effectively. As such, this literature tends to understand law's role as entirely facilitative, so that the law's threat is enlisted primarily for its deterrent capacities. The law's threatening dimension is clearly visible within command-based regimes, but it is rarely absent in its entirety, with its hidden quality perhaps most evident in prescriptive models of enforcement behavior examined in Chapter 4. So for example, in the well-known 'pyramid of enforcement' model developed by Ayres & Braithwaite, the law's role is claimed to operate most effectively when its threat is present but largely hidden, operating as a sword of Damocles, to be invoked by regulatory officials only when softer, persuasive attempts to elicit the desired behavioural response have failed. Indeed, it is partly because of the facilitative power embodied in the law's threat, emanating from its capacity to invoke the coercive power of the state against its citizens, that calls forth the need for its legitimation, reflected in various appeals to democracy referred to in Chapter 5.

But the extent to which the facilitative dimension of the law's threat may be legitimately invoked is shaped and tempered by its expressive capacity. By proscribing particular kinds of conduct on pain of sanction, the law's threat may be seen as expressing condemnation of that conduct. Condemnation of this kind is most visible in criminal laws that proscribe and sanction conduct regarded as morally wrongful. In other words, the law's threat serves an important symbolic function, one that may not be adequately replicated when alternatives to command-based techniques are adopted in order to discourage undesirable behaviour. It is the expressive dimension of the law's threatening role that is illuminated by the well-developed literature, referred to in Chapter 4, that seeks to understand the responses of regulatory enforcement officials to observed non-compliance with regulatory rules. In particular, attempts by law-makers to strengthen the facilitative capacity of the law's threat by proscribing conduct without reference to notions of moral culpability are likely to be ineffective, for it is the expressive capacity underlying the law's threat which helps to command respect and obedience by the regulated community and the public more generally.

But the law's threat, most evident in rules proscribing specified conduct, is not entirely self-executing. Its deterrent effect relies to some extent on its effective and publicly visible enforcement, in which the adverse consequences arising from a breach of the law's command are brought to bear directly on those found to have violated its commands. Accordingly, resort must be had to the law's umpiring function to establish and maintain a structured framework for free interaction between regulatory participants. In its facilitative dimension, the law's umpiring role is perhaps most clearly recognisable in the range of institutions, actors and behavioural dynamics involved in the task of monitoring and enforcing regulatory rules. But it is also at work in providing the legal infrastructure which ensures the security of voluntary transactions undertaken by market participants. Although there is a strong tendency in policy circles to view the law in opposition to the market, in which legal intervention is often characterised as an 'interference' with the market order, the latter cannot exist without a stable legal infrastructure in which the competitive forces of supply and demand may be free to operate. As institutionalist theories of regulation become more dominant, law's umpiring role becomes more central. As Teubner puts it, "the role of reflexive law is to structure and restructure semi-autonomous social systems by shaping both their procedures of internal discourse and their methods of coordination with other social systems": a classic umpiring role. And in discussing regulatory legitimation in Chapter 5, law's capacity to coordinate political dialogue encompassing multiple competing values is a crucial, umpiring facet of its facilitative role, which is at the heart of many of the approaches advocated by academic scholars in responding to the challenges of market liberalisation and globalisation.

But the law's umpiring function also displays an expressive character. That expressive character arises from the capacity of the law to institutionalise values, whether they be moral principles, community preferences chosen through democratic procedures or constitutional values. This expressive character is crucial to the legitimation of a regulatory regime. Seen in this light, tools and techniques of regulation can no longer appear as neutral, technocratic instruments of social and economic policy. Rather, they may be seen as embodying particular values, so that a preference for one policy instrument over another may be understood as allocating priority to the values associated with the former over the latter. In a similar vein, the conferral of rights of enforcement on private parties may be regarded as more than merely vehicles through which compliance with regulatory rules may be promoted, but as an important avenue through which individual members of the community may actively participate in the regulatory enterprise. And precisely because the expressive force of the law's umpiring role is crucial to micro-level facets of regulation such as enforcement and techniques, a similar importance pervades theories of regulation and judgements about regulatory legitimation. We suggested at the end of Chapter 2 that the various institutionalist theories might be understood as attempts to blend the insights of public and private interest theories into one single approach. Similarly, we can see in pluralist models of regulatory legitimation, the law's role is to provide a means for structuring dialogue between participants thereby enshrining values of openness and participation.

Once we extend our analytical framework to the supranational context, the law's contribution to regulation is significantly altered. Although the law's facilitative capacity extends to supranational regulation, its power is considerably weakened. While this dilution of the law's facilitative power is partly attributed to the largely undeveloped nature of supranational institutions for global democratic governance that may legitimately exercise coercive power at the international level, it may also be attributed to the weakness of the law's expressive capacities at that level. Although the European Union and World Trade Organisation may act as global law-making institutions, their law-making power stems from diverse and heterogeneous national communities, each represented by negotiators who define their regulatory goals in a relatively narrow, trade-focused compass. Accordingly, it is more difficult for these supranational institutions to represent affected communities than it is for national law-making institutions. In other words, the expressive capacity of law in reflecting the political and moral consensus of the community affected by that law is not well replicated at the supranational level: it is muddied by the presence of supranational regulatory dynamics.

While the absence of highly developed institutions of global governance capable of resolving conflicts between competing global policy objectives in a democratically legitimate manner may weaken the law's facilitative power, attempts at regulation above and beyond the state have nonetheless flourished in narrowly defined policy contexts, through the extensive participation by 'experts' in developing supranational regulation in specific policy sectors. In other words, the predominance of expert-driven supranational regulatory conversations in discrete policy sectors may ground shared understandings between regulatory participants and thereby help to strengthen the law's facilitative role. Although law may play a loose coordinating role across these sectors, it is yet to draw these sectors together in a unified manner. For whereas in a national context, law can facilitate a balancing of outcomes recommended by different expert discourses across different sectors, in a supranational context, the most law can do is encourage dialogue between different expert discourses. This is because it cannot, at present, make and impose policy trade-offs transparently, authoritatively and in a manner which is responsive to the community in the absence of democratically legitimate coercive supranational institutions.

Our final observation aims to clarify an ambiguity that may arise from adopting a decentred view of regulation while retaining a state-centric definition of law. Our argument about the law's role in regulation has defined law as authoritative rules backed by the legitimate coercive power of the state. In the supranational context, a state-centric understanding of law includes binding commitments voluntarily entered into between sovereign states (that is, typified by public international law) through intergovernmental agreement. But as we have seen, the law's contribution to regulation above and beyond the state is under challenge. Just as the forces of globalisation are challenging the primacy of states in both empirical reality and academic scholarship, state-centric conceptions of law are also being questioned.

This may have implications for the character of *law*, as opposed to the implications for regulation, which have been our primary focus. At the supranational level, we have observed that regulation takes place through a broad range of norms which may be thought to exert legitimate influence, although devoid of direct coercive legal force. While legal pluralists claim that such norms constitute forms of law, others have made powerful arguments in favour of retaining a narrower, state-centric conception, in order to retain a sense of the law's distinctive nature and attributes. In other words, the weakening of state-centric understandings of law raises a question: can law *persist decoupled* from the concept of coercively binding norms promulgated by a sovereign (and sometimes democratic) state legislature?

This question is not one which we have sought to address in this book. Rather, our analytical framework for exploring regulation, and its application to both domestic and supranational contexts, throws into high relief the challenges with which academic debates within law and social scientific inquiry are currently grappling. The emergence of regulation as a distinct field of scholarly inquiry occupies a particularly rich and powerful vantage point from which to explore the consequences of the pressures generating a move towards decentred accounts of regulation. Just as regulatory scholarship is strengthening its position as a placeholder for arguments about democracy and other political ideals, the familiar structures of traditional representative democracy are under strain. Similarly, just as regulatory scholarship is establishing itself as a forum for debates about the nature and role of law in collective social life, so too are the familiar structures of law under strain. Throughout this book, we have adopted a traditional, state-centric notion of law in an effort to address the first field of flux in a manner which will resonate with both lawyers and non-lawyers. In so doing, we hope that we have succeeded in making the broad and varied terrain inhabited by academic literature on regulation more accessible to newcomers, as well as demonstrating its enormous potential as a rich and fertile field of scholarly enquiry.

Index

CPSIA information can be obtained at www.ICGtesting.com
Printed in the USA
BVOW08s0254030915

416409BV00001B/68/P